I0889274

Reportage in the Chinese-Speaking World

China Understandings Today

Series Editors: Mary Gallagher and Emily Wilcox

China Understandings Today is dedicated to the study of contemporary China and seeks to present the latest and most innovative scholarship in social sciences and the humanities to the academic community as well as the general public. The series is sponsored by the Lieberthal-Rogel Center for Chinese Studies at the University of Michigan.

Reportage in the Chinese-Speaking World
Edited by Charles A. Laughlin and Li Guo

Creative Belonging: The Qiang and Multiethnic Imagination in Modern China
Yanshuo Zhang

Ethnic Minority Cinema in China's Nation-State Building
Kwai-Cheung Lo

Gendered Memories: An Imaginary Museum for Ding Ling and Chinese Female Revolutionary Martyrs
Xian Wang

Engineering Stability: Rebuilding the State in Twenty-First Century Chinese Universities
Yan Xiaojun

In Search of Admiration and Respect: Chinese Cultural Diplomacy in the United States, 1875–1974
Yanqiu Zheng

Seeking a Future for the Past: Space, Power, and Heritage in a Chinese City
Philipp Demgenski

China as Number One? The Emerging Values of a Rising Power
Yang Zhong and Ronald F. Inglehart

Paris and the Art of Transposition: Early Twentieth Century Sino-French Encounters
Angie Chau

A complete list of titles in the series can be found at www.press.umich.edu

REPORTAGE IN THE CHINESE-SPEAKING WORLD

Edited by Charles A. Laughlin and Li Guo

University of Michigan Press
Ann Arbor

Published in the United States of America by the
University of Michigan Press
First published February 2026

A CIP catalog record for this book is available from the British Library.

Library of Congress Cataloging-in-Publication Data

Names: Laughlin, Charles A., 1964– editor | Guo, Li, 1979– editor | Michigan Publishing (University of Michigan) publisher
Title: Reportage in the Chinese-speaking world / edited by Charles A. Laughlin and Li Guo.
Other titles: China understandings today
Description: Ann Arbor : University of Michigan Press, 2026. | Series: China Understandings Today | Includes bibliographical references and index. | In English, with some text in Chinese scripts or romanized.
Identifiers: LCCN 2025027376 (print) | LCCN 2025027377 (ebook) | ISBN 9780472077878 hardcover | ISBN 9780472057870 paperback | ISBN 9780472905492 ebook other
Subjects: LCSH: Mass media and culture—China | Reportage literature, Chinese—History and criticism | Reporters and reporting—China
Classification: LCC P94.65.C6 R47 2026 (print) | LCC P94.65.C6 (ebook)
LC record available at https://lccn.loc.gov/2025027376
LC ebook record available at https://lccn.loc.gov/2025027377

DOI: https://doi.org/10.3998/mpub.12992804

The University of Michigan Press's open access publishing program is made possible thanks to additional funding from the University of Michigan Office of the Provost and the generous support of contributing libraries.

Cover image: "Social Memory: Alishan" (社會記憶-阿里山, 1990), by Chang Chao-tang 張照堂 (1943–2024). Copyright National Taiwan Museum of Fine Arts, National Center of Photography and Images. Used with permission.

The authorized representative in the EU for product safety and compliance is Easy Access System Europe, Mustamäe tee 50, 10621 Tallinn, Estonia, gpsr.requests@easproject.com *for Professor Yingjin Zhang*

Contents

Digital materials related to this title can be found on the Fulcrum platform via the following citable URL: https://doi.org/10.3998/mpub.12992804

Figures

Acknowledgments

This coedited volume would not have been possible without the essential support and mentorship of the editorial team at the University of Michigan Press. We feel truly fortunate to have received the generous support of Professor Mary Gallagher and Professor Emily Wilcox, editors of University of Michigan Press's China Understandings Today series. We thank Sara Cohen for her timely and constructive suggestions, which were crucial in preparing this volume for anonymous peer review. We deeply appreciate Marcella Landri's sustained support and patient facilitation of the peer review process. We thank Delilah McCrea for her assistance in preparing the final manuscript, and are grateful to Kevin Rennells for his careful shepherding of it through production. We are also thankful to Danielle Coty-Fattal for facilitating the marketing. The anonymous reviewers of this volume have provided very helpful suggestions for the coeditors and our chapter authors. We thank them for their inspiring and beneficial feedback. Their comments helped this project grow in depth, rigor, and relevance to our audience's interests. We thank the following artists who generously granted us permission to use their images in our studies of their works: Zhang Mengqi, Yan Wang Preston, Liao Chia-chan, and Yan Hsin-chu.

The conception of this coedited volume on Chinese and Sinophone reportage using plurimedial forms of aesthetic production can be traced to an organized panel on Chinese reportage narratives at the annual meeting of the Association for Asian Studies in 2016. Extending the fruitful discussions of the AAS panel, two sessions focused on Chinese reportage studies were organized at the Rocky Mountain MLA annual meeting later in the fall of that year, expanding the coverage of reportage studies to a wide range of topics, including late Qing exploration narratives about Burma, Chinese and Sinophone documentary film, the leftist woodcut movement in the 1930s, reportage drama in the 1920s and 1930s, as well as women's prison memoirs as wartime reportage. Building on the outcomes of these two conference sessions, the coeditors of this volume organized a collaborative reading workshop in fall 2018, "Reading Chinese Reportage Across the Disciplines," funded by the Henry Luce Foundation/American Council of Learned Societies (ACLS) Program in China Studies Collaborative Reading-Workshop Grants and a University of Virginia Center for Global Inquiry and Innovation Grant. The ACLS workshop explored reportage narratives in contemporary China, Taiwan, and Hong Kong, including travel writings, environmental reportage, nonfiction works, and documentary films. One workshop outcome is the publication of seven critical essays on Chinese and Sinophone reportage works in a special issue, "Reportage and Its Contemporary Variations," in the journal *Modern Chinese Literature and Culture*, edited by Professor Kirk A. Denton in 2019. This paved the way for the current volume. In the summer of 2021, the coeditors started preparing for the current project by soliciting submissions of studies of literary, cinematic, theatrical, and media reportage in the Sinophone world. Our focus is on how the artistic processing in reportage evokes, negotiates, and refashions poetic or artistic sensibilities to process social and political critiques. Based on the received proposals, the volume editors organized a seminar of three sessions at the annual meeting of American Comparative Literature Association (ACLA) in the summer of 2022. A group of chapter contributors utilized the platform of the ACLA to garner feedback from discussants and workshopped their chapters.

Many mentors, colleagues, and friends generously provided support for this volume during its long process of preparation. We are incredibly indebted to Professor Yingjin Zhang, who served as an expert participant in the ACLS reading workshop and provided important insights on our in-progress works on plurimedial reportage and its activist sociopolitical function. Professor Zhang's pioneering scholarship on reportage studies, which was one of the major inspirations for the AAS panel on reportage in 2016, has remained a foundational part of this volume's theoretical framework. We are deeply thankful for Professor Xiaomei Chen, Professor Amy Dooling, and Professor Steve Riep, who have kindly supported our explorations of Chinese and Sinophone reportage works through their sustained mentorship. We are sincerely thankful for Professor Kirk A. Denton's exceptional editorship and generous mentorship. Professor Denton helped us refine our work on reportage studies through the *Modern Chinese Literature and Culture* special issue, the success of which led to the launch of this book-length project. We also thank Jie Guo, Tie Xiao, Lei Qin, Louisa Wei, Dorothee Hou, Harlan Chambers, Lawrence Z. Yang, and Christopher Lupke for their support of our studies of Chinese and Sinophone reportage.

INTRODUCTION

From Reportage to Nonfiction Art

New Perspectives from the Chinese-Speaking World

Li Guo and Charles A. Laughlin

This book proceeds from the premise that the serious contemplation of what reportage *is*, along with its comparable forms, compels us to rethink what we know about art and about the conceptual frameworks adopted by Euro-American scholars for approaching Chinese-language artistic expression of all kinds. These studies explore cultural practices and works that have been rendered marginal, silent, or invisible by the institutionalized study of modern Chinese culture, yet that, in their adherence to "real people, real events," embody the deepening promise of realism that has been a central impetus of that culture. Further, reportage's versatility in comprising plurimedial forms of representation (through nonfiction writing, photography, and film) lends it much expediency in amplifying intersectional accounts of marginalized individuals who struggle against multiple forms of discrimination because of race, gender, disability, age, education, class, economic status, or geocultural origins. This volume considers reportage as a plurimedial form of aesthetic production, which strives for a situated and holistic representation of actual social, political, and historical figures and events. Embracing its authors' subjective perspective and creative energies, reportage aesthetically engages its audiences in affective ethico-political exchanges with (human or nonhuman) subjects, and promotes audiences' empathetic responses to the democratic appeals of socially marginalized groups whose status, identity, or situation manifests emergent ethical challenges in the society of their time. As a critic observes, reportage in Chinese-language cultures gains prevalence because "it often fills in a role that journalism, which has been subject to concentrated political censorship in China from the late Qing to the present, cannot."[1] Charles A. Laughlin observes that readers of Chinese reportage in the 1980s looked to works of reportage as sources of knowledge about events in their own country and around the world beyond the orthodox narratives in official party-controlled media.[2] Likewise, in post–World War II Poland, writers' turn toward semifictional reportage to circumvent censorship was welcomed by the readers who could understand the intended metonymies and appreciate reportage as a venue for offering immediate information about social events.[3]

The rise of reportage, as Taiwanese scholar Shiu Wen-wei 須文蔚 (1966–) observes, is no less than "a rebellion against the canon of pure journalist writings" (對傳統純淨新聞的反動), as reportage authors endeavor to turn from coverage of short-term news events to the creation of literary productions of long-lasting value.[4] Tracing the formative influence of New Journalism in the United States in the 1960s and 1970s on Taiwan's reportage literature, Shiu argues that reportage purposefully challenges pure journalistic writings by surpassing the "news net" and conventions of news reporting, and permits authors to circumvent media authorities, misinformation, and censorship through a creative form of writing beyond the constraints of time and space.[5] Yang Kui 楊逵 (1906–1985), a founding author and theorist of Taiwan's reportage, observes that journalist writings prioritize "registrations of facts" (事實的羅列), whereas reportage literature aims to move readers through "dynamic" (動態的) and compelling representations of real events and actualities.[6] Chen Yingzhen, the renowned editor of *Ren Jian* 人間 magazine, further notes that reportage's "dynamism" is an emphatic "critical tendency" (強烈的傾向性), which distinguishes reportage as an aesthetic form from journalist productions.[7] More recently, reportage writer and theorist Yang Du 楊渡 (1958–) offers extensive discussions of the distinctions between journalism and reportage works. Whereas journalistic writings often focus on "partial, phenomenal reality" (局部的，現象性的真實), reportage strives to achieve a "holistic perception of reality" (全局的真實), which entails a critical viewpoint that seeks a balanced, in-depth understanding beyond fragmented representations.[8] Reportage's quest for reality (真實), Yang observes, includes the authors' pursuits of "on-site actualities, inner sincerity, linguistic veracity, and holistic observation of actuality."[9] Whereas journalism accentuates objectivity and impartiality, reportage establishes its persuasiveness by celebrating the author's subjective point of view, on-site interpersonal engagements, private reflections, and even sensual experiences. For Yang Du, journalism upholds the adage of objectivity and impartiality even at the price of forgoing reporters' personal responses; reportage, in comparison, embraces the authors' subjective experiences as a means of reaching for a deeper underlying veracity. In terms of style, Yang observes that, in Taiwan, partially due to the limitations of traditional news media, journalistic writings often require lucid descriptions of major events and outcomes within the first 100 or 200 words.[10] Reportage enjoys a much more varied choice in covering social instances, figures, and communities beyond current events, and may often represent a "growing embryonic social trend" through longer and sometimes serialized works in newspapers and magazines.[11] Yang notes that whereas journalist writings prioritize clarity, reportage works demand a form of narrative aesthetics and may resort to a broad array of techniques, including flashbacks, metaphor, irony, contrast, suspense, and vivid psychological depictions.[12] Detailed illustrations are often deployed in reportage at critical moments to enliven the events and figures in the works and endow the narrative with a storytelling quality.[13] Yang holds that unlike journalist writings' emphasis on contemporaneity, reportage works purposefully to reach out for a long-lasting readership who share a common interest in exploring humanist values.[14]

In reconceptualizing Chinese and Sinophone reportage, it helps to consider reportage as a medium for artistic interventions in other cultures, such as twentieth-century Korea and Japan. Sunyoung Park observes that in the early 1930s, literary reportage in Korea was largely produced to provide eyewitness accounts of forbidden spaces, including prisons and factories.[15] These leftist works complement journalistic writings in covering these marginal and unknown spaces by resorting to a wide array of reportage-like literary forms, such as prisoners' memoirs, worker-correspondents' letters, diaries, and reportage-style fiction. Such formal hybridity in Korean reportage burgeoned because of censorship in the 1920s and 1930s, and persisted because of the anticommunist cultural policy of banning all leftist writings in postcolonial South Korea. Both the historical origin and contemporary manifestations of Korean reportage resolutely express a democratic experimental aesthetic. Examples of democratic experimental aesthetics can also be found in Japanese reportage paintings by left-wing artists of the late 1950s and early 1960s. These paintings are part of "the grassroots protests opposed to Japan's incorporation into U.S. cold-war policy," including a nationwide rise of protests against US military bases.[16] Representative works include *American Soldier, Child, Barracks* (1953), *The Lucky Dragon* (1954) by Ikeda Tatsuo (1928–2020), and

Sunagawa (1955) and *The Civil War Era* (1958) by Nakamura Hiroshi (1932–), among others. Justin Jesty observes that painting provides a medium for artists such as Yamashita Kikuji (1919–1986) and others to facilitate the expression of human feelings and experiences when confronted by systematic violence, the failure of war, the Cold War, and Japan's conservative government.[17] These artists' illustrations and paintings had a clear political function: to resist violence, to bring to life the marginalized and the vulnerable, and to bring about the possibility of change.

This volume, comprising nine chapters on reportage works from mainland China, Taiwan, and overseas Chinese artists, reconsiders how reportage authors have sought to harness the cultural agency of literary narrative writing to influence society and effect change. Readers of Lu Xun's preface to his first collection of stories (*Na han* or "A Call to Arms") will see that yearning to transform society with art is fundamental to the New Culture Movement, regardless of genre.[18] Reportage could thus be considered part of a broad phenomenon in modern Chinese culture that manifests itself in other genres and forms of expression—a mode of activist artistic and cultural engagement. "Reportage" has been obscured by occasionally momentous failures to recognize it. For example, there has been confusion about whether important works by one of China's best-known practitioners of reportage, Liu Binyan 劉賓雁 (1925–2005), in the first phase of his career in the 1950s, were "reportage" or "fiction."[19] Similarly, although reportage was a well-known category in Taiwan in the 1970s (known there as *baodao wenxue*), the historical reportage "Song of the Covered Wagon" (幌馬車之歌) by Lan Bozhou 藍博洲 (1960–), about victims of the February 28 Incident in 1947 and the subsequent decades of White Terror, has often been classified as fiction both in Taiwan and in English-language scholarship.[20] Whereas the boundary between reportage and fiction can be quite fluid, it is important to consider and further pursue the *approach* taken to social intervention through the art of the real, which has been often called "reportage literature" but is significant in visual and performative as well as literary arts.

The English-language study of Chinese reportage began in 1985 with diverse efforts to define reportage as a literary genre with discussions of how it functions in social and cultural discourses. Yin-Hwa Chou delineates four types of Chinese reportage, including the subjective sketch, the objective sketch, investigative reportage, and creative reportage.[21] Xiaomei Chen asserts that the readers' "lectorial competence" played a decisive role in defining the literary status of Chinese reportage in the twentieth century.[22] Yingjin Zhang speaks of reportage's introduction of a "subversive discourse" to resist interpellation by ideological state apparatuses.[23] Since the publication of *Chinese Reportage: The Aesthetics of Historical Experience* (2002), there has been no book-length study on reportage in English. A special issue of *Modern Chinese Literature and Culture* (vol. 31, no. 2, Fall 2019) explored the subject by including seven essays covering issues of race and gender in reportage, reportage works in Taiwan, reportage and epistephilia, environmental reportage, aging in documentary film, and rural reportage. This volume blazes new trails in scholarship by including nine chapters on Chinese reportage since the 1940s, Taiwan reportage, and Sinophone reportage articulating themes of race, indigeneity, and diaspora cultures. We appropriate "reportage" as a critical tool to unify the artistic engagement of actuality in its infinite variety, and how writers and artists have used reportage to challenge, contest, and extend the scope of literary and artistic realism.[24] The variations of reportage provide lenses through which to look differently at how Chinese-language culture *in general* has been developing, especially in recent years. With its stylistic and ethical impact on narrative film and fiction, reportage has the potential to engage multiple forms of media production, including nonfiction writing, photography, documentary film, and intermedial visual and performative experiments.

Toward a New Ethico-Aesthetic Paradigm

What are the larger theoretical implications of reenvisioning reportage as a multiplicity of artistic practices across historical and national boundaries instead of as a discrete literary genre? We believe it allows us to highlight the centrality of ethical concerns to the arts of the real. This volume revisits the question of ethics in reportage and nonfiction through an *ethico-aesthetic paradigm*, to seek a deeper understanding of the function of literary and artistic reportage and the sociopolitical factors that have influenced reportage in various historical contexts. Félix Guattari argues that contemporary history's heightening sentiments of nationalism and mounting requests for "subjective singularity" in the Third World not only produced aspirations for national liberation and autonomy, but contributed new forms of "conservative reterritorialisations of subjectivity," which were often achieved at the cost of international relationships and the interests of the multitude of socially marginalized individuals.[25] As a corrective response, Guattari proposes an ethico-aesthetic paradigm to reconsider the complexities of subjectivity from the viewpoint of its production.[26] This ethico-aesthetic paradigm diverts from the traditional understanding of the subject as "the ultimate essence of individuation," "a pure, empty, prereflexive apprehension of the world."[27] Rather, this ethico-aesthetic paradigm forsakes a realist approach to lived actualities, and embraces "multi-faceted theatrical" aspects in the production of subjectivity.

Guattari alludes to Chinese students' democratic protests at Tiananmen Square in 1989 as an example of massive, theatricalized movement of subjectivization. An ethico-aesthetic engagement with this historical incident will surpass its ideological appeals and pay attention to the movement's "contagious affective charges" and its quest for "a whole [new] lifestyle, collective ethic and conception of social relations."[28] Alluding to Mikhail Bakhtin, Guattari observes that an ethico-aesthetic engagement of subjectivity abandons dualistic oppositions of subject-object, and explores the "mode of production of polyphonic subjectivity."[29] It prioritizes "a multiplicity of expressive instances," and allows the subject to "create a more authentic relationship with the other" through "the logic of affects."[30] Intentionally "shifting the human and social sciences from the scientific paradigm," Guattari deliberates on the ethical choice between a "scientifised," objectified subjectivity and a consideration of subjectivity in light of its "processual creativity," and endorses the latter.[31] This processual, creative subjectivity, for Guattari, augments individual autonomy and empowers the author in his or her aesthetic enunciation.

In response to the aforementioned rise of nativist sentiments in modern conservative quests for subjectivity, Guattari proposes a "transversalist conception of subjectivity," which embraces pluralism, polyphony, and multiplicity. It bridges the "existential" territories affiliated with the notion of subjectivity, and the "incorporeal" dimensions of subjectivity comprised of shifting value systems and their affiliated social and cultural implications.[32] This transversalist approach to subjectivity, Martin Avila observes, "eludes the individual-social distinction as well as the conception of the subject either as a person or individual."[33] Such a vision of subjectivity allows Guattari to achieve two purposes: (1) to replace the hackneyed universal representation of subjectivity propagated by capitalist colonialism, and (2) to resituate ethico-aesthetic experience beyond the discourse of otherness. Guattari's ethico-aesthetic stance recognizes "a multiplicity within oneself" and that dissonance, difference, and otherness are constitutive of subjectivity itself.[34] To be fully ethical requires an "affective sociality of embodiments" in "our bodies, our friends," as well as the "human cluster" surrounding us.[35]

Guattari's model of transversalist subjectivity highlights "the constitution of complexes of subjectivation," the multiple exchanges between individual and community, and how such complexes of subjectivation create alternative possibilities for recomposing one's corporeal existences and "resingularizing" one's self.[36] Guattari's ethico-aesthetic paradigm opens up new dimensions of understanding the transversal connections between the author and his or her targeted readership in many early-twentieth-century reportage works. By drawing attention to manifold emotional exchanges and affective bonds among the author/reporter/photographer, the narrator, and the depicted/photographed/filmed subjects, reportage considers heterogenous components that contribute to the development of the individuals and their processes of searching for autonomy in response to shifting social, economic, and geopolitical climates. Rather than seeking truth from event-based or people-based accounts, reportage explores the mutational process in which diverse social, economic, and spatiotemporal coordinates can foster friendship, empathy, imagined kinships, and reinforced sovereignty. For example, Charles Laughlin observes that in early-1930s Chinese labor reportage, reporting on labor conditions allowed writers to "develop techniques of expressing consciousness" through the illustrations of the "factoryscape" or industrial environment, while deploying the narrator as "the sensory and emotional medium" for articulating the workers' sufferings.[37] Ping Zhu, in discussing labor reportage by Zheng Guanying on Chinese overseas laborers in the 1870s, elucidates how late Qing reportage combines narrative illustration with an ethnic-aesthetical appeal to an imagined community of sympathetic conationals. In such cases, transversal communication in reportage facilitates transference of subjective experiences of pain, suffering, and angst. The relations between authors, narrators, and their imagined readers in these reportage works are constituted through intersubjective bonds, affective reversibility, and empathetic responsiveness. Affective reversibility here refers to the ability to meet with and empathize with the subject and events under one's investigation, to acknowledge one's social relationality, and to transform aesthetic experiences as meaningful encounters to spark social change.[38] As the above examples illustrate, ethical reportage authors and readers need to meet and acknowledge their own response-ability, to embrace affective responsiveness when facing differences and dissonances.

Further, Guattari's notion of affective community illuminates reportage's dialectical relationship with its imagined and historical readership/audience, by either appealing to a collective identification with the political imaginary of the Chinese nation (as in the leftist reportage of the 1930s and 1940s), or by evoking sympathetic identification with more concrete, multiplicitous, and personal contemplations of place, hearth, and senses of belonging. Guattari's vision of subjectivity as a group, i.e., an affective community, validates an ethico-aesthetic stance that recognizes dissonance, difference, and otherness as constitutive of subjectivity. As this volume demonstrates, from the minority ethnic peoples in Zhuang Xueben's photography to the images of the disabled and the marginalized peoples recorded by Liao Chia-chan's camera, the gesture of reportage plays a vital role in establishing and reinforcing an ethico-aesthetic relationship among the author/reporter, the subject, and the audience. Reportage facilitates the interventions, transposition, and circulations of desire and dissonance among pluralist subjective positions in the viewer and the subjects. Affective intensity allows transversal communication among the author, the reader/audience, and the subject in reportage. The ethics of reportage depends on its potential to conceptualize a pluralistic subjectivity through aesthetic evocation of audience responses and meaningful configurations with varied affective relations.

The current studies, rather than considering reportage from a genre-based approach, strive to explore reportage as an ethico-aesthetic mode or function that can be manifested through a plethora of written or artistic forms of expression, and can at times even strike intersectional resonances and commonalities with fiction, poetry, or narrative films.[39] In this light, Guattari's ethico-aesthetic paradigm, by emphasizing the ethico-political implications of aesthetic creations, provides a productive theoretical prism for us to reconsider the creative potentials of reportage in underexplored artistic forms, such as photography, documentary film, and nonfiction art. Whereas in fictional narratives and films, transversal relations between audiences and characters facilitate emotive exchanges or may even inspire nascent moral and political imaginings, reportage's aesthetic explorations are often aligned with its ethico-political function of representing and responding to contingent social events and achieving augmented social efficacy. The question of ethics is central to studies on Chinese-language reportage and nonfiction art. Yingjin Zhang, regarding representations of earthquakes in reportage and independent documentary, observes that documentary photography and filmmaking "foreground an urgent demand of 'response-ability' for the victims and survivors 'on the scene' (*xianchang*), at the very moments of encounter in the epicenter of the disaster."[40] Observational documentaries present a unique form of epistephilia[41] by emphasizing "the process of knowledge acquisition and the ethics of 'response-ability' ([Zhang's] term for the yet-to-be-realized capacity for response and responsibility) for both the documentarist and the viewer."[42] Such embodied "response-ability" of the documentarist or the reportage author to their environment is often "conditioned by social relationality."[43] In the environmental reportage of Xu Gang 徐刚 (1945–), the author's affective encounter with the depicted plays a positive role by addressing humanity's crisis, awakening ethical sensitivities to one's surroundings, and inspiring activist endeavors to restore landscapes that have suffered abuse and damage.

Revisiting the question of ethics through a new ethico-aesthetic paradigm facilitates a deeper understanding of the function of literary and artistic forms of reportage, their distinction from fact-based journalistic writings, and the sociopolitical factors that influenced the form of reportage in various historical contexts. A prominent example is the "Living Newspaper," a leftist reportage performance form that originated in the former Soviet Union in the early 1920s. The best-known performer of the Soviet living newspapers is the Blue Blouse Theater, named after the simple workers' shirts that performers wore. The format for this troupe's performances included presenting the news of the day in a mix of satirical songs, skits, dances, and pantomimes.[44] Living Newspaper performance, or *huobaoju* 活報劇, emerged in the 1920s in China and gained wide popularity after the Second Sino-Japanese War (1937–1945). As Xiaomei Chen argues, "Performance troupes—professional and amateur alike—traveled inland and to the battlefield to dramatize current events and mobilize for war."[45] Famous war-resistance live newspaper plays include *Put down Your Whip!* (Fangxia ni de bianzi 放下你的鞭子, 1937), *In Protest against the New Fourth Army Incident* (Fandui Ruannan shibian 反對阮南事變, 1940), and *The Normandy Campaign* (*Kaipi di'er zhanchang* 開闢第二戰場, 1944). Living Newspaper performance flourished during the Maoist era, and continues to thrive in diversified theatrical forms in China today. Since 2010, mainland Chinese playwrights have produced various forms of reportage plays (*baogaoju* 報告劇), such as anti-COVID reportage plays, situational reportage plays, and even acrobatics reportage plays.[46] These reportage plays strive to achieve affective veracity by resorting to narrative theatricality, dramaturgical coordinates, or even emotional displays through acrobatic performances. Diverging from bland propaganda-driven narratives, these plays stage theatrical conflict as a means of reviving historical actualities or social circumstances.

Many politically progressive contemporary Chinese and Sinophone reportage writings often receive affective reverberations among readers in the transnational community. *Revealing the Secrets of Poachers* (Daolie jiemi 盜獵揭秘, 2000) by Manchurian author Jiang Hao 江浩 (1954–) received the third prize of Lettre Ulysses Award for the Art of Reportage in 2003. *Will the Boat Sink the Water? The Life of China's Peasants* (Zhongguo nongmin diaocha 中國農民調查, 2003; English 2006), by Chen Guidi 陳桂棣 (1942–) and Wu Chuntao 吳春桃 (1963–), which exposed peasants' tragic living conditions under a corrupt bureaucracy, gained international acclaim overseas, receiving the Lettre Ulysses Award first prize in 2004. The reportage of Zhu Ling (朱

凌), *The Legend of a Local People's Congress Representative* (Yige renda daibiao de canzheng chuanqi 一個人大代表的參政傳奇, 2006), which recounts the political career of a member of the National People's Congress and China's dysfunctional democratic election system, received much attention through overseas media after governmental censorship. The reportage of Xu Zhiyuan 許知遠 (1976–), *The Protestors* (Kangzheng zhe 抗爭者, 2013), consists of face-to-face interviews with activists, democratic campaigners, and political dissenters from Taiwan, Hong Kong, and China, showcasing transverse communications with progressive figures from heterogenous Sinophone communities. These reportage works illustrate what Yingjin Zhang terms "a distinctively subversive discourse in Chinese reportage" and contribute to a more pluralized "intellectual trend toward subjectivity."[47] The art of reportage has the potential to cultivate a transhistorical, transsubjective affectivity, which offers authors, filmmakers, readers, and audiences alike new epistemic encounters beyond their immediate observed or lived experiences.

The ethico-aesthetic paradigm can be discerned in contemporary media reportage and its function in enacting transnational affectivity, a focus of Ran Ma's chapter in this volume. Ma probes "film and media representations of affects, emotions and affective life—examined in terms of 'affectivity'—pertaining to the Chinese *ryūgakusei* [overseas students in Japan] and migrants." Affective intensities in media reportage, as Ma illustrates in her studies of Chinese-in-Japan documentary media, embody a transhistorical, transnational potentiality of overseas Chinese's diasporic and exilic filmmaking. In documentary filmmaking, affective reverberations with the audience can be created through realist dramatization, reenactment of historical evidence, and *mises-en-scène*.[48] Affect and emotional engagement, what Bill Nichols terms "the relational intimacy of filmmaker and the subject," is an important model in a filmmaker's engagement with the digital world in the twentieth-first century.[49] Creating a visceral and affective experience through film could yield an ethico-political effect among the audience by establishing a connection between messages and their recipients, by allowing us to reframe how we think about specific issues of social justice.[50] Affective intensities in documentary media bear an ethico-political power by moving audiences into deeper understandings of social realities.

From Reportage to Nonfiction Art

Before focusing on the thematic throughlines in this book, we revisit the history of Chinese reportage practice and clarify the commonality of the endeavor of reportage writers and the creators of the proliferation of contemporary nonfiction forms. The legacy of *baogao wenxue* in mainland China is both an asset and a liability to our ongoing project. The genre's historical relationship to the cultural policy of the Communist Party of China made it into an orthodox genre of the socialist period, creating associations that repel most contemporary artists and critics. What gets lost in this is that much of what defined *baogao wenxue* in its early decades and throughout its relationship with the Chinese revolution and socialism are compelling aspects of the art of the real that draw people to it in its various forms today.

Reportage as a form of artistic expression originated principally in the work of the Czech writer Egon Erwin Kisch, whose agitational nonfiction beginning in the 1920s about industrial working conditions, war, and the harms of imperialism, became a major feature of the international proletarian literary movement supported by the Soviet Union's Communist International (Comintern). Through such international flows, Kisch's reportage as well as that of Soviet and other Eastern European revolutionary writers gained global currency and invited imitation and variation among leftist literary communities worldwide. This included that of Taisho period Japan, where reportage was enthusiastically promoted as a new revolutionary form of art, and as such quickly attracted progressive Chinese writers studying in Japan. Although all forms of reportage in some way adopted a journalistic posture, they also sharply departed from international journalistic norms of "objectivity" and "impartiality," featuring bold formal and creative innovations and a sustained focus on concrete subjective experience.

In the early days of Chinese reportage in the 1930s, the cases of Ding Ling and Xia Yan exemplify how reportage fit into the heyday of early literary progressivism in China. Both were well-known authors and members of the League of Leftwing Writers, Ding Ling being a prominent fiction writer already by the end of the 1920s, and Xia Yan a dramatist who became a major figure in the emerging film industry. Both were advocates and practitioners of reportage.

In two installments in the January and July 1932 issues of *Big Dipper* (Beidou 北斗, a progressive literary magazine edited by Ding Ling) appeared Ding Ling's reportage "Eventful Autumn" (Duo shi zhi qiu 多事之秋; the phrase is also used as an idiom for "times of trouble"). The work depicts various happenings on the streets of Shanghai after the Mukden Incident (in which the Japanese annexed Manchuria the previous year, on September 18, 1931). The text's point of view is indeterminate, moving among crowds of students, workers, office clerks, policemen, and manual laborers, whose fragmented verbal and at times physical interactions are accompanied by flashes of insight into their thoughts and feelings. The anonymous narrator expresses admiration for organized students' marching, shouting slogans, and educating the diverse throngs about the historical and political significance of the crisis with Japan as well as crises of social exploitation and authoritarianism in China. The result is a wild narrative ride that creates an effect of objectivity by making anti-Japanese, prowar, and revolutionary attitudes seem collective by distributing them among diverse voices and social actors throughout the texts' many episodes. Ding Ling also quotes from newspaper coverage of the municipal rally to highlight the function of reportage to correct the elite and commercial biases of mainstream media with visceral counternarratives of what is implied to be "the real story."

Four years later, in 1936, Xia Yan published a very different text in the first issue of *Guangming* (Brilliance) magazine, which became the best-known and most anthologized work of reportage literature of the Republican period, "Indentured Workers" (Baoshen gong 包身工). Like "Eventful Autumn," "Indentured Workers" was the length of a short story, but rather than depicting public confrontations on the streets, Xia Yan's work shows the hidden misery and inhumanity of a Japanese textile mill in Shanghai. Xia uses a mixture of description/analysis and narration, painting a picture of a system of labor extraction and exploitation focused on the suffering of one destitute teenager from the countryside, Lu Chaibang, being worked to death in the factory. The actuality of the world depicted in "Indentured Workers" is verified with statistics, scientific data, and analysis, but whether the unfortunate protagonist Lu Chaibang is a real person or a composite character based on stories about various workers is impossible to determine. Her function in the text, though, is clear: Hers is the body on which is visited every imaginable humiliation and abuse, the object of the violence that typifies industrial (and national) relations, violence that brings the facts and figures and abstract analysis disturbingly to life. The sense of objectivity brought about by the numerical data and analytical passages is balanced or belied by the narrator's consistently outraged affect, use of exclamation points, and emphasis on ironies; it is these latter aspects that both give the text impact and, along with its sensorially vivid descriptive passages, verify its status as a literary work.

War is another important early social origin for Chinese reportage. The first use of the Chinese translation of the term "reportage" as *baogao wenxue* appeared in the title of a compilation of emotionally charged accounts of the aftermath of the bombing of Shanghai on January 18, 1932, "The Shanghai Incident and Reportage" (Shanghai shibian yu baogao wenxue 上海事變與報告文學, edited by Ah Ying). When only a few years later, Japan began a general invasion of China, writers like Qiu Dongping 丘東平 (1910–1941) and Ah Long 阿壠 (1907–1967) began writing of the horrors of war from experience on the scene.

Qiu Dongping's and Ah Long's writing is not propaganda, but sober depictions of the subjective human costs of war that often use the point of view of soldiers on the battlefield as their vehicle. Both writers are among the contributors to the literary magazine *July* (Qiyue 七月), launched by Hu Feng in response to the outbreak of war with Japan in July 1937. *July* includes both fiction and reportage texts (which bear a close resemblance to each other), reflecting Hu Feng's vision of literary realism, which emphasizes the projection of subjectivity into the objective world as a means of expressing "subjective fighting spirit."[51] Qiu Dongping's "Company Seven" (Di qi lian 第七連) is a good case in point. The text presents itself as an oral account of young company commander Qiu Jun, who has nearly lost his life trying to keep his unit together and alive under relentless Japanese mortar fire. He discusses his background and the principles behind his approach to leadership and fighting, the physical and psychological struggles of his men, the disconnect between orders being radioed to him from his commander and the real battle situation, and the moral collapse of some of his men and even the commander of an adjacent company as they desert and run for their lives, while Commander Qiu and his men continue to try to hold on against impossible odds.

Other formats of reportage also began to emerge. As early as 1936, the novelist Mao Dun launched a highly successful collective writing project called *One Day in China* (Zhongguo de yiri 中國的一日). Inspired by a similar project on a global scale launched by Maxim Gorky in the Soviet Union earlier that year, Mao Dun's editorial team solicited short contributions from all over the country in major newspapers and literary magazines; participants were asked to write about their lives on May 21, 1936. Contributions could be reportage, fiction, poetry, and one-act plays. Since the project used forms of literature to create a snapshot of the whole of China in a single day, it often is thought of as a monumental work of reportage.

During the wars throughout the 1940s, the "One Day" format served as a model for other collective works, usually produced in occupied areas as well as in the various Revolutionary Base Areas, such as *One Day in Shanghai* (Shanghai yiri 上海一日) and *One Day in Central Hebei* (Jizhong de yiri 冀中的一日). There were also individual and collective works written by participants of Writer Battlefield Interview Groups and members of revolutionary-base-area communities, like Liu Baiyu's 劉白羽 (1916–2005)'s book *Life in Yan'an* (Yan'an shenghuo 延安生活, 1946), which emphasized positive themes and the superiority of the social order being created in the base areas by the Communist Party. The war reportage from the hinterland and base areas focused on selfless, lovable peasants and soldiers, and tended more toward panegyric than had previously been the case for war reportage.

Works in this era began a long departure from the critical social perspective that fueled the emergence of reportage a decade earlier. This facilitated the canonization of reportage as an orthodox socialist genre that during the war in the Communist base areas as well as after 1949 in the People's Republic, would be expected to extol socialism, the Communist Party, and Chairman Mao. The apotheosis of orthodox reportage in China can be seen in the well-known eulogies to Lei Feng and the selfless county party secretary Jiao Yulu.[52]

The first challenge to the panegyric type of reportage came in the Hundred Flowers Campaign of 1956. The invitation from the Party leadership to go beyond singing the praises of the achievements of Chinese socialism to also shed light on flaws and areas in need of improvement in Chinese society seemed tailor-made for the nonfiction genre. Amid a flood of public discourse from scientists, educators, and artists, a young journalist named Liu Binyan had been particularly inspired by the "close-ups" (*ocherki* in Russian and *texie* 特寫 in Chinese) of the Soviet reportager Valentin Ovechkin, who revealed corruption and bureaucratism in the Soviet Union.[53] Liu wrote similar long-form narrative texts such as "The Inside News of the Newspaper" and "On the Bridge Construction Sites," purportedly based on real people and situations, combining a novelist's penchant for rhetoric and imagery in dramatizing social and political tensions in a way that had never been seen before in China. The works, appearing in the conspicuous publication venues of *People's Daily* and *People's Literature*, created much controversy and played a role in the reversal of the Hundred Flowers Campaign and its tragic transformation into the Anti-Rightist Campaign. Like virtually everyone who spoke out during the Hundred Flowers campaign, Liu was censured and sent to the countryside for reeducation through labor. The crisis in the history of reportage lay in this: While the Party wished to endorse a genre based on facts and reality, the issue of who is entitled to discursively lay claim to the real made it highly perilous to make an earnest attempt like Liu's to revivify the genre.

Something that makes reportage fascinating, however, is that its story does not simply end with the suppression of prominent practitioners like Liu. The orthodox version of the genre continued to occupy space in the media landscape throughout the 1960s. After Mao's death in 1976, the ultraleftism of the Great Proletarian Cultural Revolution was generally discredited by the emergent Deng Xiaoping regime. Intellectuals, artists, and scientists who were still being persecuted in the hinterlands or in prison, Liu Binyan among them, were *rehabilitated* in the name of restoring a sense of reality in public discourse, a gesture typified by the famous slogan "seek truth from facts" (*Shishi qiu shi* 實事求是), which became a motto for the unprecedented boom in reportage writing in the late 1970s and 1980s that helped define the literature of the New Era. Liu's own 1978 text, "People or Monsters?" (*Renyao zhi jian* 人妖之間), was a lengthy autopsy of the rise of a corrupt party secretary in Heilongjiang province who was executed for amassing a fortune of embezzled funds. Although arguably more intensely critical than his works of the late 1950s, "People or Monsters?" was written with a similar approach. What distinguished Liu's mature reportage was his extensive research and the broad historical span (nearly twenty years), which may have created a template for the new wave of reportage of the 1980s.

The 1980s were a period of unprecedented productivity and popularity for the reportage genre in mainland China, one that has not been equaled since.[54] Other members of the older generation writing reportage in the 1980s, such as Xu Chi 徐遲 (1914–1996), Huang Zongying 黃宗英 (1925–2020), Li You 理由 (1935–), and Chen Zufen 陳祖芬 (1943–2019), extended the panegyric model of socialist reportage to include stories of rehabilitated scientists whose discoveries and achievements made them as worthy of recognition as model workers and party cadres, while also acknowledging their suffering and persecution during the Anti-Rightist Campaign, the great famine, and the Cultural Revolution. The younger generation, however, represented by Su Xiaokang 蘇曉康 (1949–), Qian Gang 錢剛 (1953–), Jia Lusheng 賈魯生 (1950–), and Mai Tianshu 麥天樞 (1956–), transformed the genre by focusing on marginalized groups or even drawing into question the role of the intellectual as the conscience and hope of the nation. Works such as Qian Gang's *The Great Tangshan Earthquake* (Tangshan da dizhen 唐山大地震; 1986), Su's *Freedom Memorandum* (Ziyou beiwang lu 自由備忘錄), or Jia's *The Prisons of China's West* (Zhongguo xibu de jianyu 中國西部的監獄) raised questions about distorted history and presented readers with disenfranchised characters who challenged familiar categories. While shedding light on new values such as humanism and the rule of law, their writing also reflected the persistence or resurgence of traditional *jianghu* 江湖 ("rivers and lakes") values of a nomadic detachment from mainstream hierarchies, systems, and roles by way of the freelance circuits of socioeconomic mobility. With its alternative ethics of brotherly loyalty, *jianghu* was often unleashed or embodied in the form of the new protagonist of reform and opening, the unconventional individual entrepreneur or *getihu* 個體戶.

The freewheeling frenzy of 1980s reportage came to an end with the closing down of *Reportage* (Baogao wenxue 報告文學) magazine, reportedly because of close associations with the democracy movement of spring 1989.[55] This also ensured that, officially, there was no longer space for social criticism in reportage literature. Yet even in the highly commercialized publication industry of the 2000s, one still saw significant book-length works of nonfiction whose spirit of unmasking and historical revisionism resembled that of works from the late 1980s. Such landmarks as the aforementioned *Will the Boat Sink the Water? The Life of China's Peasants* (2004; 2006 in English) by Chen Guidi and Wu Chuntao, *Tombstone: The Great Chinese Famine, 1958–1962* (Mubei: zhongguo liushi niandai da jihuang jishi 墓碑：中國六十年代大饑荒紀實, 2008; 2012 in English), by Yang Jisheng 楊繼繩 (1940–), and *China in One Village: The Story of One Town and the Changing World* (Zhongguo zai Liangzhuang 中國在梁莊, 2010; 2021 in English) by Liang Hong 梁鴻 (1973–) continually appeal to broad readerships. Though none are usually classified as "reportage," all feature the combination of extensive research and systematic analysis with the vivid narration and often passionate writing that achieved currency in reportage's heyday.

Whether it is ironic or just politically sensible that the term *baogao wenxue* has been so generally shunned in the PRC since 1989, the same practices have diversified across media and been repackaged in prose, while still serving essential functions in contemporary Chinese public discourse. The purpose of this historical sketch is to demonstrate that the practice of *baogao wenxue* in mainland China, apart from the socialist tradition of panegyric, has from the outset resembled postsocialist forms that have gone by other names, such as *jishi wenxue* and *fei xugou xiezuo* ("nonfiction writing"). This book questions the stigmatization of the term *baogao wenxue* and its gradual displacement by other terms. While many believe that *baogao wenxue is* essentially socialist panegyric, we maintain that the genre had established a substantive meaning before it was co-opted by the Chinese Communist Party, and continues to retain that meaning in both the socialist and postsocialist eras, so that it continues to be distinctive as a vibrant form of modern Chinese creative expression.

Seeing Taiwan through Reportage

Taking reportage studies outside the realm of the mainland-based leftist narrative tradition, we consider how reportage narratives, film, and media record, inspire, and respond to social currents and trends in Taiwan, Hong Kong,

China, and overseas diaspora cultures. To begin with, three chapters in this volume offer much-needed discussions of Taiwanese *baodao wenxue* 報導文學.[56] That the term is used at all in Taiwan demonstrates the need to broaden the scope of the genre's practice beyond the PRC, indicating both its historical relation to the form in mainland China as well as its independent development. The relation is embodied by the remarkable figure of Yang Kui, who emerged as a writer during the development of a new cultural movement in colonial Taiwan. Even though Taiwan had been a Japanese colony since 1895, there had been calls since the May Fourth Movement in China (beginning in 1919) for a vernacular literature and a literature reflecting the experience of common people in Taiwan. Like several authors preceding him, such as Zhang Wojun 張我軍 (1902–1955) and Lai He 賴和 (1894–1943), Yang Kui was educated in Japanese and did most of his writing in that language in journal articles published in Taiwan as well as Japan. One thing that made Yang different, though, was his encounter with the international proletarian literary movement in Japan in the 1920s, which exposed him to the form of reportage, which he passionately promoted and practiced almost to the exclusion of fiction.

However, because of the Japanese crackdown on leftism, expressions of local identity and national independence in Taiwan during the war, and then the strictures of martial law after the war when the Nationalists moved the capital of the Republic of China to Taipei, political suppression and censorship increasingly marginalized reportage literature.[57] Perhaps the most important condition for the flourishing of Taiwanese reportage was the political and social turmoil of the 1970s. Though Taiwan was still under martial law, the recognition of the PRC as the legitimate representative of China by the United Nations, the establishment of diplomatic relations with the United States, and the resulting isolation of Taiwan, along with the resurgence of local identity, nativism, and calls for independence in the form of political activism and nativism in fiction and poetry (to be followed by narrative film in the 1980s), created space for the emergence of nonfiction forms like reportage, photography, and early independent documentary as expressions of contemporary social realities, the predicaments of marginalized populations, and activism.

Current scholarship has traced the hybrid origins of Taiwan's reportage traditions. Resonating with Shiu Wen-wei's study, Lin Chi-yang 林淇瀁 (1955–) observes that Taiwan's reportage came into being under the influence of leftist reportage literature in the 1930s in mainland China, the surge of New Journalism in the United States in the 1960s and 1970s, and the impact of Japanese reportage literature and art in the 1930s on colonial Taiwan.[58] One of the earliest studies on Taiwan's reportage literature is *Exploration of Realities* (現實的

探索, 1980), a volume edited by Chen Ming-pan 陳銘磻 (1951–), which contains over thirty scholarly essays on Taiwanese reportage works. *An Introduction to Taiwan's Reportage Literature* (台灣報導文學概論, 2001) by Yang Sufen 楊素芬 is widely deemed to be the first scholarly monograph that traced the historical origin, lineage, and development of Taiwan's own reportage literature. Among recent publications, a canonic collection is *Reportage Literature: A Reader* (報導文學讀本, 2002), edited by Lin Chi-yang and Shiu Wen-wei, which comprises reportage works by sixteen Taiwanese authors. These works display shared interests in writing about calamity and disaster, including the aftermath of the 1935 Hsinchu-Taichung Earthquake, industrial pollution in Taoyuan, the endangerment of Formosa black bears, the tragedy of social activist Chung Hao-tung 鍾浩東 (1915–1950) against the backdrop of the February 28 Incident, the Siraya people's struggles against cultural displacement, the sufferings of Seqaro people after Japan's invasion of Taiwan in 1874, and politically marginalized residents in the island of Kinmen 金門 and their forsaken lives at the frontline of cross-strait relations. Such exceptional focus on calamity writing, Lin observes, reflects the shared concern of Taiwan's reportage literature in "expressing empathy for the vulnerable, oppressed, and ill-treated social communities and indignation against the politically privileged groups," ranging from "incompetent or indifferent officials, unremitting hunting and killing of black bears, [and] influences of colonialism and dominant Han ethnic cultures."[59] For Lin, canonical Taiwanese reportage has embraced narrative conventions in order to ingrain truth in fictional illustration and to preserve veracity through creative expression. Likewise, renowned Taiwanese reportage author Yang Du identifies a perpetual tension between realism and literary aesthetics in reportage literature. Reflecting on his own experience of writing reportage on Taiwan's peasant movement, Yang comments that, ironically, in some reportage works, the manifested "narrativity" (故事性) of real historical events could be even more dramatic and captivating than fictional creations.[60]

Besides reportage literature, photographic reportage (*baodao sheying* 報導攝影) in Taiwan has gained more prominent critical attention in recent decades. One of Taiwan's first women pioneers in this field is Wang Hsin 王信 (1942–), known for her photographic series on Taiwan's Tao people and their living conditions titled *Farewell, Orchid Island* (再見蘭嶼 1974–75). Wang holds that photographic reportage, if instilled with humanist values, could instigate "a form of provocation and reflection among the masses and thus promote and precipitate social reforms" in a democratic and open environment.[61] Resonantly, the photographic reportage collection *Report on Orchid*

Island 1987–2007 (Lan Yu baogao 蘭嶼報告, 2007) by Kuan Hsiao-jung 關曉榮 (1949–), initially published as a series in the magazine *Ren Jian*, brought wide social attention to the Tao indigenous community's demands to remove nuclear wastes from their homeland, Orchid Island. Another example is Lai Chun-piao 賴春標, whose photographic reportage in *Ren Jian* on Taiwan's endangered hinoki cypress and red cedar trees promoted a series of governmental reforms related to forest protection and harvesting.[62] A more recent example is *Southern Wind* (Nan feng 南風 2013), a work of photographic reportage on industrial pollution of Taixi Village in Changhua. Author Chuang Jui-lin 莊瑞琳 observes that a key function of her reportage is to draw social attention to obscure and less-understood people, events, and incidents to engage them through public discussion. Plurimedial reportage requires the author to have an interdisciplinary epistemological framework to sufficiently address complex and intersecting social issues. In the photographic reportage *Southern Wind*, these intersecting concerns include remote-area villagers' health risks, class divides, economic development, and rural population loss.

In English-language scholarship, from Yang Kui's works of the 1930s to the present, Taiwanese reportage has received limited attention. In addition to Po-hsi Chen's article on Lan Bozhou's leftist reportage in Taiwan, Lawrence Zi-Qiao Yang analyzes the agrarian origin of Richard Yao-chi Chen's documentary *Liu Pi-chia*, a Cold War *avant-garde* documentary that Yang considers an example of audiovisual reportage. This book expands current studies in this emerging field by contributing three chapters on Taiwan's reportage and photographic reportage of the late 20th century. Whereas the authors and works examined in these chapters are closely affiliated with Taiwan's reportage literature, each chapter elucidates how nonfiction writing and artistic expression in these works expose poignant authorial conflict in depictions of the marginalized subjects' predicaments and the authors' arduous negotiation between tradition and modernity, their shared aspirations for humanitarianism, and their reflections on writerly ethics in influential social campaigns during Taiwan's democratization. From the second-person narration of Gu Mengren 古蒙仁 (1951–) to *Ren Jian*'s illustration of its photojournalists collective ethical identity, from reportage by Liao Chia-chan 廖嘉展 (1962–) to the empathetic documentary photography of Yan Hsin-chu 顏新珠 (1961–), these works display how nonfiction writing and art compel the authors and the audience to ponder the ethical and political stakes of "depicting" the socially marginalized and telling their stories, and the necessity of embracing the tensions in the authors' subjective positions and their connections with real people and live events.

Intermediality, Photography, and Reportage

Whereas early studies on reportage delineated various typologies or time periods of Chinese reportage, this volume addresses modern and contemporary variations of Sinophone reportage by exploring reportage's relationship with intermedial reflexivity, as well as reportage's conscious reference to other media in representing individual or collective desires or sensibilities. As an aesthetic form of expression, reportage both bridges and problematizes the bifurcation of ornamental and persuasive speech that Yin-hwa Chou has observed. The operative function of reportage in provoking readers into taking action is widely acknowledged. For example, mainland Chinese author Xu Gang took to environmental reportage writings to raise an outcry about the crisis of land loss and desertification.[63] Likewise, *A Single Person's Battle to Protect Kunming Lake* (一個人的滇池保衛戰 2012), a reportage by Yunnan-based female writer Ye Duoduo 葉多多, is an account of a forest guard's lifelong battle against mining-related pollution and deforestation around Kunming Lake. It makes an appeal for greater public awareness for environmental protection. Critics of modern and contemporary reportage writings and documentaries in mainland China and Taiwan have explored how written and visual reportage, rather than distancing the audience/readers from the realm of imagination, engage them through diverse forms of activist encounters with social and political reality. For the reportage audience/reader, the act of commenting on or responding to social veracities is facilitated through affective encounters with the art of the real.

Chapters in this volume engage with nonfiction writing, photography, and documentary films to examine how intermediality cultivates aesthetically distinctive expressions in reportage, inviting fresh perspectives on cross-cultural empathy and ethico-political relationships between the reporter/photographer/filmmaker and his or her surroundings. The concept of intermediality, which can be traced to the notion of intertextuality, is instrumental for understanding reportage's interconnectedness with nonfiction writing and art forms. Julia Kristeva holds that intertextuality allows considerations of the text "as such within (the text of) society and history."[64] Intertextuality grants "a mechanism whereby we write ourselves into the social text, and thereby the social text writes us."[65] Often engaging diverse modalities of corporeal and affective interactions, intermediality takes our focus to the transformative potential of artworks that express their messages through two or more media forms. In modern and contemporary Chinese-language reportage, intermediality provides an expedient approach to engage reportage studies in a conversation with resonant discourses on indexicality and realisms, and on artistic fidelity and creative intimacy in nonfiction, photography, ethno-autobiography, film, and media archeology. In chapters on nonfiction documentary films (by Moran and Ma), intermediality emphasizes the representational level of images and subjects and the level of diegesis. In chapters on photography and documentaries (by Mirra, Chen, Guo, Zhang, Ma, and others), intermediality draws attention to the synesthetic resonances and mutual transpositions between different affective experiences, such as text and image, hearing and perception, and sound and colors. Intermediality creates alternative affective experiences for the reportage readers/audience, and opens up nonnormative realms of interpretations of hybrid presentations of images and texts. By yielding insights on memory, storytelling, and spectatorship, intermediality allows us to rethink nonfiction works as vehicles for the creative energies and ideals of social activism.

A major contribution of this volume to current studies of nonfiction art is its discussion of photographic reportage. Photographic reportage calls attention to the significant and complex dynamism between the photographer/reporter and the photographed subject. As Barthes reminds us, "a photograph can be the object of three practices (or of three emotions, or of three intentions): to do, to undergo, to look."[66] The photographer himself or herself is the spectator, the "measure of photographic 'knowledge,'" whereas "the person or thing photographed is the target, the referent, a kind of little simulacrum, any eidolon emitted by the object."[67] The relation between the photographer/reporter and the subject of photography or reportage invites reflections on the portrait-photograph as "a closed field of forces." The making of a portrait-photograph invites reflections on posing and obliged resistance to compromising individuality.[68] Yet photography also animates the subject and creates new forms of affective experiences, which can include a form of general commitment of a photographer to his or her surroundings, or sometimes the photographer's provocative encounters with the photographed.

Several chapters in this volume consider photographic reportage as an artistic form by using new forms and discourses to examine the interrelations between the interviewer and the interviewee and how, because of race, ethnicity, class, and gender, such interrelations become intricate and complex in facilitating new perspectives and forms of spectatorship. Li Guo considers how photographic reportage by Taiwanese reporters Liao Chia-chan and Yan Hsin-chu facilitates affective encounters with their disabled and socially marginalized subjects. The photographer/reporter's intrasubjective experience in the communication process contributes to an emotionally appealing and plurimedial reportage, allowing the audience to understand the contexts of the interviewees' experiences with possibilities for interaction and response. For Federica Mirra, photographic reportage by Yan Wang Preston on the state-sanctioned practice of transplanting trees in the "Forest Chongqing" project embraces an empathetic, documentary approach and facilitates personal, emotional connections with nonhuman species. For Yanshuo Zhang, the photographic work of Zhuang Xueben 莊學本 (1909–1984) for *Liangyou* 良友 magazine on human faces of the Tibetan and Qiang ethnic communities between 1934 and 1942 interjected a strong subjectivity, wide-ranging epistemologies, and sometimes even "spectacular curiosity" into his work, creating multifaceted images of China's western borderlands. Po-hsi Chen's study of photographic reportage by foreign photojournalists in the international section of the Taiwan magazine *Ren Jian* likewise explores the photographer/reporter as an intermediary subject, who could endow the photographed subjects with a certain degree of agency.

Photographic reportage is instrumental in reconfiguring the intrasubjective relationship between the photographer and the photographed. By providing an elastic interrelationship between text and image, photographic reportage opens up new aesthetic, spiritual, and psychic dimensions of articulating truth. André Bazin noted the apparent rivalry between photographic reporting and the use of drawings in illustrated magazines between 1890 and 1910, and endorsed photography for "freeing the plastic arts from their obsession with likeness" because it only entails a "nonliving agent" between the originating object and its reproduction.[69] The function of photographic images is to "help us to remember the subject and to preserve him from a second spiritual death."[70] And yet the penchant in photographic reportage to strive for objectivity raises questions about artistic arrangements and manipulations of personal and social spaces. As Laughlin observes, "especially in reportage, space is organized so as to bring out themes and achieve desired effects."[71] An example is Ding Ling's "Eventful Autumn," which Laughlin calls "urban protest reportage" that resorts to a theatrical mode of spatial signification. Further, the reportage text "can exploit the techniques of illustrating characters" at the scene in an event.[72] A study of photographic reportage expands the horizon of reportage works to visual materials, and engages critical inquiries about how gaze, visuality, and transmedial spectatorship are constructed to facilitate epistemic processes of knowing the Other.

Among published works on photographic reportage, a prominent example is Po-hsi Chen's 2019 essay on Lan Bozhou's leftist reportage "Song of the Covered Wagon," which includes numerous photographic works as historical evidence of the tragic fate that befell Communist activists during the White Terror in Taiwan. This volume expands studies of photographic reportage by including a wide spectrum of modern and contemporary works from mainland China and Taiwan, reflecting intersecting themes of disability, gender, race, ethnicity, and indigeneity, as well as nonhuman subjects of photography. Photographic reportage invites a renewed reflection on transmediality underlying the shifting and hybrid poetics of Sinophone reportage with the introduction of print culture and new forms of media technologies. The poetics of reportage necessarily exceeds the written tradition of reportage and entails audiences' participation at the extraliterary level. Photographic reportage could thus be considered, along with documentary film, as a form of transmedia documentary products that are distinguished not so much by a political function of effecting social changes, but by an artistic "response-ability" as meaningful interventions amid the trials of the era we live in.

Reportage on Race, Ethnicity, and Indigeneity

This volume provides a wide-reaching investigation of Sinophone reportage works on race, ethnicity, foreignness, and overseas diasporic identities, covering a broad span from reportage works on overseas Chinese coolies in the 1870s, to photographic reportage on Qiang and Tibetan peoples in the early twentieth century, to Taiwan's reportage on aboriginal peoples, and to overseas Chinese immigrants' documentary reportage in the new millennium. These chapters explore how reportage texts, images, and documentaries provide plurimedial presentations of race, ethnicity, and diasporic identities, reflecting reportage's elasticity in diverse articulations such as news media and print culture, modern photography, travel writings, independent documentary, and mass media production. Four chapters in this volume (Laughlin, Zhang, Zhu, and Ma) showcase reportage as an artistic medium that reflects on or facilitates culturally bound gazes at and through the Other. As these chapters display, encountering racial otherness activates nascent insights, be they inverted gazes of selfhood, agonizing reflections on one's own otherness, new aspirations of national or personal identity for the Other, or uncanny misrecognitions of the Other. Racial, ethnic, and indigenous demarcation of subjectivity effectively expands the empathetic horizons of reportage, by reflecting on and extending the boundaries of personal epistemic experiences, and also enhances and reinforces affective bonds between the reporter/photographer/documentary filmmaker and their audience, cultivating a profound awareness of sincerity, devotion, and care for the other. Notably, the authors expand the notion of race by engaging reportage on ethnicity in China, Taiwan, and overseas diaspora communities as a broader concept that, rather than being an external signifier for cultural Otherness, could be appropriated for expressions of a self-endorsing, native understanding of subjectivity. The ethnic subject could be endowed with the position of an author or self-reporter or filmmaker who embraces his or her own indigeneity for new possibilities of space-making and storytelling.

In a 1997 essay, Yingjin Zhang proposes a distinction between "race" and "ethnicity," suggesting a preference of "ethnicity" over "race" as "an equivalent of *minzu* in historical and social-scientific literatures in the field of Chinese studies."[73] Importantly, Zhang considers the notion of "ethnicity" to be a more fluid term that is more relational and less problematic in analyzing relationships between the Han and minorities.[74] At the heart of the study of nationhood and ethnicity, Zhang proposes, "apart from discerning the political hierarchies in majority/minority representation, is a conceptualization of the hegemonic culture not as a self-stabilizing structure but rather as negotiated, present processes whereby the geopolitical boundaries of centers and margins are periodically redrawn and the localized differences tactfully articulated."[75] The limitations of "race" as a discursive concept also have been articulated by researchers on Native American studies, as state discourses about racial notions of identity often fall short in their articulations of indigenous identity, and of how indigeneity was constructed as a cultural heritage and its attachment to land and language.[76] This volume reconsiders the cultural and historical constructions of race, ethnicity, indigeneity, and Sinophone diaspora through reportage or even self-reportage writings, photography, and film, taking reportage as an artistic prism through which different positionalities are negotiated in conversation across spatiotemporal distances.

An important contribution of this volume is the discussion of indigeneity beyond the mainland Chinese state narrative about ethnicity (*minzu*) and minority ethnicities (*shaoshu minzu*). Several chapters in this volume explore the complex parallelism between indigeneity and the cultural legacy of nativism in the greater Sinophone cultures. Laughlin's study of Gu Mengren's reportage on northern Taiwanese fishermen and indigenous Atayal people in the mountains of eastern Hsinchu contributes to theoretical reflections on indigeneity, cultural authenticity, and Taiwan's geocultural specificity in the milieu of global cosmopolitanism, by exploring the unique relationship between aboriginal reportage and the rise of Taiwan's literary nativism in the 1970s.[77] Laughlin holds that Gu Mengren's reportage is particularly valuable because of its evocation of "an analogy between the relationship of Taiwan to the global cosmopolitan mainstream, on the one hand, and that of indigenous tribes to the mainlander-dominated mainstream, on the other." Reportage is instrumental in representing this trend of "nativism" in Taiwan as a counter-discourse to the elite discourse of cosmopolitan modernism (globalism).

THIS VOLUME COMPRISES three thematic sections, including (1) Contesting Chinese Reportage, (2) Envisioning Taiwanese Reportage, and (3) Race, Indigeneity, and Border Crossings. Chapter 1 by Thomas Moran studies the documentary aesthetics in six recent documentaries of Zhang Mengqi (章夢奇 b. 1987), an active participant in the *Folk Memory Project* guided by Wu Wenguang. Moran considers how Laughlin's investigation of the production of social space in the literature of the real helps to understand Zhang's work as a kind of praxis or intervention, and how Zhang's works envision new documentary spaces that invite alternative perception, creativity, and being. Building on Yingjin Zhang's discussion on Wu Wenguang's documentary films and "the ethics of 'response-ability,'" Moran investigates how filmmakers and artists of the real, as cultural practitioners, engage with and contribute to the social debates and movements of their times.

Chapter 2 by Federica Mirra examines photographic works by UK-based Chinese photographer Yan Wang Preston, who deploys her camera to reflect on the state-sanctioned practice of transplanting trees and rewilding in China. Preston's photographic work *Forest* problematizes the ecological transformations enforced by the government under the official campaign of "Forest Chongqing" since 2008. By reducing the long-established separation between ecology and mankind, Preston's photographs envision an ecology that develops despite and alongside capitalism and urbanization. Whereas the campaign of "Forest Chongqing" is a political and commercial strategy to display national success in environmental activism, Preston's reportage spreads a holistic view of ecology, reimagining trees as interconnected with human beings and the urban space.

Chapter 3 by Federico Picerni explores contemporary nonfiction and its debt to reportage literature as an instrument for workers' narratives. Picerni examines nonfiction accounts by two worker writers who are members of the Picun Literature Group in Beijing, a space devoted to literary training and creative writing for rural-to-urban migrant laborers. Picerni is concerned with the rearticulation of authorial voice and perspective, involvement with their objects and investigation, and the "activist" functions assigned to anchor workers' nonfiction to the tradition of labor reportage. The (dis)continuity of the shift from reportage to nonfiction mirrors the transition from older workers' literature to today's migrant workers' literature, which carries forward the "task" to build a labor narrative by workers themselves.

Chapter 4 by Charles A. Laughlin studies Taiwan's "literary reportager" Gu Mengren and his best-known work, "Black Tribe," about Atayal tribesman living in the mountains at the eastern edge of Hsinchu county. Laughlin approaches the author as a social type in the tumultuous decade before the lifting of martial law in Taiwan. Gu is initially encouraged to write reportage by Huang Chunming (1935–), a key figure in nativist literature, which, like reportage, focuses the on social life of contemporary Taiwan and on the predicament of marginalized populations, unlike the modernist fiction that held sway since the 1950s. This cultural-political reversal is central to *Black Tribe*, Gu's first reportage collection. Gu focuses on farming, mining, and fishing among impoverished Han Chinese populations, but the title work concerns the indigenous Atayal tribe, hunter-gatherers as yet unrepresented in modern literature. Immersing himself among tribesmen, Gu achieves something unprecedented in Taiwan's literature.

Chapter 5 by Po-hsi Chen focuses on *Ren Jian* (1985–1989), a pioneering magazine in Taiwan that documented and participated in social campaigns, including sex workers' rights, environmental activism, and indigenous rights movements. Chen examines how *Ren Jian* situated Taiwan's photojournalism in the Third World by translating reportage from globally recognized photojournalists, such as Mitome Tadao (b. 1938), Peter Magubane (b. 1932), Dorothea Lange (1895–1965), and Higuchi Kenji (b. 1937). *Ren Jian*'s translation of these photojournalists' reportage exemplifies good reportage in writing and visual aesthetics for the magazine's reporters and readership. While analyzing the magazine's male-centered glorification of foreign photojournalists, Chen also discusses a *Ren Jian* female reporter's coverage of child prostitution, which explores a female perspective on photojournalism.

Chapter 6 by Li Guo examines reportage essays on people with disability by Liao Chia-chan, with photography by his wife Yan Hsin-chu, published in *Ren Jian* in 1986. Guo inspects these aesthetically experimental reportage works, which comprise nonfiction writing, photography, medical records, and legal documents. In *Moon Children*, Liao and Yan embrace fairytale elements in their narrative and strive for an empathetic approach in their reportage on the photographed child with albinism. Further, the mixed media of narrative portraiture and photographic images generates an interactive mode of storytelling, suturing memories and interviews with images. Another work of reportage, through representations of the blind Pig Master Ah Hsu and his affective bonds with livestock, illustrates an ekphrastic process that entails an empathetic identification with the blind and disabled.

In chapter 7, Ping Zhu traces pioneering works of Chinese reportage in late Qing autoethnographic texts and drawings in newspapers about Chinese coolies in the 1870s. As early examples of labor reportage, these works display a commitment to sincerity and a revulsion against capitalist greed as well as a growing awareness of racial or national crises. Such emotional engagement, moral certainty, and the impulse for visual representations in early journalistic writing continued in later newspaper essays and exposé novels about overseas Chinese workers, covering the mistreatment of Chinese immigrants in the United States during the Chinese exclusion period (1882–1943). They shared a strong penchant for humanist emotions and social engagement that was later shared by May Fourth literature.

Chapter 8 by Yanshuo Zhang investigates how photographic reportage, as an emerging domain of nationalistic imagination, took root in China's southwestern and northwestern ethnic frontier regions in the 1930s and 1940s. While providing aesthetic pleasure and exotic spectacles of non-Han communities to China's reading public, photographic reportage reflected an ethnographic realism, imagining the former "barbarian" ethnic frontiers as multiethnic centers of the new nation-state. Zhang studies the renowned photographer Zhuang Xueben (1909–1984) and his construction of ethnic groups in photographic reportage for *Liangyou* magazine. Driven by a desire to foster interethnic unity, Zhuang deployed artistic means and visual technologies to portray the humanity of non-Han groups.

In chapter 9, Ran Ma explores reportage-style film and media representations by and about Chinese (im)migrants in Japan since the late 1990s and early 2000s. Ma traces the history of Chinese-in-Japan documentary media and explores new perspectives on intersectional inquiries into transnational affectivity in Sinophone film and media studies. Besides discussing film and media representations of affective life pertaining to Chinese *ryūgakusei* and migrants, Ma explores the multilayered sociopolitical relations that Chinese in Japan are situated within, contending with, and working through. The chapter situates the inconsistent history of Chinese-in-Japan documentary media in relation to affectivity against the backdrop of transformations in Chinese and Japanese societies since the mid-1990s, as well as the changing media ecologies in Japan and beyond.

In Memory of Our Times

In his collection *In Memory of Our Times: Thirteen Essays on Reportage* 我們如何記憶這時代—報導文學十三講 (2024), Taiwanese reportage writer Yang Du observes that the blossoming of digital cultures, "We Media" (自媒

體), and diverse social media platforms have created an opportune climate for the development of reportage, and permitted every ordinary citizen to become a reportage author through activist endeavors. Yang celebrates the plurimedial forms of contemporary reportage and its myriad venues of dissemination, affirming that "Today's reportage serves as the testimony of how we commemorate our times" (今日的報導文學，即是我們如何記憶這時代的見証).[78] Resonating with Yang's statement, this volume explores the function of reportage as a medium for documenting and providing objective testimonies of historical events by including reportage auteurs, photographers, and filmmakers from diverse gendered, racial, cultural, and historical backgrounds. This volume expands the legacy of earlier women reportage authors, deploying reportage writing to explore "new social [and] political terrains across national boundaries" and to imagine alternative aesthetic and political sentiments beyond a nationalistic framework.[79] As Amy Dooling observes, early-twentieth-century female reportage authors, including Ding Ling, Hu Lanqi 胡蘭畦 (1901–1994), Bai Lang 白朗 (1912–1994), and Chen Xuezhao 陳學昭 (1906–1991), "offered a distinctly gendered vision of the historical crisis sweeping urban China," and resorted to wartime reportage writing to "carve out new imaginative terrain for modern Chinese women's writing."[80] Women's reportage writing played a vital role in feminist literary historiography, powerfully articulating "a sense of women engaging in the front lines of national history."[81] Whereas English-language scholarship on modern and contemporary women's reportage writing in Chinese remains scant, the current volume offers groundbreaking coverage of Chinese and Sinophone reportage in documentary film, photography, and nonfiction writing by women in four chapters (by Moran, Ran, Mirra, and Picerni). In addition, two other chapters offer significant discussion of women's reportage works in collaboration with male authors (such as Yan Hsin-chu's photography in Guo's chapter) or contributing to male-edited magazines or documentary films (such as the reportage on Taiwan's child prostitutes by female author Tseng Shu-mei 曾淑美, and reportage in Chen's chapter on documentary photography by Dorothea Lange from male author Kuo Li-hsin 郭力昕). Covering an eclectic range of reportage by women based in mainland China, Taiwan, and diaspora cultures in Europe and Japan, these chapters show that contemporary women's reportage is a rejuvenated mode of expression that seeks intersectional forms of gendered, racial, social, and environmental justice by articulating the interests of marginalized communities.

Besides drawing from and expanding Guattari's discussion on the ethico-aesthetic paradigm, this volume discusses ethics as response-ability as a renewed theoretical lens for reconsidering Chinese-language reportage and exploring new critical potentials of established scholarships in reportage studies. As discussed above, the conceptualization of this edited volume is much indebted to Yingjin Zhang's studies on ethics as response-ability in Wu Wenguang's documentary and the mode of epistephilia in observational documentaries representing earthquakes, to his pioneering inquiry regarding reportage's political function in exploring a subversive discourse to resist ideological interpellations, and to his seminal distinction between the concepts of "race" and "ethnicity" and reconsideration of "ethnicity" as a more elastic, relational term in describing the Han-minority relationships.[82] Drawing synergic vigor from Zhang's contributions, this volume continues Zhang's scholarly bequest in two aspects. First, six chapters (by Moran, Mirra, Chen, Guo, Zhang, and Ma) focus on exploring reportage as a plurimedial form of expression by focusing on photography and documentary films. Second, four chapters (by Laughlin, Zhu, Zhang, and Ma) engage race, ethnicity, and indigeneity as theoretical prisms in considering Chinese-language reportage across cultural, national, and geopolitical boundaries. This volume considers reportage as an aesthetically and politically progressive form that could facilitate what bell hooks called "mindful awareness to bonding across differences" of identity, while fostering empathy, solidarity, and conscious border-crossing.[83] In particular, contributors to this volume contest and expand established understandings of race and ethnicity in Chinese-language reportage; question the complexity of the racialized gaze in visual, cinematic, and narrative representations of marginalized communities; and make cases for the new ethico-political obligations of reportage in navigating interspersing spaces of visibility and power.

NOTES

1. The authors of the introduction are indebted to an anonymous reviewer of this volume for this observation.
2. Laughlin, "Reportage and the Forms of Nonfiction Art," 190.
3. Frukacz, "Literary Reportage or Journalistic Fiction?," 7.
4. Shiu, "Reportage in Taiwan," 121.
5. See Tuchman, "The News Net," 253–76.
6. Yang Kui, "Q&A on Taiwan's Reportage Literature."
7. Chen Yingzhen, "Yang Kui and Taiwan's Reportage Literature."
8. Yang Du, *In Memory of Our Times*, 88–89.
9. Yang Du, *In Memory of Our Times*, 96.
10. Yang Du, *In Memory of Our Times*, 415.
11. Yang Du, *In Memory of Our Times*, 416.
12. On literary devices in reportage, see Yang Du's discussion of "Wang Jingwei

in Front of the Camera" (開麥拉之前的汪精衛, 1939), by Huang Gang 黃鋼 (1917–1993), *In Memory of Our Times*, 74–80.

13. Yang Du's emphasis on reportage's aesthetic forms here resonates with Mao Dun's discussion of reportage's celebrated "imaging quality" (形象化). See Mao Dun, "About 'Reportage Literature.'" Yang Kui uses very similar language around the same time; see chapter 4 in this work.

14. Yang Du, *In Memory of Our Times*, 550.

15. Sunyoung Park, "A Forgotten Aesthetic," 273–87.

16. Linda Hoaglund, "Protest Art in 1950s Japan."

17. See Jesty, *Art and Engagement in Early Postwar Japan*, 2018.

18. Lu Xun, "Preface to the First Collection of Short Stories, *A Call to Arms*," 6.

19. Liu Binyan, "On the Bridge Construction Sites"; Liu Pin-yen, "The Inside News of the Newspaper," 411–64.

20. Po-hsi Chen, "Chanting Slogans with Muted Voices," 91–94.

21. Chou, "Formal Features of Chinese Reportage," 203–5.

22. Chen, "Genre, Convention, and Society," 97.

23. Zhang, "Narrative, Ideology, Subjectivity," 231.

24. The term "realism" has taken on diverse forms and interpretations in Chinese and Sinophone literary and artistic works since the twentieth century, ranging from *xianshi zhuyi* 現實主義 to *xieshi zhuyi* 寫實主義. In China, Taiwan, and Hong Kong, the relationships of works of reportage to diverse literary and artistic realisms have remained tenuous and contested in heterogeneous social, political, and historical contexts. In mainland China, Liu Binyan's reportage promoted a form of "critical realism" (批判現實主義) and was dismissed as a rightist false realism because of Liu's focus on darker social realities and diversion from the Maoist model of "socialist realism" (社會主義的現實主義) promulgated in Mao Zedong's "Talks at the Yenan Forum on Literature and Arts" (在延安座談會上的講話, 1942). The resurgence of Taiwanese reportage in the 1970s, marked by a general trend of "returning to realities" (回歸現實), could be traced to a series of earlier debates about "realism" (寫實主義) in Taiwanese literature, including Yang Kui's defense of Taiwan's grassroots realism as a more grounded native alternative to the Japanese aesthetic of realism in his response to Mitsuru Nishikawa; the influence of Chinese leftist literature and its submission to political propaganda under the Kuomintang regime after 1949; and the impact of modernism and comparative literature in Taiwan's burgeoning studies of foreign literature (Hsiao, "The Recurrence of Realism"). Likewise, Shiu Wen-wei considers the renovation of Taiwan's reportage after World War II as a form of "elevated expression of the trend of realism" (寫實主義思潮的昇華) (Shiu, "Reportage in Taiwan," 127) that distinguishes itself from realisms in both 1930s Chinese leftist reportage and the Maoist model of socialist realism. As mainland Chinese literary thought in the 1930s and 1940s suffered political censorship and suppression in the 1950s in Taiwan, authors such as Chen Yingzhen and Chiang Hsun 蔣勳 (1947–), among others, seek to explore an alternative form of realism (寫實主義) rooted in Taiwan's social and political realities. In sum, reportage's development in Chinese and Sinophone contexts manifests pluralist forms of realism and invites situated considerations in diverse specific social, political, and historical circumstances.

25. Guattari, *Chaosmosis*, 3.

26. Guattari, *Chaosmosis*, 1.

27. Guattari, *Chaosmosis*, 22.
28. Guattari, *Chaosmosis*, 2.
29. Guattari, *Chaosmosis*, 16.
30. Guattari, *Chaosmosis*, 9.
31. Guattari, *Chaosmosis*, 13.
32. Guattari, *Chaosmosis*, 4.
33. Avila, "Three Ecologies Diffracted: Intersectionality for Ecological Caring," 3.
34. Guattari, *The Guattari Reader*, 216.
35. Guattari, *The Guattari Reader*, 216; Bertelsen and Murphie, "An Ethics of Everyday Infinities and Powers," 153).
36. Guattari, *Chaosmosis*, 7.
37. Laughlin, *Chinese Reportage*, 115.
38. The term "affective reversibility" could be traced to Anya Daly's *Merleau-Ponty and the Ethics of Intersubjectivity* (Palgrave, 2016). Daly deploys the term "affective reversibility" to describe a form of "pro-social responsiveness" in intersubjective relations that promotes empathetic connections between the subject and the other. Affective reversibility emphasizes the "interdependences" and "intersections" between linguistic subjects and provides a nondualistic approach to understanding the relationship between the subject and object (Daly, *Merleau-Ponty and the Ethics of Intersubjectivity*, 24).
39. On reportage as a mode of aesthetic expression in narrative films such as *24 City* and *A Simple Life*, see Laughlin, "Images of Aging."
40. Zhang, "Perseverance through Aftershocks," 132.
41. "Pleasure of knowing," as opposed to "pleasure of seeing." The distinction is made by Bill Nichols, *Issues and Concepts in Documentary*, 178. As Thomas Moran observes in chapter 1 of this volume, the latest edition of Nichols and Baron, *Introduction to Documentary*, updates this word to "epistemophilia."
42. Zhang, "Perseverance through Aftershocks," 147. An earlier discussion on ethics as response-ability in Chinese-language documentary appears in Kuei-fen Chiu and Yingjin Zhang's study of Wu Wenguang's "ethics of self" and a Levinasian "response-ability" for the other in Wu's works (Chiu and Zhang, *New Chinese-Language Documentaries*, 79–98).
43. See Chambers, "The 'Liang Village Series,'" 267.
44. Mally, "The Americanization of the Soviet Living Newspaper," 5.
45. Xiaomei Chen, *Performing the Socialist State*, 217.
46. See Liu Yican, "Reportage Plays on Stage."
47. Zhang, "Narrative, Ideology, Subjectivity," 211, 236.
48. Nichols, *Speaking Truths with Film*, 36.
49. Nichols, *Speaking Truths with Film*, 74.
50. Nichols, *Speaking Truths with Film*, 215.
51. Shu, *Buglers on the Home Front*.
52. Laughlin, *Chinese Reportage*, 255–62.
53. Nicolai Volland notes that, after publishing an article on new reportage from the Soviet Union by Boris Polevoy in 1953, reportage became a popular form in *Translation* (Yiwen 譯文) magazine. Volland, *Socialist Cosmopolitanisms*, 172–73.

54. Information in this and the following paragraph on reportage in the PRC in the 1980s is based on Thomas Moran's 1994 doctoral dissertation, "True Stories: Contemporary Chinese Reportage and its Ideology and Aesthetic," which is still the only English-language work on this important phase of reportage history.

55. Moran, "True Stories," 426–27.

56. Regarding the translation of reportage in Taiwan as *baodao wenxue*, Po-hsi Chen observes, "When reportage was introduced to colonial Taiwan in the late 1930s, Yang Kui rendered it as *hōkoku bungaku* (which, in kanji, are the same characters as in *baogao wenxue*)" (Chen, "Lan Bozhou's 'Song of the Covered Wagon,'" 105). Yet the term *baodao wenxue* came to be more commonly used in Taiwan. Chen argues that for leftist reportage author Lan Bozhou, "the difference between *baogao* and *baodao* is not merely semantic but rather also embodies entirely different historical trajectories and ideologies of literary development" (See Chen, "Lan Bozhou's 'Song of the Covered Wagon,'" 105).

57. For discussion of reportage published from 1960s to the late 1970s in Taiwan, see note 17 in Li Guo's chapter "Reportage, Photography, and the Ekphrastic Encounter: On *Moon Children* by Liao Chia-chan and Yan Hsin-chu."

58. Lin Chi-yang, "Fictional Narrative Conventions in Taiwanese Reportage," 31.

59. Lin Chi-yang, "Fictional Narrative Conventions in Taiwanese Reportage," 39.

60. Yang Du, *In Memory of Our Times*, 56. An example of literary depiction in reportage is *Liao Binghan's Life and Death* (*Liao Binghan shengqian sihou*) 廖秉漢生前死後, by Hong Kong writer Li Guowei 李國威 (1948–1993), a reportage on Liao Binghan, an officer at Yau Ma Tei Police Station who reportedly committed "suicide" by jumping off a balcony of Hong Ming Building in 1977. Addressing suspicions of his death as a murder related to the conflicts between police and the Independent Commission Against Corruption, Li resorts to first-person narration from Liao's perspective, deploying fictional depiction to fill in the gap of narration when it is impossible to have truthful accounts from the deceased victim. See Wong, "Accounts of Everyday Life."

61. Wang Hsin, *Farewell, Orchid Island*, 11.

62. Lai, "Site Visit Report on Logging and Deforestation in Danda Forest Region," 25–42.

63. Li Guo, "From the Margins to the Hearth," 163.

64. Kristeva, *Desire in Language*, 37.

65. Bazerman, "Intertextualities," 54.

66. Barthes, *Camera Lucida*, 9.

67. Barthes, *Camera Lucida*, 9.

68. Barthes, *Camera Lucida*, 11, 13.

69. Bazin, *What Is Cinema?*, 13.

70. Bazin, *What Is Cinema?*, 10.

71. Laughlin, "Narrative Subjectivity," 28.

72. Laughlin, "Narrative Subjectivity," 28.

73. Zhang, "From 'Minority Film' to 'Minority Discourse,'" 74–75.

74. Zhang, "From 'Minority Film' to 'Minority Discourse,'" 76.

75. Zhang, "From 'Minority Film' to 'Minority Discourse,'" 82.

76. Forte, "Introduction: 'Who Is an Indian?,'" 18.

77. See Gu, *Black Tribe*; Shih Shu-mei, "Globalisation," 143–53; Kuei-fen Chiu, "Cosmopolitanism and Indigenism," 159–78.

78. Yang Du, *In Memory of Our Times*, 27.

79. Dooling, "Introduction," 12.

80. Dooling, "Introduction," 12. On wartime reportage by Hu Lanqi and Bai Lang, see Guo, "Women's Wartime Life Writing."

81. Dooling, "Introduction," 13.

82. On reportage representing the intersection of race and femininity, see Jie Guo "Reportage, Ethnicity, and Feminine Subjectivities," 1–40.

83. hooks, *Writing Beyond Race*, 146.

REFERENCES

Avila, Martin. "Three Ecologies Diffracted: Intersectionality for Ecological Caring." *Nordic Design Research* 8 (2019): 1–8.

Barthes, Roland. *Camera Lucida: Reflections on Photography*. Trans. Richard Howard. New York: MacMillan, 1981.

Bazerman, Charles. "Intertextualities: Volosinov, Bakhtin, Literary Theory, and Literacy Studies." In Arnetha F. Ball and Sarah Warshauer Freedman, eds., *Bakhtinian Perspectives on Language, Literacy, and Learning*, 53–65. Cambridge: Cambridge University Press, 2010.

Bazin, André. *What Is Cinema?* Trans. Hugh Gray. Berkeley: University of California Press, 1967.

Bertelsen, Lone, and Andrew Murphie. "An Ethics of Everyday Infinities and Powers: Felix Guatarri on Affect and the Refrain." In Melissa Gregg, Gregory J. Seigworth, Sara Ahmed, Brian Massumi, Elspeth Probyn, and Lauren Berlant, eds., *The Affect Theory Reader*, 138–60. Durham: Duke University Press, 2010.

Chambers, Harlan. "The 'Liang Village Series': Postsocialist Dynamics of Liang Hong's Rural Investigation." *Modern Chinese Literature and Culture* 21.2 (2019): 249–92.

Chen Ming-pan. *Exploration of Realities* (Xianshi de tansuo 現實的探索). Taipei: San Min Book Co., 1980.

Chen, Po-hsi. "Chanting Slogans with Muted Voices: Lan Bozhou's 'Song of the Covered Wagon' and Untimely Leftist Reportage in Taiwan." *Modern Chinese Literature and Culture* 21.2 (2019): 81–128.

Chen, Xiaomei. "Genre, Convention, and Society: A Reception Study of the Chinese *Reportage*." *Yearbook of Comparative and General Literature* 34 (1985), 85–105.

Chen, Xiaomei. *Performing the Socialist State: Modern Chinese Theater and Film Culture*. New York: Columbia University Press, 2023.

Chen, Yingzhen. "Yang Kui and Taiwan's Reportage Literature" (Yang Kui yu Taiwan baodao wenxue 楊逵與台灣報導文學). *China Tide* 夏潮, October 22, 2005.

Chiu, Kuei-fen. "Cosmopolitanism and Indigenism: The Uses of Cultural Authenticity in an Age of Flows." *New Literary History* 44.1 (2013): 159–78.

Chiu, Kuei-fen, and Yingjin Zhang. *New Chinese-Language Documentaries: Ethics, Subject and Place*. New York: Routledge, 2015.

Chou, Yin-hwa. "Formal Features of Chinese Reportage and an Analysis of Liang Qichao's 'Memoirs of My Travels in the New World.'" *Modern Chinese Literature* 1.2 (1985): 201–17.

Chung, Jae Won Edward. "Maps of Life and Abjection: Reportage, Photography, and Literature in Postwar Seoul." *Journal of Asian Studies* 79.2 (2020): 335–75.

Daly, Anya. *Merleau-Ponty and the Ethics of Intersubjectivity*. New York: Palgrave, 2016.

Dooling, Amy. "Introduction." In Amy Dooling, ed., *Writing Women in Modern China: The Revolutionary Years, 1936–1976*, 1–34. New York: Columbia University Press, 2005.

Forte, Maximillian C. "Introduction: 'Who Is an Indian?' The Culture Politics of a Bad Question." In Maximilian C. Forte, ed., *Who Is an Indian? Race, Place, and the Politics of Indigeneity in the Americas*, 3–51. Toronto: University of Toronto Press, 2014.

Frukacz, Katarzyna. "Literary Reportage or Journalistic Fiction? Polish Reporters' Struggles with the Form." *Literary Journalism Studies* 11.1 (2019): 7–24.

Gu, Mengren. *Heise de buluo* (Black tribe). Taipei: Shibao wenhua chuban shiye youxian gongsi, 1978.

Guattari, Félix. *Chaosmosis: An Ethico-Aesthetic Paradigm*. Trans. Paul Bains and Julian Pefanis. Bloomington: Indiana University Press, 1995.

Guattari, Félix. *The Guattari Reader*. Ed. Gary Genosko. London: Blackwell, 1996.

Guo, Jie. "Reportage, Ethnicity, and Feminine Subjectivities: Ai Wu's Journey to the South and Its 'Sequels.'" *Modern Chinese Literature and Culture* 21.2 (2019): 1–40.

Guo, Li. "Women's Wartime Life Writing in Early Twentieth-Century China." *CLCWeb: Comparative Literature and Culture* 17.3 (2015): http://dx.doi.org/10.7771/1481-4374.2637

Guo, Li. "From the Margins to the Hearth: A Study of Xu Gang's Environmental Reportage." *Modern Chinese Literature and Culture* 21.2 (2019): 162–206.

Hoaglund, Linda. "Protest Art in 1950s Japan: The Forgotten Reportage Painters" (抗議する美術—忘れられた1950代日本のルポルタージュ画家). *Asia-Pacific Journal: Japan Focus*. 12.43 (2014). https://apjjf.org/2014/12/43/Linda-Hoaglund/4203.html

hooks, bell. *Writing Beyond Race: Living Theory and Practice*. New York: Routledge, 2013.

Hsiao Jun-yi. "The Recurrence of Realism: Reportage Literature and Historical Ruptures" (Xieshi de fanfu: baodao wenxue yu lishi liekou 寫實的反覆: 報導文學與歷史裂口). *The Merit Times*, July 17, 2017.

Jesty, Justin. *Art and Engagement in Early Postwar Japan*. Ithaca: Cornell University Press, 2018.

Kristeva, Julia. *Desire in Language: A Semiotic Approach to Literature and Art*. Ed. Leon S. Roudiez. Trans. Thomas Gora, Alice Jardine, and Leon S. Roudiez. New York: Columbia University Press, 1982.

Kuan Hsiao-jung. *Report on Orchid Island 1987–2007* (Lan Yu baogao 蘭嶼報告: 1987–2007). Taipei: Ren Jian, 2007.

Lai Chun-piao. "Site Visit Report on Logging and Deforestation in Danda Forest Region" (Danda linqu kanfa xianchang baogao 丹大林區砍伐現場報告). *Ren Jian* issue 23 (September 1987): 25–42.

Lan Bozhou. "Song of the Covered Wagon I" (Huangmache zhi ge: shang 幌馬車之歌: 上). *Ren Jian* 3.11 (1988): 157–68.

Lan Bozhou. "Song of the Covered Wagon II" (Huangmache zhi ge: xia 幌馬車之歌: 下). *Ren Jian* 3.12 (1988): 141–47.

Laughlin, Charles A. "Narrative Subjectivity and the Production of Social Space in Chinese Reportage." *boundary 2* 25.3 (1998): 25–46.
Laughlin, Charles A. *Chinese Reportage: The Aesthetics of Historical Experience*. Durham: Duke University Press, 2002.
Laughlin, Charles A. "Writing the Actual." In Ban Wang, ed., *Words and Their Stories: Essays on the Language of the Chinese Revolution*, 135–48. Leiden: Brill, 2011.
Laughlin, Charles A. "Images of Aging and the Aesthetic of Actuality in Chinese Film: Reportage, Documentary, and the Art of the Real." *Modern Chinese Literature and Culture* 21.2 (2019): 207–48.
Laughlin, Charles A. "Reportage and the Forms of Nonfiction Art in China." In Yingjin Zhang, ed., *A World History of Chinese Literature*, 185–95. New York: Routledge, 2023.
Laughlin, Charles A., and Li Guo. "Reportage and Its Contemporary Variations: An Introduction." *Modern Chinese Literature and Culture* 21.2 (2019): v–xvi.
Lin Chi-yang. "Fiction Narrative Conventions in Taiwanese Reportage" ("Taiwan baodao wenxue de xugou xushi guiyue" 台灣報導文學的虛構敘事規約). *Taiwan Studies in Literature and History* no. 6 (2013): 25–47.
Lin Chi-yang and Shiu Wen-wei, eds. *Reportage Literature: A Reader* (*Baodao wenxue duben* 報導文學讀本). New Taipei City: Fish & Fish Co., 2002.
Liu Binyan. "On the Bridge Construction Sites" ("Zai qiaoliang gongdi shang" 在橋樑工地上). *Renmin wenxue,* vol. 1956, no. 4.
Liu Binyan. "The Inside News of the Newspaper" ("Benbao neibu xiaoxi" 本報內部消息). *Renmin wenxue,* vol. 1956, no. 6.
Liu, Binyan. *Two Kinds of Truth*. Ed. Perry Link. Bloomington: Indiana University Press, 2006.
Liu, Binyan, and E. Perry Link. *People or Monsters? And Other Stories and Reportage from China after Mao*. 1st Midland Book. Bloomington: Indiana University Press, 1983.
Liu Pin-yen [Liu Binyan]. "The Inside News of the Newspaper." In Hualing Nieh, ed., *Literature of the Hundred Flowers*, vol. II, 411–64. New York: Columbia University Press, 1981.
Liu, Yican. "Reportage Plays on Stage: Currents of the Era in Performance" (*Wutai baogao ju, fangcun zhijian kuijian shidai bolan* 舞台報告劇，方寸之間窺見時代波瀾). http://yn.people.com.cn/BIG5/n2/2020/1111/c372458-34407612.html
Lu Xun. "Preface to the First Collection of Short Stories, *A Call to Arms.*" In Joseph S. M. Lau and Howard Goldblatt, eds., *Columbia Anthology of Modern Chinese Literature*, 3–6. 2nd ed. Trans. Gladys Yang and Yang Xianyi. New York: Columbia University Press, 1997.
Mally, Lynn. "The Americanization of the Soviet Living Newspaper." *Carl Beck Papers in Russian and East European Studies*, no. 1903 (2008): 1–40.
Mao Dun. "About 'Reportage Literature'" (Guanyu "baogao wenxue" 關於"報告文學"). *Zhongliu* 中流 11 (1937): 15.
Moran, Thomas Elton. "True Stories: Contemporary Chinese Reportage and Its Ideology and Aesthetic." PhD diss., Cornell University, 1994. ProQuest 9501300.
Nichols, Bill. *Representing Reality: Issues and Concepts in Documentary*. Bloomington: Indiana University Press, 1991.

Nichols, Bill. *Speaking Truths with Film: Evidence, Ethics, Politics in Documentary.* Berkeley: University of California Press, 2016.

The Office for the Investigation of Historical Open Cases. "What Does Non-fiction Writing Mean to Taiwan?" (*Fei xugou xiezuo zai Taiwan yiwei zhe shenme?* 非虛構寫作在臺灣意味著什麼?). Office for the Investigation of Historical Open Cases. January 31, 2018. https://ohsir.tw/632/

Park, Sunyoung. "A Forgotten Aesthetic: Reportage in Colonial Korea, 1920–1930." In Heekyoung Cho, ed., *The Routledge Companion to Korean Literature*, 273–87. New York: Routledge, 2022.

Shih, Shu-mei. "Globalisation and the (in)significance of Taiwan." *Postcolonial Studies* 6.2 (2003): 143–53.

Shiu Wen-wei. "Reportage in Taiwan, 1949–1994" (Baodao wenxue zai Taiwan 報導文學在台灣). *Mass Communication Research* 新聞學研究 51 (1995): 121–42.

Shu, Yunzhong. *Buglers on the Home Front: The Wartime Practice of the Qiyue School.* Albany: SUNY Press, 2000.

Tuchman, Gaye. "The News Net." *Social Research* 45.2 (1978): 253–76.

Volland, Nicolai. *Socialist Cosmopolitanism: The Chinese Literary Universe, 1945–1965.* Studies of the Weatherhead East Asian Institute, Columbia University. New York: Columbia University Press, 2017.

Wang Hsin. *Farewell, Orchid Island* (Lan Yu, zaijian 蘭嶼，再見). Taipei: Chun wenxue chubanshe (Pure Literature Press), 1985.

Wong Shuk-han 黃淑嫻, "Accounts of Everyday Life? Historical Injustices and Hong Kong's Reportage Literature." (Shenghuo wenxue? Chenyuan daixue: Xianggang baogao wenxue 生活文學? 沉冤待雪：香港報告文學). *Ming Bao*, May 12, 2017. https://www.mingpaocanada.com/Tor/htm/News/20170512/HK-gfk1_er_r.htm

Yang Du. *In Memory of Our Times: Thirteen Essays on Reportage* (Women ruhe jiyi zhe shidai: baodao wenxue shisan jiang 我們如何記憶這時代—報導文學十三講). EPUB. Taipei: Homeward Publishing, 2024.

Yang Kui. "A Visit to the Disaster Area of the Taiwan Earthquake" ("Taiwan dizhen zaiqu kancha weiwen ji" 台灣地震災區勘察慰問記, 1935; originally published in Japanese). *Lianhe bao fu kan.* Trans. Qiu Zhenrui, 2000.

Yang Kui. "Q&A on Reportage Literature" (Baodao wenxue wenda 報導文學問答). *New Taiwanese Literature* 台灣新文學 2.5 (1937).

Yang, Lawrence Zi-Qiao. "Soil and Scroll: The Agrarian Origin of a Cold War Documentary Avant Garde." *Modern Chinese Literature and Culture* 21.2 (2019): 41–80.

Yang, Su-fen. *A Brief Introduction to Taiwanese Reportage Literature* (Taiwan baodao wenxue gailun 台灣報導文學概論). Taipei: Daoxiang, 2001.

Zhang, Yingjin. "Narrative, Ideology, Subjectivity: Defining a Subversive Discourse in Chinese Reportage." In Liu Kang and Xiaobing Tang, eds., *Politics, Ideology, and Literary Discourse in Modern China: Theoretical Interventions and Cultural Critique*, 211–42. Durham: Duke University Press, 1993.

Zhang, Yingjin. "From 'Minority Film' to 'Minority Discourse': Questions of Nationhood and Ethnicity in Chinese Cinema." *Cinema Journal* 36.3 (1997): 73–90.

Zhang, Yingjin. "Thirdspace Between Flows and Places: Chinese Independent Documentary and Social Theories of Space and Locality." In Carlos Rojas and Eileen

Chow, eds. *The Oxford Handbook of Chinese Cinemas*, 320–42. New York: Oxford University Press, 2013.

Zhang, Yingjin. "Perseverance through Aftershocks: Epistephilia in Chinese Reportage and Independent Documentary." *Modern Chinese Literature and Culture* 21.2 (2019): 129–61.

I

Contesting Chinese Reportage

ONE

The Poetics and Praxis of Zhang Mengqi's Documentary Films

Thomas Moran

Zhang Mengqi 章梦奇 (b. 1987) is a participant in the Folk Memory Project (*Minjian jiyi jihua* 民间记忆计划), the collaborative endeavor begun in 2010 and guided by Wu Wenguang 吴文光 (b. 1956) that has recorded village elders' memories of the famine of 1959–1961, the history of which has been "erased," Zhang says in her 2020 video lecture *Blue House*.[1] The project was first called the Starving Project (*Ji'e jihua* 饥饿计划) because the people involved in it were "starving" not only for knowledge of the suppressed history of the famine, but also for an outlet for creative expression, and through 2022, project participants had, in addition to recording oral histories, created sixty-one documentary films.[2] What follows is a discussion of Zhang Mengqi's poetics (the aesthetic of her films) and her praxis (how her filmmaking becomes community-building social activity). This chapter joins the discussion begun in the introduction to this volume of the ethico-aesthetic paradigm and the ethics of reportage and other forms of nonfiction art.

In the 1980s, Chinese reportage was moving into television, and the term *jishi wenxue* 纪实文学, which Laughlin and Guo translate as "documentary literature," was coming into wider use.[3] Reportage by a narrow definition was understood to be timely, agenda-driven reporting that to some fell short of being objective journalism and to others lacked literary quality.[4] It could not completely escape its heritage as "the work of the biased, passionate observer, who deliberately injects the revolutionary temperament of the author . . . into the reportage."[5] The issue was put this way in a 1986 article in *Reportage* (*Baogao wenxue* 报告文学): "[I]n general, reportage is propagandistic literature with a very clear bias. If it is not exposé, then it is panegyric." The author, Wu Liang, argued that *jishi wenxue* was more neutral and objective than *baogao wenxue*.[6]

By the mid-1980s, the term "TV reportage" (*dianshi baogao wenxue* 电视报告文学) was in use.[7] After the success of China Central Television's (CCTV's) 1988 *River Elegy* (*Heshang* 河殇), reportage authors who joined *River Elegy* coauthor Su Xiaokang 苏晓康 in moving into television included Jia Lusheng 贾鲁生, Hu Ping 胡平, Qian Gang 钱钢, Zhao Yu 赵瑜, and Zhang Shengyou 张胜友.[8] After June 4, 1989, Su Xiaokang joined Liu Binyan 刘宾雁 in exile, Qian Gang was forced to retire from the PLA, the journals *Reportage*, the *New Observer* (*Xin guancha* 新观察), and *Literary Monthly* (*Wenhui yuekan* 文汇月刊) closed, and the television projects on which Jia et al. had been working were canceled,[9] which brings us to an origin story of China's independent documentary film movement.

In 1988, CCTV launched "a number of large-scale documentary productions" to mark the fortieth anniversary of the founding of the PRC, but after June 4, 1989, films "that were considered untimely or inappropriate" were "shelved," including *The Chinese* (*Zhongguoren* 中国人), on which Wu Wenguang had been working.[10] Using CCTV equipment, Wu filmed his friends, and this turned into the 1990 *Bumming in Beijing* (*Liulang Beijing* 流浪北京), "often described as marking the birth of the New Documentary Movement."[11] That movement was one of what Chris Berry and Lisa Rofel call "the major transformations . . . in all kinds of actuality-based visual culture—from television news to the internet" that began in the early 1990s.[12]

The legacy of 1980s *baogao wenxue* is evident in broadcast television and independent documentary film. Reportage as exposé is in the films of documentarians such as Hu Jie 胡杰, and reportage as panegyric survives in CCTV productions such as the 2018 *Amazing China* (*Lihaile, wode guo* 厉害了，我的国). On a list of issues addressed by 1980s print "social issue reportage" (*shehui wenti baogao wenxue* 社会问题报告文学) compiled by reportage scholar Xie Yong 谢泳 are the highway system, the college entrance exam, threats to the environment, mental illness, and disability;[13] to Xie's list, one may add prostitution, rural poverty, government corruption, and the legal system. These topics have all been addressed in independent documentary films.

Lin Xu-dong writes that *Bumming in Beijing* was "a foray into a truly fringe world of filmmaking," which introduced to China a new documentary film form "that afforded the filmmaker the widest possible latitude for his artistic intuition about the events happening in the lives of his characters."[14] This "artistic" approach is seen in the subjective, creative, artistic work that is part of the Folk Memory Project, including Zhang Mengqi's "fringe" filmmaking. Zhang, who was trained as a dancer, joined the Folk Memory Project at twenty-three. From 2010 to 2021, Zhang directed, shot, and edited ten films in her Self-Portrait Series (*Zihuaxiang xilie* 自画像系列). The nine about her paternal grandfather's village are the focus of this study. We can infer from Zhang's films that the government has failed rural people; rural women have suffered because of the patriarchy; and the future is uncertain for rural children, girls in particular. But the people in Zhang's work are not in any sense merely vehicles for the expression of a message or protest. The most significant function of Zhang's films is to make us aware of our ignorance about the lives of the people in the films, and to make us emotionally cognizant of their dignity and beauty.

Laughlin and Guo argue that Chinese genres of the real "embody a distinctive epistephilic aesthetic that could be said to be a deeper and more meaningful characteristic than their purported veracity."[15] This is in reference to Bill Nichols's idea that unlike feature films, which titillate our scopophilia (our love of looking), documentaries also appeal to our epistemophilia (our desire to know).[16] We watch documentary film, in part, as a pursuit of knowledge. The influence of classic "voice-of-God" documentary film can, however, lead to the misunderstanding that this pursuit of knowledge ends with the acquisition of facts and truth. Documentary films such as Zhang Mengqi's appeal to and reinforce a contrary idea that our pursuit of knowledge has emotional and aesthetic components and is not intended to arrive at any single truth.

A way to get at the "deeper and more meaningful" something in documentary film is to shift emphasis to Nichols's assertion that there is "no hard and fast boundary between fiction and nonfiction." Indeed, one of the main modes of documentary filmmaking defined in *Introduction to Documentary* is poetic. In the latest edition of this book, Nichols and his coauthor, Jaimie Baron, write that the poetic mode "stresses mood, tone, and affect" and has the "expressive, sometimes performative, quality of avant-garde" film.[17] In Werner Herzog's opinion, documentary should not be about the "superficial 'truth of accountants' based in objectively observable facts" but must pursue "a deeper, 'ecstatic truth' that can only be reached 'through fabrication and imagination and stylization.'"[18] Like Herzog, Zhang Mengqi did not attend film school, and like Herzog, she makes poetic documentaries that are experimental, personal, and avant-garde.

Fig. 1.1. Zhang and her grandfather in *Dancing* (0:50:30). (© 2012, reprinted by permission of Zhang Mengqi.)

Beginning with her second film, *Self-Portrait: At 47 KM* (*Zihuaxiang: 47 gongli* 自画像: 47公里, 2011), all of Zhang's films, which she shoots and edits as a crew of one, have been made in and are about her paternal grandfather's village of Diaoyutai 钓鱼台村 in Hubei. The rest of the films are as follows—all of the titles begin "Self-Portrait" (自画像) followed by a colon, but I have omitted this in the following list: *Dancing at 47 KM* (*47 gongli tiaowu*, 47公里跳舞, 2012); *Dreaming at 47 KM* (*47 gongli zuomeng*, 47公里做梦, 2013); *Building the Bridge at 47 KM* (*47 gongli da qiao*, 47公里搭桥, 2014); *Dying at 47 KM* (*47 gongli zhi si*, 47公里之死, 2015); *Birth at 47 KM* (*Sheng yu 47 gongli*, 生于47公里, 2016); *Sphinx in 47 KM* (*47 gongli Sifenkesi*, 47公里斯芬克斯, 2017); *Window in 47 KM* (*47 gongli de chuanghu*, 47公里的窗户, 2019); and *Fairy Tale in 47 KM* (*47 gongli tonghua*, 47公里童话, 2021).[19]

These nine films may be considered as a fourteen-hour, expressive documentary engagement with the lives of some of the people who lived in one village over the course of a decade. Later films assume we remember earlier films and can be fully understood only if we have seen the previous work. Zhang's niece Ding Qixuan is the first villager to appear in front of Zhang's camera in the first 47 KM film, and ten years later she is with Zhang in the last shot of *Fairy Tale*; villager Fang Hong is in all the films from the 2013 *Dreaming*, made when Fang was eight, through the 2021 *Fairy Tale*, made when she was sixteen. "47 KM" is not a name used by the villagers. Zhang did not grow up in the village and had not visited it often before her first trip there to film; she did not know what the village was called. She knew only that she was to be met at the 47 KM marker along the highway from Suizhou. The village became "47 KM" in her films. That she uses an invented name for the village is appropriate, given that Zhang's films are not primarily about the documentation of fact or actuality. Neither are Zhang's films conventional "self-portraits," because they are more about other people than about her. Zhang gives us little information about her life in the village until the 2021 *Fairy Tale*, in which she for the first time shows us the room she lives in, describes how she works, and shares the emotions she had at the beginning of her project. The "self-portrait" in Zhang's titles might refer to the fact that Zhang's process of engaging others—sitting with them, talking to them, doing yoga and dancing with them, helping them with chores, playing and laughing with them, filming them—is a process of self-discovery. Zhang's reference to herself in her titles might also be a way of calling attention to the economic, educational, linguistic, and cultural gap that lies between her and the people of the village.

Zhang's films show us her relationship with her grandfather, what elders remember about the famine, how Zhang collected money for a memorial tablet for villagers who died in 1959 and 1960, and her interactions with several of the village's older women and several children. Zhang asks people to talk about their dreams and aspirations, and she comes to terms with her dual identity as both Zhang Mengqi (Zhang is her mother's surname) and Ding Qi 丁琪, the daughter of Ding Zuhua 丁祖花, from whom Zhang's mother is divorced and Zhang is estranged. We come to understand the people in Zhang's films gradually and partially and only by inference, because Zhang includes little in the way of exposition. Likewise, Zhang does not include establishing long shots to help us grasp the village's geography. Only after seeing several films do we have some idea of the layout of the village, and only at the end of *Fairy Tale* does Zhang show us most of the village in a single frame.

The nine films of Zhang's 47 KM series I am discussing may be divided into two parts based on aesthetics. The last four, *Birth* through *Fairy Tale*, are longer, more slowly paced, and include fewer people, fewer stories, and fewer total shots than do the first five. Features of Zhang's cinematography, however, are present in all the films I am considering here. Almost everything is shot with a normal lens; the number of zoom shots can be counted on one hand. Zhang's camera is almost always steady, even when hand-held and even when she is moving. She pans and tilts only infrequently, to follow a person who begins to move or let us read a slogan on a wall or follow her point of view. She shoots village buildings in full shots and fields in full shots and long shots that are steady and still. The camera angle is straight and head-high, the light is ambient, and the focus is deep. Shots of people are often composed with doorways as frames. Interviewees are shot in a mix of close-up, medium close-up, and medium full shots. Zhang frequently uses two-shots, often of herself and a villager, as well as tableaux or group shots, often with Zhang in the group. In shots of villagers she seems to be catching in the midst of daily activities, Zhang emphasizes her subjective approach by using point-of-view tracking shots and by talking from behind her camera.

Zhang's films move at a steady pace, with cuts coming at regular intervals, but this approach is interrupted by shots that last far longer than the average and so demand attention and thought. Zhang sometimes tests our patience; in *Sphinx* there is a seven-minute shot of a young man staring into a well and stirring its water with a stick. Many shots seem to be without a connection to anything in particular—shots of crows flying, a dog napping in the sun, pigs in a pen, chaff burning in a harvested field, chickens going to roost, a man putting stone on a dirt road, a shepherd with sheep—and such shots function as caesuras that give us time to think. Zhang makes use of montage, leaving it up to the audience to find meaning in the juxtaposition of shot and shot or shot and voice. For example, in *Birth*, a woman talks about giving birth to each of her children over shots of felled poplar trees; we have to decide for ourselves what this means. Tong Wang argues that Zhang's use of the "empty shot" (a shot with no person in it) allows the "traumatic past a full entry into the present" and transfers the "burden of memory" from the filmmaker to the viewer.[20] I take instruction from this insight but believe that while Zhang's films invite us to think about the traumatic past, they remind us that it is never accessible in the present, especially to those of us who did not live it.

Zhang's films cross-cut between two different sorts of shots and sequences that I will call "observational" and "performative."[21] By "observational," I mean footage of what might be seen in the village anytime: people talking, eating, and working; dogs barking; streams flowing; and so on. By "performative" I mean shots and sequences scripted or staged by Zhang Mengqi. Often, a performative shot or sequence appears before the opening title; examples include large photographs of village elders that are hung on trees, beneath which Zhang dances; a silent, black-and-white shot of Zhang lying in a field; and a series of dissolves between shots in which women of several generations dance with stalks of bamboo.

Zhang makes use of song, poetry, and prose that is sung or read aloud. For example, in *Bridge*, Fang Hong recites Tang and Yuan Dynasty poems that offer images of the countryside as a pastoral refuge and world of toil, both of which describe aspects of village life as depicted in Zhang's films. In *Dying*, Fang Hong recites these poems and others on similar themes, including a Meng Jiao 孟郊 (751–814) poem about a mother missing her son that connects to the film's reference to the village men and women who have left for jobs elsewhere. In *Dying*, three village women listen as a fourth reads from the Chinese Union Version of the Bible:

> [T]he cities of the nations fell, and God remembered great Babylon, to make her drain the cup of the fury of his wrath. And every island fled away, and no mountains were to be found; and great hailstones, heavy as a hundred-weight, dropped on men from heaven, till men cursed God for the plague of the hail, so fearful was that plague.[22]

We are left to wonder, What God? Whose fury? Who has been cursed with what plague? A plague that has happened or that will come? Or is the shot simply to show that the villagers will reach for any ideology that allows them psychological escape from difficulty?

Early in Zhang's first 47 KM film, elder Guo Chuanfu is interviewed. Before Guo is settled in his seat, a young man leans in and, because Guo is almost deaf, shouts a question, using a common euphemism to refer to the famine years: "Were you hungry during the period of grain transition?" Guo says he cannot remember, then says he cannot speak about the past and then looks at the camera and says that during the famine he ate husks, peanut leaves, and cotton leaves. He says, "We ate grief" (*Chi kui* 吃亏). Looking at the camera, he says his brother starved to death. He repeats this, then Zhang cuts away. Zhang has quickly established the difficulty of communication with famine survivors, the taboo against talking about the famine, the immediacy with which the famine is still remembered, and the humanity and individuality of the village elders.

Fifty minutes into Zhang's first 47 KM film, made in 2011, Zhang's grandfather tells her she should not pursue her project. Of the famine, he says, "1959 was about repaying a debt, repaying a debt to the Soviet Union. There was no choice; the grain had to be all shipped out; people had nothing to eat." Zhang cuts to a skinny, shirtless man who steps out of a doorway and then back into it; she cuts to a child eating and then to a close-up, tracking pan along a slogan on a wall that reads "Without the Communist Party, There Would Be No New China!" This is followed by a close-up of a television on which a newscaster is talking about a mudslide in Gansu province that killed more than 1,000 people.

On the TV are the words "Heavy at Heart, We Mourn." Zhang's juxtaposition of shots suggests that, in contrast, the famine victims of sixty years ago have not been properly mourned.

Li Guiting (b. 1933) appears at the start of the 2019 *Window*, which cuts back to him periodically from start to finish. Zhang puts Li's name on the screen in the first shot of him, and each time Zhang returns to Li and his story, text on the screen gives the year and his age at the time of what he is recounting. She does this in no other interview in any film. Instead of showing Li speak or putting his voice over empty shots, which is how she handles interviews in all other films, Zhang puts Li's voice over footage of him sitting alone in a room in a shaft of sunlight. He glances back now and again at the portrait of Mao that is in the shadows behind him. The devices Zhang uses to present Li and his story can be understood to alienate this interview, by which I mean that Zhang's choices call our attention to the element of artificiality in any documentary interview, which has its entrenched conventions and cannot be expected to offer uncompromised access to historical truth. As Li goes through the years of his life, we are left not knowing exactly what to think. We do not know what to make of Li's repeated glances back at the poster of Mao. Li was born poor, and he suffered. The revolution of 1949 made his life better, and he was put in a leadership position because of his class background, but this resulted in an attack on him during the Cultural Revolution. When Li gets to 1959, he says exactly what Zhang's grandfather says in her 2011 film: foreign debt forced China to export all its grain, leaving the people with nothing to eat. After eight years, nothing has changed in the way the villagers talk about the famine in public.

Li Guiting is one of only a few men who receive attention in Zhang's oeuvre, which focuses on women. *Self-Portrait with Three Women* (*Zihuaxiang he sange nüren* 自画像和三个女人, 2010), Zhang's first film, is about Zhang, her mother Zhang Yan 章燕, and her maternal grandmother He Jinxiu 何锦秀. Lidan Hu writes that Zhang "foregrounds the presence of the female filming subject" and argues that while "Zhang has never regarded herself as a feminist filmmaker, the sensitivity to gender-related issues in her work reveals an 'unconscious feminism.'"[23] It is possible that Zhang is conscious of her ideas about gender but does not speak of herself as a "feminist" filmmaker because this term carries meanings and associations that are particular to the Western world and do not align with Chinese experience. In any event, more than she puts herself—the female *filming* subject—in the foreground, Zhang foregrounds the presence of the female *filmed* subject.

Zhang shows us people who have been made invisible several times over because they are poor, rural, old, and female. When women are interviewed in Zhang's films, they speak of their suffering during the famine and their mistreatment by their husbands and sons. In *At 47 KM*, Yu Xiantang (b. 1926) tells Zhang that her children do not take care of her, and in *Dancing*, we learn that the children of Jiang Wangying (b. 1931) do not take care of her. Shu Jiaqing (b. 1934) appears in several of the films. She lives in a small, unheated shed that has no electricity and is near her son's brick and concrete house.[24] In *Dreaming*, a neighbor says Shu's three sons have money and live in two-story houses but keep their mother in a shack. In the 47 KM films, we hear stories of women who killed themselves rather than continue to suffer; one is told by Shu in *Bridge*, in which another woman says that the way her son mistreats her makes her want to die.

Birth at 47 KM (2016) is a double portrait of Lei Xianzhen (b. 1945) and the young mother Fang Yuan, older sister of Fang Hong. Lei appears in four of Zhang's 47 KM films, including the first one. She has kyphosis or a similar issue that causes her to walk with a severe stoop. The account of her life that Lei gives in *Birth* continues the story she begins to tell in the previous film, *Dying*. As Lei does household chores, she tells Zhang Mengqi that Zhang is lucky to be young and free and not looking for a husband. In answer to a question from Zhang, she says no man is dependable and a woman must rely on herself. Lei says her father forced her to marry and her life has been one of suffering. Her husband beat her. She divorced and left with their children. Her father forced her to come back to her husband. Her husband tried to drown her. She mentions women who suffered similar abuse and killed themselves. She says she hopes to see her husband die a miserable death. This is followed by a cut to a two-shot of Lei and, we infer, her husband sitting in a doorway. Lei is eating; her husband is plucking a dead chicken. The next cut is to Fang Hong, which invites us to think that surely her future as a woman has to be better.

Birth crosscuts between Lei telling of each time she gave birth and Fang Yuan talking about her life when she was unmarried and what life has been like since she met and married her husband; the narration is over empty shots. Lei says she had her first child, a daughter, in 1966, when she was twenty-one. About nine minutes into the film, we see a pregnant Fang Yuan, and when we next see her, about ten minutes later, she is holding her newborn, while her other child, a toddler, plays at her feet. The cross-cutting continues: Lei describes giving birth alone with no doctor or midwife; Fang Yuan talks about working in a factory when she was fifteen, and the narration is over a shot of certificates commending her younger sister Fang Hong for academic excellence (Fang Hong is seen at play, drawing, and sitting with her sister, but does not speak in this film); Lei Xianzhen describes giving birth in a pigpen; Fang Yuan says she does not like working but needs the income.

This juxtaposition of the stories of Lei Xianzhen and Fang Yuan, along with the shots of the silent Fang Hong, continues throughout the film and allows us to think about the traditional forms of misogyny and servitude in marriage that lasted into the People's Republic, reminding us that rural woman continue to have to cope with the expectation that they marry and raise children while at the same time facing pressure to leave home to find the work and income they and their families need. The expectation that they have children and the demand for their labor threaten the dreams of girls such as Fang Hong.

About ninety minutes into *Birth*, a sequence begins that lasts for the final fifteen minutes of the film and has something of what Werner Herzog might mean by "ecstatic truth." There is a close-up of Lei Xianzhen's hands, worn from work. After a cut, there is a forty-second shot of Lei's hands holding Zhang's hands. We hear rhythmic, soft exhaling, and there is a cut to the hands moving together in close-up. We see Zhang's forearms and hands following Lei's as they move in a flapping-wing motion. A low humming mixes with the sound of breathing. There is a cut to Zhang's hands above Lei's, mimicking the movements of Lei's hands. The hands move more rapidly and playfully. The humming becomes plosive, sputtering nonsense sounds. There is a two-shot of Zhang and Lei, sitting, facing each other, eyes closed as they make the sounds with their lips. Zhang makes exaggerated smacking sounds, at which Lei opens her eyes, leans back, and laughs, which makes Zhang laugh and giggle. They close their eyes and breathe deeply.

Zhang cuts to the shot of a burning field that opens the film; next are shots of Zhang and Fang Hong, Zhang and Fang Yuan, Zhang and two other village women, and Zhang and a group of women and children who move, stretch, and dance as they smile and laugh. There is a shot of Lei singing and a close-up of Fang Yuan and her baby. In the final shot of the film are Fang Yuan and her children and Fang Hong, who is lip-synching to "Grateful Heart" (*Gan'en de xin* 感恩的心), a song that expresses gratitude to an unnamed "you" for providing companionship and support. This poetic fifteen-minute sequence demonstrates that Lei Xianzhen is a complex person who cannot be reduced to an example of the typical fate of women of her generation; it shows how closely connected Zhang is to Lei and the other villagers, despite their clear differences, and it adds emotions of love, gratitude, and joy to the end of a film that deals with dark and difficult subject matter.

The stories told by Lei Xianzhen and other village women are about the past, but Zhang's films are also concerned with the present moment and the

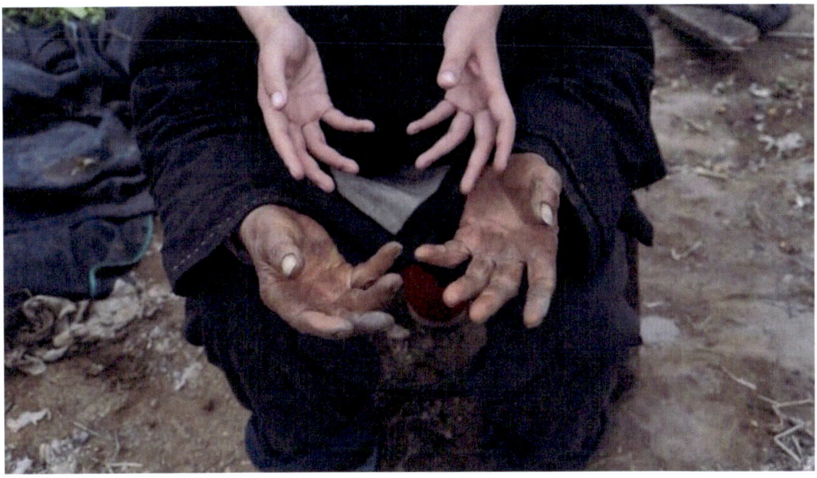

Fig. 1.2. The hands of Zhang and Lei Xianzhen in *Birth* (1:29:57). (© 2016, reprinted by permission of Zhang Mengqi.)

future. They show a village empty of adults, who have left for urban areas for work; they invite us to reflect on the damage done to individual lives by China's development, which in its long initial phase was driven by low-cost, low-skilled labor provided by migrant workers. Zhang's later films quite literally ask when communism will finally come and what "-ism" (what political philosophy) will save China. The former question is asked in *Window* by interviewee Li Guiting after his account of his difficult life, and the latter question is addressed in *Bridge* and *Sphinx*.

Zhang shows us the wreckage and relics of the Maoist past with her favored montage of shots in juxtaposition, and while it is impossible to know what Zhang expects us to make of these shots, they seem to ask why the revolution failed to improve the lives of the rural poor, if the belief in the ideals of socialism still survives, and if those ideals might rescue people left behind or victimized by China's economic rise. In the 2012 *Dancing*,[25] after Zhang's uncle says Zhang's effort to put up a memorial tablet for victims of the famine will make people think she is against the Party, there is a cut to a shot of a ruined wall on which part of a painted quotation remains. The characters for "class contradiction" are prominent in the frame. This is followed by Jiang Wangying speaking of officials wasting food during the famine and a cut back to the quotation for a close-up of the Chinese for "Marx." There is a cut to Shu Jiaqing speaking of a man who hanged himself during the famine and a cut to a close-up of the last words in the quotation, which are "[Party] line." Seven years later, in *Window*, someone (most likely Fang Hong) films Zhang as Zhang films the slogan and reads it. It is about the struggle between socialism and capitalism on the long road toward socialism, and it calls for vigilance against efforts to resurrect capitalism.[26] The shot seems not a mocking dance on the grave of Marxism, Leninism, and Mao Zedong thought, but rather an invitation to ask what might bring a better future: the ideals of the old socialism or a version of a resurrected capitalism that is not as merciless, amoral, and exploitative as what we have at present?

In the 2013 *Dreaming*, a man recounts the political movements that have punctuated his life and says the government does not provide any help (we assume he means to the elderly). There is a cut to Shu Jiaqing speaking of the politically motivated abuse her family suffered; Shu speaks over a shot of a ruined building and a doorway lintel on which there is a five-pointed Communist Party star and the slogan "Serve the People." Then there is a cut to a shot of a house on which a slogan has been painted. Where two characters once were there is now a door, and so the slogan reads, "Only □ ism Can Save China" (*Zhi you □ zhuyi cai neng jiu Zhongguo* 只有 □ 主义才能救中国). Fifty-one minutes into the next film, *Bridge*, there is a shot of thirteen-year-old Zou Xuesong standing in front of the house. From behind the camera, Zhang reads the slogan, filling in the blank, "Only Socialism Can Save China." She asks if Zou understands. Zou says he does and explains, "Only society . . . only if we have a society can we get New China established and make New China even stronger." Zhang does not correct Zou's misunderstanding. Zhang's exchange with Zou might elicit three questions. First, what "ism" will save us? Second, does Zou not understand the word "socialism"? And third, has the village been so changed by the events of the past thirty years that Zou thinks it lacks a "society"?

Seventeen minutes later, Zhang's camera is on a tripod for a medium full shot of Zou Xuesong, another boy about Zou's age named Wang Yifei, Fang Hong, Zhang, and Zhang's grandfather. They are sitting outside in chairs arranged in a semicircle facing the camera. When the shot begins, Wang Yifei is reading aloud from a book. He reads (in Chinese), "No animal must ever live in a house, or sleep in a bed, or wear clothes, or drink alcohol, or smoke tobacco, or touch money, or engage in trade. All the habits of Man are evil." He trails off and hands the book to Zou Xuesong. Zhang cuts to a close-up of Zou reading from the book, which we see is George Orwell's *Animal Farm*. Zou reads as Zhang cuts to a close-up of her grandfather, now standing. He turns and looks at the camera in a long take.[27] Over this shot, Zou reads (in Chinese):

> Many years ago, when I was a little pig, my mother and the other sows used to sing an old song of which they knew only the tune and the first three words. I had known that tune in my infancy, but it had long since passed out of my mind. Last night, however, it came back to me in my dream. And what is more, the words of the song also came back—words, I am certain, which were sung by the animals of long ago and have been lost to memory for generations. I will sing you that song now, comrades. I am old and my voice is hoarse, but . . .

Zou does not read the rest of the passage, which is in the first chapter of Orwell's book and continues "when I have taught you the tune, you can sing it better for yourselves. It is called 'Beasts of England.'" The song is, of course, an allusion to *The Internationale*.

Zhang happened to be reading *Animal Farm* at the time, and she chose the passages that she had Wang and Zou read.[28] She also appears to have reversed the order of shots in editing. Zou reads twice, and in Orwell's text what Zou reads first comes after what Zou reads second. This sequence is Zhang's creation, and it implicitly applies Orwell's critique of the Soviet Union and Stalinism to contemporary China. It lampoons the hypocrisy and cruelty of communism in practice, while also reminding us of the fight for freedom, justice, and equality that Orwell never abandoned.

The 2017 *Sphinx* begins with a shot of the "Only □ ism Can Save China" house that lasts ninety seconds. Twelve minutes later, Zhang returns to a full shot of the house. A woman walks out of the house and sits on a chair in front of it. After thirty seconds of silence, she says, "We are people who have lived pitiable lives. We are sufferers. My son is dead." Seven times Zhang returns to this shot of the woman in front of the building as she tells the story of her son. She says her son was a kind boy who left to work in a city factory. He was cheated out of his pay and in a resulting confrontation killed a man. He was arrested and executed. The woman's telling of the story of her son is steadily cross-cut with shots of sixteen-year-old Zou Xuesong and twelve-year-old Fang Hong.

The boy's story is an extreme version of the reality for many migrant workers. Zou Xuesong is shown in a series of long shots in which he is idle. Only in one shot does he speak. We worry for Zou Xuesong as he withdraws into himself. His future is uncertain. Fang Hong is shown in close-up, drawing and creating stories for what she has drawn. On a brick wall, she paints a village with ponds, trees, haystacks, and two girls, one in a red hood and one, smaller, in black, whom Fang Hong calls the *monü* (魔女), the witch. An hour and ten

Fig. 1.3. From the first shot of *Sphinx* (0:01:03). (© 2017, reprinted by permission of Zhang Mengqi.)

minutes into the film, there is a scene in which Fang Hong, wearing a red coat with a hood, and Zhang Mengqi's young niece, Ding Qixuan, all in black, stand in a harvested field. They appear and disappear in a series of dissolves as they take turns recounting things they dreamed they were. They say, "In my dream I became a" . . . river, brick, tree root, characters on an oracle bone, fish, clay Buddha, cat, vampire, and more. They giggle and laugh. Fang Hong and Ding Qixuan remain full of the dreams and creative potential of childhood but, we wonder, what "-ism" will help them realize their dreams and potential?

In the final scene of *Bridge*, each of several children talks about the "village of their imagination." They imagine a village that is not deforested or polluted, in which houses do not leak in the rain, where everyone is good-hearted, altruistic, and equal, and where there are many children who have many toys and no homework. A boy begins, "The best village . . . ," but he stops and hangs his head in shyness or confusion or both, and then there is a dissolve to a slow-motion shot of Zhang and the children flapping their arms as if to take off and fly away.

In a full discussion of Zhang's depiction of children, I would argue that Zhang has created an extended documentary take on the lives and dreams of young people that contests socially constructed ideas of "childhood" and invites us to think about the class and gender politics of the adult world that

Fig. 1.4. Fang Hong (*left*) and Ding Qixuan say what they dreamed of in *Sphinx* (1:12:36). (© 2017, reprinted by permission of Zhang Mengqi.)

impact children. More interesting to explore, however, would be the idea that the younger people who appear in Zhang's films are her collaborators in creative play. Zhang's 2021 *Fairy Tale* is the most recent of Zhang's films that I am considering, and it is her most joyful. It was filmed, the credits say, by Zhang Mengqi, Fang Hong, and Ding Qixuan. In Zhang's films, children represent, embody, and enact the sort of imaginative, artistic approach to living that the films celebrate as an answer to or a temporary release from the struggles of life.

In *Blue House*, Zhang is wearing a T-shirt with the slogan "100% LIFE 零% ART" (100% life, 0% art). I take the slogan as an assertion that creative activity is or should be an integral part of all lives, rather than something reserved for the solitary genius who produces transcendent art for us to admire. The slogan is the expression of an idea much like Félix Guattari's "ethico-aesthetic paradigm," which term comes from the title of his book that explores "the existential role of creativity in daily life, world politics, science, society, and psychoanalytic practice."[29] I do not have room here for a deep dive into Guattari's theory of the pursuit of liberation from the impoverishment of subjectivity under capitalism "through the unleashing of singularizing processes which would transform existence in all its dimensions by releasing mutant creative energies,"[30] but a definition of the key term has been provided by Stephen J. Goldberg, who writes:

> In China creativity is construed as an ethico-aesthetic practice in which signifying acts of self-presentation . . . are evaluated as to their efficacy in fostering harmonious relations of social exchange within specific historical occasions. To say this is to call attention to the performative dimension of aesthetic creativity; to recognize, beyond its constative meaning, the force of an expressive act to produce effects that profoundly affect its recipients.[31]

I understand the ethico-aesthetic paradigm—and Zhang's T-shirt—as articulating the belief that aesthetic activity is an essential part of the development of healthy, liberated, individual personhood that encourages empathy for and solidarity with others and so builds communities. This belief seems to inform the Folk Memory Project in general and Zhang Mengqi's filmmaking in specific.

The Folk Memory Project's home is the Caochangdi Workstation (*Caochangdi gongzuozhan* 草场地工作站) (CCD), which was founded in 2005 by Wu Wenguang and dancer and choreographer Wen Hui 文慧 (b. 1960).[32] CCD was a physical place from 2005 to 2014, after which it was "no longer a physical location, but rather a name for the creators working together on the Folk Memory Project."[33] In the two decades of the CCD and the fifteen years of the Folk Memory Project, Wu and his collaborators have created a community and have created spaces—actual, virtual, and in the mind—in which they can work outside of governmental and commercial constraints. Jiayun Zhuang argues that in the English name for the project we should drop the word "folk" and instead refer to the "Minjian Memory Project" to preserve the specific meaning of *minjian* (民间, among the people), because this Chinese word "registers the very idea of a society that exists and thrives both among the people and outside of the state."[34]

Wu Wenguang's 2013 *Because of Hunger: Wu's Diary* (*Yinwei ji'e: Wu riji* 因为饥饿：吴日记) shows us project filmmakers as they discuss their experiences in the villages, review and edit their footage, exchange criticism and advice, and rehearse and perform "Memory: Hunger" (回忆: 饥饿), a dance and spoken-word piece in which the filmmakers act out the stories of their interviewees and of their own "homecoming journeys."[35] The film documents ethico-aesthetic practice in action; we see the integration of aesthetic activity into everyday life, and we see its power to create connections among people. During the pandemic, CCD filmmakers met and exchanged ideas and shared their work online. This has continued post-pandemic. In a January 2023 email to CCD's allies, Wu wrote that during 2022, eighteen filmmakers attended the weekly CCD online editing workshops, and at the start of 2023, eight of them had finished their films, and the rest were in editing.

Xi Jinping became president of the PRC the year Wu released *Because of Hunger*, and in the years since, the free, uncensored exchange of art, information, opinion, and ideas in any medium in China, whether television, radio, film, online, or social media, has become increasingly difficult. Space for society to merely exist "among the people and outside of the state," let alone thrive, has contracted almost to the vanishing point. In 2020, Qian Gang, one of the most thoughtful and professional of the journalists who contributed to the flourishing of reportage in the 1980s, observed that Xi Jinping "has revived many red terms from the Mao era, including phrases like: 'East, west, south, north and center, Party, government, military, society and education—the Party rules all.'"[36] In a January 20, 2024, WeChat message to me, Zhang Mengqi wrote, "The environment for [online and social-media hosted] independent screenings is increasingly bad. What we are trying to do feels a bit like 'online tunnel warfare,' but still, everybody is full of enthusiasm." Zhang's joke about CCD's efforts to avoid censors is a reference to the 1965 film *Tunnel Warfare* (*Didao zhan* 地道战), in which Chinese villagers use tunnels to hide from and resist the Japanese invaders.

In the introduction to *New Chinese-Language Documentaries: Ethics, Subject and Place*, Kuei-fen Chiu and Yingjin Zhang write that while "documentary filmmaking can be and has been practiced as creative art, it always involves commitments and responsibility and is inevitably implicated and complicated by ethics in various forms."[37] Zhang Mengqi has demonstrated a fully realized and exemplary capacity in her creative art for an ethical response to and responsibility for the people who appear in her films. She has devoted more than a decade of her life, hours of hard work, and great emotional energy to get to know Yu Xiantang, Shu Jiaqing, Lei Xianzhen, and others. These women and others in Zhang's 47 KM films have been given an opportunity to make their voices heard. Zhang's work has fostered connections in the village between the younger and older generations and perhaps has inspired Fang Hong and other young villagers. Zhang's films have prompted members of Zhang's audience to donate money to help improve lives in the village. Zhang had a memorial to village famine victims erected, gave clothing to village elders, organized the establishment of a reading room for the village children, and got electricity wired into an elderly woman's home.

Zhang's 2021 *Fairy Tale* is about the construction in Diaoyutai of her Blue House (*Lan fangzi* 蓝房子), a space where village children can come to learn and play. It was paid for with prize money for the award Zhang won for *Sphinx*

Fig. 1.5. Zhang (*left*) and her young collaborators at the end of *Fairy Tale* (1:47:38). (© 2021, reprinted by permission of Zhang Mengqi.)

at the DMZ Documentary Film Festival in South Korea. *Fairy Tale* shows the Blue House moving from the minds, drawing paper, and tablet screens of her young friends to brick and mortar. Twenty-one minutes into *Fairy Tale*, Zhang and Fang Hong visit the ground on which the house will be built; Zhang tells Fang Hong she envisions a deck in front of the house as a "public space" (公共空间) where anyone can sit, talk, rest, or play cards; she tells Fang Hong that she will give her a key to the house, which she says will be a safe place for Fang Hong to keep her computer and edit the films she may make. At the end of *Fairy Tale* there is a shot of the house, painted a rich blue, surrounded by the vivid greens of summer, a first for Zhang's films, the rest of which were shot in winter and early spring. In the last shot, Zhang stands with Fang Hong, Ding Qixuan, and two other children as they look down on the village. They say, "I see our space in 47 KM!" (*Wo kandaole women de 47 gongli de kongjian* 我看到了我们的47公里的空间!).

In December 2024, Zhang was editing her latest film, which is about the building—with money raised by CCD and Zhang—of the "Seniors' Canteen" (老年食堂), which offers village elders shelter and food. Zhang and Chiu paraphrase Michael Renov's definition of documentary filmmaking as "an ethical encounter with the other—an encounter that prioritizes the questions of justice, responsibility, and being-for-the other" and asks "what constitutes the ethical production of truth?"[38] The real work that Zhang Mengqi has done in

Diaoyutai places her ethics above reproach, and so to close, I will ask, what constitutes the ethical *consumption* of documentary film? One answer is that those of us who watch, write about, and teach Chinese independent documentary film have an ethical responsibility to be as financially supportive of filmmakers as we can. I also believe that an ethical way for the undergraduates in my course on Chinese documentary film to respond to the films on the syllabus is to engage in ethico-aesthetic practice and make films about subjects that matter to them. This, more than writing critically about the films, perhaps makes them more empathetic viewers, which is an ethical way for people in a small town in Vermont to engage films made a world away in a small town in Hubei.

NOTES

1. *Blue House* was made for the streamed lecture series "Lola Arias: My Documents."
2. Wu Wenguang, "Guanjianci: duli → ziyou → xingdong," 219, 223.
3. Moran, "True Stories," 147–48.
4. Moran, "True Stories," 137.
5. Monteath, "The Spanish Civil War and the Aesthetics of Reportage," 74. Monteath is writing about Egon Erwin Kisch, one of the creators of modern reportage.
6. Wu Liang, "Guanyu jishi wenxue ji baogao wenxue de duanxiang," 71.
7. Zhang Chi, "Di shier jiang," 56.
8. Zhang Chi, "Di shier jiang," 56.
9. Moran, "True Stories," 50, 449–51.
10. Lin, "Documentary in Mainland China."
11. Reynaud, "Translating the Unspeakable," 158.
12. Berry and Rofel, "Introduction," 3.
13. Xie's list is in his 1988 unpublished manuscript, *From Liu Binyan to Su Xiaokang: Rethinking Reportage* (Cong Liu Binyan dao Su Xiaokang: baogao wenxue xin lun 从刘宾雁到苏晓康：报告文学新论). In 1992, Xie privately printed 100 copies of a revised version as *Shouting in Shackles: Chinese Reportage 1976 to 1989* (Jingu xia de nahan: 1976–1989 nian de Zhongguo baogao wenxue 禁锢下的呐喊：1976–1989年的中国报告文学).
14. Lin, "Documentary in Mainland China."
15. Laughlin and Guo, "Reportage and Its Contemporary Variations," xii.
16. Nichols and Baron, *Introduction to Documentary*, 38. The term is given as "epistephilia" in earlier editions of this book, which were by Nichols alone.
17. Nichols and Baron, *Introduction to Documentary*, 1, 174.
18. Church, "Werner Herzog."
19. Zhang's most recent film is her 2023 *Self-Portrait: 47 KM 2020*, which I do not discuss because *Fairy Tale* is a summing-up of the phase of Zhang's career that is my focus.
20. Wang, "Looking Back While Marching Forward," 95–96.

21. Nichols and Baron, *Introduction to Documentary*, 133.
22. Revelation 16: 19–21, Revised Standard Version.
23. Hu, "Self-Portraiture and Historical Memory," 32, 35.
24. Zhang paid to have electricity run to Shu's home.
25. For a close reading of *Dancing*, see Kissel, "The Memory Project and Other Ways of Knowing."
26. The quotation is from a June 1967 *Red Flag* editorial commemorating the tenth anniversary of Mao's "On the Correct Handling of Contradictions Among the People."
27. He died before Zhang made her next film.
28. Zhang told me this in a WeChat message.
29. Watson, "*Chaosmosis: An Ethico-Aesthetic Paradigm*," 62.
30. Watson, "*Chaosmosis*, 63.
31. Goldberg, "Chinese Aesthetics," 225.
32. According to Pernin, to "some extent, [the] interplay between documentary and performance, and the historical theme of the Folk Memory Project, derive from Wen Hui's approach to contemporary dance and theatre." Pernin, "Performance, Documentary, and the Transmission of Memories," 18.
33. Zhang Mengqi, "Guanjianci: gongzuofang," 288.
34. Zhuang, "Remembering and Reenacting Hunger," 120.
35. Zhuang, "Remembering and Reenacting Hunger," 129.
36. Qian Gang, "The Politics of Gratitude."
37. Chiu and Zhang, *New Chinese-Language Documentaries*, 4.
38. Chiu and Zhang, *New Chinese-Language Documentaries*, 4.

REFERENCES

Berry, Chris, and Lisa Rofel. "Introduction." In *The New Chinese Documentary Film Movement: For the Public Record*, edited by Berry, Lu Xinyu, and Rofel, 3–14. Hong Kong: Hong Kong University Press, 2010.

Chiu, Kuei-fen, and Yingjin Zhang. *New Chinese-Language Documentaries: Ethics, Subject and Place*. London: Routledge, 2015.

Church, David. "Werner Herzog." *Senses of Cinema*, 2006. Great Directors. https://www.sensesofcinema.com/2006/great-directors/herzog/

Goldberg, Stephen J. "Chinese Aesthetics." In *A Companion to World Philosophies*, edited by Eliot Deutsch and Ron Bontekoe, 225–34. Malden, MA: John Wiley and Sons, 1999.

Hongqi. "Editorial: A theoretical weapon for undertaking revolution under the dictatorship of the proletariat—commemorating the tenth Anniversary of the publication of "On the correct handling of contradictions among the people" (Shelun: wuchan jieji zhuanzheng xia jinxing geming de lilun wuqi: jinian 'Guanyu zhengque chuli renmin neibu maodun de wenti' fabiao shi zhounian 社论:无产阶级专政下进行革命的理论武器—纪念《关于正确处理人民内部矛盾的问题》发表十周年). *Hongqi*, no. 10 (June 21, 1967): 32–39. https://www.bannedthought.net/China/Magazines/Hongqi/index.htm#1967

Hu, Lidan. "Self-Portraiture and Historical Memory: Zhang Mengqi's Documentary

Practice." *Critical Arts* 33, no. 2 (2019): 29–41. https://doi.org/10.1080/02560046.2019.1671887

Kissel, Laura. "The Memory Project and Other Ways of Knowing: Filmmaking, Affect, and Embodied Knowledge." In *Filming the Everyday: Independent Documentaries in Twenty-First-Century China*, edited by Paul G. Pickowicz and Yingjin Zhang, 99–115. Lanham, MD: Rowman and Littlefield, 2017.

Laughlin, Charles, and Li Guo. "Reportage and Its Contemporary Variations: An Introduction." *Modern Chinese Literature and Culture* 31, no. 2, Special Issue on Reportage and its Contemporary Variations (Fall 2019): v–xvi. https://www.jstor.org/stable/10.2307/26895770

Lin, Xu-dong. "Documentary in Mainland China." Translated by Cindy Carter. Documentary Box, #26 (August 2005). https://www.yidff.jp/docbox/26/box26-3-e.html

Monteath, Peter. "The Spanish Civil War and the Aesthetics of Reportage." In *Literature and War*, edited by David Bevin, 69–85. Amsterdam: Rodopi, 1990.

Moran, Thomas Elton. "True Stories: Contemporary Chinese Reportage and Its Ideology and Aesthetic." PhD diss., Cornell University, 1994. ProQuest 9501300.

Nichols, Bill, and Jaimie Baron. *Introduction to Documentary*. 4th ed. Bloomington: Indiana University Press, 2024.

Orwell, George. *Animal Farm*. New York: Harcourt Brace, 1946. Project Gutenberg Canada ebook #785. Posted May 12, 2011. https://www.gutenberg.ca/ebooks/orwellg-animalfarm/orwellg-animalfarm-00-h.html

Pernin, Judith. "Performance, Documentary, and the Transmission of Memories of the Great Leap Famine in the Folk Memory Project." *China Perspective*, no. 4 (100) (2014): 17–26. https://www.jstor.org/stable/24055647

Qian, Gang. "The Politics of Gratitude." China Media Project. (March 23, 2020). https://chinamediaproject.org/2020/03/23/the-politics-of-gratitude/

Reynaud, Bérénice. "Translating the Unspeakable: On-Screen and Off-Screen Voices in Wu Wenguang's Documentary Work." In *The New Chinese Documentary Film Movement: For the Public Record*, edited by Chris Berry, Lu Xinyu, and Lisa Rofel, 157–76. Hong Kong: Hong Kong University Press, 2010.

Wang, Tong. "Looking Back While Marching Forward: Reconfiguration of Selfhood in the Folk Memory Project." In *Filming the Everyday: Independent Documentaries in Twenty-First-Century China*, edited by Paul G. Pickowicz and Yingjin Zhang, 87–98. Lanham, MD: Rowman and Littlefield, 2017.

Watson, Janell. "*Chaosmosis: An Ethico-Aesthetic Paradigm*." In *The Deleuze and Guattari Dictionary*, by Eugene B. Young, with Gary Genosko and Watson, 62–63. London: Bloomsbury, 2013.

Wu, Liang. "Guanyu jishi wenxue ji baogao wenxue de duanxiang 关于纪实文学及报告文学的断想" (Some thoughts about documentary literature and reportage). *Baogao wenxue*, no. 12 (December 1986): 70–71.

Wu, Wenguang. "Guanjianci: duli → ziyou → xingdong 关键词：独立→自由→行动." Translated by Michelle Deeter as "Keywords: Independence → Freedom → Activism." *Chinese Independent Cinema Observer* 1, no. 3 (2022): 216–24.

Zhang, Chi. "Di shier jiang: baogao wenxue de fazhan qushi 第十二讲：报告文学的发展趋势" (Lecture twelve: the trend in the development of reportage). *Baogao wenxue*, no. 12 (December 1984): 54–56.

Zhang, Mengqi. "Guanjianci: gongzuofang. 'Ganxing yinlu, lixing zhaoliang'—wode gongzuofang jishi 关键词:工作坊. '感性引路,理性照亮'—我的工作坊纪事." Translated by Michelle Deeter as "Keyword: Workshop. 'Feelings guide the way, rational thought lights the way': My Workshop Notes." *Chinese Independent Cinema Observer* 1, no. 3 (2022): 281–90.

Zhuang, Jiayun. "Remembering and Reenacting Hunger: Caochangdi Workstation's Minjian Memory Project." *TDR: The Drama Review* 58, no. 1, Performing Shanghai and Beyond: Special Consortium Issue (Spring 2014): 118–40. https://www.jstor.org/stable/24584921

TWO

Forest Chongqing

A Photographic Reportage by Yan Wang Preston

Federica Mirra

This chapter examines the photographic work *Forest* (2010–17) by Chinese artist Yan Wang Preston, who documents the ecological transformations in Chongqing enforced by the Chinese central government. By showing her work in the sociohistorical context of Chongqing and the origins of photographic reportage, this chapter reveals how Preston's long-term project can provide a more complicated narrative than the state-sanctioned, unilateral view of a sustainable, green, and hence beautiful city.[1] Specifically, her photos problematize how trees and, more widely, ecology are exploited for political, economic, and aesthetic goals. Though Preston's artistic practice documents the transplanting of vegetation from Dali in Yunnan province and Sanhe in Beijing to parts of Europe (i.e., West Yorkshire and Romania, to name just two),[2] this paper concentrates on the area of Chongqing municipality. By reducing the long-established separation between humankind and the natural environment, Preston's photos envision a "feral ecology"—that is, a more holistic view of ecology that can develop "despite capitalism" and alongside urbanization.[3]

Introduction

Counting nearly twenty-three million residents, Chongqing is a new-first-tier city situated in the west of the People's Republic of China (PRC).[4] It is located between rivers and mountains and has a distinctive urban landscape integrating the built and natural environment. Historically, Chongqing belongs to China's less-developed internal regions.[5] However, since the 1990s, the city has rapidly turned into a global metropolis under the direct control of the central government. Today, it has one of the highest GDPs in the PRC thanks to the ambitious engineering project of the Three Gorges Dam and a centralized development model.[6]

In 2008, the Chongqing Municipal Government and its former party secretary, Bo Xilai, launched the campaign "Forest Chongqing" to rebrand the city as a model for environmental protection. Creating ninety-five ecological forest towns, Forest Chongqing is part of a bigger project that aims to pursue "Five Chongqing(s)": a Safe, Livable, Forested, Healthy, and Convenient Chongqing.[7] Since its launch, green trees have suddenly materialized, transforming the city into a sustainable, aesthetically pleasing urban forest. Though the promotion of this campaign stopped after Bo Xilai's scandal in 2012, it still shapes the party direction.[8] Even nationally, as early as 2005, Xi Jinping, as Zhejiang party secretary, started promoting more sustainable development through the slogan "*lüshui qingshan jiushi jinshan yinshan* 绿水青山就是金山银山" (clear waters and green mountains are as good as mountains of silver and gold).[9] Moreover, since 2012, he has promoted the idea of a "Beautiful China" (*meili Zhongguo* 美丽中国). Through broad guidelines and evocative campaigns referring to Chongqing as the "City of Mountains and Water," "Forest," and "Beautiful Chongqing," local authorities today attempt to tackle the ecological crisis while boosting the city image.

Before delving into qualitative, empirical, and visual analysis of Preston's photographs, a brief contextualization of her work in the wider discourse of photography and reportage in China is due. Photography reached China around the time of the Nanjing Treaty (1842) and spread among diplomats and military officials as well as traders.[10] Historically, photography was initially deployed for portraits and in commercial studios to then "become an increasingly pervasive presence in everyday life" at the turn of the 20th century.[11] During the Maoist era, the aim of photography shifted to visualizing "'reality as it should be' in order to mobilize the masses."[12] After a period of crisis for reportage, in April 1979, the exhibition *Nature. Society. Man.*, organized by the April Photography Society in the Orchid Room of Zhongshan Park, Beijing, marked the discussion around photography as an independent artistic genre.[13] This event was followed by other exhibitions and by the emergence of numerous groups of photographers, including the Everybody Photography Society in Guangzhou, the Square City Photography Group in Xi'an, and the China Modern Photo Salon, to name a few.

Art historian Claire Roberts refers to this new phase as "people's photography";[14] it captured everyday moments ranging from social concerns to the trauma of the Cultural Revolution (1966–76). Chinese art historian Wu Hung explains this shift partly in terms of Mao Zedong's death (1976) and China's opening up to the outer world. Artists and intellectuals could finally access Western theories and literary sources on modern art, including Magnum photographers and the documentary movement in the US in the 1930s.[15] Moreover, many of the fine arts graduates who often found jobs in the news and publishing industries started experimenting with photography.[16] Roberts argues that those young artists experienced "confusion and bewilderment" due to the gap between their commercial professions and their artistic aspirations.[17] This confusion, alongside the changing sociohistorical circumstances in China and the increasing popularity of the camera, led to what Wu calls a "documentary," independent, and experimental turn for photography.[18]

Whilst reportage initially emerged in China in the 1930s as a new literary genre "that could respond rapidly to social and historical change," by the 1970s it had infiltrated photography and assumed increasing aesthetic value.[19] Whereas photographer Guenther Cartwright defines photojournalism as a "journalism in which the written word is subordinate to pictorial usage,"[20] artist Jeff Wall argues that photojournalism was photography's "post-Pictorialist phase" due to its utilitarian and instantaneous images.[21] Many photojournalists at the time were self-taught photographers who wanted to observe and record the changes around them.[22] Li Guo reports Ding Xiaoyuan's observation that after the 1970s reportage works in Taiwan shifted from being driven by political and ideological ideas to being more attentive to the "author's negotiations about subjectivity and writing."[23] Reportage writers experimented with their style and content and reflected on their own role in China's changing society, and Chinese photography and visual arts similarly tested the "limits of artistic freedom" while moving away from a state-sanctioned context.[24] Reportage became a method in itself and "found expressions in a nexus of genres, from late imperial exploration narratives [. . .] to the search for truthful cinema in documentary filmmaking."[25]

Today, scholars such as Lawrence Buell (in an interview with Qingqi Wei) recognize the added value of visual arts to reportage, namely the ability to synthesize complex themes through imagination, participation, and empathy, while also encouraging multiple interpretations and dialogue.[26] Focusing on documentary films in the Sinophone world, Charles Laughlin explains that this genre can grasp "inarticulable traces of veracity through ambient sound or unintentionally captured images."[27] According to Laughlin and Guo, documentary reportage is a practice that strives for knowledge while retaining its aesthetic qualities, adding a significant function to reportage's search for truth.[28] Moreover, for Guo, reportage can induce transformations by "allowing reportage writers [and artists] to participate in information gathering for the achievement of good governance."[29] Though a concrete impact on governance might be hard to attain immediately, Preston's photographic reportage is extremely significant in advancing a more holistic understanding of ecology.

In the wider Chinese artistic context, contemporary works addressing ecological concerns include Yin Xiuzhen's *Washing River* (1995). In her public performance in Chengdu, Sichuan province, the artist and local community cleaned cubes of frozen water coming from a polluted river. Washing the dirty water was futile, of course, because the water used for the cubes was polluted and the cubes melted. However, the ineffectiveness and ephemerality of the cleaning served as an invitation to the local community to act on their ecological concerns and amplified their experiences. With a similar intent, Zheng Bo, who belongs to a younger generation of socially engaged artists, imagines sustainable and inclusive futures through his practice.[30] His projects range from the work *Plants Living in Shanghai* (2013), which converts Shanghai's Cement Factory into a botanical garden for educational and public activities, to *Pteridophilia* (2016–), an exploration of eco-queer potentialities. His actions reconfigure the circular ecology that humans and nature are both part of through the perspective of plants and other marginalized living beings. Yin's and Zheng's works contribute to an aesthetics that does not passively depict nor exploit the nonhuman, but rather actively encourages an inclusive and hands-on approach to ecology.[31]

Overall, environmental reportage, and visual arts more widely, contain cues to encourage a more responsible awareness and organic understanding of ecology. Specifically, I align with critic Susan Sontag's argument that "to take a photograph is to participate in another person's (or thing's) mortality, vulnerability, mutability."[32] Preston's long-term project of mapping trees, *Forest* (2010–2017), can attest to the "vertiginous rate of change" and join in the spatial transformations in and of Chongqing through the camera.[33] As those who manage the urban landscape become increasingly obsessed with the color green, the artist observes magnificent gingko trees mushroom around the city to embellish the already-attractive skylines and waterfronts. Rather than portraying a "tamed, endangered, mortal" nature,[34] Preston focuses on a rebirth and re-adaptation of trees as vegetation merges with Chongqing's concrete jungle.

Humanizing Trees

Born in China, Preston currently lives in England and works as a photographer and lecturer at the University of Huddersfield. Unlike the reporters and documentary photographers of the 1970s and 1980s, who were often-self-taught, she decided to study photography after years working as an anesthesiologist in Shanghai. She was inspired by the powerful black-and-white shots of French photographer and cofounder of Magnum Photos, Henri Carter-Bresson, and of American landscape photographer Ansel Adams.[35] After moving to the UK, she completed her MA in visual arts at Bradford College, Leeds Beckett University, in 2009, and was awarded her PhD in photography by the University of Plymouth in 2018. Her practice-based PhD included the photographic work, *Mother River*. *Mother River* was a photographic reportage on the Yangtze River, which toured through twelve international exhibitions. Since 2015, Preston has participated in numerous international shows, including the 56th Venice Biennale (2015) and the LOOK photo Biennial, Liverpool (2019). She won several prizes, including the Professional Landscape prize from the Sony World Photography Awards (2019) and the Syngenta Photography Award (2017), among others. Today, her work features in catalogs, articles, and websites in both English and Chinese.[36]

Her photographic project, *Forest,* visualizes the state-sanctioned process of foresting and greening Chongqing between 2010 and 2017. It overlaps with reportage in its informative and illustrative function, its empathetic approach, and its use of text. Her project aims first to understand and document the visual and ecological impact of "Forest Chongqing" by combining her photographic practice with ethnographic research. Specifically, Preston was inspired by photographer Tyrone Martinsson's notion of repeat photography and visual storytelling.[37] In 2001, when Martinsson traveled to Spitsbergen to create a commissioned work on the historical expedition of Nils Strindberg, he coined the term "rephotography" to refer to the way earlier, archived photographs of the mountain served as a comparative tool to show the implications of global warming in the region.[38] Rephotography "create[d] a dialogue with history through stories of place and journeys through time, connecting the archives and collections with the places that produced them."[39] While Preston traveled to a very different region, the China-born artist understood Martinsson's rephotography as a key method to capture "certain trees, woodlands, and areas [. . .] repeatedly over the course of seven years from comparable angles and weather conditions."[40]

Preston further adapted Martinsson's photographic method—as a dialogue "with time, history and memory"—by using ethnographic methods.[41] The artist regularly stayed in Chongqing for several months, talking to taxi drivers and locals, exploring the surroundings, and consulting maps, local magazines, and newspapers to collect informal, grassroots, site-specific evidence.[42] By staying for longer periods in Chongqing and having a wide network of contacts, Preston was able to enter the outside area of an apartment block and talk with photojournalists who worked for state-sanctioned media. While Preston's research-informed practice certainly influenced her own positionality and understanding of the official practices of rewilding and afforesting, her collection of selected photographs over seven years provides an alternative to the dominant narrative of a green and hence beautiful Chongqing.

The artist's earlier photographs are loaded with strong personal and emotional connotations. Her first photographic encounters with transplanted trees are permeated with a sense of sadness and impotence. They are medium-shot portrayals of transplanted trees that seldom leave space for other elements in the composition. As the artist states, "across nearly eight years [. . .] what I saw was, at first, half trees everywhere because 2011 [. . .] was the peak of Chongqing's Forest City policy" (see fig. 2.2).[43] The novelty and ubiquity of such sights meant that Preston could not entirely keep her emotions to herself while taking the pictures. The sympathy toward the trees, as if they were human beings with their arms chopped off, was the catalyst to start *Forest*, and similar sentiments can also be detected in her earlier pictures.

For instance, in *Central Park, University City, Chongqing, China* (fig. 2.1), three trees are wrapped in a semi-transparent fabric and turn into undefined, loose shapes. The fine material covers and blurs the contours of the trees and leaves, but it lets light pass through, partly exposing what is underneath, namely trees damaged and adapting to a new soil. The ambiguous outlines of the trees provide a sense of grandeur thanks to the low-angle shot and the slightly higher focal point. Preston shoots an overexposed picture where the light is bright and ethereal, and the sky looks impenetrable in its compact off-whiteness. The triptych of trees in a slightly elevated position, the veil covering them, and the silvery shade of sky give the overall picture a sense of detachment, spirituality, and fragility.[44] The surrounding landscape seems still, expressionless, and sterile. With cut branches, supporting structures, and nets wrapping them, the trees appear as damaged, unstable, suffocating beings fighting for survival. Preston's crude and unembellished portraits of trees depict a still and suspended afterlife, a dystopian, deserted land where humankind has urbanized plants and vegetation but perhaps also endangered its own survival.

Fig. 2.1. Central Park, University City, Chongqing, China, 2011. (From the *Forest* series [2010–2017]. © Yan Wang Preston, reprinted with permission.)

Preston's photographs seem to suggest two meanings for "nature," as either "denaturalized," harmed, and unembellished, or as a decorative, glorious symbol of wealth and modernity for the apparent benefit of an urban elite. The sense of distance and hopelessness, and the fragile appearances of the trees in what looks like a wasteland, invite further reflection on the biased understanding of "nature" as something separate from humankind. Philosopher Timothy Morton argues that "the environment was born at exactly the moment when it became a problem."[45] As nature was viewed as something pure and uncontaminated and, hence, separate from humankind, that separation allowed a powerful minority to impose their imagined superiority and deny their responsibility to the environment, the result being a worsening of the ecological footprint.[46] This perspective reflects the bias that Western nations stand outside "nature" and colonize it, whereas the East was and still is largely assumed to retain spiritual harmony with the environment.[47] Contrary to this narrative, as early as the fourth century representations of "landscape" in Chinese paintings and literary works reflected the human desire to reconnect with a long-vanished "nature," which was also evident in scientific studies.[48]

Heiner Rotz, professor of the history and philosophy of China, believes that "grief at the destruction of nature is . . . never to be understood only as allegorical, but also in its direct sense."[49] The "sympathetic feeling for nature [. . .] was simply a reaction against the course being taken in an entirely opposite direction by reality as it developed."[50] This sympathetic feeling is an essential part of what Li Guo calls "affective encounters" with ecology.[51] For Guo, an affective encounter "not only includes emotional interaction, but also comprises learning to apply cognitive skills to familiarize oneself with one's immediate environment, to recognize 'the resilience and fragility' of wildlife and to develop an empathetic thinking."[52] Specifically, empathy becomes the access point for the photographer to establish an ethical-aesthetic connection between viewers and their surroundings.[53]

As mentioned above, in Preston's earlier photographs (2010–2014), the transplanted trees convey a feeling of frailty and loneliness. In *Longan Woodland, University City, Chongqing, China* (fig. 2.2), for example, Preston captures what looks like a battlefield of injured trees, wrapped in white bandages and kept upright by supporting structures.[54] The cut and barren branches look like amputated limbs with open wounds. Moreover, the point of view and composition of the photograph reduce the distance between the spectator and the trees, metaphorically inviting the former to become one with the landscape. Six years later, Preston returned to the site to find fully grown trees adorned with green leaves. It is not only the sight, but the artist's attitude that had changed. As Sontag argues, once the photographer notices a certain image, they become so accustomed to it that the picture becomes less and less real.[55] However, rather than less truthful, the story that Preston decides to narrate is more complex. As she states:

> It's quite easy to keep producing very sad looking tree pictures. They will always look sad. But that for me [. . .] was not quite complex or complete enough. So, I made a few decisions after the first two or three years. I thought I would like to observe how the city may or may not develop with these trees and, you know, what I realized is that some of them do adapt, they do survive.[56]

Overall, Preston's photographs demonstrate her transitioning positionality within the changing environment and her ability to recognize and communicate the resilience of the trees.

Fig. 2.2. Longan woodland, University City, Chongqing, China, 2011. (From the *Forest* series [2010–2017]. © Yan Wang Preston, reprinted with permission.)

Three photos stand out for their empathetic, as well as informative, dimension thanks to the presence of written text, namely *Frank* and *Goldie* (figs. 2.3–2.5). Before analyzing the pictures, a few words on the function of text in Preston's work are in order. *Forest* integrates photographs with explanatory text in the form of titles, captions, and short passages and essays included in the exhibition space and catalog. The choice of English can be explained, first, by the artist's desire to "face international audiences" and to respond to the universality of ecological recovery and tree transplantation,[57] and second, by the sensitive nature of the project, which is critical of the official practice of transplanting trees in Chongqing. Whereas most titles inform the reader of the geographical location where an image was shot, *Frank* and *Goldie* are exceptions. They allow viewers to develop empathetic feelings toward the trees. Even more significantly here, the inclusion of a written element provides essential information to decode the visual message and understand the context in which the photo was taken.

The story of *Frank* (figs. 2.3 and 2.4) presents an extreme case where a

Fig. 2.3. Frank_1, Lijiang, China, March 2013. (From the *Forest* series [2010–2017]. © Yan Wang Preston, reprinted with permission.)

300-year-old tree was removed from a small village, Xialiu in Lijiang, and transplanted in Dali Bai Autonomous Prefecture in Yunnan. The goal was to embellish the facade of a future five-star hotel with the sight of a lush, ancient tree. To help it adapt to the new soil, Frank was deprived of its crown and leaves, but it died in 2017. After Frank, another tree was transplanted, which also died, failing to provide the sensation of being surrounded by green vegetation in the city. Preston dedicates three photographs to Frank. The first—*Frank_1, Lijiang, China, March 2013*—depicts the lush tree in its original habitat, where it grew for three centuries alongside the villagers. In the picture, Frank is tall and imposing and seems to overlook the ordinary life in the village, such as the two elderly women conversing, and the children sitting at the base of the tree (fig. 2.3). In the second picture—*Frank_2, Binchuan, China, June 2013*—Frank still dominates the photograph. However, this time the branches have been exposed and deprived of any leaves, the tree trunk is wrapped in bandages, and the surroundings are in the process of being developed (fig. 2.4). In the last image, taken in November 2017, Frank has disappeared. The only sign of its

Fig. 2.4. Frank_2, Binchuan, China, June 2013. (From the *Forest* series [2010–2017]. © Yan Wang Preston, reprinted with permission.)

existence is the red soil on the right, which is partly covered by more construction tools and equipment. The sequential photographs of Frank are Preston's artistic strategy to provide a more complex visual narrative on ecological practices and "to observe how the city may or may not develop with the trees."[58]

Whereas the story of *Frank* is exceptional and moving, *Goldie, A Fake Old Tree, Chongqing, China* (2017) has a more ironic connotation. Even though at first glance the photo seems to portray a lush, big oak tree, Goldie (fig. 2.5) is formed of several smaller oak trees planted very close to each other to resemble a single ancient tree.[59] Old trees are often protected, and when they are not, they are very expensive to buy. Goldie is a smart solution to avoid complications and attach immediate cultural value, giving a sense of identity to a new building or street. In the picture, the tree stands undisturbed on the grass next to some bamboo. Even though it takes center stage, the fence and part of a condominium at the sides suggest that the tree is situated in the urban space. The gold wrap around Goldie's trunk is the only warm color in the picture and stands out against the gray building and pale sky. Furthermore, it hides this

Fig. 2.5. Goldie, a fake old tree, Chongqing, China, 2017. (From the *Forest* series [2010–2017]. © Yan Wang Preston, reprinted with permission.)

escamotage and even gives the tree a regal appearance. Maintaining that "irony has an 'evaluative edge' that elicits an emotional response from those who 'get it' and those who do not," *Goldie* is able to make people smile, evoking empathy while presenting a critical view of the visual deceit.[60]

Preston's giving the tree a human name achieves two outcomes. On one hand, she makes the trees and their stories more memorable and approachable to the public; on the other, she denaturalizes the trees and affirms a holistic understanding of ecology. In other words, by giving trees a human name, Preston invites the audience to identify themselves with nature and treat the trees as living beings, in an effort to reiterate the interdependence between humanity and ecology. Critic Roland Barthes argues that words "can shift a sentence from description to reflection," while the "Photograph [. . .] immediately yields up those 'details' which constitute the very rare material of ethnological knowledge."[61] In Preston's case, the text provides theoretical grounding and criticality to her work, whereas the visual language has the potential to express Laughlin's "inarticulable traces" of reality.[62] Through her documentary and empathetic approach, Preston's photographs simultaneously unveil the instantaneity, violence, and humanity of transforming Chongqing into a "Forest City."[63]

Forest(ing) Chongqing

Preston's project investigates the stark presence of (and perhaps obsession with) the color green, which has come to signify wealth, modernity, and success.[64] Throughout the years, she has discovered that the local government and private businesses have transplanted many trees in Chongqing to make the city greener and to promote the narrative of a mountainous city crossed by two rivers. Photographs like *Frank* expose the fact that trees are often acquired from rural villagers through compensation, or they are illegally taken from the mountains to the city center. The large sum of money compensates for the removal of the tree from its original site, the emotional loss to the community, and the potential death of the plant after transplantation. In return, trees provide green areas, and visually demonstrate real estate developers' mission to conserve and restore the environment.[65] For Preston green becomes a means to associate the neighborhood, city, and to a wider extent the nation, with the ecological imperative. However, besides the good intent to create a more sustainable reality, "other needs override," and ecological recovery becomes a means for a minority to "make some money."[66]

One can more easily observe the long-term political and economic impact on the landscape in Preston's later photographs. The close-up shots that characterized her earlier images are replaced by wider views where the green of trees and the grey of concrete merge into the same scene (figs. 2.6 and 2.7). Preston argues that casting her "gaze towards a wider landscape" is one of her strategies, alongside repeating photographs over time, to weave a more complex narrative about the official campaign.[67] In later pictures, the bushes and trees look less majestic against the suspended multilane motorways and imposing skyscrapers. At the same time, the built and natural environment seems better integrated; the vegetation seems to have recovered, and in some

Fig. 2.6. Egongyan Park, Chongqing, China, 2017. (From the *Forest* series [2010–2017]. © Yan Wang Preston, reprinted with permission.)

cases it is even an essential part of the recreational spaces used for social and collective interaction.

For instance, in *Egongyan Park, Chongqing, China* (2017) (fig. 2.6), the green is delimited within a circumscribed area, which embellishes the surroundings and supplements another kind of forest made of concrete. The picture integrates three kinds of landscape. First, in the hazy background one can glimpse construction works, yellow cranes, and green nets covering a rising building; second, in the middle ground, there are solid, gray concrete columns sustaining the elevated motorways, which look massive and imposing; last, in the foreground vegetation and people interact and green and gray merge together. At the center of the picture, a circular elevated area hosts several lush trees as well as two columns, whose bases are covered by climbing ivy. Around the circular platform, families with children play, and elderly people dance and practice outdoor activities. Preston's later photographs capture and problematize the instantaneity and ease with which officials and developers have built ecological cities to serve their agenda, but they also attest to the ability of trees to adapt to their surroundings.

Fig. 2.7. Yangtze Riverside Road, Chongqing, China, 2011. (From the *Forest* series [2010–2017]. © Yan Wang Preston, reprinted with permission.)

China expert Elizabeth Economy refers to the interlinkages between ecology and policymaking as "environmental governance," a strategy that exploits "nature" for economic gain.[68] Today, being able to protect and restore a thriving ecology and develop high-end cities by advancing clean technologies and renewable sources has become a source of pride for modern nations. Environmental governance reiterates established discourses and representations of an external "nature" for political and economic ends. On one hand, these policies address city dwellers' concerns about the hazards of pollution and aim to prevent potential uprisings due to the spread of malcontent.[69] On the other, green urban practices become part of an international strategy to increase nations' soft power by projecting the image of an aesthetically pleasing and lush city center. However, these green initiatives, though aesthetically pleasing, do not often get to the root of the problem as they may present contradictions, lack feasibility, or be motivated by economic gain.[70]

Since Rio de Janeiro Earth Summit in 1992, manifold conversations and strategies have emerged to reduce the ecological footprint attributed to major polluters, though they have often proved inadequate.[71] In China, the central government has taken significant steps in environmental policy to raise the nation's credibility and power by promoting green strategies such as introducing the green GDP, increasing the pricing of natural resources, and instituting the National Environmental Model City program.[72] The GreenWatch program, supported by the State Environmental Protection Agency and the World Bank, has successfully reduced emissions by publicly disclosing firms' environmental performances.[73] Overall, China's local and central governments have exploited the ecological crisis to validate their political mandate and attract investment.

In Chongqing, the official campaign for a forest city has visually translated into the sudden appearance of parks, trees, and green everywhere. Preston argues that "trees display a political landscape," where "nature" assumes a set of meanings and services, ranging from the ecological to the political and the cosmetic.[74] Sadly, she states, "it is all green washing. I felt disgusted every time I saw green in China because I knew; I knew that every time you see a new part of green, there's probably a sad story behind it."[75] The picture *Yangtze Riverside Road, Chongqing, China* (2011) (fig. 2.7) reveals the sudden appearance of two curving rows of frail trees in a desolate, human-made scene. The trees have narrow, slender trunks that stretch across the horizon and are wrapped as well as supported by triangular structures. Despite their naked and fragile look, there are branches and green leaves at the top, signs of recovery from the transplantation. Juxtaposed to concrete buildings and delimited by a walking path in the process of being paved, the living, breathing trees become additional elements in the urban design. Displaced from their natural habitat, they try to adapt to another soil, the only function being to please the eye of city dwellers and investors. Through her unembellished photographs, the artist shows how trees, and to a wider extent ecology, have become symbols of sustainable development and, as such, are able to attract capital.

Although ecology becomes one victim of prioritized economic gain, the death and decay of certain ecological communities are seldom given much consideration. The inevitable losses are counterbalanced by the visions of a greener environment, and ultimately justified by financial expectations.[76] Throughout a long-established process, ecology today is intentionally exploited, objectified, and reproduced to produce more capital than ever. Neil Smith refers to this tactic as "green capitalism" or the "financialization of nature."[77] This externalized "nature" constructed through modern capitalism is turned for all intents and purposes into a commodity.[78] The Marxist discourse around capitalist production is useful to explain this process of separation: "much as the real subsumption of labor strips the laborer of individuality, the real subsumption of nature, through its capitalization and financialization, strips nature of its specificity."[79] As a social product, "nature" reflects the uneven development of capitalism, which is responsible for the overexploitation of land, water flows, and other raw resources, and produces unequal development across countries. In this context, the villagers who were separated from the previously mentioned tree—*Frank*—in exchange of capital metaphorically stand for the factory workers who cannot afford the product they produce.[80]

Through Preston's epistemophilic and empathetic approach, the artist is capable of articulating the complex dynamics behind the top-down policy of Forest Chongqing. Whereas her close-up shots in the first part of her project are more evocative and imbued with emotions, her latter photographs seem permeated by a sentiment of acceptance, reflecting her prolonged exposure to the changing landscape of Chongqing. Those images do not treat trees as the main subjects. Instead, Preston produces pictures of a more intricate landscape where gray and green are combined for the sake of political and economic gains.

Conclusion

To reiterate my argument, it is worth examining one last photograph, which is part of a set of images shot by Preston in 2017, the final year of the project. This set of lively and colorful photographs captures the holistic vision of people, trees, and the built environment coexisting altogether. More hopeful and optimistic regarding the future, *Jiulong Square, Chongqing, China* (2017) (fig. 2.8) shows a more integrated landscape and, arguably, Preston's vision. In the picture, families relax and children play around a water fountain in the foreground, whereas tall, lush trees occupy the middle ground. In the distance, just behind the central tree, a green horizontal line leads to a concrete urban jungle where condominiums, high-rises, and vegetation coexist and complement each other. Contrary to the previous pictures dominated by a cold, gray, undersaturated tone, Jiulong Square is colorful and vibrant. Hit by a suffused pink glow, the green lights of the fountain and the abundance of people give vitality to the overall scene. The photographer captures an instant of everyday life in Chongqing: the playfulness and liveliness of children, who are running, touching the water, and socializing; the public space that hosts a variety of activities and is embellished with green vegetation; and a distant concrete

Fig. 2.8. Jiulong Square, Chongqing, China, 2017. (From the *Forest* series [2010–2017]. © Yan Wang Preston, reprinted with permission.)

wall, which suggests a different reality in which the frenetic urban rhythms leave little space for slow-paced leisure activities in the square. Instead of photographing spectacular urban landscapes or mourning trees, Preston records fragments of heterogeneous lives in Chongqing that are relatable and hopeful.

Whereas this photograph alone could be interpreted as a celebration of the state-sanctioned policy Forest Chongqing, Preston's long-term visual and artistic engagement suggests a more complex and critical outlook. It is a reminder that "yes, you've got all these wonderful woodlands now, but please don't forget where they come from."[81] It is a visual narrative that conveys oscillating and at times contradictory feelings, ranging from sadness and vulnerability to irony and hope. Preston's changing trajectory in her photographic work also reflects the understanding that in the natural environment change is more frequent and more dominant than harmony and balance. Anthropologist Anna Tsing explains that whereas in the 1950s and 1960s "the idea of ecosystem equilibrium seemed promising [. . .], in the 1970s [. . .] attention turned to disruption and change, which generate the heterogeneity of the landscape."[82] Maintaining this, the highly cosmetic and economically driven practice of transplanting trees could ironically point to and shape more inclusive ecosystems. Indeed, the coexistence of trees, urban space, and people can reinforce an understanding of ecology as a web of interconnected linkages. This overarching ecology resists humankind's exceptionalism and understands the universe as an interlinked entity where human and nonhuman coexist and are interdependent.[83] Preston's later work seems to capture and join in these continuous exchanges and transformations. By becoming more optimistic and confident about our ecosystems' ability to adapt, Preston depicts trees as healing and resilient beings in our interlinked ecology.

Overall, this chapter has examined Preston's photographic reportage to reflect on the specific ecological practices in the municipality of Chongqing between 2010 and 2017, showing how nonhuman ecological communities have been pivotal to project the image of a beautiful, green city center. Under the national imperative of pursuing a "Beautiful China," environmental conservation has been deeply intertwined with policymaking, economics, and ultimately, the realization of a modern nation. However, the exchanges seem to be mostly unidirectional and fail to recognize the multilateral linkages that we are all part of, transforming ecology into a set of tools to materialize attractive and sustainable cities and boost national soft power.

In the words of Preston, today "the whole concept of trying to be green is being abused."[84] Preston's photographic project is invaluable in privileging and narrating the exploited and underrepresented lives of trees. Whereas some of her first photographs convey sorrow and a sense of powerlessness in front of transplanted trees' barren, naked branches, her prolonged exploration of Chongqing allows her to gather a multiplicity of stories in which vegetation readapts to the urban soil and blossoms. In addition to having a significant documentary and informative function, Preston's reportage has the capacity to collect and communicate these stories in a meaningful manner. From the ironic encounter with *Goldie* to the optimistic and lively image of Chongqing residents playing and resting in green spaces, Preston's practice can reduce the constructed distance between human beings and trees and recognize the intricate living webs that sustain the globe. For more sustainable futures, we need to imagine multiple and interdependent ways of life,[85] which is what the photographic reportage by Preston and works in other visual arts can do.

ACKNOWLEDGMENTS

This research was made possible through the AHRC/Midlands3Cities Doctoral Training Partnership and the feedback of Prof. Jiang Jiehong and Dr. Theo Reeves-Evison. I also wish to thank the artist Yan Wang Preston, who kindly agreed to meet and discuss her work on several occasions.

NOTES

1. Methodologically, this article deploys qualitative, empirical, and visual analysis, semi-structured interviews with the artist, and critical theory and philosophical investigation.

2. Preston, *Forest.*

3. Tsing, *The Mushroom at the End of the World*, viii.

4. The tier city ranking aims to categorize China's metropolises into four different orders. The criteria include GDP, population, political administration structure, commercial and urban residents' activities, as well as urban lifestyle; Sun, "2017 Xin Yixian chengshi." Rather than a standard official mechanism, it works as an arbitrary tool to measure something as nebulous as urban success. According to the Chongqing Municipal People's Government website, at the end of 2023 the population of the entire municipality, including rural areas surrounding the city, was 34,093,500, while long-term residents in the urban area numbered 22,874,500. http://wap.cq.gov.cn/zjcq/sqgk/cqsq/202412/t20241231_14378524.html (accessed July 4, 2025).

5. Guo and Liu, "Guangzhou's Special Path to Global City Status," 59–76. Geographical inequalities have perhaps even worsened since Deng Xiaoping's set of socio-economic reforms, which focused on overall national development; see Long, "China's Changing Regional Disparities during the Reform Period," 69; Hui, "Changing regional rural inequality in China 1980–2002," 387.

6. Lim and Horesh, "The Chongqing vs. Guangdong Developmental 'Models,'" 372–95.

7. Chreod Ltd., *People's Republic of China: Provincial Development Strategies for Chongqing Municipality*, 3. Bo Xilai was Communist Party secretary of Chongqing between 2007 and 2012. In 2012, Bo was found guilty of corruption and abuse of power and removed from the party; his wife was accused of murdering the British businessman, Neil Heywood. See Jacobs and Buckley, "Chinese Official at Center of Scandal Is Found Guilty and Given a Life Term."

8. Zhang, *Branding Chongqing*, 217.

9. Geall, "Clear Waters and Green Mountains: Will Xi Jinping Take the Lead on Climate Change?"; Huang Runqiu, "Jianchi 'lü shui qing shan.'"

10. Roberts, *Photography and China*, 7.

11. Schaefer, *Shadow Modernism*, 3.

12. Li, *Utopian Ruins*, 105. This chapter offers insight into photography during the Maoist era.

13. Roberts, *Photography*, 129; Wu, *Zooming In*; Chen, "Departing from Socialist Realism." For a discussion of the initial emergence of photography as a fine art in the 1920s and 1930s in Beijing and Shanghai, see Kent, "Early Twentieth-Century Art Photography in China"; Schaefer, *Shadow Modernism.*

14. Roberts, *Photography*, 121.

15. Wu, *Zooming In*, 13–14.

16. Through interviews and exchanges with Chinese artists during my fieldwork in Beijing and Shanghai in 2019 and online, it has emerged that many artists born before the 1980s and experimenting with the camera were hired as news reporters or photojournalists. These include Xing Danwen, Jiang Zhi, and Jiang Pengyi, among others.

17. Roberts, *Photography*, 139.

18. Wu, *Zooming In*, 13–14.

19. Laughlin and Guo, "Reportage and Its Contemporary Variations," x. Charles A. Laughlin links Chinese reportage to the writers of the Leftwing League; see Laughlin, *Chinese Reportage*, xxiv.

20. Cartwright, "Photojournalism," 339.

21. Wall, "'Marks of Indifference,'" 248.

22. Roberts, *Photography*.

23. Guo, "From the Margins to the Hearth," 167.

24. Wu Hung argues that the political dimension of contemporary Chinese experimental art is not straightforward to recognize. He states that "although some experimental art conveys political criticism and intends to challenge official ideology, [. . .] such challenges are subtle, realized mainly through deconstructing typical images in official art"; see Wu, *Transience*, 12. Gao Minglu, among other scholars, refers to experimental art as "avant-gardes"; see *Total Modernity and the Avant-Garde in Twentieth-Century Chinese Art*.

25. Laughlin and Guo, "Reportage," viii.

26. Laughlin, *Chinese Reportage*; Wei, "Opening Ecocriticism's Sino-America Dialogue," 76–90.

27. Laughlin and Guo, "Reportage," xii.

28. Laughlin and Guo, "Reportage," xii.

29. Guo, "From the Margins to the Hearth," 172.

30. Data on Yin Xiuzhen and Zheng Bo were collected by the author in spring 2019 at the Asia Art Archive, Hong Kong. For more information on Yin Xiuzhen, see Olivier Krischer, "Contending Nature: The Environment as 'Found Object' in the Practices of Song Dong and Yin Xiuzhen," in *The River Project*, 156–62 (Campbelltown Arts Centre, 2010); Nancy P. Lin, "Keepers of the Waters: Experiments in Xianchang Art Practice in 1990s China," *Journal of Contemporary Chinese Art* 7, nos. 2–3 (2020): 325–43; Xiuzhen Yin, *Yin Xiuzhen* (London: Phaidon Press, 2015). For Zheng Bo, see Tess Edmonson, "Post-Nature—A Museum as an Ecosystem," *E-Flux*, 2019, https://www.e-flux.com/criticism/250396/post-nature-a-museum-as-an-ecosystem; Zheng Bo, "E-Catalogue," *Kiang Malingue*, 2023, https://kiangmalingue.com/wordpress/wp-content/uploads/2019/05/Zheng-Bo_e-catalogue-5.pdf; Zheng Bo and Sohl Lee, "Contemporary Art and Ecology in East Asia," *Journal of Contemporary Chinese Art* 3, no. 3 (2016): 215–22.

31. Federica Mirra examines the works by Ye Funa and Na Buqi and argues that they shed light on and play with the exploitation of "nature," especially in relation to tourism. See Mirra, *Urban Imaginaries*, chapter 5.

32. Sontag, "In Plato's Cave," 11.

33. Sontag, "In Plato's Cave," 11.

34. Sontag, "In Plato's Cave," 10.

35. Author's online interview with Yan Wang Preston, January 31, 2020.

36. See Andreasson, "Yan Wang Preston's Best Photograph"; Barth, *Yan Wang Preston*; "Capturing the Environment"; "Mapping China's Frontline"; Preston, *Forest*; Preston, "Forest: Re-Seen"; Ying, "Huayi sheying shi"; Ma, *Wang Yan*; Warner, "Into the Forest with Yan Wang Preston." However, apart from exceptions such as Preston, "Forest: Re-Seen," there is little academic literature on her photographic practice.

37. Preston, "Forest Re-Seen," 346.
38. Martinsson, "Introduction," 9.
39. Martinsson, "Introduction," 13.
40. Preston, "Forest Re-Seen," 349.
41. Martinsson, "Introduction," 9.
42. Author's online interview with Yan Wang Preston, January 31, 2020.
43. Author's online interview with Yan Wang Preston, January 31, 2020.
44. Even though there is no direct connection, the translucency of the fabric around the trees could be reminiscent of the exquisite shroud on Giuseppe Sanmartino's *Veiled Christ* (1753) in Sansevero Chapel in Naples or of Giovanni Strazza's *Veiled Virgin* (19th century).
45. Morton, *Ecology without Nature*, 140.
46. Morton, *Ecology without Nature*; Elvin, *The Retreat of the Elephants*; Tan, "Landscape without Nature," 223–41.
47. Hudson, "Urbanism in the Anthropocene," 299–313. For instance, Yin argues that whereas *ziran* originally meant "spontaneity" and "all living beings" in the Daoist tradition, it gained the additional definition of a separate and different "nature" with the 1864 translation of *Elements of International Law* by American jurist Henry Wheaton (2017).
48. Elvin, *The Retreat of the Elephants*; Tan, "Landscape without Nature."
49. Cited in Elvin, *The Retreat of the Elephants*, 323.
50. Cited in Elvin, *The Retreat of the Elephants*, 324.
51. Guo, "From the Margins."
52. Guo, "From the Margins," 171.
53. See the introduction to this volume for a further discussion of Guattari's ethical-aesthetic paradigm.
54. Her trees are reminiscent of Liu Jianhua's sculptures, *Transformation of Memories* (2003). Liu's work was inspired by the sudden tearing down of trees and buildings in Jingdezhen, China. Gathering trunks, branches, and other fragments from the ground, Liu used them to make molds to give trees another life. Although denaturalized and converted in ceramic sculptures, the trees become fragile yet eternal sculptures. Author's in-person interview with Liu Jianhua, artist's studio, Shanghai, May 8, 2019.
55. Sontag, "In Plato's Cave," 15.
56. Author's online interview with Yan Wang Preston, January 31, 2020.
57. Author's email exchange with Yan Wang Preston, July 6, 2022. In China's authoritarian regime, her project could be deemed confrontational with the CCP's power. Preston preferred English to Mandarin because the scope of the project goes beyond the PRC; Chongqing is a case study in widespread afforesting instances around the world. Moreover, English was preferred in order to control the production quality of catalogs and other published materials.
58. Author's online interview with Yan Wang Preston, January 31, 2020.
59. Preston, "Forest Re-Seen," 345–66.
60. Cited in Duffy, "Ai Weiwei's Furniture-Sculpture," 84.
61. Barthes, "Camera Lucida," 28.
62. Laughlin and Guo, "Reportage," xii.

63. Preston, "Forest."

64. One can even interpret the color green as a marker of the ecological mission by officials, urban planners, and real estate developers, who deploy it extensively in the urban space. Mirra observes that construction sites are often surrounded by green billboards and panels of fake grass, perhaps in an attempt to counterbalance urban ruins and amplify the sense of being in a green environment. See Mirra "The Art of Billboards in Urbanized China," 290–91.

65. Preston, *Forest*.

66. Author's online interview with Yan Wang Preston, January 31, 2020.

67. Author's online interview with Yan Wang Preston, January 31, 2020.

68. Economy, "Environmental Governance."

69. Zhao, "The China Model: Can It Replace the Western Model of Modernization?"

70. For instance, Preston observes that after a tree dies, the authorities just plant another without anyone even noticing. During my stay in Chongqing in spring 2023, I also came across this practice of replacing trees at night.

71. UNFCCC, "Paris Agreement."

72. Economy, "Environmental Governance." The concept of Green GDP was established by the United Nations to measure the environmental impact of economic activities. According to the System of Environmental-Economic Accounting, "the 'Green GDP' is derived from Net Domestic Product (NDP), – which is obtained by subtracting the depreciation of produced assets such as machines and buildings from GDP – by deducting the cost of depletion of natural resources and degradation of ecosystems"; United Nations, "The Quest for Green GDP." The National Environmental Model City recognizes the prestige "attained by meeting a set of highly specific environment and development targets" within China, see Economy, "Environmental Governance," 178.

73. Wang, Bi, Wheeler, Wang, Cao, Lu, and Wang, "Environmental Performance Rating and Disclosure." A Greenpeace report in 2018 shows that the PRC has made significant reductions in fine particle levels and in 2018 owned the "most numerous and far-reaching monitoring network"; see IQAir AirVisual, "2018 World Air Quality Report."

74. Preston, "Forest Re-Seen."

75. Author's online interview with Yan Wang Preston, January 31, 2020.

76. Wong, "Eco-Cities in China."

77. Smith, *Uneven Development*; Smith, "Nature as Accumulation Strategy."

78. Though the idea of several "representations of nature" could imply the existence of a real nature, it is worth stressing that this "nature" might never have existed in the first place. Quoting Reeves-Evison and Bowsher, "the actual nature" is "an already-externalized product of the Nature-Society distinction set in motion by capitalist modernity," see "On Capital's Watch," 41.

79. Smith, "Nature as Accumulation," 29.

80. The metabolic rift is a term developed by scholars to describe the Marxist analysis of the labor process between humans and nature; see Foster, "Marx's Theory of Metabolic Rift."

81. Author's online interview with Yan Wang Preston, January 31, 2020.

82. Tsing, *The Mushroom at the End of the World*, 160–61.

83. Tsing, "Feral Atlas."
84. Warner, "Into the Forest."
85. Lindner and Meissner, *The Routledge Companion to Urban Imaginaries.*

REFERENCES

Andreasson, Kevin. "Yan Wang Preston's Best Photograph: A Chinese Village's Ancient Tree—Sold for 25,000." *The Guardian*, 2017. https://www.theguardian.com/artanddesign/2017/mar/09/yan-wang-preston-best-photograph-a-chinese-village-tree-syngenta-award

Barth, Nadine. *Yan Wang Preston: Mother River*. Berlin: Hatje Cantz, 2018.

Barthes, Roland, ed. "Camera Lucida: Reflections on Photography." In *Camera Lucida: Reflections on Photography*, 85–91. London: Vintage Books, 1993.

Berghuis, Thomas. *Performance Art in China*. Hong Kong: Timezone 8 Limited, 2006.

"Capturing the Environment." *BBC News*, 2017. https://www.bbc.com/news/in-pictures-39179576

Cartwright, Guenther. "Photojournalism." In *The Focal Encyclopedia of Photography: Digital Imaging, Theory and Applications, History, and Science*, edited by Michael R Peres, 339–401. Burlington: Taylor & Francis, 2007.

Chen, Shuxia. "Departing from Socialist Realism: April Photo Society, 1979–1981." *Trans Asia Photography* 8, no. 1 (2017).

Chreod Ltd. *People's Republic of China: Provincial Development Strategies for Chongqing Municipality*. Asian Development Bank and Chonqing Municipal Finance Bureau. May 2011. https://www.adb.org/sites/default/files/project-documents//42139-012-prc-tacr-02.pdf

Duffy, Owen. "Ai Weiwei's Furniture-Sculpture: Radical Ambiguity and the Function of Critique." *Journal of Contemporary Chinese Art* 5, no. 1 (2018): 77–91.

Economy, Elizabeth. "Environmental Governance: The Emerging Economic Dimension." *Environmental Politics* 15, no. 2 (2006): 171–89.

Elvin, Mark. *The Retreat of the Elephants: An Environmental History of China*. New Haven: Yale University Press, 2004.

Foster, John B. "Marx's Theory of Metabolic Rift: Classical Foundations for Environmental Sociology." *American Journal of Sociology* 105, no. 2 (1999): 366–405.

Gao, Minglu. *Total Modernity and the Avant-Garde in Twentieth-Century Chinese Art*. Cambridge, MA: MIT Press, 2011.

Geall, Sam. "Clear Waters and Green Mountains: Will Xi Jinping Take the Lead on Climate Change?" Lowy Institute Analyses, Lowy Institute for International Policy, November 1, 2017. http://www.jstor.org/stable/resrep17555

Guo, Li. "From the Margins to the Hearth." *Modern Chinese Literature and Culture* 31, no. 2 (2019): 162–206.

Guo, Xiangmin, and Changtao Liu. "Guangzhou's Special Path to Global City Status." In *Aspects of Urbanization in China: Shanghai, Hong Kong, Guangzhou*, edited by Gregory Bracken, 59–76. Amsterdam: Amsterdam University Press, 2012.

Huang Runqiu. "*Jianchi 'lü shui qing shan jiu shi jin shan yin shan' linian cujin jing ji shehui fazhan quanmian lüse zhuanxing*" 坚持"绿水青山就是金山银山"理念促进经济社会发展全面绿色转型 [Adhere to the Concept of 'Clear Water and Green

Mountains Are as Good as Golden and Silver Mountains' to Promote a Comprehensive Green Transformation of Economic and Social Development]. Xinhua, 2021. http://www.xinhuanet.com/politics/2021-01/15/c_1126985515.htm

Hudson, Mike. "Urbanism in the Anthropocene: Ecological Urbanism or Premium Ecological Enclaves?" *City* 14, no. 3 (2010): 299–313.

Hui, Liu. "Changing Regional Rural Inequality in China 1980–2002." *Area* 38, no. 4 (2006): 377–89.

IQAir AirVisual. "2018 World Air Quality Report: Region & City PM2.5 Ranking." IQAir, 2018. iqair.com/dl/pdf-reports/world-air-quality-report-2018-en.pdf?srsltid=AfmBOoqZ1lCU5c3cYOB3X_ZImhIV9eNS16yBFum7V0QHnA6TYwQ1HQWB

Jacobs, Andrew, and Chris Buckley. "Chinese Official at Center of Scandal Is Found Guilty and Given a Life Term." *New York Times*, September 22, 2013. https://www.nytimes.com/2013/09/22/world/asia/bo-xilai-official-is-found-guilty-of-all-charges-and-given-life-term.html

Kent, Richard K. "Early Twentieth-Century Art Photography in China: Adopting, Domesticating, and Embracing the Foreign." *Trans Asia Photography* 3, no. 2 (2013): n.p.

Laughlin, Charles. *Chinese Reportage: The Aesthetics of Historical Experience*. Durham: Duke University Press, 2002.

Laughlin, Charles, and Li Guo. "Reportage and Its Contemporary Variations: An Introduction." *Modern Chinese Literature and Culture* 31, no. 2 (2019): x–xvi.

Li, Jie. *Utopian Ruins: A Memorial Museum of the Mao Era*. Durham: Duke University Press, 2020.

Lim, Kean Fan, and Niv Horesh. "The Chongqing vs. Guangdong Developmental 'Models' in Post-Mao China: Regional and Historical Perspectives on the Dynamics of Socioeconomic Change." *Journal of the Asia Pacific Economy* 22, no. 3 (2017): 372–95.

Lindner, Christoph, and Miriam Meissner. *The Routledge Companion to Urban Imaginaries*. New York: Routledge, 2019.

Long, Gen Ying. "China's Changing Regional Disparities during the Reform Period." *Economic Geography* 75, no. 1 (1999): 59–70.

Ma, Yalan. "Wang Yan: yuqi shuo sheying, zhe geng xiang shi yi chang xiuxing" [Wang Yan: It's More Like a Practice than Photography]. *Guo wang tupian zhongxin* (China Image Centre), April 20, 2017. http://cic.china.com.cn/pic/2017-04/20/content_9445225.htm

"Mapping China's Frontline: The Yangtze at 100 km Intervals—A Photo Essay." *The Guardian*, 2018. https://www.theguardian.com/world/2018/jun/26/yangtze-at-100km-intervals-a-photo-essay

Martinsson, Tyrone. "Introduction." In *Arctic Views: Passages in Time*, 7–16. Stockholm: Art and Theory.

Mirra, Federica. "The Art of Billboards in Urbanized China." *Journal of Contemporary Chinese Art* 7, nos. 2–3 (2020): 281–306.

Mirra, Federica. *Urban Imaginaries: Contemporary Art and Urban Transformations in China since 2001*. PhD diss., Birmingham City University, 2022.

Morton, Timothy. *Ecology Without Nature: Rethinking Environmental Aesthetics*. Cambridge, MA: Harvard University Press, 2007.

Preston, Yan Wang. *Forest*. Yan Wang Preston, n.d. https://www.yanwangpreston.com/projects/forest-images

Preston, Yan Wang. "Yangtze the Mother River: Photography, Myth and Deep Mapping." PhD diss., Plymouth University, 2017.

Preston, Yan Wang. *Forest*. Berlin: Hatje Cantz, 2018.

Preston, Yan Wang. "Forest Re-Seen: From the Metropolis to the Wilderness." *Journal of Contemporary Chinese Art* 7, no. 2–3 (2020): 345–66.

Reeves-Evison, Theo, and Josh Bowsher. "On Capital's Watch: Derivative Ecology and the Temporal Logic of Biodiversity Credits." *New Formations* 99 (2020): 33–51.

Rios, Maria Elvira. *A Chinese Buddhist Ecological Narrative and the "Beautiful Country" of Xi Jinping*. The 12th International Convention of Asia Scholars (ICAS 12), online symposium, 2021.

Roberts, Claire. *Photography and China*. Hong Kong: Reaktion Books, 2013.

Schaefer, William. *Shadow Modernism: Photography, Writing, and Space in Shanghai, 1925–1937*. Durham: Duke University Press, 2017.

Smith, Neil. "Nature as Accumulation Strategy." *Socialist Register* 43 (2007): 1–36.

Smith, Neil. *Uneven Development: Nature, Capital, and the Production of Space*. Athens: University of Georgia Press, 2008.

Sontag, Susan, ed. "In Plato's Cave." In *On Photography*, 1–19. New York: RosettaBooks, 1973.

Sun, Qi. "*2017 Xin yixian chengshi paihang bang fabu Chengdu, Hangzhou, Wuhan chanlian sanjia Zhengzhou, Dongguan xin jin ru bang*" 2017 新一线"城市排行榜发布成都、杭州、武汉蝉联三 甲郑州、东莞新晋入榜 [2017 List of 'New First Tier Cities Announced: Chengdu, Hangzhou and Wuhan at the Top, while Zhengzhou and Dongguan Enter the List"]. Yicai Global, 2017. https://www.yicai.com/news/

Tan, Chang. "Landscape without Nature: Ecological Reflections in Contemporary Chinese Art." *Journal of Contemporary Chinese Art* 3, no. 3 (2016): 223–41.

Tsing, Anna. *The Mushroom at the End of the World: On the Possibility of Life in Capitalist Ruins*. Princeton: Princeton University Press, 2015.

Tsing, Anna. "Feral Atlas and the More-than-Human Anthropocene." Art in the Anthropocene International Conference, Trinity College, Dublin, June 7–9, 2019. https://feralatlas.supdigital.org/?cd=true&bdtext=feral-atlas-and-the-more-than-human-anthropocene

UNFCCC. "Paris Agreement—Status of Ratification." UNFCCC, accessed January 24, 2020. https://unfccc.int/process/the-paris-agreement/status-of-ratification

United Nations. "The Quest for Green GDP." System of Environmental Economic Accounting, accessed March 21, 2025. https://seea.un.org/events/quest-green-gdp

"Urban Forest." MAD, 2009. http://www.i-mad.com/work/urban-forest/?cid=4

Wall, Jeff. "'Marks of Indifference': Aspects of Photography in, or as, Conceptual Art." In *Reconsidering the Object of Art, 1965–1975*, edited by Ann Goldstein and Anne Rorimer, 247–67. Los Angeles: Museum of Contemporary Art, 1995.

Wang, Hua, Jun Bi, David Wheeler, Jinnan Wang, Dong Cao, Genfa Lu, and Yuan Wang. "Environmental Performance Rating and Disclosure: China's GreenWatch Program." *Journal of Environmental Management* 71, no. 2 (2004): 123–33.

Warner, Marigold. "Into the Forest with Yan Wang Preston." *British Journal of Photography*, 2018. https://www.bjp-online.com/2018/06/yan-preston-forest/

Wei, Qingqi. "Opening Ecocriticism's Sino-America Dialogue: An Interview with Lawrence Buell." *Tamkang Review* 36, no. 3 (2006): 76–90.

Wong, Tai-Chee. "Eco-Cities in China: Pearls in the Sea of Degrading Urban Environments?" In *Eco-City Planning, Policy and Development*, edited by Tai-Chee Wong and B. Yuen, 131–50. London: Springer, 2011.

Wu, Hung. *Transience: Chinese Experimental Art at the End of the Twentieth Century*. Chicago: University of Chicago Press, 1999.

Wu, Hung. *Zooming In: Histories of Photography in China*. London: Reaktion Books, 2016.

Wu, Meichun, and Zhijie Qiu. "The Rise and Development of Video Art and the Maturity of New Media Art." In *Reinterpretation: A Decade of Experimental Chinese Art, 1990–2000*, edited by Hung Wu and Karen Smith, 52–60. Guangzhou: Guangdong Museum of Art, 2002.

Ying, Zi. "Huayi sheyingshi Wang Yan zuopin 'Muqin he' huojiang" 华裔摄影师王岩作品母亲河获奖 [China-Born Photographer Wang Yan's Work 'Mother River' Wins the Award]. *Zhongguo sheyingjia xiehui wang* 中国摄影家协会网 [China Photographers Association Network], April 8, 2014. https://www.cpanet.org.cn/detail_news_82555.html

Zhang, Bowen. "Branding Chongqing: Understanding Chinese Place Branding from a Government Perspective." PhD diss., University of Leicester, 2019.

Zhao, Suisheng. "The China Model: Can It Replace the Western Model of Modernization?" *Journal of Contemporary China* 19, no. 65 (2019): 419–36.

THREE

Reincarnations of Labor Reportage

Nonfiction by Chinese Migrant Worker Authors

Federico Picerni

Literary reportage and workers' literature have historically been imbricated in a productive relationship. In this chapter, I approach nonfiction (*feixugou* 非虛構) as a contemporary genre (that roughly came about in the 2000s), highlighting its thematic and stylistic connections to industrial-themed reportage literature and especially its function as an instrument for workers to construct *self*-narratives, thus participating in reportage art's active (and often critical) intervention in the social space where it is produced (see Chen's, Mirra's, and Moran's chapters in this volume). As case studies, I present nonfiction accounts written by two workers, Meng Yu 夢雨 and Yuan Wei 苑偉. Both are members of the Picun Literature Group (*Picun wenxue xiaozu* 皮村文學小組), a collective devoted to literary training and creative writing for rural-to-urban migrant laborers. Based in Beijing at an organization promoting cultural production and participation in the urban periphery known as the Migrant Workers Home (*Gongyou zhi jia* 工友之家), this group helps give voice to nonprofessional writers in China.[1]

Meng Yu's and Yuan Wei's stories are framed by the publications of the literature group as nonfiction (they are generally included in the *feixugou* category of the group's self-made anthologies and journals). This association is clearly aimed at inserting them into a recognized discursive context, given that nonfiction has a considerable popularity in today's literary scene. Its consecration as a distinct genre came in 2010, when China's most important literary journal, *Renmin wenxue* 人民文學, launched a project dedicated to the subject. In an attempt to establish more scholarly rigor, it has been argued that nonfiction should be understood as a hybrid writing practice at the intersection between literature per se (meaning, fictional literature), sociohistorical reality, and documentary.[2] Such characteristics are indebted to the core pursuits of literary reportage, as admitted by Li Jingze 李敬澤, who championed nonfiction in *Renmin wenxue*.[3]

Through these case studies, I aim to demonstrate that workers' nonfiction can be read as a continuation of labor reportage, especially if we understand reportage not only as a body of works with shared characteristics and produced within a clearly recognizable timeframe, but also as a set of political (and thus also ethical), social, and aesthetic premises—in other words, as an ethical-aesthetic paradigm. This approach is both consistent with and draws from Li Guo and Charles Laughlin's proposal (in the introduction to this volume) to reenvision reportage not as a discrete literary genre, delimited in time (and possibly even space), but as a "multiplicity of artistic practices" that transgress "historical and national boundaries." The point is how (workers') nonfiction contains some of the ethical aspirations and aesthetic functions assigned to early-20th-century labor reportage, while reinventing other aspects, above all the relationship between observer and observation, investigator and investigated.

Labor, Reportage (and Nonfiction): Past and Present

Workers' literature, a denomination used in this chapter to denote literary output by workers themselves, is often considered to be substantially akin to reportage—social commentary written in verse or some other form, but not ascribable to the amorphous entity properly called "literature." This understanding (requiring also a separate discussion on the "literariness" of reportage, which I will address shortly) flattens workers' literature to a superficial reading and obscures the variety of genres and forms that worker authors engage with. Nevertheless, there are two points that make the association between workers' literature and reportage meaningful. First, it highlights the fact that authors coming from subaltern contexts write with a vividness possible only to those who have actually experienced the circumstances they represent—a proximity to factual truth also sought by reportage.[4] Second, it is grounded in the historical fact that reportage literature and workers' cultural production have a long history of interrelation.

Closely connected to the popularization of culture (*dazhonghua* 大眾化) championed by some of the intellectuals who emerged from the May Fourth Movement, reportage was taken up by leftist writers of the 1920s and 1930s "to resolve the gap between theory and practice" and "produce polemical literary works that reflected the experience of the proletariat," as Laughlin puts it.[5] The development of Chinese labor reportage was considerably influenced by international figures, most from the "proletarian literature" movement in the Third International, but it also had "local" antecedents in the late Qing period (illustrated in Zhu's chapter). Important writers such as Ding Ling 丁玲 (1904–86) and Xia Yan 夏衍 (1900–95) participated in the creation of labor reportage, but attempts were also made to train workers to do the job themselves. One prominent case was the workers' correspondence movement (*gongren tongxun yundong* 工人通訊運動) during the 1930s and '40s, later joined by nonprofessional (*yeyu* 業餘) proletarian writers trained at state institutions following the establishment of the People's Republic, with Cao Ming 草明 (1913–2002) as one of the most visible representatives of industrial literature from the period.[6] Reportage was held to be a suitable artistic form and method to represent the living realities of labor, but in certain cases, it was also seen as an instrument to overcome the gap that prevented illiterate and untrained laborers from participating in the actual creation of literature. Within a literary movement informed by the ideological context of the Chinese revolution, with the centrality it assigned to the working class, reportage could generate literature *about* and at times *by* laborers, and insofar as it was connected to proletarian politics, *for* laborers as well.

Following the end of the Mao era (1949–76)—during which it was tasked with extolling the virtues of the new state, ostensibly "led by the working class"—reportage literature witnessed a flourishing resurgence; but, as Laughlin and Guo write, it generally lost its critical edge after 1989, when it "could no longer be used as a weapon of critique or resistance," and therefore suffered "a drastic loss of legitimacy."[7] Around the same time, workers' literature (*gongren wenxue* 工人文學) was discarded as politicized writing with no literary value. But were these two genres really gone for good? As a matter of fact, in China, forms that would have traditionally belonged to reportage, such as pieces of investigation, memoirs, social inquiries, etc., are now generally grouped under "nonfiction." And in this context (but not only this context) we have been witnessing a resurgence of workers' self-narratives in postsocialist China, in a more spontaneous way with respect to the bureaucratic constraints applied by the party-state that limited previous workers' literature in terms of style and content. Of course, present-day workers are much different in their social composition and political centrality from the subjects of early-20th-century reportage. The vast majority are migrants from rural areas, employed not only in factories, but also in the urban service sector (care work, gig economy, etc.). Marginalized by the obliteration of class politics, they are nevertheless highly productive in terms of literary activity, mostly in amateur form. Their output is generally categorized under the name of *dagong wenxue* 打工文學 (loosely translatable as "precarious workers' literature," or "battlers' literature" in van Crevel's translation), although crucially, some have been using *xin gongren wenxue* 新工人文學 (new workers' literature) precisely to stress the continuity with previous generations and highlight the historical role of the working class.[8]

Nonfiction's general interest in the objective representation of the subaltern classes[9] and its reliance on direct experience of facts and situations[10] also foregrounds its interest in the living conditions of the working class. While workers are generally targets for investigation, they are also active as producers of creative (nonfictional) output. In fact, a considerable portion of labor-related or social-themed nonfiction is written by migrant workers themselves. One of the first and most visible examples of workers' nonfiction is *Qingchun yizhan* 青春驛站 (*Station Youth*) by Anzi 安子 (b. 1967), published in 1991, which oscillates somewhat between a vivid account of a female migrant worker's ordeals and a typically neoliberal narrative of individual success. Another remarkable example is *Cidian: nanfang gongye shenghuo* 辭典：南方工業生活 (*A Dictionary: Life in the Industrial South*) by Xiao Xiangfeng 蕭相風 (b. 1977) in 2011, in the inspiring form of a dictionary, reminiscent of Han Shaogong's 韓少功 (b. 1953) partly nonfictional masterpiece, *Maqiao cidian* 馬橋辭典 (*A Dictionary of Maqiao*). In particular, the memoir of Fan Yusu 范雨素 (b. 1973), *Wo shi Fan Yusu* 我是范雨素 (*I Am Fan Yusu*, 2017), which went viral in 2017 following its publication online, displayed the critical sharpness ascribable to traditional reportage. The most recent case would probably be Hu Anyan's 胡安焉 *Wo zai Beijing song kuaidi* 我在北京送快遞 (*I Deliver Parcels in Beijing*, 2023), written from the perspective of someone who spent time working in a vital sector of today's urban service economy.

The marked presence of autobiographical elements is one of the attributes that differentiates this kind of nonfiction from traditional reportage, which sought to discuss the greater problems of history, society, and the nation.[11] With this consistent element of narrative self-construction, workers' nonfiction rearticulates problems of representation and authenticity. Mediation was a central tenet of reportage literature and much of postsocialist nonfiction as well,[12] because the investigator was often (but not always) an intellectual who explored certain situations and environments. In the case of workers' nonfiction, the investigator and the investigated tend to be combined into the same subject. Writers are not external observers, but individuals who generally talk about their own experience, and when it is not exactly their own, it is that of a common group—a social class most of them tend to identify with.[13] This fact brings renewed attention to the notion of "authenticity," which Wagner considers an attribute of traditional reportage in its "not hav[ing] a plot in the sense of an invented action."[14] In workers' nonfiction, "authenticity" can rather be associated with authors' claims of direct experience, further "restricting [reportage] to the phenomena that can be observed and proved."[15] Of course, "authenticity" (even as a sort of firsthand vividness) should never be taken uncritically, given the number of agents (instructors, trainers, publishers, editors, etc.) intervening in the production, publication, and distribution of workers' nonfiction.

While there is a clear historical continuity between traditional labor reportage and present-day workers' nonfiction, the two also share an aesthetic problem—the relation between social engagement and the aesthetic level that a literary work is generally supposed to present. This is a problem that lies at the heart of the genre's intelligibility as *literature*. In fact, Laughlin points out that reportage challenged watertight dichotomies between extraliterary (social) relevance and artistic quality per se. What he terms "*literary construction of social space*" (italics in the original)[16] shows that reportage's fidelity to facts does not automatically exclude its "literariness," as the author's subjective perception "creates new possibilities for imaginative literary expression, not the least of which are the exploration of modes of consciousness and identity other than individuality and a shift of focus in the production of meaning from characters to places and events."[17] This principle is also active in contemporary Chinese workers' nonfiction. Even more relevant, though, is the fact that the relation between society and art is in the very nature of workers' literature. As already mentioned, workers' literature is often seen, or misunderstood, as (self-)ethnography—a collection of sources of biographical information with an essentially documentary role.[18] While this is true (and it is nothing negative per se), overemphasis on the "empirical value" leads to missing its poetics—its essential literary characteristics—just as in reportage.[19] The artificial opposition of factual and fictional, documentary and imaginary, distracts from a dialectical approach to these literary realities as organic entities. The fruitful integration of these binaries, on the contrary, constitutes one of the most compelling and recognizable traits of the ethical-aesthetic paradigm where the labor reportage–nonfiction dis/continuum can become intelligible.

To sum up, on the one hand, we have the historical role of reportage in representing social life, particularly that of the working class. On the other, both reportage/nonfiction and workers' literature challenge dominant aesthetic conceptions regarding producing a form of literature that heavily relies on social engagement, without relinquishing its artistic refinement. A difference may be found in the fact that while social engagement was an ethical imperative for leftist writers in the early 20th century who wrote labor reportage, it constitutes an aesthetic premise in workers' nonfiction, often read on the assumption that it will provide a window into the otherwise obscured or ignored lives of society's downtrodden.[20] This is yet one more encouragement to consider the combination of nonfiction and workers' narratives as a valid ground for analysis.

The Merging of Investigator and Investigated: Meng Yu

Meng Yu's literary work is one example where these issues of representation and mediation appear quite lucidly. Born in Gansu in 1968, she worked for several years in Beijing as a housekeeper or domestic worker (*jiazhenggong* 家政工; also called nanny, *baomu* 保姆), Meng Yu is a pen name for Li Wenli 李文麗, who has also published with her real name, and as Li Yu 李玉. In addition to belonging to the aforementioned Picun Literature Group, while in Beijing she was extremely active in a marginal but lively scene managed by female housekeepers who carried out various sorts of cultural activities, called Swan Goose's Home (*Hongyan zhi jia* 鴻雁之家). In 2025, one year after she left Beijing and returned to Gansu, Meng Yu published her first book by her real name, Li Wenli, *Wo zai Beijing zuojiazheng* 我在北京做家政 (*A Domestic Worker in Beijing*), with an official publishing house, Duzhu chubanshe.

She mostly writes memoirs or reportages from her native place, in the Gansu countryside, or accounts of her daily activities either at work or while engaging in artistic endeavors. Her depictions of the working history of her "sisters'" and her own experiences reveal lives completely subsumed by a heavy work schedule, paired with contempt or harassment by employers, which she attributes to her rural origin.[21] Rural provenance clearly epitomizes her outsider status in the city, and bespeaks the structural inequality existing in the urban social space. Although quite different from the images of factory labor typically associated with wage exploitation, Meng Yu's stories reflect the new realities of a mobile workforce employed not only on the shop floor, but in the service industry for the new urban bourgeoisie. It comes as no surprise, then, that social relations in the city are a fundamental part of her nonfiction.

"Zheli ye you chuntian laiguo" 這裏也有春天來過 ("Spring Has Been Here Too"), for example, depicts Meng Yu observing migrants bustling through the lower levels of the city from her employers' home, from which she looks down to imagine their circumstances and schedules. By making up these strangers' backstories, Meng Yu prompts the reader to scratch below the surface of observation. What motivates her is no mere sympathy, but an awareness of belonging to the same social group. Although the physical distance (her being on the upper level of her employers' home in a high building) seems to encourage her observer's status, it is annulled by her social proximity to the observed individuals. This identification is especially made explicit in a conversation that Meng Yu reports having with her employer, who hopes that migrants' shabby lodgings can be demolished to improve the area:

> Immediately I said: "Madam, certainly they've got no other option than living there! Of course they don't wish to live there!"
>
> "What do you mean, no other option? Isn't it better for farmers to stay home and plough the land? Do they really have to come to Beijing, make trouble, and create a filthy environment for the good and decent locals?" said the baby's mother furiously.
>
> "Hey, Madam, you make it sound as if we people from the countryside are all beggars! If it wasn't for us, would the urbanites have their skyscrapers? They're all built by them! Who would look after your baby if I wasn't here?" I hated the way she was speaking and hurried to object.
>
> The lady laughed. "Ah, I didn't mean you! I was referring to those people who live downstairs. Don't be offended!"
>
> Humph! How could I not be offended! "And why can't they live there? When you have a place to shield you from the wind and the cold, and you're together with your family, your rice would taste good even if it had sand in it!" Speaking of them I was actually speaking of myself. Those words made me feel uncomfortable. But then what could I do? What can be effectively changed by a victory with words? I felt in a gloomy mood, and disheartened.[22]

Although Meng Yu insists that she writes in a rush, in the little free time she has left after work (her pieces are, in fact, all very short), without paying much attention to technical craft,[23] the strategy displayed here says otherwise. Throughout Meng Yu's work we find a considerable amount of dialogue and direct speech, often with the goal of clarifying the moral message she wants to convey, which is frequently made explicit in the closing of the story. Other examples that show her "technical" awareness include elaborate descriptions, the use of irony to reinforce the narration, or beginnings *in medias res*. We do not always see such sophistication in Meng Yu's works, but some show a strong formal investment that compels us to approach them from a literary point of view, not just as a sociological document.

One of the most evident examples of narrative technique is the trope of home; the image occurs repeatedly, skillfully articulated along with the many meanings that it has for housekeepers: workplace, lodging, biological family, or the family that employs them. Implicitly, it is possible to find a contrast between her lack of an actual home in the city, caused by structural inequality, and her newfound spiritual home among the "sisters" with whom she shares conditions and aspirations. When she is with them, she feels "as if I were back home" (感覺回到了家) and describes her sensation as "like reuniting with family after a long separation" (久別重逢的家人一樣).[24]

Most crucially, it is her combination of (distant) observation and (class) proximity that merges the roles of the narrator/investigator and the informant/observed. She sketches out the idea in another piece, significantly titled "Jiaru wo shi yi ming jizhe" 假如我是一名記者 ("If I Were a Journalist"). In the story, she interviews three housekeepers she knows and reports their stories, detailing their motivations for moving to Beijing, be it recovering from a marital loss, earning money after a husband's death, or paying back debts to friends and family. In the first paragraphs, Meng Yu clarifies her own interest in recording fellow housekeepers' stories by saying "I am a housekeeper, people I'm in contact with are housekeepers too," but "no one truly tries to understand all they've been through, no one is able to calm their own hearts to listen to their voices"; therefore, she has to take up the task herself.[25] It is important to emphasize again, however, that she does so not simply out of sympathy, but more relevantly, because she implies that having firsthand experience provides a depth of understanding and an all-around viewpoint that would otherwise be unattainable.

The inseparability of the individual and the social is reinforced, for example, by another piece in which Meng Yu tells her own story. The piece is made up of seventeen very short segments, each detailing a part of her life. The fragmentary technique is also interesting, probably motivated by the author's attempt to extract from her life individual episodes that have particular significance. She sets off from her life in the countryside, then moves to her first experiences as a waitress, nurse, worker at small workshops, and finally housekeeper. Throughout this time, she lives in Lanzhou, Yinchuan, and Inner Mongolia before finally reaching Beijing. There, thanks to contacts found by her local Women's Federation branch, she attends a professional school for housekeepers and finally gets a job that allows her to pay her children's school fees.

The title of this fragmented story is "Jiazhenggong de gushi" 家政工的故事, translatable both as "A Domestic Worker's Story" (or "My Story as a Domestic Worker") and "The Story of Domestic Workers." The indeterminacy of the Chinese language unintentionally reveals a powerful social ambiguity between the singular and plural. On the one hand, Meng Yu is clearly telling her own story. However, she is also adamant that the conditions described go beyond her, which she makes clear in a diegetic intervention where she directly addresses the reader: "Do you find these girls in the picture pretty? Do you know what they do at their age? You don't, right? [. . .] Then let me tell you the stories of us housekeepers."[26] This statement is consistent with Meng Yu's intention to record housekeepers' stories "to let more people understand their ordeals and hardships that often go unnoticed."[27] The ambiguity between the private and the social, the movement between intimacy and exhibition, is developed into a primary socioaesthetic component of her work. Her accuracy is warranted precisely by her belonging to the social group, which she reaffirms with tears shed at hearing fellow housekeepers' stories of pain: "I felt our minds had come even closer and more intimate, almost as if we had become one person."[28]

In this dialectics of subalternity and belonging, Meng Yu's own "literary construction of the urban space" is based on representation of physical spaces (as seen above), but also on the social relations of such spaces, which was similarly a key aesthetic attribute of early-20th-century reportage.[29] Fundamentally, this means coming to terms with her (rural) outsider status in the city. One way to do so is by contesting the idea that migrant workers have a low *suzhi* 素質, or quality of character. In what is probably her most outspoken piece, "Wo bu shi kangsu ye bu shi tiaoti wo zhi shi shihuashishuo" 我不是抗訴也不是挑剔我只是實話實說 ("I'm Not Complaining or Being Fussy, I'm Just Being Honest"), Meng Yu, while admitting that she is satisfied with her job and thankful to her employers for treating her well, portrays several episodes of injustice and mistreatment by employers in general, thus describing a sort of class mood that goes beyond individual specificities. As a counterbalance, she stresses, "Who actually decides the quality of life in a family are precisely nannies, these small individuals unworthy of attention,"[30] and she insists that migrant housekeepers care for others' children, "tak[ing] even more trouble than with their own children."[31] This is proof of hard work, demonstrating clear adherence to the moral standards required by society.

It makes sense to consider Meng Yu's nonfiction to be a social act aimed at building grassroots solidarity.[32] At the same time, she is lucidly aware that her writings will be read by upper-class individuals, which makes her feel responsible as a representative and spokesperson for other housekeepers, portraying and persuading readers of their cultural quality:

> Here I wish to declare on behalf of my house-keeping sisters: we hope that more people in society will take an interest in us, understand us, and reflect on problems from our point of view. I also hope that employers will no longer despise and misunderstand us. . . . [T]his way, won't our society grow more harmonious and prosperous?[33]

As we have seen, many works by Meng Yu exhibit this extremely explicit "verbal/artistic construction of the event" through which the writer "imparts the tendentious message to it."[34] This fact, drawn from the practice of reportage, especially clarifies the functions of nonfiction for a nonprofessional migrant-worker author like her. Meng Yu's stories undoubtedly have social value; they display a very practical goal of inviting others to understand domestic workers and to see that they can also produce culture (again, contesting their supposedly low *suzhi*). They also fully express reportage's role in highlighting identities otherwise marginalized (see, e.g., Laughlin's chapter in this volume). Perhaps most significant, given the increasing stratification of Chinese society, they are predominantly a vehicle through which members of the working class can express their view of the world.

The Fiction of Nonfiction: Yuan Wei

A carpenter hailing from Shandong, where he was born in 1985, Yuan Wei (also known by his *nom de plume*, Wei Chen 微塵) has produced a small but significant number of literary works. A general characteristic of his oeuvre is the constant blending of nonfiction and (auto)fiction, to the point that in some cases it becomes difficult to discern what comes from Yuan Wei's life experience and what is supplemented by his imagination. In some instances, he makes up different characters and spells out that he is writing fiction, but the distinction is not always so clear. In this sense, his writing plays with a basic feature of nonfiction as the unity of artistic technique, creative imagination, and factual fidelity.[35] After all, genres are malleable; a rigidly formalistic delimitation cannot capture their complexity, which is especially true for post-1980s Chinese nonfiction.

A signal that the work we are reading is nonfictional often comes when the piece is introduced by a temporal statement that localizes the action to a moment of Yuan Wei's life. "Cengjing shuiguo de difang" 曾經睡過的地方 ("The Place Where I Slept"), for example, which documents his adventurous arrival to Beijing, opens quite brusquely: "At the end of spring 2002, I didn't get into high school and had no intention of going anyway, so I just quit."[36] The abrupt start anticipates the emotionally detached and observant style that characterizes most of Yuan Wei's accounts. The story continues detailing his preparations to move to Beijing, where a job found by his cousin awaits. As paperless migrants, though, Yuan Wei and the others who make the journey with him have to travel hidden in the back of a truck. The apprehension felt by the traveling migrants as the truck speeds up to avoid a police patrol is vividly expressed, as is the description of them clinging to each other for warmth. Although the story is autobiographical, Yuan Wei tells it all from a perspective of narrative distance (a fictitious distance, in this case),[37] replaced by a more emotional recollection only in the closing lines:

> Pressed against each other in the bed of the truck, no one spoke, seemingly sleeping, or as if we were lost in our thoughts, or maybe in a memory. Perhaps we were thinking of a placid night, or a warm folded quilt on a hot *kang* [bed-stove].[38]

Yuan Wei never supplements narration with his comments. He resorts to other devices to create the mood he wants to convey. In the passage cited above, for example, the tense and contemplative silence of migrants packed in the truck actually acts to decry the dehumanizing conditions of labor migrancy. Indirect speech, used as a narrative technique, is another way to express the feelings of the individuals in the stories, while at the same time maintaining a sense of factuality by avoiding "made-up" dialogues. Sometimes, however, Yuan Wei makes use of direct speech, too, reporting what the other travelers are saying. Formally, this strategy is still one of narrative detachment, but it allows the mindset of observed individuals to emerge in a fast sequence of exclamations:

> "Had I known sooner, I would not have gone with him."
> "A boss from Tianjin was looking for me. Had I known, I would have gone!"
> "Are we really going on this truck?"

"It's just because the bosses moved all the motorbikes over here to make looking for work easier," someone explained.

The temperature on the truck fell, and people started covering themselves with the quilt.

"Don't worry too much about the quilt. The construction site will be dirtier than here."

"How did they calculate the transport fee? I'm too embarrassed to ask."

"A hundred per person, the rest is shared by the three bosses."

"Fuck, it's even more expensive than the bus!"

"Don't let the bosses hear you. It's so cold, let's squeeze together."[39]

The lack of extradiegetic comments or narratorial interventions like those of Meng Yu (who repeatedly insists that the facts she narrates are true) maintains a facade of fiction. Formally, even in first-person narratives, the narrator's voice is seldom heard, never openly taking a stance on the facts described (as we find with Meng Yu). In terms of content, Yuan Wei never declares the truthfulness of his stories, leaving it to be inferred partly from the first-person narrative (by itself no indication of nonfiction), and partly from the autobiographical elements found throughout.

The effects of this deliberate blurring of the fictional and nonfictional are particularly evident in "Beijing Thoughts" ("Beijing suixiang" 北京随想), written as a sort of sequel to the previous story to document Yuan Wei's vicissitudes after getting to Beijing. The main elements confirming its nonfictional character are clear: The first-person narrator, called Yuan ge 苑哥, specifies he has been in the capital for fifteen years since arriving in 2003, "after a night-long ride in the truck" (躺了一夜的貨車),[40] which corresponds to what Yuan Wei wrote in 2018. Other autobiographical elements include the narrator eventually ending up in Picun, where Yuan Wei lived at the time of writing the story. The story follows his troubles as an undocumented migrant without a temporary residence permit, especially during the SARS epidemic in 2003, and his attempts to find a fulfilling job. It is plausible that Yuan Wei supplemented the nonfictional recollection with imaginary dialogues or actions to improve the narration while taking nothing away from its fidelity to real life experience. But he also makes full use of the memoir as a type of nonfiction, allowing for, in Eakin's words, "an intricate process of self-discovery and self-creation."[41]

Self-discovery is especially evident in the story through a reflection on death, which appears first as a lurking threat in connection with the SARS epidemic, and then in the store that Yuan Wei's cousin wants to buy, taking advantage of its cheap price because the previous owner killed a local burglar in it. Yuan Wei spends a night there to inspect the facility and has a disturbing vision of the bloody event. Then his life is threatened when a wood board catches fire as he sleeps. The fact is not further commented on, but this strong presence of death mirrors the material conditions of extreme insecurity that a precarious migrant laborer faces in daily life, especially given that such deadly events are not uncommon among rural-to-urban migrants in China.[42] Such conditions of precarity and the constant threat of bodily harm are transformed into another form of alienation when Yuan Wei finds work in a wood-carving factory. However, the menial and repetitive job, metonymically represented by the machines, produces feelings of uncertainty and alienation:

> Only after I started working did I realize the work was not done by hand, but it was all mechanized. I learned to use the machines pretty well—there was no need for manpower, I just had to sit facing a computer, like a white-collar worker. I carried on one year, and learned nothing valuable about engraving and milling, I was just watching machines [. . .] I gave up, I could not waste my time there.[43]

This explicit reflection on the relationship between a manual worker, frustrated in his artisanal spirit, and the means of production, echoes a similar trope present in early-20th-century labor reportage. This trope is also one of its most distinctively *literary* attributes, allowing social experience to be accessed via the narrator's mind "as the sensory and emotional medium,"[44] exposing the sociopsychological dimension shared by laborers.

In a different fashion, another story, "No Money for You" ("Bu gei qian" 不給錢), displays an almost overt utilitarian function, although still filtered through the narrative devices of the nonfiction memoir. The story details the struggle of a worker, a former colleague of the narrator (here in the role of witness), to obtain his unpaid salary. This is the first element distinguishing this story from the previous one, viz., the fact that the first-person narrator is not also the main protagonist of the action. Even more interestingly for what concerns its utilitarian function, the story includes at least two passages that contain explicit advice to other laborers in the same situation to avoid getting cheated by ruthless bosses:

> The old boss had politely said that he would pay after a few days. Now the deadline had come, but he persisted in not paying. [He] regretted not having the boss sign an IOU in front of the police in the first place[.]
>
> I asked him, "What's up, did you file the complaint?"

> But he said with a bitter smile, "I went to the supervisors' team and even consulted a lawyer, but without a contract, a working certificate, or a wage slip, there's nothing they can do. I'm on my own."[45]

This kind of indirect, "activist" advice then reveals another use for workers' nonfiction—sharing information on real (as in this case) or fictional events that can help laborers solve real-life problems or avoid problematic situations in the first place. Although different from Meng Yu's solidarity narratives, Yuan Wei also develops a form of social commitment, because he provides practical instructions about how workers should protect their own interests. Both passages warn workers that they should insist on proper documentation, be it an IOU or a formal working contract or certificate, to prevent employers from fraudulently withholding their salary. In contrast to Meng Yu's stories—more socially motivated than Yuan Wei's private recollections, but also more explicitly directed at upper-class readers—this sort of literary mutual aid found in Yuan Wei's "No Money for You" implies a readership sharing the same social status as the author, who may directly benefit from practical advice. Of course, whether this target readership is eventually reached is an entirely different matter.

Yuan Wei has also written a third, longer instalment about his life story, "The Road" ("Lu" 路), which steers much more decisively toward autofiction, like other nonautobiographical stories in his *oeuvre*. In autofiction, the author, the narrator, and the protagonist share the same identity and are supposed to tell real-life stories from the author's past, but the narration makes ample use of fictive episodes, invented dialogues, and other fictional elements that would otherwise be absent from nonfiction.[46] "Lu" corresponds to this description as it expands the stories already told by Yuan Wei in the works discussed in this section, adding more direct speech (which plays a much larger role), more detailed descriptions and episodes (where it is possible that the imagination supplements what memory cannot provide), and more indirect speech. The story retraces the narrator's and his friends' attempt to realize an ideal of individual self-ownership by becoming small, artisanal entrepreneurs. Eventually, however, they need to come to terms with the city's unequal class relations. Their eventual resignation is effectively expressed by the gloomy atmosphere of the following passage from "Lu":

> Looking at the advertisements plastered on the utility poles, there was no longer any passion, and there was even a bit of discouragement. [. . .] We didn't have specific wage demands; we accepted the price he

> offered. Our only requirement was payment upon completion, and he agreed. In reality, we didn't negotiate the terms of payment; as soon as we entered, we had already lowered our heads.[47]

As we have seen, supplementing factual information with imagined episodes or descriptions more proper to autofiction is a general trait of Yuan Wei's nonfiction writing practice. Indeed, the boundary between the two genres is quite thin. In Yuan Wei's specific case, this negotiation is due to his interest in increasing his legitimacy as a writer by producing stories with more literary flourishes than just the pure observation or recollection of facts. Yuan Wei thus represents yet one more manifestation of workers' nonfiction, which makes full use of the genre's purposeful combination of methods and devices borrowed from multiple narrative traditions.

Conclusion

In the case studies above, the rearticulation of authorial voice and perspective, the authors' involvement with and proximity to their objects of investigation, and the "activist"/utilitarian functions assigned to nonfiction anchor workers' nonfiction to the tradition of labor reportage, albeit with significant developments deriving from the characteristics of its new writing subjects. For example, the factoryscape that dominated early-20th-century reportage is now part of a larger, globalized economic environment with variegated forms of labor indenture. Even more important, though, is the complete overhaul of mediation—no longer happening "through the consciousness of the reporter"—since the conflation of investigator and investigated already "bring[s] the voice and subjective experience of the worker to the reader intact."[48] This does not, however, automatically produce immediacy; the constant balancing between the two poles of the referential and the expressive brings about quite different solutions. In the two cases presented in this chapter, we have seen Meng Yu's vocally personal accounts, but also Yuan Wei's skilled effort to maintain, or rather produce, the impression of authorial distance, in part through the use of fictional elements.

A particularly significant and necessary consequence of this overhaul of mediation is the rearticulation of the ways through which the ethical impulse to recount reality develops into an aesthetic approach. An ethical imperative of traditional labor reportage, written by engaged intellectuals, was epistephilia, well described by Zhang (with reference to the observational documentary) as "the process of knowledge acquisition and the ethics of 'response-ability.'"[49] In workers' nonfiction, the conflation of investigator and investigated does not eliminate the need for knowledge acquisition (as we have seen, worker authors do not write exclusively about what has happened to them individually), but it can redirect their "response-ability" to individuals with whom they share the same social belonging. That is evident in Meng Yu's feeling of responsibility toward fellow housekeepers and Yuan Wei's more "utilitarian" passages.

Contemporary authors seem much less interested in producing the class awakening sought by early-20th-century reporters—a typical postsocialist contradiction, because while there are now more individuals with access to the means of cultural production who can write starting from their direct experience of inequality and exploitation, this is not automatically translated into political consciousness, due to the party-state's negation of class politics in China and the absence of impactful organizations pursuing such politics. Readership is therefore ambiguous; we find certain works explicitly imagining upper-class readers, but in other instances there are displays of activist concern addressed to fellow workers. Leaving this discussion of intended readership aside for now and following Jie Guo's observation that *collective voice* is a vital component of reportage's creative potential,[50] it is worth noting that both Meng Yu's and Yuan Wei's stories clearly speak of a reality with which a multitude of individuals can identify. In this regard, workers' nonfiction foregrounds an effort to single out the elements of social commonality from reported private experiences. It acknowledges and reinterprets a collective dimension that helps break through the isolation and anomie many workers feel in China today.

After all, the age of "farewells" to the political and cultural practices of the revolutionary era, which included reportage literature,[51] has not erased the basic needs this practice expressed. In a way, the continuity/discontinuity matrix of the shift from reportage to nonfiction partly mirrors the transition from older workers' literature to today's migrant/new workers' literature. Even as it displays huge differences, this new impulse to record, synthesize, and transform personal experience into a collective expression carries on the fundamental "task" to build a labor narrative by workers themselves. What connects 20th-century labor reportage and 21st-century workers' nonfiction is an endeavor informed by the same concerns and ambitions, or the same "ethical-aesthetic paradigm": to tell social reality as it is, with a critical view and the valuable perspective of lived experience, welcoming nonfictional literary techniques to do so in a more efficacious way.

NOTES

1. Dong, "Repoliticizing the Depoliticized"; Picerni, "Picun Migrant-worker Poets," "From the Periphery of Literature"; Qian and Florence, "Migrant Worker Museums in China"; Wang and Qiu, "Kongjian, jiqiao, yu shengyin"; Ting, "The 'Unlikely Writers' from Picun"; van Crevel, "Debts."
2. Li Chaoquan, "Xiaoshuo yu feixugou de hunrong," 64–68; Zhang Huiyu, "Qingting taren"; Zhang Wendong, "'Feixugou' xiezuo," 43–47.
3. Zhang Hong, "Lingpiao," 128.
4. Wagner, *Inside a Service Trade*, ch. 15.
5. Laughlin, *Chinese Reportage*, 13.
6. Xie Baojie, "'Xin wenxue liliang' de peiyang."
7. Laughlin and Guo, "Reportage and Its Contemporary Variations," vi, vii.
8. For a panoramic overview of these literary realities, see for example Iovene and Picerni, "Chinese Workers' Literature in the 20th and 21st Centuries," 1–30.
9. Song Xueqing, "'Feixugou' de liliang," 55.
10. Li Yunlei, *Xin shiji "diceng wenxue" yu Zhongguo gushi*, 204.
11. He Ying, "Baogao wenxue de qiantu," 30–40; Li Yunlei, *Xin shiji "diceng wenxue,"* 208.
12. Laughlin, *Chinese Reportage*, 144, 199.
13. Lin, "'Feixugou' xiezuo," 78–83.
14. Wagner, *Inside a Service Trade*, 248.
15. Wagner, *Inside a Service Trade*, 249.
16. Laughlin, *Chinese Reportage*, 29.
17. Laughlin, *Chinese Reportage*, 3.
18. Sun, *Subaltern China*, ch. 7.
19. Tran, "Sex in the City," 172.
20. Picerni, "From the Periphery of Literature"; Sun, *Subaltern China*, ch. 7.
21. Meng Yu [Li Yu], "Wo bu shi kangsu."
22. Meng Yu, "Zheli ye you chuntian laiguo," 113.
23. Meng Yu, Interview with the author in Beijing, November 30, 2019.
24. Meng Yu, "Hongya zhi jia: shengming xiangyu," 121.
25. Meng Yu, "Jiaru wo shi yi ming jizhe," 105.
26. Meng Yu, "Hongya zhi jia: shengming xiangyu," 123.
27. Meng Yu, "Jiaru wo shi yi ming jizhe," 104.
28. Meng Yu, "Hongya zhi jia," 120.
29. Laughlin, *Chinese Reportage*, 29.
30. Meng Yu, "Wo bushi kangsu," 201.
31. Meng Yu, "Jiazhenggong de gushi," 124.
32. Xiao, "Caring for the Small," 46–57.
33. Meng Yu, "Wo bushi kangsu," 201.
34. Laughlin, *Chinese Reportage*, 15.
35. Li Chaoquan, "Xiaoshuo yu feixugou de hunrong," 66.
36. Yuan Wei, "Cengjing shuiguo de difang," 95.
37. Genette, *Narrative Discourse*, 162.
38. Yuan Wei, "Cengjing shuiguo de difang," 95.

39. Yuan Wei, "Cengjing shuiguo de difang," 95.
40. Yuan Wei, "Beijing suixiang," 287.
41. Eakin, *Fictions in Autobiography*.
42. Song, Zhang, and Li, "Beijing Evictions."
43. Yuan Wei, "Beijing suixiang," 281.
44. Laughlin, *Chinese Reportage*, 115.
45. Yuan Wei, "Bu gei qian," 93–94.
46. Lecarme, "L'Autofiction."
47. Yuan Wei, "Lu," 279.
48. Laughlin, *Chinese Reportage*, 144.
49. Zhang, "Perseverance through Aftershocks," 147.
50. Jie Guo, "Reportage, Ethnicity, and Feminine Subjectivities," 5.
51. Chambers, "The 'Liang Village Series,'" 252, 257–58.

REFERENCES

Chambers, Harlan. "The 'Liang Village Series': Postsocialist Dynamics of Liang Hong's Rural Investigation." *Modern Chinese Literature and Culture* 31, no. 2 (2019): 249–92.

Dong, Yuxiang. "Repoliticizing the Depoliticized: Social Practices of New Workers in Picun." In *Socially Engaged Public Art in East Asia: Space, Place, and Community in Action*, edited by Meiqin Wang, 241–71. Wilmington: Vernon Press, 2022.

Eakin, Paul John. *Fictions in Autobiography: Studies in the Art of Self-Invention*. Princeton: Princeton University Press, 1985.

Genette, Gerard. *Narrative Discourse: An Essay in Method*. Ithaca: Cornell University Press, 1980.

Guo, Jie. "Reportage, Ethnicity, and Feminine Subjectivities." *Modern Chinese Literature and Culture* 31, no. 2 (2019): 1–40.

He Ying 何英. "Baogao wenxue de qiantu: yi Xinjiang baogao wenxue yanjiu wei zhongxin" 報告文學的前途——以新疆報告文學研究為中心 ("The Future of Reportage Literature: A Focus on Studies on Xinjiang Reportage"). *Wenxue pinglun* 3 (2018): 30–40.

Iovene, Paola, and Federico Picerni. "Chinese Workers' Literature in the 20th and 21st Centuries." *Oxford Research Encyclopedia of Literature*, 1–30. Oxford: Oxford University Press, 2022.

Laughlin, Charles A. *Chinese Reportage: The Aesthetics of Historical Experience*. Durham: Duke University Press, 2002.

Laughlin, Charles A., and Li Guo. "Reportage and Its Contemporary Variations." *Modern Chinese Literature and Culture* 31, no. 2 (2019): v–xvi.

Lecarme, Jacques. "L'Autofiction: un mauvais genre?" In *Autofictions et cie*, edited by Serge Doubrovsky, Jacques Lecarme, and Philippe Lejeune, 227–49. Paris: Université de Paris, 1993.

Li Chaoquan 李朝全. "Xiaoshuo yu feixugou de hunrong ji qi wenti chaungxin yiyi" 小說與非虛構的混融及其文體創新意義 ("The Fusion of Novel and Nonfiction and the Creative Relevance of Its Style"). *Zhongguo wenyi pinglun* 1 (2018): 64–68.

Li Yunlei 李雲雷. *Xin shiji "diceng wenxue" yu Zhongguo gushi* 新世紀"底層文學"與中國故事 (*"Subaltern Literature" of the New Century and the China Story*). Guangzhou: Zhongshan daxue chubanshe, 2014.

Lin Xiuqin 林秀琴. "'Feixugou' xiezuo: geti jingyan yu gonggong jingyan de kunjiong" "非虛構"寫作：個體經驗與公共經驗的困窘 ("Nonfiction: The Uncertainty of Personal and Shared Experience"). *Jiangxi shehui kexue* 11 (2013): 78–83.

Liu Liu 劉瀏. "'Feixugou' de shinian taolun yu Zhongguo feixugou wenxue yanjiu" "非虛構"的十年討論與中國非虛構文學研究 ("Ten Years of Debates on Nonfiction and Chinese Nonfiction Literature Studies"). *Yue Gang'ao dawanqu wenxue pinglun* 2 (2020): 68–77.

Meng Yu 夢雨 [Li Yu 李玉]. "Wo bu shi kangsu ye bu shi tiaoti wo zhi shi shihuashishuo" 我不是抗訴也不是挑剔我只是實話實說 ("I'm Not Complaining or Being Fussy, I'm Just Being Honest"). In *2018 laodongzhe de shi yu ge*, 197–201. Beijing: Gongyou zhi jia (unofficial), 2018.

Meng Yu 夢雨. "Zheli ye you chuntian laiguo" 這裡也有春天來過 ("Spring Has Been Here Too"). In *2019 laodongzhe de shi yu ge*, 112–14. Beijing: Gongyou zhi jia (unofficial), 2019.

Meng Yu. Interview in Beijing, November 30, 2019.

Meng Yu. "Hongya zhi jia: shengming xiangyu" 鴻雁之家——生命相遇 ("The Swan Goose's Home: Encounters of a Life"). In *2019 laodongzhe de shi yu ge*, 120–24. Beijing: Gongyou zhi jia (unofficial), 2019.

Meng Yu. "Jiaru wo shi yi ming jizhe" 假如我是一名記者 ("If I Were a Journalist"). In *2019 laodongzhe de shi yu ge*, 105–9.

Meng Yu. "Jiazhenggong de gushi" 家政工的故事 ("A Domestic Worker's Story"). In *2019 laodongzhe de shi yu ge*, 124–28.

Picerni, Federico. "Strangers in a Familiar City: Picun Migrant-worker Poets in the Urban Space of Beijing." *International Quarterly for Asian Studies* 51, no. 1–2 (2020): 147–70.

Picerni, Federico. "From the Periphery of Literature: Marginal Urban Lives and Recognition(s) in the Picun Literature Group." In *China from the Margins: New Narratives of the Past and Present*, edited by Emily Williams and Loredana Cesarino, 137–53. London: Routledge, 2024.

Qian, Junxi, and Eric Florence. "Migrant Worker Museums in China: Public Cultures of Migrant Labor in State and Grassroots Initiatives." *Journal of Ethnic and Migration Studies* 47, no. 12 (2021): 2706–24.

Song, Jiani, Shuchi Zhang, and Qiaochu Li. "Beijing Evictions: A Winter's Tale." *Made in China Journal* 3, no. 1 (2018): 28–33.

Song Xueqing 宋學清. "'Feixugou' de liliang: nongmingong wenxue zhong de feixugou xiezuo" "非虛構"的力量——農民工文學中的非虛構寫作 ("The Power of 'Nonfiction': Nonfiction within Rural–Urban Migrant Workers' Literature"). *Zhengzhou shifan jiaoyu* 6, no. 7 (2018): 54–59.

Sun, Wanning. *Subaltern China: Rural Migrants, Media, and Cultural Practices*. Lanham, MD: Rowman and Littlefield, 2014.

Ting, Chun Chun. "The 'Unlikely Writers' from Picun: Reinventing Literature and Politics at the Migrant Workers Home." *positions: asia critique* 31, no. 2 (2023): 333–55.

Tran, Richard Quang-Anh. "Sex in the City: The Descent from Human to Animal in Two Vietnamese Classics of Urban Reportage." *International Quarterly for Asian Studies* 51, no. 1–2 (2020): 171–92.

Van Crevel, Maghiel. "Debts: Coming to Terms with Migrant Worker Poetry." *Chinese Literature Today* 8, no. 1 (2019): 127–45.

Wagner, Rudolf. *Inside a Service Trade: Studies in Contemporary Chinese Prose*. Cambridge: Harvard University Press, 1992.

Wang Hongzhe 王洪喆 and Qiu Linchuan 邱林川. "Kongjian, jiqiao, yu shengyin: xinlao gongren jieji wenhua kongjian de bijiao yanjiu" 空間、科技、與聲音：新老工人階級文化空間的比較研究 ("Space, Technology, and Voice: A Comparative Research into Old and New Working-Class Cultural Spaces"). *Chuanbo wenhua yu zhengzhi* 2 (2015): 27–60.

Xiao, Hui Faye. "Caring for the Small: Gendered Resistance and Solidarity through Chinese Domestic Workers' Writings." *Chinese Literature Today* 10, no. 2 (2021): 46–57.

Xie Baojie 謝保傑. "'Xin de wenxue liliang' de pieyang: yi shiqinian shiqi Cao Mingyu yu Anshan gongren zuozhe de chengzhang wei lie" "新的文學力量"的培養——以十七年時期草明與鞍山工人作者的成長為例 ("Nurturing the 'Power of the New Literature': The Case of Cao Ming and the Growth of the Anshan Worker Writers in the Seventeen Years"). *Wenyi lilun yu piping* 2 (2018): 81–88.

Yuan Wei 苑偉 [Wei Chen 微塵]. "Cengjing shuiguo de difang" 曾經睡過的地方 ("The Place Where I Slept"). In *Laodongzhe de shi yu ge*, 95–96. Beijing: Gongyou zhi jia (unofficial), 2017.

Yuan Wei. "Bu gei qian" 不給錢 ("No Money for You"). In *Laodongzhe de shi yu ge*, 93–95.

Yuan Wei 苑伟. "Beijing suixiang" 北京随想 ("Beijing Thoughts"). In *2018 laodongzhe de shi yu ge*, 286–93. Beijing: Gongyou zhi jia (unofficial), 2018.

Yuan Wei. "Lu" 路 ("The Road"). In *Diyijie laodongzhe wenxue jiang huojiang zuopinji*, 272–81. Beijing: Gongyou zhi jia (unofficial), 2019.

Zhang Hong 張弘. "Lingpiao: jujiao baogao wenxue yu feixugou" 零票：聚焦報告文學與非虛構 ("Zero Votes: A Focus on Reportage Literature and Nonfiction"). *Shehui kexue luntan* 12 (2014): 125–34.

Zhang Huiyu 張慧瑜. "Qingting taren: feixugou xiezuo yu xinwen jiaoyu de jiehe" 傾聽他人：非虛構寫作與新聞教育的結合 (Listening to the Other: Nonfiction Writing and Journalism Education Combined). *Xiezuo* 1 (2020): 17–22.

Zhang Wendong 張文東. "'Feixugou' xiezuo: xin de wenxue kenengxing?—Cong *Renmin wenxue* de 'feixugou' shuoqi" "非虛構"寫作：新的文學可能性？——從《人民文學》的"非虛構"說起 ("Nonfictional Writing: A New Possibility for Literature? Starting from the Nonfiction [Column] in *Renmin wenxue*"). *Dangdai wentan* 3 (2011): 43–47.

Zhang, Yingjin. "Perseverance through Aftershocks: Epistephilia in Chinese Reportage and Independent Documentary." *Modern Chinese Literature and Culture* 21, no. 2 (2019): 129–61.

II

Envisioning Taiwanese Reportage

FOUR

Gu Mengren and Reportage in 1970s Taiwan

Charles A. Laughlin

Gu Mengren (古蒙仁, pen name of Lin Riyang 林日揚, b. 1951), was a central figure in the remarkable wave of reportage literature (*baodao wenxue* 報導文學) in Taiwan that began in the 1970s. Much of Gu's work centered on his immersion among marginalized communities in Taiwan and communicating their perspectives to readers; "Black Tribe" (Heise de buluo 黑色的部落, 1977), which depicts the daily life and struggles of the Atayal people in mountainous central Taiwan, is his best-known work.

The history of literary reportage in Taiwan is nearly as long as in mainland China, although not as continuous.[1] Decades before Gu Mengren's emergence on the scene, the literary ferment of the 1930s in the midst of Japan's 50-year colonization of Taiwan included robust nonfiction writing that leaned into social inequities and historical struggles. It involved such writers as Yang Kui 楊逵 and Wu Xisheng 吳希聖, Yang Kui being an explicit promoter of the genre under the influence of the proletarian literary movement in China. In a Japanese-language article entitled "What Is Reportage?" (Hôkoku bungaku wa nani ka 報告文学とは何か) in the *Taiwan shinmin po* 台湾新民報 of April 25, 1937, Yang exhorted socially engaged nonfiction writers to focus on the reader, use facts as a basis, but also have a passionate understanding of the fact or event to convey to the reader. He cautioned them that although reportage may embellish and choose among facts, it should not fabricate them. At the same time, he argued that reportage must not simply relate facts like journalistic reporting; its literary nature lay not in fictionality but in the use of "figurative images" (形象 *keishô*) to illustrate facts in a lively manner. Finally, reportage should not be too complicated, but written to convey the content and ideas easily, correctly, and efficiently to the minds of readers.[2]

However, shortly after Yang published works of reportage and articles such as the above in 1937, the Japanese began their invasion of China and imposed stricter censorship policies, leaving little room in the colony of Taiwan for the publication of the kind of critical documentary writing Yang espoused. In the years after the Japanese surrender at the end of the second world war, Yang had once again tried to promote writing about the lived reality of the present under the rubric of *shizai de wenxue* (實在的文學 "true-to-life literature"), but he was arrested and imprisoned for twelve years in 1948 by the Nationalist government for his involvement with the "Peace Manifesto" and alleged association with dissident student groups. In the period that followed, the trends of anticommunist fiction and ostensibly apolitical literary modernism dominated Taiwan's literary scene, and nonfiction literature was almost nonexistent.[3]

The Protect Diaoyutai movement in 1971, which originated among Taiwanese students studying abroad in the United States, helped create the conditions for the reemergence of reportage. In two provocative review articles on new collections of modern poetry and criticism published in the *Renjian* 人間 literary supplement of *China Times* 中國時報, critic Guan Jieming complained that contemporary literature had lost touch with reality in an era of increased political agitation and social awareness. These articles sparked a lively debate in the literary community, and in May 1973, the *Renjian* literary supplement was taken over by Kao Hsin-chiang 高信疆, who initiated the reportage column *Zai xianshi de bianyuan* (在現實的邊緣 "On the Frontiers of Reality").[4] Although still under the White Terror, this was an era of unprecedented social activism, not only in the literary scene, but in the whole of Taiwanese society. In 1977, the literary magazine *Xiachao* (夏潮 China Tide) was established, advocating "critical realism" and publishing several reportage works by Gu Mengren and others. It was also at this time that the *xiangtu* (鄉土, nativist) movement in Taiwan literature emerged, and reportage can be viewed as a significant aspect of that movement.[5] When Kao Hsin-chiang became the general editor of *China Times*, he initiated the *China Times Literary Prize*, which included a reportage category, and the winners of the *China Times Literary Prize* for reportage (one of the first of whom was Gu Mengren for "Black Tribe") for the next several years were among the most notable authors during reportage's heyday in the 1970s and early 1980s.[6]

Lianhe bao's 聯合報 literary supplement, taken over by Ya Xian 瘂弦 in 1978, also promoted reportage and related forms, and in the same year *Minsheng bao* 民生報, a newspaper devoted to practical everyday advice for readers, was established; it often featured nonfiction writing on the environment and endangered species. But political backlash came after the *Formosa* Incident of 1979, including the closing down of politically engaged magazines such as *The 1980s* and *China Tide*. As described by Shiu Wen-wei, after these closings, "the environment of public discourse became tense, and the subject matter for reportage literature confined itself to writing about indigenous peoples, culture, marginalized populations, ecology and environmentalism, and was unable to make the leap into deeper public issues about labor, farming, and even politics."[7] Due to the conservatism of commercial media, exacerbated by the strictures of censorship and martial law, reportage literature trended away from sensitive topics, and the writings that were published and received awards shifted from "reports from the field" toward "reports from academia."[8]

As reportage scholar Li Ruiteng 李瑞騰 puts it, Taiwanese reportage in the 1970s was "several socially-conscious (憂民淑世的) new generation intellectuals who stepped off campus and became trailblazers in the cultural scene; their enthusiasm and idealism combined to form moral courage, using every form at their disposal to illuminate the space they inhabited."[9] Shiu Wen-wei expands on this to point out that, more than a resurgence of realism, the wave of reportage might rather be viewed as a new form of praxis that arose from new trends in literary theory. This coincides with Gu Mengren's account in an interview of the impact of several conversations with Huang Chunming 黃春明 that led him to begin writing reportage, having previously published several works of fiction; it was time for reportage in Taiwan.[10] The 1970s and early 1980s was the period of Gu Mengren's most prolific reportage writing.

Literary reportage exemplifies a particular moment in contemporary Taiwan history, a moment that helped define an ongoing part of contemporary Taiwan consciousness focused on the cultural dissemination of local actuality in written and visual form. Gu Mengren's collection, *Black Tribe*, includes a number of photographs of the places included in the respective reports; he continued this practice in the 1984 collection *Shiqu de shuiping xian* (Lost horizon; 失去的水平線).[11] In these ways, reportage resisted the discourse of cosmopolitan modernism that prevailed over the literature of the previous two decades. In short, what we have in literary history referred to primarily as fictional nativism in Taiwan resonates to a significant extent with the contemporary literary reportage.

In connection with this trend toward critical-realist nativism and reportage emerged a cultural type we might call the "literary reportager," of whom Gu Mengren is a representative case. Gu is a native of southern Taiwan, growing up on a sugar plantation in Yunlin County near Tainan. He attended Fu-jen University (in Taipei), majoring in Chinese literature, in the mid-1970s. As Gu writes in his preface to the 1978 collection *Black Tribe*, he had the opportunity to meet the nativist novelist Huang Chunming, when Huang gave a lecture at Fu-jen.[12] Gu had already been publishing stories and essays in literary magazines throughout college, but this encounter inspired him as never before to shift his attention to nonfiction to reveal the true texture and atmosphere of the hidden corners of Taiwan. Before graduation, he had traveled with some friends to a remote fishing village (Bitoujiao 鼻頭角, or "Nose Point"), and he was so taken with the place that he pitched the idea of an extensive report to Kao Hsin-chiang, the editor of the *Renjian* literary supplement of *China Times*, for Kao's new reportage column "On the Frontiers of Reality" in 1975. Embedding himself in the village and nearby communities for three weeks, Gu wrote an essayistic description of his experiences there, the fishing industry, education, and generational differences, that was published to much fanfare. Gu's collection *Black Tribe* includes this work as well as several other travel reports depicting farming, fishing, mining communities, and the unique existence of indigenous mountain tribes—parts of a comprehensive writing/travel plan.

On completing his military service in the hills of Kinmen, Gu Mengren was already a well-known author of literary nonfiction and was beginning to publish book-length collections of his works. He could now add the famous novelist and later founder of *Ren Jian* magazine, Chen Yingzhen 陳映真, to his circle of acquaintances. Like Huang Chunming, Chen Yingzhen straddled the periods of modernism and nativism in Taiwan; his anti-capitalist and pro–mainland Chinese political views got him imprisoned for seven years.[13] Chen's release from prison roughly coincided with the reportage trend and Gu Mengren's emergence onto the scene. Both Li Guo and Po-hsi Chen's articles in this volume discuss aspects of Chen's epoch-making magazine *Ren Jian*, in rich detail.

The essays in *Black Tribe* are arranged in chronological order, but also according to the itinerary of Gu Mengren's journey southward throughout Taiwan, with only one or two interruptions. "A Nose that Doesn't Snore: The Tribulations of Bitou Fishing Village," and the long essay that follows it, "Shattered Dreams of Gold Digging: The Past and Present of Jiufen and Jinguashi," are the first two chapters; they are geographically focused on a small area in the northeastern tip of Taiwan, not far from Taipei. The first essay is concerned with the author's observations of an isolated fishing village at Bitou and his attempts to understand the texture of its inhabitants' lives, ultimately by accompanying them on midnight fishing expeditions. But an equally conspicuous layer of this text is the author's comparison of the young people of the village to their counterparts from the city, including reflections on his own status as a young, educated outsider trying to understand the local people. After discussing how the "bizarre" clothing and lifestyle of intellectuals and urban students conceals anxieties about the world and Taiwan's place in it, he compares this to the predicament of young people in the small fishing village in contrast to their local elders:

> The younger generation, witnessing the gradual decline and fall of an ancient fishing village from the glories of its past, have lost their confidence. For old fishermen, their lifetime of toil has brought them nothing more than hard-won food and shelter. The leaps of progress, with its deep-sea ships and massive nets, have invaded their world, already threatening their environment and economic structure. It is a cruel reality. Aging fisherman who strove their whole lives on the sea have no other options, even as desperate as their predicament is, and so just grit their teeth and press on. The younger generation have begun to rebel; they can neither endure the loneliness of going out to sea, nor resist the temptations of the city. With their wings grown, they have begun to strike out into those broader horizons.
>
> The young go out, bathed in the wind and rain, the coal smoke and the stench of oil, the luxuries and extravagance of the city. The boys go to factories, the girls to restaurants: they learn machinery, tailoring, smoking and drinking, miniskirts and high heels. Each month they send their wages back, and on holidays or weekends they bring their friends, all dressed to the nines, back to the fishing village for an excursion. They invite their friends for seafood dinners, stroll about the fishing harbor, then say "bye-bye" and flutter away like butterflies.[14]

This is a vivid depiction of the unraveling of the village community via the effects of economic change on the younger generation. The author's exasperation at the youths' failure to support their elders is intertwined with his awareness of the inevitability of change. Later in the essay, the author shifts his attention to young tourists from Taipei and other cities, who also embody the vast difference between urban and rural in 1970s Taiwan:

> From the point of view of the fishermen, these tourists create a lot of disruption, and the worst are the young couples. They are students from middle and high school, and college too, with most being college students. These arrogant young intellectuals, once they stride into a fishing village, consciously or unconsciously put on the aloof airs of the traditional gentry; in words and actions they express the insolence and pomposity of the little intellectual. Whether from reflex or habit, or deliberately expressing how special they are, they bring a peculiarly unhealthy atmosphere of college campuses with them. With hair down to their shoulders, flowery shirts, bright red T-shirts, wire-rimmed sunglasses, they croon foreign pop songs, swaggering around the villages in packs. When they stay in fisherman's houses, they always smoke and play cards, and when the spirit moves them, they have dance parties, noisily jabbering and shouting, keeping the fishermen awake.
>
> When they stay at the school, they're even more inconsiderate. To their minds, "primary school" represents immaturity and ignorance; it's a big joke. See them laugh and chatter, opening and knocking on doors and windows, and getting up to all kinds of mischief in the classrooms. Some play the organ, others play flutes, and still others sing at the top of their lungs; the noisy visitors are separated by only a thin wall from the shabby dormitories of the young schoolteachers, yet they don't care about disturbing their sleep. One night I was sleeping in the principal's office and at two or three in the morning the noise of a fierce argument awakened me—it was a fed-up schoolteacher who wanted to shut them up. I only could vaguely make out one sentence—"We're college students! You should show some respect!" In the darkness I felt my gut twist: college students everywhere were shamed by these words. I really wanted to get up and smack him in the face, and break his jaw—do people like this belong in college?[15]

Young people fall into many categories here: We have seen the young villagers in the previous passage; here we have urban youth in the form of tourists and schoolteachers, as well as the author himself, who can be said to belong to yet another category. We can sense that the author's disdain for these tourists is wrapped up in an insecurity about his own identity and role vis-à-vis this urban-rural division. The project of Gu's writing seems to be to resolve this dilemma, continually performing the act of bridging the gap between elites and marginal populations through observation, sympathy, and understanding, conveyed to a readership that can be assumed to be young, educated people like himself. In the end, his message about the communities he visits is often one of acknowledging their pride and right to persist in their own way of life, despite the encroachment of homogenizing global modernity. Already in this, his first published reportage work, Gu appeals to the imagery of illumination to affirm the dignity of ordinary people:

> Reassuringly, Bitou Point is making great strides on the way to becoming a beautiful fishing village or a scenic destination. As long as there are lives with real substance, and individuals with an innate and pure goodness, no amount of poverty or ignorance, no disdain or animosity can conceal the brilliance (*guanghui* 光輝) that comes out of them. There will be a day when these (now) obscure auras will shine forth myriad rays of love and warmth and illuminate the earth and warm humanity. For Bitou Point, which I truly adore, to the lovable friends I have come to know there, the purpose of my writing this essay, is nothing more than to shed a little light upon it, to remind the world to pay attention to it, telling them, this is a nice place, and it has everything that you need.[16]

The local populace emanates light, despite the darkening effects of encroaching industrial development and urbanization. The author, too, wishes to "shed a little light" on them through his essay, which will have the effect of amplifying the light of the locals themselves and, it is hoped, ensure a future that both dignifies and enriches them. This echoes the reference to light in the title of Gu's preface, "Moving Step by Step to a Brighter Place," in which he explains the serendipitous sequence of events that led him on the path to his first book-length collection of reportage.

The larger significance of Gu's engagement with the Bitou fishing village becomes clear when the author uses his own efforts to understand fishing through experiencing it as a metaphor for reportage writers' relation to the world and to human communities, as he uses the second person to put the reader in the author's shoes:

> What you want to learn is the entire process of becoming a complete fisherman, the history of the fishing village's struggles, and not merely being a tourist or a traveler.
>
> In the fishing village, beneath the life background and experience you never had, at the very beginning, perhaps curiosity or novelty motivated you, an emotional yearning or surge of excitement. On the one hand, you may have been misled by the abstract theories and reso-

> nant slogans of social reformers; on the other, you may have been intoxicated with Taoistic ideas of returning to nature and the self. But in the end, you discover that these passions are all false, empty ideals. You are not only fooling yourself, but also the fishing village. At this point you finally realize that feelings cannot be forced or faked. Forcing yourself, or putting on a mask, is painful and foolish.
>
> In the end, a fishing village is just a fishing village. For over 100 years, it curled itself up here, wrapped up in its little happiness, little disasters, and little dreams. All you can do is open your arms and bravely stride toward it, embracing it, and dissolving yourself in it. Listen to its breathing, feel its pulse, and only then will you have the authority to say, I've come, I've truly come into its embrace, for the sake of the ideals and the enthusiasm we adhere to.[17]

In effect, Gu is articulating the purpose and the value of reportage: It is harmful to rely on abstract, preexisting conceptions or the words of others ("social reformers" and "Taoists"); the only way to do justice to places like Bitou Point is to experience them firsthand with respect and an open mind, or to read the account of someone—a reportager—who has experienced the living value of the place and its people on the readers' behalf. As the author approaches the end of the piece, he includes a mysterious interlude about an allegedly haunted house, then returns to the theme of his role as a writer and what he needs to convey to the reader, giving us also a hint of how that differs from what would have been familiar to readers of literature:

> Behind the Fisherman's Club, there is a dilapidated house, well-known to be haunted. The story goes that there was a quack doctor whose treatments killed two children, whose spirits have haunted the place ever since. A year ago, a *fengshui* master passed by the place, and they say that he saw a female ghost in a long, white gown, floating along three feet off the ground, which created a furor in the village for quite some time, putting everyone on pins and needles. I visited there several times, walking around for quite a while, and the place is certainly gloomy—you get goosebumps passing by there even in broad daylight. But now there is an old woman living in there; she has a severe hunchback and curls up in a dark corner not moving a muscle—you would almost think *she* was a ghost. I wanted to interview her, but never had a good opportunity; what a shame![18]

Given Gu's consistent emphasis on gathering information, ideas, and feelings from conversations with the local people, it seems odd that he reports never having interviewed the old woman, but the mention of her in her situation resonates with the larger situation of the essay—that he is experiencing a place that most people would never see, and about which there might be a lot of baseless and silly ideas floating among the population. The old woman, in turn, is like the actuality of Bitou Village and its people, not really magical or mysterious but in fact struggling through a life that is often very hard. In the final section of "A Nose that Doesn't Snore," the author contemplates the meaning of his visit on his last night in Bitou Village:

> You all might think it strange; what did this sloppily dressed young man come here for? A head of messy hair, a light blue, hooded sweat jacket with brown shorts, always strolling alongside the harbor, carrying a little notebook, sitting on the harbor benches, writing. Some kids would play the wise guy and announce, "He's a reporter!" or "he's an author!" Some of them would go as far as to say, "He's a rich kid, here for a vacation!" In fact, I'm nothing at all; I came here to learn from you how to become a fisherman; how to live; how to struggle; nothing more than these.
>
> Perhaps you would laugh again; what could you possibly pick up in 20 days? You think you can become a fisherman just like that? The idea is ridiculous; but you can't deny that I did learn a great deal here. At least I learned what a fisherman is, what a fishing village is, as well as that I cannot become a good fisherman, nor can a lot of young people of my generation.[19]

Here we can see that the above-mentioned abstract passions and concepts that can mislead one in fact were part of the author's own struggle as part of an educated urban elite to open himself up to the living reality of the places he visits. He takes the lessons he learned, we are to understand, to more hidden and marginal communities throughout the island, where the author will continue to discover himself through the struggles and environments of others.

The second essay in the collection, "Shattered Dreams of Digging Gold: Past and Present in Jiufen and Jinguashi," concerns a pair of small towns so close to Bitou that the author must have traveled to them immediately after it. There the author has his first encounter with the hidden world of a coal mine. After descending hundreds of meters in an elevator and entering the tunnels, Gu narrates his fearful progress into the mine:

> Bracing myself, I continued to crawl forward. Mr. Jian was waiting for me ahead, and he asked me how I was doing. I said I'm okay, and we resumed crawling forward. My heart was still gripped with terror, and I was still being crushed under the weight of despair. Facing the looming shadows of loneliness, despair, and terror, one is more able to perceive how small and vulnerable humanity is. Where, after all, was human pride and dignity? While I struggled with my doubts, I began to hear the faint sound of digging up ahead, one shovelful at a time, slow and dull. It was only when we got close that I was able to clearly discern two miners lying on their backs beneath the coal bed, laboriously wielding their tools in a space so narrow as to barely be able to turn. I fell flat on the coal bed, my head, hands, and flesh pressed against the damp, hard surface. They both laughed at me, and it was only then that I was able to believe that here, 350 meters below ground, there were still us four living men. A wave of human warmth quickly flowed through my whole body. All that terror and insecurity, loneliness and despair, disappeared completely. In their smiling faces and mild eyes, I saw the pride and dignity of man. Man's will and wisdom breaks through strata of stone and chunks of coal, all the way to this unbelievable space. It is neither a miracle nor a myth, but the product of these men working their fingers to the bone, a hoe, and a shovel, a drop of sweat and a drop of blood at a time.[20]

Notably, it is through the reader's apprehension of the author's affective and corporeal experience of the alien environment of the actual mine that he or she is able to perceive the admirable dignity of the miners. Gu's reportage succeeds where it presents a virtual sensorium to the reader that is more visceral and palpable than we usually find in the imagined worlds of fiction.

Of particular interest here is Gu Mengren's best-known and impactful work, "Black Tribe," about Atayal people living in the mountains at the eastern edge of Hsinchu county. "Black Tribe" was one of the first influential literary works to highlight the lives of aboriginal people in contemporary Taiwan.[21] In discussing the issue of indigeneity in the work of the Tao tribe writer Syaman Rapongan, Kuei-fen Chiu has suggested a connection between the nativist trend in Taiwanese literature in the 1970s and the indigenous movement, which she says began in 1983 or 1984; yet this connection is full of tensions.[22] These tensions can be observed in the writing of Gu Mengren, as I will show.

The title of Gu's essay on Xiuluan village, which also gives his collection its title—*Black Tribe*—presents a different perspective on the imagery of light and illumination introduced in the earlier works. Gu's approach to the indigenous community he visits in the mountainous eastern extremity of Hsinchu county is similar to that of the previous reportage works, in that he devotes considerable space in the beginning to the history and geography of the people he is writing about, followed by sections dedicated to the various aspects of Atayal contemporary life, such as their farming, hunting, housing, and education. People in Taiwan often refer to indigenous groups as "compatriots in the mountains" (*shanbao* 山胞), as the plains in Taiwan have been largely urbanized. The term *bao* ("compatriots") deemphasizes ethnic difference in favor of national unity. Indigenous populations are concentrated in mountain areas that at the time of Gu's writing were extremely remote. As a result, Gu's first extended section is devoted to his arduous journey to the areas depicted, which again concentrates the focus on the author's affective and corporeal experience of the community's environment. This has the double result of creating a vivid picture of the environment to the reader, but also carving out a dramatic image of the author as adventurer.

"Black Tribe" is not written with an overt agenda or in a way that romanticizes the Atayal or their way of life. Instead, Gu's style can be described as realistic, scientific, and confined to the facts as much as possible. Nevertheless, the metaphor of light and darkness continues from the previous texts. At the end of an introductory section describing his long journey through the forest toward Xiuluan Village and providing a history of the Atayal tribes in the area, the author prepares to relate the Lidong Mountain Incident, a series of bloody Atayal retaliations between 1911 and 1913.

> Among these dim and blurry tribal villages, history does not have any particular meaning; except for what is expressed as the bloodshed in the competition for survival, evolution leaves no special traces either. How could the Atayals of Xiuluan Village hidden in this darkness be any different?
>
> However, after murderous cries from Lidong Mountain arose and shocked the world, this page of the history written in blood by the Atayals took on a special meaning.[23]

The incident, about which little has been written in English or Chinese, was the outcome of the Japanese colonial governor Sakuma Samata's five-year campaign (*aiyongxian de qianjin jihua* 隘勇線的前進計畫) to "advance the boundary" separating the mountain tribes from the settler population so as to facilitate the extraction of valuable lumber and camphor from the mountains and to control the "barbarian" aborigines. The Japanese were continuing a Qing Dynasty practice of maintaining a physical barrier (called 土牛溝 *tuniu-gou* "diking and ditching"), but by the early 1900s the Japanese were using electrified fencing.[24] Early attempts to move the fence into Atayal territory led to unexpected Atayal raids on the Japanese command posts and the killing and beheading of their soldiers and officers. Subsequent waves of Japanese attacks over the next two years led to further and more widespread bloody retaliations and counterattacks, which often prevented the Japanese from advancing their positions at all. This ultimately led to a full-scale military offensive in 1913 in which massive numbers of Atayal were slaughtered by artillery fire into their villages. Gu's detailed account illustrates that no matter how much lethal force the Japanese brought to bear on the Atayal, many of their communities, including the *knazi* (基那衣, the group visited by Gu Mengren), continued to attack, throwing themselves against the bullets and artillery shells, knowing they would die in the effort.

For Gu, although the battlements and remains of the fallen had long since been overgrown in the mountains and were no longer plain to see, they served as a "spiritual fortress" for the Atayal. The Atayal, described as "hidden in darkness," are brought to the world's attention only through the violence of "history written in blood." In a world divided between light and darkness, light is conventionally associated with civilization and darkness with primitive savagery. But Gu says the attempt of the Japanese to wipe out the tribal darkness led to a "special meaning," which could be understood as the historical agency of the Atayal—their pride, prowess, determination, and resistance.

Nevertheless, the Atayal people of the time of Gu's writing in 1975 are still cast in the imagery of darkness, raising doubts about the author's message:

> The dark side of history will eventually be hidden away. Over more than 60 years, the Atayal of Xiuluan Village have endured the rule of the Japanese and the [Taiwan] government, but now the shadow cast over their faces has disappeared forever. The chimney smoke of Xiuluan Village curls skyward as before; abiding in their original village, they are like hermits secluding themselves from the world outside. Although they are backward and poor, they are happy and contented.[25]

By emphasizing the image of smoke curling from chimneys, a common Chinese image of pastoral tranquility, Gu affirms the continuity of tribal life while also dissociating it from the dark and shadowy culture of the Atayal.

His Sinicization of indigenous terms is difficult to avoid, but also contributes to the domesticating effect. The author again seems ambivalent about the legitimacy of the Atayal's full identity, affirming their right to abide in their traditional folkways while still trying to expel the dark shadow of their brutality in battle, symbolized by facial tattooing and the ritual decapitation of enemies and rivals.

This leads Gu to reflect on the problem of alcohol abuse among the Atayal men, associating it with the loss of their traditional masculine rite of passage—bringing home the head of an enemy.

> Today's Atayal people no longer perform ritual decapitation, and so they are increasingly anesthetizing themselves in alcohol. Drink and your worries disappear; the world through drink-heavy eyelids has become their best refuge to which to escape from their troubles. Drinking, provoking, fighting are already Xiuluan Village traditions. You can go without food, but can't miss your daily drinks. The rice wine in the little shops can't keep up with the demand; drunken men stumble to the left and fall to the right. The Atayal are so difficult to understand.
>
> As night's curtain falls, the village gradually fades from the grayish dimness of dusk to a bottomless inky black. The nights of this deep mountain village are gloomy and terrifying. The world disappears and the candles and torches lit by the Atayal faintly burn. It's not long after they've eaten dinner before they must climb in bed and sleep. Because what God gave them is a completely dark village; the arm of Edison cannot reach into these deep mountains, and the light is still very far away![26]

Gu doesn't explain the logic of alcohol substituting for violent rituals, but seems to imply that the deprivation of the rite of passage has painfully emasculated the Atayal men (their "troubles"), a pain that drinking and brawling assuages, if destructively.

Gu wrote a reprise to "Black Tribe" in 2014, when an environmental foundation invited him to join an excursion to Xiuluan Village; the foundation was celebrating the Atayal's successful development of the area into a socially responsible, green tourist destination. The opportunity brings Gu a flood of feelings; memories of his journey of forty years before were bittersweet: It was a life-changing experience, but also entailed loneliness, adversity, and disappointment.[27] Gu travels to the village with a group of over a dozen in a minibus about four hours from the nearest town along a route he had to negotiate on foot over a twenty-four-hour period on his initial visit. They encounter over 100 other green tourists there. On the way to a cleansing ceremony to welcome the visitors, Gu is invited by the village chief and elder to participate in the ritual as an honored dignitary. The group is taken to an activity center, where they are treated to dance performances by local children and a trivia game about Atayal culture. The village chief then takes the stage and announces that he has a special prize for someone in the audience. It is an exquisitely crafted bamboo Atayal headpiece, a token of gratitude and respect for the author, who is rendered speechless by the unexpected gesture. The speech from the village chief tells how Gu's month-long journey forty years before drew the public's attention to their community, and without it they might not have experienced development (improved transportation, electrification, cash crops, tourism). Gu writes that for him, neither his prestigious literary award nor the attention it brought to him as a writer could equal this moment of seeing the positive effects of his writing on the community that was its subject, and their sincere personal gratitude to him for it.[28]

The image Gu Mengren projects in his reportage is that of an immersive traveler—not a tourist—and also of a self-aware member of mainstream society troubled by his possible complicity in the marginalization of local people. He uses his immersive travel to both unlearn his urbanity and to gain new, authentic knowledge and perspectives from locals. In "Black Tribe," Gu describes his exposure to Atayal hunting as occurring in stages, starting with day trips for small game in the vicinity of Xiuluan Village, followed by his shadowing a hunting party on a multiday hunt deep into the mountains, once he has demonstrated that he is not a liability.

Pointing the literary spotlight toward the living conditions of marginal communities harmed and neglected through Taiwan's capitalist development was a common theme of writing at the time, but it was unprecedented for cultural mass media to turn their attention to the lives of indigenous tribes in the mountains.[29] This is significant not only for reasons of politics and public discourse, but also literary aesthetics. Gu Mengren's above-mentioned encounter with Huang Chunming opened his eyes to an aesthetics of documentary realism—not just shifting his *fictional* attention to marginalized people and places, but overhauling the whole writing process, shifting writerly attention to the actual conditions of people, and presenting them in a different way than the fictional plots to which readers were accustomed.[30] This epiphany led to many years of literary productivity that had a unique impact on the literary scene; Gu had found his voice.

This was not simply a move from literature to journalism; Gu's resulting reportage was clearly literary and was published in neither the manner nor the venues of journalism. In this respect Gu's paradigm shift resembles the genesis of Chinese reportage in the mainland around 1930—it would never have been conceived of by its advocates or practitioners as a form of journalism; on the contrary, it was explicitly conceived as a *corrective* to the hidden biases and hypocrisy of mainstream newspaper journalism. This is why the term *baodao wenxue*, arguably similar in meaning to the mainland Chinese term *baogao wenxue*, deploys literature to play a journalistic role, but in a way that diverges sharply from that of professional journalism. When Gu emerged onto the literary scene in the 1970s, the absence of freedom of the press would also have made such a corrective in literary form highly attractive and impactful among readers.

Equally important, the new literary territory that opened up to Gu on his encounter with Huang Chunming represented a consequential breakthrough in artistic realism, where the frequently burdensome gap between fictional imagination and actual world of society is potentially breached and a mode of socially operative literary writing comes into being. On the level of rhetoric, ethics, and logic, though, there are issues and even contradictions to explore and work through. Reading the reportage works included in *Black Tribe* from today's perspective, Gu Mengren appears (often unconsciously) conflicted about the predicaments of his subjects and how to address them.

Gu's writing plan—from fishing village to coal mine to Atayal mountain village to farms, and finally back to delivery men on motorbikes in the city—had the effect of equating indigenous peoples with Han and Hakka villagers and workers. To be sure, the marginalized communities do have much in common, and Gu Mengren is not by any means trying to say they all face the same challenges. On the contrary, *Black Tribe* offers a cornucopia of marginalized experiences. But the meaning of matters such as rural poverty, the harms of capitalism, and the challenges of providing education differ significantly in the case of ethnically Chinese subjects and those of other ethnicities, and the distinction is further concealed by the choice of primarily rural settings.

For example, all the communities featured in the collection face challenges in providing education in the absence of adequate funding and teachers. Each essay presents young schoolteachers, in some ways underprivileged and underpaid, in a heroic light, and shows their students' dedication to learning. But when it comes to the piece on the Atayal mountain tribe, it may seem ironic to the reader of today to see the author's delight at hearing Atayal children loudly reciting their Mandarin Chinese lessons: "In this materially impoverished, culturally backward mountain district, to hear Atayal children with their awkwardly-accented Chinese, reading aloud in unison of the boyhood stories of the father of our country [Sun Yatsen], can be quite moving."[31] Given the time and the circumstances, it is understandable that he would write this, but he seems to overlook how this could be seen as an affront to Atayal cultural identity, comparable to the period of Japanese occupation. Although Gu's attention to the lives and world of the indigenous people is a breakthrough, the author seems to accept the goal of their assimilation into modern (Chinese) society, and the role of mainstream national education as an avenue out of the mountains into society. This conflicts with his lament regarding the departure of Bitou Point's younger generation for the city as well as his resentment of college kids disrupting the serene purity of Bitou Point's fishing villages. Are those kids, whom Gu says he wants to "smack in the face," not also the products of mainstream society and the benefits it gives access to?

The irony runs deep in the imagery of light and darkness that pervades the essay on the Atayal. The word "black" that appears in the title is literally the absence of light. The bamboo houses of the Atayal village, we are reminded repeatedly, are pitch black inside, but the metaphorical potential of this darkness as the absence of "enlightenment" is never far from Gu's rhetoric. The mountain jungles in which the Atayal hunt are also significantly darkened by natural foliage, and the prospects for the younger generation are conceived of as "brilliant," even if their auras as yet shine only dimly. Such imagery seems innocent enough, viewing knowledge and civilization as light that illuminates the darkness of ignorance, but when you consider that the Atayal were considered to be "savage" headhunters until modern waves of "enlightenment"—such as the Japanese colonial occupation—you begin to perceive the imagery's unconscious alignment with imperialism and capitalist/industrial development, which are often the ostensible target of Gu Mengren's criticism.

By contrast, Hu Tai-li's 胡台麗 (1950–2022) *Voices of Orchid Island* (Lanyu guandian 蘭島觀點, 1993), a documentary filmed about fifteen years later than the journeys that comprise *Black Tribe*, reveals a profound and overt opposition and gap of understanding between mainstream Taiwan and indigenous people, in this case the Tao people of Orchid Island.[32] The film was also made years after the lifting of martial law in 1987, the restoration of freedom of the press, and political democratization. Orchid Island as a tropical tourist attraction is shown to suffer from daily direct impacts from unscrupulous tourism, and is also secretly exploited by the energy company Taipower, which cordons off a part of the island without informing its inhabitants and then begins dumping nuclear waste there. One could hardly imagine a starker or more adversarial standoff between tradition and modernity, between aboriginal worldviews and scientific progress.

Hu Tai-li's central aim in the film is to provide a platform for the diverse voices of Orchid Island to speak their truth. The harms of external encroachment are symbolized by tour guides' preposterous mangling of Tao folk traditions and cavalier invasion of locals' privacy (tourists often want to make a spectacle of the Taos' scanty loincloths, surreptitiously taking pictures and spreading them in the media). On the other hand, the above-mentioned Tao author Syaman Rapongan—one of Hu's collaborators—openly expresses his resentment toward external attention of *any* kind—even that of anthropologists like Hu—as exploitative, stating flatly at the outset that he does not think the film will do any good. We also see local activists taking political action into their own hands, holding demonstrations against Taipower, and against the government's failure to right their wrongs.

In short, *Voices of Orchid Island* is the product of a new era, in which the universality and legitimacy of mainstream Han elites and modernization may be openly questioned. As early as the 1990s, authors from the Atayal, Puyuma, Bunun, Paiwan, Ami, and other indigenous tribes have emerged on the (Chinese-language) literary scene, and their prose works frequently take the forms of nonfiction and reportage.[33] This may have had the effect of eclipsing the contributions of Han authors such as Gu Mengren, who a generation earlier had drawn attention to their peoples. Yet in his preface to Gu Mengren's latest book, *The Call of Smangus: Return to The Black Tribe*, in which the title work narrates Gu Mengren's 2014 return to Xiuluan Village after forty years, the Puyuma poet and political figure Paelambang Danapan (known in Chinese as Sun Dachuan 孫大川) gives enthusiastic credit to Gu Mengren for this epoch-making contribution.[34] Shiu Wen-wei, another practitioner of reportage who has published many studies and collections of the genre, also contributed a preface, and the title of Shiu's preface, "Writing Darkness, Ushering in the Light" adopts Gu's imagery of light and darkness, while Paelambang's, which is focused entirely on the progress of indigenous people and their literature since the publication of *Black Tribe*, does not use this imagery at all.[35] This new era would be the new normal in Taiwan, at least up to the present, but it is a new normal that owes its existence in part to "Black Tribe" for its recognition of the agency and subjecthood of Taiwan's indigenous peoples, made possible by Gu Mengren's groundbreaking reportage work.

ACKNOWLEDGMENTS

I am grateful to have received a Taiwan Fellowship from the Ministry of Foreign Affairs of the Republic of China in 2020, which contributed greatly to this research.

NOTES

1. See Charles A. Laughlin, *Chinese Reportage*, 1–19, 33–36.
2. Shiu Wen-wei, "Zaixian Taiwan tianye de jiti jiyi," 14. All translations are my own.
3. Shiu Wen-wei, "Zaixian Taiwan tianye de jiti jiyi," 14–15.
4. Lawrence Zi-Qiao Yang, "Soil and Scroll: The Agrarian Origin of a Cold War Documentary Avant-Garde," 46.
5. Shiu Wen-wei, "Zaixian Taiwan tianye de jiti jiyi," 17.
6. See also the introduction to this volume. Li Guo's article in the present volume also offers more perspective on the genesis and nature of reportage in Taiwan, especially on page 163 and 187n17.
7. Shiu Wen-wei, "Zaixian Taiwan tianye de jiti jiyi," 19.
8. Shiu Wen-wei, "Zaixian Taiwan tianye de jiti jiyi," 20.
9. Shiu Wen-wei, "Zaixian Taiwan tianye de jiti jiyi," 20.
10. Ding Wan, "Xingzhe de lu: benbo zai baodao wenxue lu shang de Gu Mengren (The path of the sojourner: Gu Mengren on the road of reportage)," 269–81.
11. The further development of photography in connection with Taiwanese reportage is explored chapters 5 and 6 of this volume. See also Federica Mirra's study of contemporary mainland photographic reportage in chapter 2.
12. Gu Mengren, "Yibu yibu zouxiang geng guangming de difang—Heise de buluo zixu (Going to a brighter place one step at a time: preface to *Black Tribe*)," 14–15.
13. Yvonne Sung-sheng Chang, *Modernism and the Nativist Resistance*, 160.
14. Gu Mengren, "Meiyou hansheng de bizi: Bitou yucun cangsang (A nose that doesn't snore: the tribulations of Bitou fishing village"), 16–17. This article also appears in an abridged form in the 2022 collection, *Simakusi de huhuan—chongfan heisede buluo* (The call of Smangus: return to the black tribe), 33–56, but the passages I quote here were not included.
15. Gu Mengren, "Meiyou hansheng de bizi," 31.
16. Gu Mengren, "Meiyou hansheng de bizi," 33.
17. Gu Mengren, "Meiyou hansheng de bizi," 34.
18. Gu Mengren, "Meiyou hansheng de bizi," 41.
19. Gu Mengren, "Meiyou hansheng de bizi," 59–61.
20. Gu Mengren, "Taojin mengsui: Jiufen, Jinguashi de yuanmao," 78.
21. I am referring here to works within the system of Chinese-language literature published in Taiwan after the Republic of China made Taipei its capital in 1949. Writers in other languages had previously given significant attention to Taiwan's indigenous peoples, notably George Leslie Mackay in the 1890s and Kondo Katsusaburo in the 1930s (Mackay and Macdonald, *From Far Formosa: The Island, Its People and Missions*; Barclay, *Kondo the Barbarian: A Japanese Adventurer and Taiwan's Bloodiest Uprising*). I want to thank an anonymous reviewer for drawing my attention to these fascinating works. Li Guo and Po-hsi Chen's contributions to this volume reflect the persistent attention to indigenous people in *Ren Jian* magazine and in book-length projects produced by its contributors.
22. Chiu, "The Production of Indigeneity: Contemporary Indigenous Literature in Taiwan and Trans-Cultural Inheritance," 1071–88.
23. Gu, "Heise de buluo," 178.

24. National Museum of Taiwan History, "Aiyongxian de qingkuang 隘勇線的情況 (The confinement of natives situation)." Apart from this background, the following summary is based on the text of Gu's article.

25. Gu, "Heise de buluo," 96. I am indebted to Darryl Sterk of Lingnan University and Liu Yunan 劉宇南, who answered many of my questions about the Lidong Mountain Incident and Atayal terminology.

26. Gu, "Heise de buluo," 178.

27. Gu Mengren, "Simakusi de huhuan: chongfan heise de buluo," 181.

28. Gu Mengren, "Simakusi de huhuan: chongfan heise de buluo," 187. In light of later shifts in attitude toward indigenous people and the emergence of indigenous writers in the Chinese-language literary scene, it may be noted that "Black Tribe" and other early works included in Gu's 2022 collection were abridged and edited in ways that could be seen as accommodating those shifts in attitude.

29. Not that this was unprecedented in *any* language; see note 21 above.

30. Gu Mengren, "Yibu yibu zouxiang geng guangming de difang—Heise de buluo zixu," 14–15. I am extrapolating based on my reading of Gu's writing practice.

31. Gu Mengren, "Heise de buluo," 194–95.

32. Hu Tai-li, dir. *Lanyu guandian* (Voices of Orchid Island).

33. See John Balcom and Yingtsih Balcom, *Indigenous Writers of Taiwan: An Anthology of Stories, Essays, & Poems*, Modern Chinese Literature from Taiwan (New York: Columbia University Press, 2005).

34. Paelambang Danapan (Sun Dachuan), "'Wenxue' gongxian gei yuanzhu minzu de liwu," 7–10.

35. Shiu Wen-wei 須文蔚, "Shuxie heian; jieyin guangming," in *Simakusi de huhuan: chongfan heise de buluo*, by Gu Mengren, 13–17.

REFERENCES

Barclay, Paul D. *Outcasts of Empire: Japan's Rule on Taiwan's "Savage Border," 1874–1945*. Oakland: University of California Press, 2018.

Barclay, Paul D. *Kondo the Barbarian: A Japanese Adventurer and Taiwan's Bloodiest Uprising*. Manchester: Eastbridge Books, 2023.

Chang, Yvonne Sung-sheng. *Modernism and the Nativist Resistance: Contemporary Fiction from Taiwan*. Durham: Duke University Press, 1993.

Chiu, Kuei-fen. "The Production of Indigeneity: Contemporary Indigenous Literature in Taiwan and Trans-Cultural Inheritance." *China Quarterly (London)* no. 200 (December 1, 2009): 1071–88.

Ding Wan 丁琬. "The Path of the Sojourner: Gu Mengren on the Road of Reportage" (Xingzhe de lu: benbo zai baodao wenxue lu shang de Gu Mengren 行者的路——奔波在報導文學路上的古蒙仁). In *Files on Taiwan Society* (Taiwan shehui dang'an 台灣社會檔案), edited by Gu Mengren, 269–81. Taibei Shi: Jiu ge chubanshe, 1983.

Gu Mengren 古蒙仁. *Black Tribe* (Heise de buluo 黑色的部落). Taibei Shi: Shibao wenhua chuban shiye youxian gongsi, 1978.

Gu Mengren 古蒙仁. "A Nose that Doesn't Snore: First Visit to Bitou Fishing Village"

(Meiyou hansheng de bizi: Bitou yucun chulü 沒有鼾聲的鼻子——鼻頭漁村初旅). In *Black Tribe* (Heise de buluo 黑色的部落), by Gu Mengren 古蒙仁, 13–61. Taipei: Shibao wenhua chuban shiye youxian gongsi, 1978.

Gu Mengren 古蒙仁. "Shattered Dreams of Gold-Digging: The Real Face of Jiufen and Jinguashi" (Taojin mengsui: Jiufen, Jinguashi de yuanmao 淘金夢碎–九份、金瓜石的原貌). In *Black Tribe* (Heise de buluo 黑色的部落), by Gu Mengren 古蒙仁, 63–121. Taipei: Shibao wenhua chuban shiye youxian gongsi, 1978.

Gu Mengren 古蒙仁. "Going to a Brighter Place One Step at a Time: Preface to *Black Tribe*" (Yibu yibu zouxiang geng guangming de difang—Heise de buluo zixu 一步一步走向更光明的地方–黑色的部落自序). In *Black Tribe* (Heise de buluo 黑色的部落), by Gu Mengren 古蒙仁, 13–23. Taipei: Shibao wenhua chuban shiye youxian gongsi, 1978.

Gu Mengren 古蒙仁. "The Call of Smangus: Return to the Black Tribe" (Simakusi de huhuan: chongfan heise de buluo 司馬庫斯的呼喚–重返黑色的部落). In *The Call of Smangus: Return to the Black Tribe* (Simakusi de huhuan: chongfan heise de buluo 司馬庫斯的呼喚–重返黑色的部落), 180–88. Taipei: Times Culture, 2022.

Hu Tai-li 胡台麗 (Director). *Voices of Orchid Island* (Lanyu guandian 蘭嶼觀點. [Video/DVD] Documentary Educational Resources (DER, 1993). Retrieved from https://video.alexanderstreet.com/watch/voices-of-orchid-island

Laughlin, Charles A. *Chinese Reportage: The Aesthetics of Historical Experience*. Durham: Duke University Press, 2002.

Mackay, George Leslie, edited by J. A. Macdonald. *From Far Formosa: The Island, Its People and Missions*. Cambridge: Cambridge University Press, 1896.

National Museum of Taiwan History. *The Confinement of Natives Situation* (Aiyongxian de qingkuang 隘勇線的情況). Online Museum of Taiwan History, n.d. https://the.nmth.gov.tw/nmth/zh-TW/Item/Detail/28da7409-8acd-436a-bb58-cd8570ae2f7c#:~:

Paelambang Danapan (Sun Dachuan 孫大川). "The Gift Given to Indigenous Peoples by 'Literature'" ('Wenxue' gongxian gei yuanzhu minzu de liwu '文學'貢獻給原住民族的禮物.) In *The Call of Smangus: Return to the Black Tribe* (Simakusi de huhuan: chongfan heise de buluo 司馬庫斯的呼喚–重返黑色的部落), by Gu Mengren 古蒙仁, 7–10. Taipei: Times Culture, 2022.

Shiu Wen-wei 須文蔚. "Representing Taiwan's Collective Memory in the Field: Taiwan Reportage History from Social Movements and Representation Theory" (Zaixian Taiwan tianye de jiti jiyi: cong shehui yundong yu zaixianlun kaochaxia de Taiwan baodao wenxue shi 再現台灣田野的集體記憶–從社會運動與再現論考察下的台灣報導文學史." In *The Reportage Reader*, rev. ed. (Baodao wenxue duben: zengding ban 報導文學讀本:增訂版), edited by Shiu Wen-wei 須文蔚 and Xiang Yang 向陽, 8–44. Er yu wen hua. Taibei shi: Eryu wenhua chuban, 2012.

Shiu Wen-wei 須文蔚. "Writing Darkness, Guiding the Light" (Shuxie heian; jieyin guangming 書寫黑暗,街引光明). In *The Call of Smangus: Return to the Black Tribe* (Simakusi de huhuan: chongfan heise de buluo 司馬庫斯的呼喚–重返黑色的部落), by Gu Mengren 古蒙仁, 13–17. Taipei: Times Culture, 2022.

Xiang Yang 向陽 and Shiu Wen-wei 須文蔚, eds. *The Reportage Reader*, rev. ed. (Baodao wenxue duben 報導文學讀本：增訂版). Er ban. Taibei: Eryu wenhua chuban, 2012.

Yang, Lawrence Zi-Qiao. "Soil and Scroll: The Agrarian Origin of a Cold War Documentary Avant-Garde." *Modern Chinese Literature and Culture* 31, no. 2 (2019): 41–80.

FIVE

Stoic Heroism

Making "Photojournalist" a Professional Identity in Ren Jian *Magazine's International Section*

Po-hsi Chen

Ren Jian (Human World), founded by novelist Chen Yingzhen (1937–2016), has been hailed as the pioneering photojournalist magazine in Taiwan. During its brief but eventful existence (1985–1989), the magazine not only documented but actively shaped Taiwan's democratization movement through groundbreaking social advocacy. *Ren Jian* pioneered a new form of visual journalism in Taiwan, covering pressing social issues ranging from environmental devastation to child prostitution, while paying particular attention to marginalized communities, including indigenous people and people with disabilities (see also chapters 4 and 6). Decades after its closure, both public and private sectors still celebrated and paid tribute to *Ren Jian*'s enduring legacy. In 2015, the National Human Rights Museum held a special exhibition to commemorate the thirtieth anniversary of its founding. In 2021, the Taiwan International Documentary Festival bestowed the Special Contribution Award on the magazine.

To date, discussions about *Ren Jian* have largely centered on its best-known coverage of and participation in *local* activism. The magazine's approach to social justice is perhaps best illustrated through its coverage of the Tang Yingshen (1967–1987) case in 1987. When Tang, a young Tsou indigenous man working in Taipei, was convicted of murdering his employer's family, *Ren Jian*'s coverage transcended mere documentation. The magazine's photojournalists used the case to expose Taiwan's stark urban-rural divide and the deep-seated inequities between Han and indigenous communities. Going beyond traditional journalistic boundaries, the *Ren Jian* team campaigned against Tang's death sentence. Even after his execution, the reporters continued their involvement, accompanying his ashes back to his southern Taiwan hometown and facilitating reconciliation between Tang's father and the victim's family. Tang's case demonstrates how *Ren Jian* redefined photojournalism in Taiwan—not as passive documentation, but as active participation in social transformation.

While *Ren Jian*'s place in Taiwanese society is indisputable, focusing solely on its local impact risks overlooking its broader universalistic implications, encoded in its very title—"human world"—not to mention its Japanese cognate, *ningen*, which refers to the entirety of humanity. In the 1970s, before founding *Ren Jian* in the mid-1980s, Chen founded the political magazine *China Tide* (*Xia chao*) where he first established his leftist critique of capitalism. By the mid-1980s, as Taiwan's economic miracle generated mounting social costs—urban-rural disparities, indigenous impoverishment, and environmental degradation—Chen turned to photojournalism as a powerful visual medium to expose these contradictions. The inaugural issue of *Ren Jian* opens with what would become the defining manifesto of photojournalism in Taiwan:

> Over the past two decades, our society's collective labor has created unprecedented prosperity in Taiwan—a level of affluence previously unknown *in Chinese history*. Yet this achievement, worthy of pride though it may be, has extracted its price. Our highly organized division of labor has severed the bonds between individuals, fragmented production sectors, and isolated markets from one another. The deep solidarity, mutual passion, and care connected through flesh and blood have withered away.
>
> Moreover, in an era of mass consumption, humans have been reduced to *Homo consumens*, processing an endless parade of commodities. Life has lost its meaning, existence its purpose. Our cultural life grows increasingly vulgar and superficial; our spiritual civilization withers day by day into desolation.[1]

This Marxist critique of global capitalism would become *Ren Jian*'s ideological cornerstone, though its reception would revolve dramatically over time.[2]

While initially widely acclaimed, it later polarized critics from different political camps. Chen's former colleagues at *Ren Jian*, now often labeled as the "pro-unification Left" (*zuo tong*, i.e., proponents of unification with China), championed the magazine's anticapitalist and left-wing humanitarian spirit. Critics advocating Taiwanese autonomy, however, viewed this humanitarianism as rhetorical cover for Chen Yingzhen's pro-China stance. In his critique of Chen's political identification, Chen Mingcheng challenges the common view that financial difficulties led to *Ren Jian*'s closure,[3] and instead hastily concludes that the magazine's persistent framing of local Taiwanese struggles within modern Chinese historical narratives—evident even in the manifesto's reference to "Chinese history"—ultimately alienated readers invested in a distinct Taiwanese identity.[4]

While both poles claim to deal with the relationship between humanitarianism and local society, neither seriously analyzes how that humanitarian discourse was mediated through the interplay of (visual) photography and (textual) reportage, or the combination of the two. In fact, whether *Ren Jian* is local-centric or pro-China, its photojournalism did not come out of the blue. As the first of its kind, the magazine needed to draw inspiration from exemplary photojournalist reportage in other contexts at a time when photojournalism had yet to be institutionalized as a discipline. As the magazine developed its collective ethical and stylistic standards, it was trying to define what constitutes good photojournalist reportage. From its inaugural issue, *Ren Jian* dedicated a special section titled "Selected Works from World-Renowned Photojournalism" (*Shijie baodao mingzuo xuandu*), a regular feature that ran through its first dozen issues. Guan Xiaorong, a former *Ren Jian* photojournalist, is one of the few people who noticed the historical significance of the international section, noting that it represented a "major breakthrough in an intellectual arena heavily dominated by the military martial-law regime."[5]

The international scope of this section was remarkable, featuring luminaries such as Japanese photographers Mitome Tadao (1938–2022) and Higuchi Kenji (b. 1937), South African documentarian Peter Magubane (b. 1932), Hungarian-born André Kertesz (1894–1985), Americans Dorothea Lange (1895–1965) and Michael Williamson (b. 1957), and French master Henri Cartier-Bresson (1908–2004). Positioned strategically toward the end of each issue, these translated reportage pieces concluded one issue while paving the way for the next and established standards of excellence in reportage writing and photography for *Ren Jian*'s practitioners and readers alike.

While *Ren Jian* underscored the distinctive identities of foreign photojournalists, it consciously deemphasized the individual voices of its own contributors. As Chang Shih-lun (Zhang Shilun) observes in his landmark study of Taiwanese photography, despite the differences in their idiosyncratic styles, *Ren Jian*'s photographers maintained such consistent social concerns and visual approaches that "not a single photographer's individual identity is made prominent." Instead, their work was celebrated as, and absorbed into, a collective *Ren Jian* aesthetics, with the left-wing idealism in their photography attributed to Chen Yingzhen's founding vision (Chang Shih-lun 2021, 375).

This tension between emphasizing individual photographic styles and the collective humanitarian goal raises fundamental questions about photojournalistic identity and purpose. How does one perceive "photojournalist" as a professional identity? After all, traditional discussions of photojournalism often focus on photography's capacity to transmit reality—however problematic that concept may be—and center on the subjects before the lens rather than those behind it.[6] In other words, it is those foregrounded by the camera who are the wretched of the earth, not the photographers. As Charles Laughlin and Li Guo note in this volume's introduction, "the penchant in photographic reportage for striving for objectivity raises questions about artistic arrangements and manipulations of personal and social spaces." This leads to a central paradox: Does emphasizing individual photographic style undermine the social mission of documentary photography? If we deemphasize aesthetic considerations, what exactly are we celebrating when we label these photojournalists "humanitarian"—a term frequently associated with the *Ren Jian* coterie?

The magazine's approach suggests an intriguing answer: Its humanitarian discourse rests not only on the suffering of its photographic subjects but on the portrayal of photographers themselves as heroic figures. This chapter examines this dual dynamic between humanitarianism and heroism, and between the photographers and their subjects, showing how *Ren Jian* negotiated the tensions between individual artistic expression and collective social purpose.

After the closure of *Ren Jian*, Chen Yingzhen reflected on its legacy and identified its key innovation in "two already mature but not yet developed literary and artistic forms": photojournalism (*baodao sheying*) and reportage literature (*baodao wenxue*).[7] Of these two forms, reportage literature has received more theoretical attention, due both to Chen's acknowledgment of his left-wing predecessor Yang Kui (1906–1985), a pioneering figure in colonial Taiwan's reportage tradition, and to the relatively recent institutionalization of documentary photography studies. Chen argued that martial law had suppressed the development of reportage literature because of its left-wing orientation toward social intervention. In this context, he saw *Ren Jian*'s significance in establishing an "institutional publication" (*jiguan kanwu*) that legitimized reportage through its "in-depth reports on the laborers and the people who were harmed," finally providing an organizational home for this marginalized genre.[8]

Scholarly work has largely followed Chen's own emphasis on reportage literature, leaving *Ren Jian*'s photojournalistic innovations and accomplishments comparatively understudied.[9] Critical acclaim for the magazine often circles in a tautological loop: *Ren Jian*'s photojournalism addressed social problems because it followed *Ren Jian*'s humanitarian doctrine; its photojournalism was humanitarian because it addressed social problems. This circular reasoning illuminates the nature of neither photojournalism nor humanitarianism. The magazine's international section, however, offers a way out of this impasse by showing how *Ren Jian* helped define both photojournalism and humanitarianism for the new magazine.

This chapter examines how *Ren Jian* selected, translated, and characterized foreign photojournalists' work, creating a dialogue between international and local documentary practices. Striking parallels emerge: Guan Xiaorong's coverage of disparities between the Han and indigenous peoples echoes Peter Magubane's documentation of South African apartheid; Tseng Shu-mei's (Zeng Shumei) reports on Taipei's child prostitutes parallel Mary Ellen Mark's work with Indian sex workers; W. Eugene Smith's Minamata coverage and Alon Reininger's on AIDS documentation find local resonances. Rather than mere imitation, these parallels reveal *Ren Jian*'s deliberate construction of professional ethics through translation and interpretation of foreign models.

I develop this analysis by examining how *Ren Jian* drew on two major international photography organizations—the Farm Security Administration and Magnum—to establish its conception of photojournalistic practice and humanitarian ethics. I introduce the concept of "stoic heroism" to analyze how the magazine portrayed photographers such as Smith, Dorothea Lange, and Mary Ellen Mark as heroic, solitary figures. The work of two female photojournalists, Lange and Mark, proves particularly significant in revealing a gendered dimension to documentary practice, offering an instructive contrast to Chen's approach. While *Ren Jian*'s overall editorial tone, influenced by Chen's approach, tended to pathologize its subjects, these foreign photographers—especially women—developed more nuanced approaches that recognized their subjects' agency.

Taiwan's Magnum and the Farm Security Administration: Stoic Heroism in *Ren Jian*'s International Vision

The genealogy of *Ren Jian*'s international influences runs deeper than as it first appears. Two major photography collectives functioned as crucial models: the Farm Security Administration, which produced the most searing images through its New Deal documentary project during the Depression, and Magnum Photos, the pioneering photojournalist cooperative founded by Robert Capa in 1947.[10]

Lange, featured in *Ren Jian*'s fifth issue, was a cornerstone of the Farm Security Administration. Henri Cartier-Bresson, introduced in the fourteenth issue, was Magnum's defining voice. W. Eugene Smith had ties with both groups. Even Higuchi Kenji, the magazine's Japanese connection, traced his artistic lineage to Capa. Through these choices, *Ren Jian* positioned itself within what Nadya Bair calls the "global imagery" of postwar photojournalism groups such as Magnum.[11]

Ren Jian's construction of foreign photojournalists as having heroic images resonates with the presentation of photographers such as Cartier-Bresson made famous by Magnum. Cartier-Bresson famously described taking an ideal photograph as a skillful photographer capturing a "decisive moment." Recent studies, however, suggest that such emphasis on photographers' individual talent ignores the network behind them, such as Magnum's editors and agents, and even photographers' spouses.[12]

In contrast, *Ren Jian*'s own local photojournalism downplayed the identity and presence of its own crew to avoid overshadowing its coverage. Furthermore, as Chang Shih-lun notes, the photojournalists' aesthetic signatures were subordinated to a unified *Ren Jian* style—sometimes at the expense of their individual aesthetics. This tension suggests that the international section served to establish a professional and ethical model for *Ren Jian*'s own crew, thereby legitimizing the magazine's collective professional ethics through association with globally recognized masters.

Ren Jian's international section broke from documentary convention beginning with its inaugural issue by foregrounding foreign photojournalists themselves alongside their reportage. In other words, their identity as photojournalists is not hidden. This dual focus crystallizes in "Hunger: Emergent Report from Ethiopia" by Mitome Tadao. The opening page is squarely split in half (fig. 5.1): On the right is the black-and-white close-up of an Ethiopian woman ravaged by hunger, while on the left is a translated

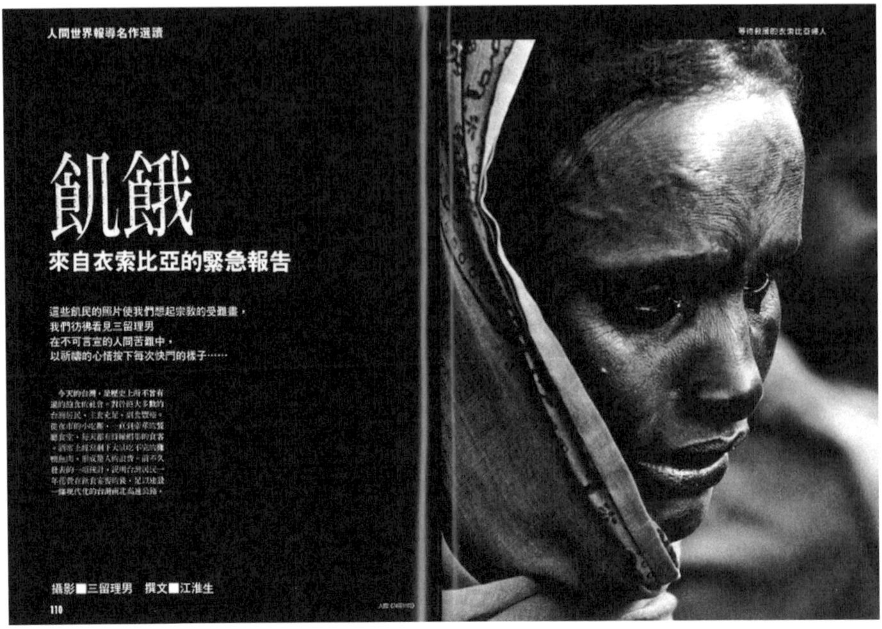

Fig. 5.1. "Hunger: An Emergent Report from Ethiopia," photography by Mitome Tadao. (Reproduced from *Ren Jian* [1985].)

report prefaced by what appear to be Chen Yingzhen's own words: "The photos of these refugees remind us of crucifixion. We seem to see Mitome Tadao, amid unspeakable human world suffering, press the shutter as if he were praying. . . ."[13]

The framing subtly inverts traditional power dynamics of documentary photography. Where media theory typically positions the photographer as the wielder of the camera's authority, determining how the subjects should be captured, *Ren Jian* recasts Mitome as a supplicant; he is compared to a person praying to Jesus. In this sense, the introductory remarks turn the photographic subjects into the ones in power. The description demands not just witness to the refugee woman's despairing facial expression, as vividly captured by the picture, it also invites us to take a step back to envision the melancholic response from the cameraman—Mitome Tadao—taking photos behind the lens. The imagined presence of the photojournalist immediately asks us to note that the photo is mediated through *someone's lens*. By making visible the mediating presence behind the lens, *Ren Jian* refuses the myth of photographic objectivity.

The Christian connotations in this opening page deserve further attention. The magazine's inaugural issue opened with a piece of Chen's, "Because We Have Faith, Hope, and Love . . ."—a clear echo of Corinthians, a biblical reference later dismissed by some critics as camouflage for his radical politics.[14] Yet in the introduction to Mitome's work, the crucifixion metaphor serves to yoke together two forms of suffering: that of the photographed subjects and, equally importantly, that of the witnessing photographer.

The interplay between text (reportage) and image (documentary photography) transcends simple documentation. What Li Guo calls the "ekphrastic process" of documentary photography "deconstructs the binary conception of the image/text relation" (see chapter 7), creating a dialogue between visual and verbal narratives. This text-and-image layout sets the tone for the magazine's later translated photojournalist reportage in the international section: While the photo zooms in on the photographed groups of people, the accompanying texts step back to position the photojournalist as an intermediary figure between subject and viewer. Karin E. Becker's analysis of tabloid photography illuminates their relationship: "the text seems to carry the greater authority; it tells us what we are 'really' seeing in the photographs. The text here *illustrates* the image, instead of vice versa."[15] *Ren Jian* pushes this dynamic further. As shown in Mitome's case, the foreign photojournalists' presence is often made known in *Ren Jian*'s section on world-renowned photojournalism. Throughout its world-renowned photojournalism section, translators and editors devote substantial space—often in prominent positions at the beginning or middle of pieces—to crafting portraits of photojournalists as lone heroes. These biographical sketches function as more than contexts: They establish a parallel narrative that places photojournalists on an equal footing with their subjects.

The construction of foreign photojournalists as heroic figures reaches its apex in *Ren Jian*'s introduction to W. Eugene Smith, the American photojournalist most famous for bringing to light the Minamata mercury poisoning crisis in Japan. The magazine's seventh issue of 1986 features "The Minamata Elegy" with a telling subtitle, "Eugene Smith and His Minamata Reports." As with Mitome's Ethiopia coverage, the photojournalist's identity shares equal billing with the crisis itself: It is Smith "and his" Minamata reports. In the same vein, the prologue sets the tone:

> To bear witness to this pollution-ravaged Japanese town, Eugene Smith lived among its ailing and helpless people, sharing their meals and living together. He spent his honeymoon conducting interviews. . . . For four years, despite the lack of food and clothing as well as injury from

> physical assault, he pressed on undaunted. He exerted the *humanitarian quality* [*rendao pinzhi*] *of a photojournalist* to the extreme.[16]

Rather than focusing on Minamata per se, this prologue foregrounds the photojournalist Smith's character as a respectful, humanitarian figure. But what constitutes the "humanitarian quality of a photojournalist," to be exact? The answer seems not to be detached observation but shared suffering with the subjects.

Smith's entrance into the narrative unfolds like theatrical staging, marked by the dramatic subtitle: "Eugene Smith—A Relentless Witness—Appears."[17] The article explains the philosophy behind his work ethic:

> Smith believed that, in news reports, nothing is absolutely objective. When reporting on a series of events, a serious reporter would inevitably commit his spirit and even emotions. He once said, "We should deeply trust human emotions. [. . .] I believe that wisdom must be triggered by emotions to rectify the major errors in this world." This was evidenced by how he spent years tracking Minamata; he was to petition for tens of thousands of patients. When he was conducting interviews in Japan, Smith was beaten by the staff of the nitrogen company, who broke his spine, which did not deter his work a bit. He exerted the *humanitarian character* of a photojournalist to its fullest.[18]

Again, the biographical account portrays an awe-inspiring, devoted photojournalist who would risk his life reporting on life-threatening incidents. This portrait of the photojournalist as martyr became a template for *Ren Jian*'s own practitioners, who would reiterate this work ethic even after the magazine shut down. For instance, in a book published one year after *Ren Jian*'s closure, aptly titled *Returning to the Scenes of the Human World*, Zhong Qiao again invokes Smith's relentlessness:

> His professional attitude was a crucial factor that determined the quality of his work. [. . .] His spine was broken by the violent act incited by the factory. However, the sensational report triggered attention and discussion from the entire world.[19]

Zhong's comment hints at what I term "stoic heroism" in the work ethics valorized by *Ren Jian*, by which I mean the lionization of photojournalists through portraying their physical and mental ordeal. In the framing of this opening, the attention to Minamata was predicated on the violent suffering of a photojournalist. I take the term *heroism* from *Ren Jian*'s introduction of Tom Cooper's interview with Smith. When translated by *Ren Jian*, it was retitled "The Story Behind the Hero."[20] While Smith is foregrounded as a "heroic" reporter, the Minamata crisis is to some extent relegated to the background, as a story "behind the hero." However, if one compares the translated interview in *Ren Jian* with the original, there is no such reference to heroism in Cooper's interview; it was simply titled "Eugene Smith."[21]

The ethic of stoic heroism extends to *Ren Jian*'s portrayal of other international photojournalists. The July 1986 issue that features Mary Ellen Mark's award-winning reportage on sex workers in Bombay, translated from her *Falkland Road: Prostitutes of Bombay*, opens with a similar beginning:

> For ten years I tried to take photographs on Falkland Road and each time met with hostility and aggression. The women threw garbage and water and pinched me. Crowds of men would gather around me. Once a pickpocket took my address book; another time I was hit in the face by a drunken man.[22]

Like Smith, Mark's narrative emphasizes repeated returns to the scene and eventually reconciliation with her targeted interviewees. She recounts how on later visits, "crowds of men around me and the women alternately hurl[ed] insults and garbage at me." Yet the hostile situation gradually ameliorated: "as the days passed and people saw my persistence, they began to get curious. Some of the women thought I was crazy, but a few were surprised by my interest in and acceptance of them. And slowly, very slowly, I began to make friends."[23]

This emphasis on evolving relationships with subjects marks a crucial difference between foreign photojournalists and *Ren Jian*'s own approach. While the magazine celebrated Mark's growing intimacy with the sex workers on Falkland Road, its own coverage of prostitution deliberately avoided such personal connections, maintaining a critical distance from what it viewed as an inherently oppressive system.

The Agency of Photographed Subjects

How documentary subjects appear in photographs—and how photographers and editors interpret those appearances—reveals crucial tensions in pho-

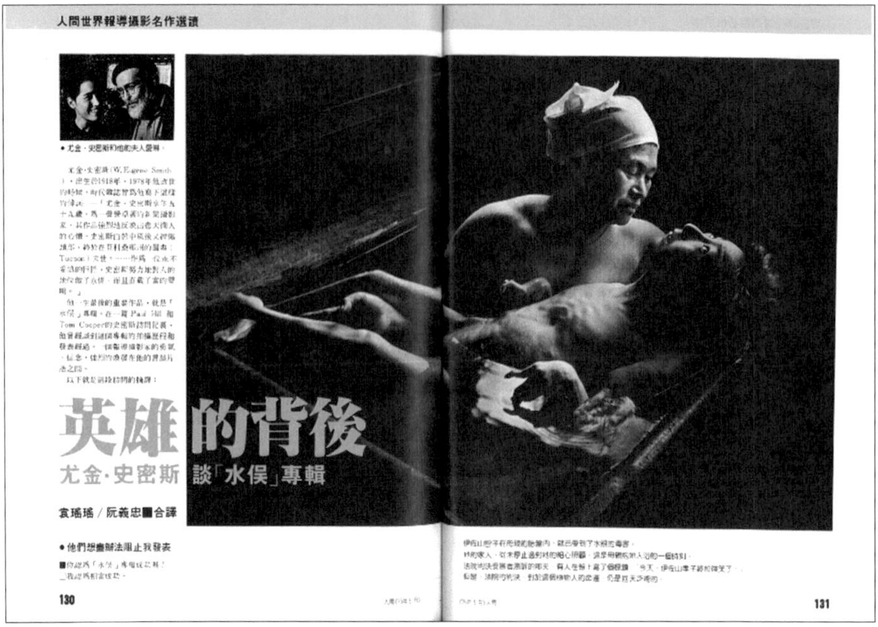

Fig. 5.2. "Behind the Hero: Eugene Smith on Minamata." (Reproduced from *Ren Jian* [May 1986].)

tojournalistic practice. This dynamic clearly surfaces in *Ren Jian*'s editorial choices, particularly in how the magazine interpreted images of suffering. The "decisive moment" came in 1983, when Chen first experienced the profound visual impact of Smith's photojournalism at the University of Iowa, which directly led him to found *Ren Jian*:

> A passionate colleague showed me a collection of famous reportage photographers' photobooks at the Department of Journalism. It was the first time I encountered such photos and I was very astounded by them. [. . .] When I saw those photos in the United States, I realized that photos could be taken in such a way that they had a strong and unforgettable impact.

The striking image that "astounded" Chen was Smith's Minamata image of a mother bathing her mercury-poisoned daughter. Chen described it as a scene of maternal melancholy, recalling "a mother *gazing at her daughter with profound sadness*. Photos like these are unforgettable once you see them."[24] Yet

Smith's actual photo shows something quite different—a tender, even loving maternal gaze, contrary to Chen's melancholic characterization. Indeed, Smith himself emphasized that he meant to capture familial intimacy, not tragedy. This gap between Smith's intention and Chen's interpretation shows *Ren Jian*'s tendency to read suffering into its subjects, even when the images themselves suggest different emotional landscapes.

The initial impression imposed by the founder on photojournalism did not entirely determine the perspectives of other translators regarding the relationship between photojournalists and their subjects. Although the overall tonality of *Ren Jian* emphasizes sympathetic pathos, an analysis of translated works by international photojournalists shows a nuanced understanding of the photographic subjects. Ironically, these translated pieces sometimes attributed more agency to photographic subjects than the original accounts warranted.

Just like the introduction of Mitome and Smith, *Ren Jian*'s piece on the FSA photojournalist Lange, written by Kuo Li-hsin—the "passionate colleague" who showed Chen Yingzhen Smith's photojournalism—opens with a biographical account:

> The young girl's [i.e., Lange's] mind was deeply affected by two tragedies. At seven, she was struck by polio. She accepted the fact and had been troubled by it for the rest of her life. While other children with similar bodily defects were prone to withdrawing from life's challenges, the misfortune instead helped steel Lange's character. She firmly believed that a limp need not lead a stumbling life [. . .]. Then at twelve, Lange's father suddenly abandoned the family and never returned. This cast another shadow across her childhood.[25]

In his *Ren Jian* introduction to Lange, Kuo's selective translation (or sometimes even mistranslation) amplifies the photographic subjects' agency. Consider Lange's 1960 account, "The Assignment I'll Never Forget," recalling her first encounter with a migrant mother:

> I saw and approached the hungry and desperate mother, as if drawn by a magnet. I do not remember how I explained [my] presence or my camera to her, but I do remember she asked me no questions. I made five exposures, working closer and closer from the same direction. I did not ask her name or her history. She told me her age, that she was thirty-two.[26]

The first sentence already puts the photographed mother in an active position, which *magnetized* the photojournalist to capture herself. Kuo may have unintentionally emphasized the agency of the subjects in his translation. This is most striking in the part where he (mis)translated Lange's description of how the mother appeared to understand the magical power of photography:

> *Lange's original*
>
> There she sat in that lean-to tent with her children huddled around her, and seemed to know that my pictures might help her, *and so she helped me. There was a sort of equality about it.* (Lange 1996 [1960], 152; my emphasis)
>
> *Kuo's translation*
>
> There she sat in that lean-to tent. Her children gradually huddled around her, and seemed to know that my pictures might help *them*, and so *they helped me construct this picture*. (Kuo 1986, 125; my emphasis)

Lange establishes a reciprocal relationship—"equality"—between photographer (herself) and subject (the migrant mother). The mother "helped" Lange with the understanding that "my [Lange's] pictures might help her."

While Lange claimed there was "a sort of equality" in her encounter with Florence Thompson—the woman who would become known as the "Migrant Mother"—recent studies unveil a far more troubling reality. As Lennard J. Davis demonstrates in a recent *Los Angeles Review of Books* article, Lange's account of a brief, spontaneous encounter masks the photograph's careful orchestration.[27] The complete series of images reveals multiple setups and deliberate staging. More significantly, crucial details in Lange's account proved to be false—from her claim that the family had sold their car tires for food to her portrait of them as recent Dust Bowl refugees, when in fact they had actually been in California for a decade. The gap between Lange's myth of reciprocity and Thompson's experience of exploitation raises fundamental questions about documentary ethics and the politics of representation.

Kuo's translation does more than reframe photographer-subject dynamics—it radically redistributes agency. By shifting focus from mother to children, his version creates a paradox: Those presumed to be least capable of understanding documentary photography's power become its conscious collaborators. Kuo's alteration of Lange's original essay works on multiple levels. First, it transfers creative agency from mother to children. Second, it replaces Lange's explicit "equality" with an even more radical vision in which subjects traditionally seen as powerless and less knowledgeable—children—comprehend the power of documentary photography and even actively assist the professional photographer in framing the photo, thus shaping their own representation. This reading inverts conventional power relations inherent in the photographic gaze, elevating subjects from observed to observers, from captured to creators.

However, the sole photograph from Lange's "Migrant Mother" series featured in *Ren Jian* places the titular melancholic woman front and center, occupying the foreground of the medium shot, while casting her gaze slightly away from the camera. This particular framing situates the woman in the being-gazed-at position, rather than in a position of active engagement with the camera. Her two children, meanwhile, can be seen leaning against her shoulders with their faces turned *away* from the camera (fig. 5.3). The careful staging of the photograph and Thompson's later testimony contradict both Kuo's translated text and Lange's own narrative of spontaneous collaboration. Rather than showing subjects helping to "construct this picture," the image represents a carefully orchestrated composition that primarily served the photographer's aesthetic aims. While the photograph did generate widespread sympathy and draw attention to Depression-era poverty—potentially serving broader social interests—Thompson's family later emphasized that they personally received no tangible benefits or assistance from the image's fame and circulation. This rupture between societal impact and personal benefit calls attention to the ethics of documentary representation, where images might simultaneously advocate for a group while potentially exploiting specific individuals.

This emphasis on the dynamic between photojournalist and photographic subjects is also evident in Mary Ellen Mark's award-winning reportage on child prostitutes in India. Mark notes that her acquaintance with the "transvestites" was facilitated by their "exhibitionistic" tendencies: "*seduced* by the sight of me pacing up and down with my camera, they ultimately came out and asked to be photographed."[28] Though this characterization risks reducing complex gender identities to performative behavior, it acknowledges their agency in initiating photographic encounter as a mutual "seduction."

Mark's documentation of Bombay's sex workers complicates standard narratives of documentary practice. While she presents her gradual acceptance by the community in terms of mutual "seduction" and eventual sisterhood, we should examine these claims carefully. Her statement that the transgender sex workers were "*seduced* by the sight of me pacing up and down with my camera" reveals

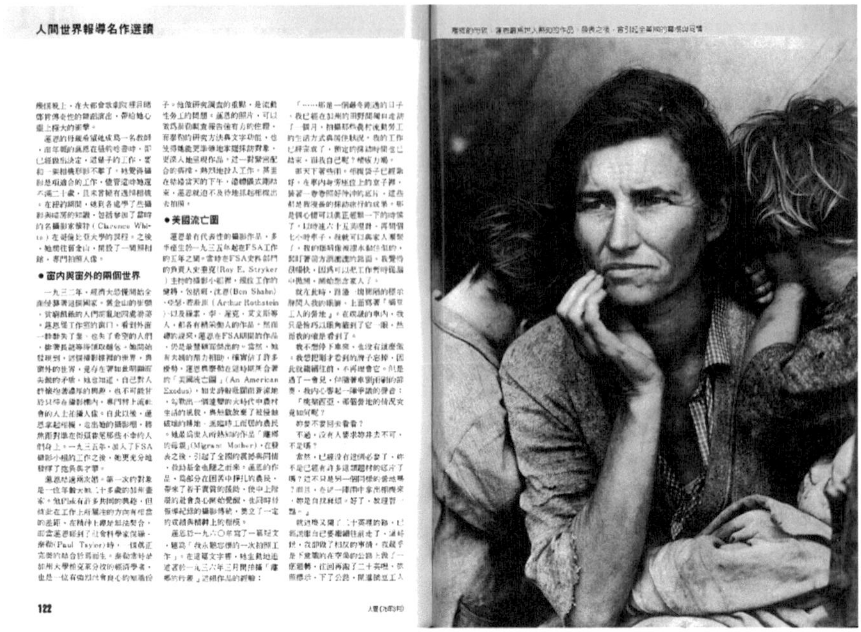

Fig. 5.3. Dorothea Lange's "Migrant Mother" as featured in *Ren Jian* (1986).

lingering orientalist tropes even as it attempts to grant them agency. Her account of developing intimacy with a madam deserves similar scrutiny:

> Saroja never asked me anything personal. No one did. They wanted to know only my age, why I didn't wear a brassiere, and why I *wasn't married*. I think the reason I was finally accepted was that *I was single—alone in the world like they were*. One madam told me, "We are sisters. You and I are fated for the same life. Every night I say my prayers and I sleep alone."[29]

This interaction markedly differs from Lange's encounter with Thompson, though not in the way previously understood. Where Lange's staged portraits and later mythmaking obscured the real power dynamics at play, Mark's subjects actively shaped the terms of their documentation, transforming the photographer-subject relationship. Her relationship with the madam—a former sex worker now managing others—exemplifies this complexity. Despite their mutual understanding, the subject refrains from prying into the photojournalist's personal life. Their connection is portrayed as a gradual mutual recognition of shared loneliness, even though their singlehood significantly differs. This marks a rare moment where the photographer comes closest to revealing as much of her own private life as her subject's.

The contrast between *Ren Jian*'s editorial approach and that of international photographers illuminates a fundamental tension in documentary practice. Where Chen's perspective tended to cast subjects as victims requiring sympathy, photojournalists like Mark cultivated more reciprocal relationships with their subjects. However, Lange's coverage of Thompson shows how even apparently sympathetic documentation could perpetuate forms of objectification, particularly when shaped by institutional demands and preconceptions. Their works demonstrate how photographic subjects could actively engage with the photographer to shape their own representation, often displaying sophisticated understanding of the power of photography to help their cause. This nuanced approach moves beyond simple documentation toward a collaborative practice where both photographer and subject participate in creating meaning. Through their rejection of purely pathological frameworks, these photographers pioneered methods that acknowledged the full humanity of their subjects, establishing documentary photography as a medium of exchange rather than mere observation.

Sisterhood in Documentary Practice

The contrast between international and local approaches to documenting sex work illuminates deeper tensions within *Ren Jian*'s photojournalistic practice. While foreign photojournalists like Mark established intimate connections with their subjects, *Ren Jian*'s own coverage displays divisions along gender lines. Female reporters brought personal, intimate perspectives to sensitive topics, while their male colleagues favored broader sociopolitical narratives.

This divergence is most salient in *Ren Jian*'s coverage of child prostitution in 1980s Taipei, where rural girls were trafficked into urban sex work. As this phenomenon surfaced as a crucial human rights concern, Tseng Shumei's groundbreaking March 1987 reportage offered one of the earliest full-length accounts that refrained from sensationalizing the plight of the girls. Her assignment to the red-light district itself embodies a gendered aspect: The magazine's editors considered her, as one of their few female journalists, to be better suited to approach young trafficking victims. Looking back in a recent interview, Tseng reflected on the gendered dynamics within the *Ren Jian* workplace:

> I felt like *Ren Jian* was quite a *masculine* group. Men liked to deal with impactful, contentious events, like the Tang Ying-shen incident. Hearing the stories beside them, I was of course deeply shaken and moved, but found it hard to discuss the details with them.[30]

Here, Tseng explicitly foregrounds her female identity and distinguishes it from the predominantly male *Ren Jian* photojournalists' image. Her testimony offers a valuable window into *Ren Jian*'s gendered dynamics, complicating our understanding of the magazine's documentary practice. While previous accounts presented the magazine's documentary practice as a gender-neutral process, her perspective explores its "masculine" aspect. According to Tseng, this male-dominant atmosphere manifested in a peculiar ideology of purity:

> A highly idealistic group would compete internally over some notion of purity (*chuncuixing*). If one came off as less than pure, she would be consciously or unconsciously criticized. Back then, I was like a little girl who wasn't too serious and just wanted to be romantically involved, and was probably hurt a bit as a result.[31]

Yet what Tseng frames as a gender division might also represent competing but complementary approaches to documentary practice. This remark further parallels the previously established gender dichotomy with different value systems: In Tseng's relatively binary (self-)understanding, female reporters tend to be more emotional, while her male colleagues' emotions were encompassed by loftier ideals. Her ability to forge intimate connections with trafficking victims, while shaped by gender, contributed essential depth to the magazine's coverage. Though Tseng's gender granted her unique access to trafficking victims, her work was thoroughly mediated by men: She was paired with male writer Chung Chun-sheng, her work was filtered through male photographers' lenses, and it was framed by Chen Yingzhen's editorial introduction. Chang Shih-lun's observation about the magazine's monolithic collective identity takes on fresh significance through this lens. This gendered structure adds a new dimension to *Ren Jian*'s "stoic heroism." What was presented as universal professional ethic now appears to be distinctly masculine.

Placed at the beginning of the March 1987 issue, Tseng's reportage opens with the accusation that prostitution is a form of slavery, under the title "Child Prostitutes: A Record of the Slaves' Plea to Heaven." Chinese readers could immediately identify the title as an allusion to late Qing writer Lin Shu's translation of *Uncle Tom's Cabin* as *A Record of the Slaves' Plea to Heaven* (Heinu yü tian lu), which emphasizes Uncle Tom's identity as a slave. This literary allusion frames child prostitution as a form of modern slavery, a comparison the prologue makes explicit:

> Within Taiwan's civilized, developed, and prosperous façade lurks a new, miserable slavery system: the slavery system of indigenous child prostitution. Girls as young as eleven, twelve, thirteen . . . are thrown into that cannibalistic purgatory[. . . .] The existence of child prostitution slavery stands as our greatest shame, an indictment of the Chinese people in Taiwan and our most unforgivable crime![32]

The following pages proceed to anatomize how underage indigenous girls, marginalized in Han-dominated Taiwanese society, became commodities in an increasingly mercantile society.[33] The sociologically minded analysis stands in sharp contrast to Mark's intimate narrative in *Falkland Road*. Where Mark begins candidly with personal encounters—her initial hostility from the Bombay brothels and her gradual acceptance by local sex workers—*Ren Jian* opens with systematic critique. Six pages of sociological analysis dissect the commodification of young girls as menial labor, expose trafficking networks, and indict structural discrimination against indigenous communities.

Despite her central role in the coverage, Tseng Shu-mei describes a complex editorial process:

> When [Chen Yingzhen] was revising our articles, he wouldn't change the specific details of our stories. Instead, he might try to reframe the story in terms of theoretical issues. For example, we could find a critique of the slavery system in the opening paragraph of this report. This is definitely his work. The critical perspective that Chen used as an introductory remark gives a better focus to the story, underpinning its narrative with sociological concerns.[34]

This editorial pattern points to a distinctive split in *Ren Jian*'s approach: While its "world-renowned photojournalism" section foregrounded photojournalists' personal experiences, local coverage opened with sweeping political-economic analysis. This divergence served multiple purposes. The international profiles established models of "heroic" photojournalism for local emulation, while the theoretical framing of domestic stories positioned them within larger social movements. The child prostitution coverage exemplifies this duality: Tseng's intimate reporting becomes a systematic critique through

Chen's lens. This synthesis reflects *Ren Jian*'s larger project: combining documentary intimacy with rigorous social analysis to create a distinctive form of engaged photojournalism.

The visual strategies of *Ren Jian*'s child prostitution coverage sharply diverge from Mark's Bombay work. Where Mark employs full color, *Ren Jian*'s black-and-white images suggest furtive documentation in dimly lit corridors. The photographs create a stark dialectic: shadowed bodies but clearly identifiable visages, intimacy forced by the narrow spaces, yet distance maintained by iron bars. These bars, present in both Mark's and *Ren Jian*'s images, serve as powerful metaphors for confinement, though the latter framing emphasizes systematic imprisonment over individual stories. The photo sequence builds from these claustrophobic portraits to a broader context: nocturnal shots of Taipei's Huaxi Street red-light district, culminating in images of public protests against child trafficking.

This visual progression mirrors the magazine's editorial stance. Where Mark cultivated intimate bonds with her subjects, particularly the madam, *Ren Jian* initially tried to maintain critical distance. While Mark's sisterhood with the madam is touching, it somewhat downplays prostitution as an oppressive institution. *Ren Jian* intends to maintain its critical force and hence does not foreground the presence of its own journalists and photographers. Only in the final moments of each interview do we catch a glimpse of their interaction.

After the opening sociological analysis, the report is followed by six testimonies from teenage victims (with the interviewees' names altered). Their accounts of being sold or coerced into prostitution by family members and strangers illuminates the cruel intersection of poverty, lack of education, and indigenous marginalization. While the photographers and journalists remain in the background, the girls' voices pierce through in moments of direct address. Their questions to Tseng become questions to society: "I don't know where I can hide. Do you know how to protect me?" "I don't know what I can do after leaving the women's employment training center?" "Can you buy me some chocolates the next time you visit me?" and "Do you want to see my child?"[35] These second-person addresses transform journalistic distance into interpellative human connection. Despite the lack of emphasis on the journalists and photographers who covered the child prostitution report, the powerful voices of the interviewed child prostitutes themselves speak volumes. These questions are a call to action, urging readers to not only read and listen but to take steps to protect and support these vulnerable members of society.

This coverage crystallizes larger patterns in *Ren Jian*'s documentary practice. The tension between intimate documentation and systemic critique played out differently across gender lines. While the magazine's male editors privileged broad social analysis, women documentarians like Mark and Tseng often sought more nuanced engagements with their subjects. The myth of Lange's "equality" with Thompson actually reveals how institutional frameworks could co-opt and reshape even female photographers' work. Yet perhaps these very tensions—between intimacy and analysis, between institutional demands and personal connection—gave *Ren Jian* its distinctive character as a documentary project.

Legacy of a Documentary Revolution

While *Ren Jian*'s local activism was widely seen as its most prominent contribution, this chapter argues that the international section was equally important and reinforced the local sections. At a time when the concept of photojournalism was still unfamiliar, *Ren Jian* introduced a series of photojournalists through its "Selected Works by World-Renowned Photojournalists," which traced the genealogy of photojournalists to the Farm Security Administration and Magnum. This connection served multiple purposes: It set an ethical ideal for professional photojournalists for *Ren Jian*'s own crew while awakening early post-martial-law Taiwan to possibilities of social critique through images.

Central to this ideal was what I term "stoic heroism," embodied by the personal experiences of W. Eugene Smith. The narrative of photojournalists who endured harassment or even brutality but persevered in their mission of documenting injustice became more than inspiration—the ideal was celebrated by a generation of Taiwanese documentarians emerging from *Ren Jian*. This emphasis on photojournalistic identity marked a theoretical shift, positioning the photographer's role as crucial to the relationship between camera and subject.

The magazine's influence persisted long after its closure. Former *Ren Jian* employees went on to become accomplished photojournalists in their own right. Guan Xiaorong, who had already published a series of photographs about indigenous rural-to-urban migration before joining the team, later compiled into a book his *Ren Jian* reportage on the exploited indigenous people of Orchid Island. Likewise, Tsai Ming-te's (Cai Mingde's) works were collected into a stand-alone album. Ruan Yizhong contributed sketches (*suxie*) (with photography but not reportage) and later founded *Photographers International*. Many of these photographers also held their own special exhibitions while maintaining a "family" resemblance—black-and-white photography that focuses on underprivileged people—that could be traced back to their time at *Ren Jian*. In a sense, they were refashioning themselves in a way similar to how *Ren Jian*'s world-renowned photojournalism section had depicted Mitome, Smith, and Lange—as heroic but alienated loners, highlighting the continuity of *Ren Jian*'s legacy in shaping the professional identity of photojournalists.

Yet *Ren Jian*'s legacy resists simple categorization. While often viewed as a uniform, if not anonymized, collective, the magazine fostered diverse approaches to documentary practice. Gender dynamics proved particularly significant: Though male perspectives dominated institutional structures, female journalists like Tseng brought essential perspectives and methods to the magazine's coverage. Understanding *Ren Jian* requires acknowledging both its unifying vision and the varied voices that gave that vision life.

GLOSSARY

baodao sheying 報導攝影
baodao wenxue 報導文學
Chen Ying-ho 陳映和
chuncuixing 純粹性
Heinu yü tian lu 黑奴籲天錄
Higuchi Kenji 樋口健二
Mitome Tadao 三留理男
ningen 人間
Ren Jian 人間
rendao pinzhi 人道品質
Renjian shijie baodao mingzuo xuandu 人間世界報導名作選讀
Ruan Yizhong 阮義忠
suxie 速寫
Tang Yingshen 湯英伸
Tsai Ming-te (Cai Mingde) 蔡明德
Tseng Shu-mei (Zeng Shumei) 曾淑美
Xia chao 夏潮
zuo tong 左統

ACKNOWLEDGMENTS

Part of the chapter was presented at the Photography as Knowledge (Re-)Production in Twentieth-Century East Asia conference, held at the University of Heidelberg in 2022. I would like to thank the participants for their insightful suggestions. Shu-mei Lin, Leo Chu, Lillian Tsay, and Chung-wei Yang kindly read an earlier version of the chapter. I am also indebted to Li Guo and Charles Laughlin for their invitation for submission, and to the two anonymous reviewers for their comments.

NOTES

1. Chen Yingzhen, "Yinwei women xiangxin, women xiwang, women ai . . ." [Because we believe, we hope, we love . . .], *Ren Jian* 1 (1985): 2; italics in original.

2. For the latest exploration of the relationship between capitalism and photography, see Kevin Coleman and Daniel James, eds., *Capitalism and the Camera: Essays on Photography and Extraction* (New York: Verso, 2021).

3. See for instance Chen's own account in Chen Yingzhen, untitled, *Lianhe bao*, December 1, 1999, 14, where he explicitly acknowledges the financial support provided by his brother Chen Ying-ho (Chen Yinghe).

4. Chen Mingcheng, *Chen Yingzhen xianxiang: guanyü Chen Yingzhen de jiazu shuxie ji qi guozu rentong* [The Chen Yingzhen phenomenon: Chen Yingzhen's family writing and his national identification] (Taipei: Qianwei, 2013), 308–34.

5. Guan Xiaorong, "Xiangnian da Chen, zaixian *Ren Jian*" [Remembering Old Chen, representing *Ren Jian*], in *Renjian fengjing Chen Yingzhen*, ed. Feng Deping (Taipei: Wenxun, 2009), 250.

6. Julianne H. Newton, *Burden of Visual Truth: The Role of Photojournalism in Mediating Reality* (New York: Routledge, 2012).

7. Quoted in Lin Qiyang, *Zhaojian renjian buping—Taiwan baodao wenxue shilun* [*Shedding light on inequality of the human world—on the history of reportage in Taiwan*] (Tainan: Guoli Taiwan wenxue guan, 2013), 121.

8. Lin, *Zhaojian*, 123.

9. Liu Yi-chieh, "*Ren Jian* zazhi yanjiu" [A study on *Ren Jian* magazine] (master's thesis, Soochow University, 2000); Lin, *Zhaojian*; Zhong Qiao, *Huidao renjian de xianchang* [*Returning to the Scenes of the Human World*] (Taipei: Shibao, 1990): 306.

10. Sara Blair and Eric M. Rosenberg, *Trauma and Documentary Photography of the FSA* (Berkeley: University of California Press, 2012).

11. Nadya Bair, *The Decisive Network: Magnum Photos and the Postwar Image Market* (Oakland: University of California Press, 2020), 47.

12. Bair, *The Decisive Network*, 6.

13. Jiang Huaisheng, photography by Mitome Tadao, "Ji'e: laizi Yisuobiya de jinji baogao" [Hunger: an emergent report from Ethiopia], *Ren Jian* 1 (1985): 110.

14. Chen Yingzhen, "Yinwei women xiangxin, women xiwang, women ai . . ." [Because we believe, we hope, we love . . .], *Ren Jian* 1 (1985).

15. Karin E. Becker, "Photojournalism and the Tabloid Press," in *The Photography Reader*, ed. Liz Wells (Abingdon: Routledge 2003), 303.

16. W. Eugene Smith, "Youjin Shimisi he tade 'Shuiyü bing' baodao," [Eugene Smith and his Minamata report], trans. Liu Zongpu, *Ren Jian* 7 (1986): 120; my italics.

17. Smith, "Youjin Shimisi," 124.

18. Smith, "Youjin Shimisi," 126.

19. Zhong, *Huidao renjian de xianchang*, 311.

20. Smith, "Youjin Shimisi," 130.

21. Eugene Smith, "W. Eugene Smith," in *Dialogue with Photography*, interviewed by Paul Hill and Tom Cooper (Manchester: Cornerhouse, 1979).

22. Mary Ellen Mark, *Falkland Road: Prostitutes of Bombay* (New York: Alfred A. Knopf, 1981), 11–12; Mary Ellen Mark, "Mengmai jinü" [Prostitutes of Bombay], trans. Song Biyun, *Ren Jian* 9 (July 1986), 138.

23. Mark, *Falkland Road*, 12; Mark, "Mengmai jinü," 138.

24. Chen Yingzhen, "Fulu: Chen Yingzhen fangwen gao" [Appendix: interview with Chen Yingzhen], interview by Liu Yi-chieh, "*Ren Jian*," 107–8; my emphasis.

25. Kuo Li-hsin, "Lixiang de muqin: Taolexiya Lian'en yü ta de sheying guan" [Migrant mother: Dorothea Lange and her ideas of photography], *Ren Jian* 5 (1986): 120.

26. Dorothea Lange, "The Assignment I'll Never Forget," in *Illuminations: Women Writing on Photography from the 1850s to the Present*, ed. Liz Heron and Val Williams, 152 (London: I. B. Tauris, 1996 [1960]); my emphasis.

27. Lennard J. Davis, "Migrant Mother: Dorothea Lange and the Truth of Photography," *Los Angeles Review of Books*, March 4, 2020, https://lareviewofbooks.org/article/migrant-mother-dorothea-lange-truth-photography/. I thank Jiaqi Yao for directing me to this article.

28. Mark, *Falkland Road*, 13; Mark, "Mengmai jinü," 139, my emphasis.

29. Mark, *Falkland Road*, 17; Mark, "Mengmai jinü," 143, my emphasis.

30. Chang Tzu-wu, "A Return to the Human World: Chen Yingzhen's Utopia and Four Ren Jian Journalists," trans. Po-hsi Chen, in *Taiwan Gazette*, February 23, 2022, https://www.taiwangazette.org/news/2022/2/20/a-return-to-the-human-world-chen-yingzhens-utopia-and-four-ren-jian-journalists (my emphasis).

31. Chang, "A Return to the Human World."

32. Tseng and Chun-sheng, "Chuji nuli yü tian lu: Taiwan chuji de xuelei zhengyan" [Child prostitutes' plea to heaven: testimonies of child prostitutes in Taiwan in blood and tears], *Ren Jian* 17 (1987): 8. The introductory remarks are credited to Ji Kunquan 紀昆泉, arguably Chen Yingzhen's pseudonym.

33. Tseng and Chun-sheng, "Chuji nuli," 10–11.

34. Chang, "A Return to the Human World."

35. Tseng and Chun-sheng, "Chuji nuli," 15–21.

REFERENCES

Bair, Nadya. *The Decisive Network: Magnum Photos and the Postwar Image Market*. Oakland: University of California Press, 2020.

Becker, Karin E. "Photojournalism and the Tabloid Press." In *The Photography Reader*, edited by Liz Wells, 291–308. Abingdon: Routledge, 2003.

Blair, Sara, and Eric M. Rosenberg. *Trauma and Documentary Photography of the FSA*. Berkeley: University of California Press, 2012.

Chang, Shih-lun 張世倫. *Xianshi de tanqiu: Taiwan sheying shi xinggou kao* 現實的探求：台灣攝影史形構考 [*The search for reality: An investigation into the history of photography in Taiwan*]. Taipei: Yingyan she, 2021.

Chang, Tzu-wu. "A Return to the Human World: Chen Yingzhen's Utopia and Four Ren

Jian Journalists." Trans. Po-hsi Chen. *Taiwan Gazette*, February 23, 2022. https://www.taiwangazette.org/news/2022/2/20/a-return-to-the-human-world-chen-yingzhens-utopia-and-four-ren-jian-journalists

Chen Mingcheng 陳明成. *Chen Yingzhen xianxiang: guanyü Chen Yingzhen de jiazu shuxie ji qi guozu rentong* [The Chen Yingzhen phenomenon: Chen Yingzhen's family writing and his national identification]. Taipei: Qianwei, 2013.

Chen Yingzhen 陳映真. "Yinwei women xiangxin, women xiwang, women ai . . ." 因為我們相信、我們希望、我們愛…… [Because we believe, we hope, we love . . .]. *Ren Jian* 1 (1985): 2–3.

Chen Yingzhen 陳映真. Untitled. *Lianhe bao* 聯合報, December 1, 1999, 14.

Chen Yingzhen 陳映真. "Fulu: Chen Yingzhen fangwen gao" 附錄：陳映真訪問稿 [Appendix: interview with Chen Yingzhen]. Interview by Liu Yi-chieh [Liu Yijie] 劉依潔. "*Ren Jian* zazhi yanjiu" 《人間》雜誌研究 [A study on *Ren Jian* magazine]. Master's thesis, 104–15. Department of Chinese, Soochow University, 2000.

Davis, Lennard J. "Migrant Mother: Dorothea Lange and the Truth of Photography." *Los Angeles Review of Books*, March 4, 2020. https://lareviewofbooks.org/article/migrant-mother-dorothea-lange-truth-photography/

Guan Xiaorong 關曉榮. "Xiangnian da Chen, zaixian *Ren Jian*" 想念大陳、再現《人間》 [Remembering Old Chen, representing *Ren Jian*]. In *Renjian fengjing Chen Yingzhen* 人間風景·陳映真, edited by Feng Deping 封德屏, 248–54. Taipei: Wenxun, 2009.

Jiang Huaisheng 江淮生. Photography by Mitome Tadao. "Ji'e: laizi Yisuobiya de jinji baogao" 飢餓：來自衣索比亞的緊急報告 [Hunger: an emergent report from Ethiopia]. *Ren Jian* 1 (1985): 110–21.

Kuo, Li-hsin 郭力昕. "Lixiang de muqin: Taolexiya Lian'en yü ta de sheying guan" 離鄉的母親：桃樂西亞·蓮恩與她的攝影觀 [Migrant mother: Dorothea Lange and her ideas of photography]. *Ren Jian* 5 (1986): 116–28.

Kuo, Li-hsin 郭力昕. "Politicising Documentary Photography: *Ren Jian* and Guan Xiao-Rong in late 1980s Taiwan." *Javnost—The Public* 14, no. 3 (2007): 49–64.

Lange, Dorothea. "The Assignment I'll Never Forget." In *Illuminations: Women Writing on Photography from the 1850s to the Present*, edited by Liz Heron and Val Williams, 151–53. London: I. B. Tauris, 1996 [1960].

Lin Qiyang 林淇瀁. *Zhaojian renjian buping—Taiwan baodao wenxue shilun* 照見人間不平——台灣報導文學史論 [*Shedding light on inequality of the human world—on the history of reportage in Taiwan*]. Tainan: Guoli Taiwan wenxue guan, 2013.

Liu Yi-chieh [Liu Yijie] 劉依潔. "*Ren Jian* zazhi yanjiu" 《人間》雜誌研究 [A study on *Ren Jian* magazine]. Master's thesis, Soochow University, 2000.

Mark, Mary Ellen. *Falkland Road: Prostitutes of Bombay*. New York: Alfred A. Knopf, 1981.

Mark, Mary Ellen. "Mengmai jinü" 孟買妓女 [Prostitutes of Bombay]. Trans. Song Biyun 宋碧雲. *Ren Jian* 9 (July 1986): 132–44.

Newton, Julianne H. *Burden of Visual Truth: The Role of Photojournalism in Mediating Reality*. New York: Routledge, 2012.

Smith, W. Eugene. "W. Eugene Smith." In *Dialogue with Photography*, interviewed by Paul Hill and Tom Cooper, 200–220. Manchester: Cornerhouse, 1979.

Smith, W. Eugene. "Youjin Shimisi he tade 'Shuiyü bing' baodao" 尤金·史密斯和他的「水俣病」報導 [Eugene Smith and his Minamata report]. Trans. Liu Zongpu 劉宗圃. *Ren Jian* 7 (1986): 120–29.

Smith, W. Eugene. "Yingxiong de beihou: Youjin Shimisi tan 'Shuiyü' zhuanji" [Behind the hero: Eugene Smith on Minamata]. Interviewed by Paul Hill and Tom Cooper. Trans. Yuan Yaoyao 袁瑤瑤 and Ruan Yizhong 阮義忠. *Ren Jian* 7 (1986): 130–34.

Tseng Shu-mei [Zeng Shumei 曾淑美] and Chung Chun-sheng [Zhong Junsheng 俊陞]. "Chuji nuli yü tian lu: Taiwan chuji de xuelei zhengyan" 雛妓奴隸籲天錄：台灣雛妓的血淚證言 [Child prostitutes' plea to heaven: testimonies of child prostitutes in Taiwan in blood and tears]. *Ren Jian* 17 (1987): 8–23.

Zhong Qiao 鍾喬. *Huidao renjian de xianchang* 回到人間的現場 [*Returning to the scenes of the human world*]. Taipei: Shibao, 1990.

SIX

Reportage, Photography, and the Ekphrastic Encounter

On Moon Children *by Liao Chia-chan and Yan Hsin-chu*

Li Guo

Reflecting reportage across diverse artistic forms, this study explores three short reportage essays on people with disability by Liao Chia-chan 廖嘉展, published in the magazine *Ren Jian* 人間 in 1986. The term "moon children" was initially used by people in the San Blas Islands of Panama to refer to people born with albinism, who, rejected by the tribal community because of their physical features and vision defects, were forced to work in the evenings and not allowed to marry. Reportage works by Liao, which included photography by his wife Yan Hsin-chu 顏新珠, transformed this term into a distinctive emblem for people with albinism, and urgently called for public awareness of the social stigma and workplace discrimination against the albinist community, the disabled, and aboriginal peoples in 1980s Taiwan. These works can be considered socially experimental reportage that bridge nonfiction writing and photography and incorporate medical records and legal documents. This chapter explores how Liao and Yan's plurimedial reportage responds to social challenges and government inefficiencies through sustained intervention. Drawing from their photography, field-note sketches, archival sources, and on-site interviews, Liao and Yan's creative work invites an empathetic gaze at the interviewed subjects, with whom they maintained a trustful, participatory interaction. Diverting from *Ren Jian*'s sociopolitical editorial framing, Liao and Yan invite their audiences to consider on a more concrete level the aesthetic and political significance of reportage as an intermedial artistic form and its allied complex forms of spectatorial engagement and responses.

Liao Chia-chan was born in 1962 in Yunlin and graduated with a degree in journalism from Chinese Culture University.[1] In 1986, on editor and writer Kao Hsin-chiang's invitation, he started working for the journal *Ren Jian* as photography editor, interview editor, and associate manager of the press. Yan Hsin-chu was born in 1961 in Luchu, Kaohsiung, and holds a degree in journalism from Chinese Culture University. Interested in "small worlds and little things," Liao and Yan cast their focus of investigation toward people and communities who suffer social stigma because of a certain kind of "disability."[2] Their documentary photography in *Moon Children* recalls socially committed realist photography, which is characterized by a form of "double indexicality" in that the photograph points both to its referent and back to the photographer, thus mediating between the subject and the world.[3] This tension between presentation and representation problematizes the photographer's position and his or her relationship with the interviewee.[4] Compelled to recall his sensory experiences at every scene, Liao emphasizes the notion of *xianchang* ("on-site" experiences)—that is, situatedness built on the photographer's participatory stance.[5] This self-positioning bespeaks a feature of social documentary photography, in that the photographer engages with the complexities of representing the subjects by consciously establishing communications with them.

While Chen Yingzhen, the editor of *Ren Jian*, envisions Liao's and Yan's work as valuable criticisms of the impact of capitalism on urban and quotidian realities, Liao and Yan seek to promote the reportage authors' participatory engagement with firsthand interviews and revive their audiences' extrasensory experiences through artistic endeavors. J. A. W. Heffernan and W. J. H. Mitchell observe that ekphrasis is a "verbal representation of visual representation."[6] Leo Spitzer defines ekphrasis as "a poetic description of a pictorial or sculptural work of art."[7] For Spitzer, ekphrasis is a process of reproduction that transposes artistic forms and makes the objects of art "sensuously perceptible" through "the medium of words."[8] The term is further expanded by Murray Krieger, who suggests that ekphrasis permits readers to "look into the illusionary representation of the unrepresentable" through linguistic representations.[9] For Mitchell, ekphrasis as a poetic mode gives "voice to a mute art object," or offers "a rhetorical description of a work of art."[10] Ekphrasis functions as an aesthetic principle that resorts to varied descriptions that enable readers to visualize people, places, and images in their mind.[11] The poetic mode of ekphrasis transcends the image/text division and cultivates alternative, synthetic forms of aesthetic expressions. Mitchell's approach to ekphrasis bridges the divide between private photography and public photography, allowing the audience to grasp contexts of the interviewees' experiences while allowing them possibilities for interaction and response.

This chapter resituates ekphrasis as an aesthetic mode of expression in plurimedial reportage. The introduction of this volume, alluding to Félix Guattari, argues that ethics in reportage could be reconsidered through an ethico-aesthetic paradigm, which emphasizes the mode of production of a polyphonic subjectivity. Liao and Yan's ekphrastic reportage bespeaks this ethico-aesthetic paradigm, through its illustration of "a processual, creative subjectivity," the theatricalized aspects of subjectivization, and its embrace of affective sociality in human relationships. Liao and Yan's ekphrastic reportage uses image/text dialectics to activate audiences' understandings of interviewees' subjective experiences; it facilitates the translation and exchange of visual and verbal expressions, and explores new ethical strategies and response-abilities in the act of representation. Rather than establishing verbal and visual representations as antithetical paradigms, ekphrasis utilizes "the figure of the image/text to pry open the heterogeneity of media and of specific representations" and "asks what the function of specific forms of heterogeneity might be."[12] The reportage works by Liao and Yan are plurimedial works of this sort, in which the reciprocity and mediation of verbal and visual representations create a triangulated, trans-sensory, and heterogeneous relationship between the authorial self, the visual object/interviewee, and the reportage reader. Liao and Yan's photographic reportage on albinist interviewees such as Chu Sheng-ho, Liao Hong-lin, Li Huan-tien, and the blind and disabled Pig Master Ah Hsu, based on the author's on-site interview and participatory interaction with them, adds interpretative potential to the definition of ekphrasis. For Mitchell, an ekphrastic encounter in language (mostly in writing and print media, such as poetry) relies on the verbal structure of the texts to describe a visual object. Ekphrastic encounter in photography considers the relationship between image and language that takes place in the representations of a visual object via the pictorial medium. Reportage authors' on-site engagement with the interviewees, interpersonal bonds with them, and subjective experiences of photographing and interviewing them expands the notion of "social encounter" for a photographer or writer.[13] As composite art works, plurimedial reportage registers a form of ekphrastic encounter with the socially marginalized subjects. Their dynamic exchanges with the artist/author yield insights on one's ethico-political tactics, the limit of representation, and the complex writerly and readerly response-abilities in making "othered" subjects visible.

Liao and Yan demonstrate how the ethico-aesthetic paradigm in reportage expands our understanding of authorial epistemic anxiety about representing socially "invisible" subjects, and how reportage, by giving authority and power to albinist and disabled people, challenges normative discourses of disability and bodily impairment. As the introduction of this volume observes, reportage's "versatility in comprising plurimedial forms of representations (through nonfiction writing, photography, and film)" grants it power in portraying marginalized groups because of their intersectional positionalities of race, gender, disability, age, and other circumstances. Liao's approach to transcribing visual information in verbal depictions through plurimedial representations invites a reading of his reportage as an ekphrastic process that engages verbal and nonverbal modes of expression. He immerses the reader in reexperiencing the subjects through multidimensional sensory encounters, which could be considered a form of literary ekphrasis. Liao and Yan's emphasis on enlivening on-site sensory experiences facilitates transference between visual and verbal expressions. Ekphrasis activates an empathetic identification with the reported objects and events, and reinscribes images, instants, and events into a collective social memory. Ekphrasis transforms the reporter from a dissociated recorder into an empathetic speaker for the interviewed subjects.

Addressing the camera's function of defining reality as a spectacle or an object of surveillance in a capitalist society, John Berger calls for alternative practices of photography that "put a photograph back into the context of experience, social experience, social memory."[14] Reporters' resilience in immersing themselves in the "nowness" and "situatedness" of an interview's context allows space for photo dynamism and performative interplay between the impassive and the engaged. Liao and Yan's reportage has a plurimedial texture because of their masterful skill in enlivening the portrayals of the site and scenes of the interview. In accounting for local histories and memories, reportage reengages the readers in the site and scene of the time. This allows readers to perceive how the author visualizes objective observations and transforms them into sensory depictions. In this process, empathetic identification occurs. Liao's works often entail multiple layers of narrative and explore the reporter's intrasubjective experiences through his communicative exchanges with the interviewees.[15] Liao and Yan's effort to create reportage grounded on empathetic communications with the interviewees recalls Laughlin's discussion of reportage as a form of "active expression of experience."[16] In Liao and Yan's reportage, the subjective aspect of socially committed reportage is amplified through interview excerpts, documentary photography, and empathetic illustrations of people, events, and their surroundings.

Moon Children as Ekphrastic Reportage

Reportage, according to Shiu Wen-wei 須文蔚 (1966–), is a "literary form that utilizes news reportage to carry out in-depth news and events exploration and interpretation."[17] Shiu traces the forerunner of reportage literature to the "true-to-life literature" (實在的文學) of Yang Kui 楊逵 (1906–1985). Chen Yingzhen reiterates that *Ren Jian*'s engagement with "people's photography and people's reportage" is a response to a time of extreme commercialization and materialism. In this volume, the introduction argues that reportage is "a plurimedial form of aesthetic production" that "engages its audiences in affective ethico-political exchanges with (human or nonhuman) subjects, and promotes audiences' empathetic responses to the democratic appeals of socially marginalized groups whose status, identity, or situation manifests emergent ethical challenges in the society of their time." Po-hsi Chen (chap. 5, this vol.) observes that *Ren Jian* played a seminal role in "documenting and often participating in influential social campaigns during Taiwan's democratization," including participating in local activism and advocating for a transnational left-wing humanitarianism. Charles A. Laughlin (chap. 4, this vol.) proposes that the rise of reportage in Taiwan "helped define an ongoing part of contemporary Taiwan consciousness focused on the cultural dissemination of local actuality in written and visual form." Reportage works by Liao and Yan exemplify a form of social intervention that redeems the value of humanism "by recording the masses' experiences and serving the purpose of social justice."[18]

From 1985 to 1989, *Ren Jian* magazine published many special issues on a wide range of social topics, such as the forty-first anniversary of the Hanaoka Massacre (June 30, 1945) (issue 9), female Filipino domestic workers in Taiwan (issue 12), the protection of Taiwan's Yuanshan prehistoric site (issue 14), and the anniversary of the People Power Revolution in the Philippines in 1986 (issue 16). Each issue covers varied topics through sketches, cover-image reports, featured interviews, and serialized reportage works on covered topics. The reportage works by Liao and Yan in the collection *Moon Children* (1992) first appeared in issues 23 and 24 in *Ren Jian* (1987), as part of the "Series on Human Rights of the Disabled Peoples." The cover of the collection *Moon Children*, featuring a girl with albinism gazing hopefully

Fig. 6.1. Cover of *Moon Children*. (Reprinted by permission of Liao Chia-chan.)

toward a distant off-screen subject, questions the reliability of socially committed photography reportage and its ethico-political obligations. Typically, close-up shots of the aged, ill, and underprivileged expose the hierarchical relation between the photographer/viewer and the subjects under the camera's objectifying lens, or even reinforce unequal relationships between the viewer and the photographed. The cover image, however, disrupts this visual hierarchy by suggesting alternative spectatorial engagement and highlights a precious moment of "nowness." This moment enables heightened perception of the subject, and an urgent empathetic response to the photographed child from both the off-screen photographer and viewers of the image. The iconic image of the smiling child and her hopeful gaze invite an interpretative response *and* inquisitive scrutiny from the audience about the uncertain future of Taiwan's albinist community.

Liao and Yan's collection contains twelve short reportage writings on topics including blindness, albinism, environmental emergency, "imported brides" in remote villages, and declining aboriginal tribes. Differing from traditional long-form reportage, *Moon Children* comprises condensed individual pieces and plurimedial illustrations of the reportage subjects. In the collection, two opening pieces on people with albinism each begin with an evocative prologue, as follows:

> *Moon Children*
>
> The Indian tribes call people with albinism "Moon Children."
> Medical records indicate that those with albinism are not different from ordinary people.
> Yet what are their real situations like in our society?
> Those with albinism are still suffering from stigma and prejudice.
> Please help them step out of their pallid lives. It is not sympathy that they seek
> But rather a fair chance.[19]
>
> *Do Not Let That Child Lose Hope: A Sad Song for the "White Crane Child" Chu Shen-ho*
>
> Bronze hair, pale skin, underneath which pink blood veins are visible.
> Amid a people of yellow skin and black hair, he looks like an alien.
> Chu Shen-ho blinked those eyes of his that are afraid of sunlight, and endured prejudice, fear and frustrations
> These born agonies will torture him for the rest of his life,
> Until one day he cried out bravely, "I am also human!"[20]

These two prologues deploy the poetic mode of ekphrasis, transcribing the albinist interviewees' presences into verbal depictions, and contesting the social perceptions of people with albinism and their often misread "visibility." Ekphrasis as an intermedial mode of expression demonstrates the need to rethink "visibility" and its engrained preconceptions as a social construct, when it comes to ethically representing socially vulnerable and marginalized groups. As these prologues display, ekphrasis transcends the paradigms of visual representation and its epistemological constraints; it invites readers to have synesthetic encounters with the interviewees or even allows the interviewed subjects to speak for themselves. Whereas the first prologue projects a reporter's voice speaking *for* the subjects, the second prologue, in a more creative style, foregrounds the voice of the interviewee Chu Shen-ho himself. Chu's expressive nickname "White Crane Child" highlights his sociopolitical vulnerability: his heightened visibility to others dispossesses him of his humanness, reducing him to an alien kind. In "A Sad Song for the 'White Crane Child' Chu Shen-ho," the author describes his first meeting with Chu:

> Indeed, the first time I met Chu Shen-ho, his unusual appearance deeply stunned me. Whenever meeting sunlight, his eyes would ceaselessly roll. His fair complexion set off the minute blood veins underneath, which are like red threads, making the veins even more discernible. When I gazed with some puzzlement at his light brown hair, and a few threads of white hair in the midst, as if seeing through my bewilderment, he explained with shyness, "A young man with white hair is too eye-catching. I dyed my hair to reduce unwanted attention."[21]

In a strongly ekphrastic account, Liao describes meeting Chu, using textual and visual elements to evoke readers' perceptions. This textual moment is ekphrastic in using "visual language" from the author's viewpoint to inscribe Chu through figurative description as if viewing a painting. Yet Chu's response to this embedded gaze (of the first-person narrator and the reader) explains his choosing to dye his hair to resist being perceived only in terms of his albinism. This is a moment of ekphrastic encounter in reportage, when the interviewed subject questions the politics of inscription and displays a desire to resist and reconfigure the regime of representation. The ekphrastic process is saturated with epistemic anxiety as it explores the interplay between the risks of gazing and the social invisibility of the interviewed. Chu's response to the interviewer's perplexed gaze reveals the diverse levels of gazing experienced by people with albinism when they are subjected to social attention and are aware that they may encounter possible stigmatization and objectification. The text's description of the photographer's uneasiness while gazing at Chu recalls what Mitchell calls "ekphrastic fear."[22] For Mitchell, ekphrastic fear occurs when preserving "the differences between the verbal and visual mediations becomes a moral, aesthetic imperative."[23] Ekphrastic fear entails a moral anxiety around remediating the real from one medium into another, and a skepticism regarding the representability of underprivileged subjects, whose "visibility" must be achieved with inevitable sacrifices of dignity, privacy, and self-esteem.

Chu Shen-ho graduated with a degree in economics from Tamkang University before he passed the employee's entrance exam of the Farmers' Association in Alian 阿蓮 District and worked there as an accountant.[24] Seven months later, Chu was fired on the pretext that he had "innate visual impairment" and as a result was ineffective in daily work management (because he had to use an magnifying lens with his left hand while working with his right hand). This shocked Chu and his family, including his third sister (a graduate from a business college) and his youngest brother (a student in Tainan Business College), who are all albinist. Chu's mother, whose children have been called "white-hair kids" (白毛仔), worked tirelessly to support her children, and talks of them with pride: "Even though my children have albinism, every one of them is kindhearted, hardworking, and behaves well (unlike some other young men). They are all optimistic, and talented in playing guitar and singing."[25] Mrs. Chu's candid interview conveys the earnestness of her voice, affirming the truthfulness of the account of Chu Shen-ho's unfortunate experiences. The mother's account is juxtaposed with a photo of the four siblings at the Chu's, taken by Liao himself (fig. 6.2).

In ekphrastic reportage, photography is not an isolated pictorial medium separated from verbal expressions, and photographs in plurimedial reportage should not be treated as singular samples of image/texts. Rather, as displayed in this example, the photograph of the Chu siblings, together with Mrs. Chu's account of her children being treated as "white-hair kids," constitute the reportage's heterogeneous form in seeking a holistic representation of interviewed subjects beyond the boundary of language and vision. The interplay between different media of representation not only operates between the captions and images, it comprises a complex process in which textual and visual mediations evoke, substitute, or even reshape each other in the reportage as a whole. In this photo, the gazes of the Chu siblings meet the camera (positioned on the lower left) at eye level. A serene light shines on them from the top left, creating layers of visual presentations of the photographed. The two elder brothers (Chu Shen-ho is on the left) are seated in the front row, gaz-

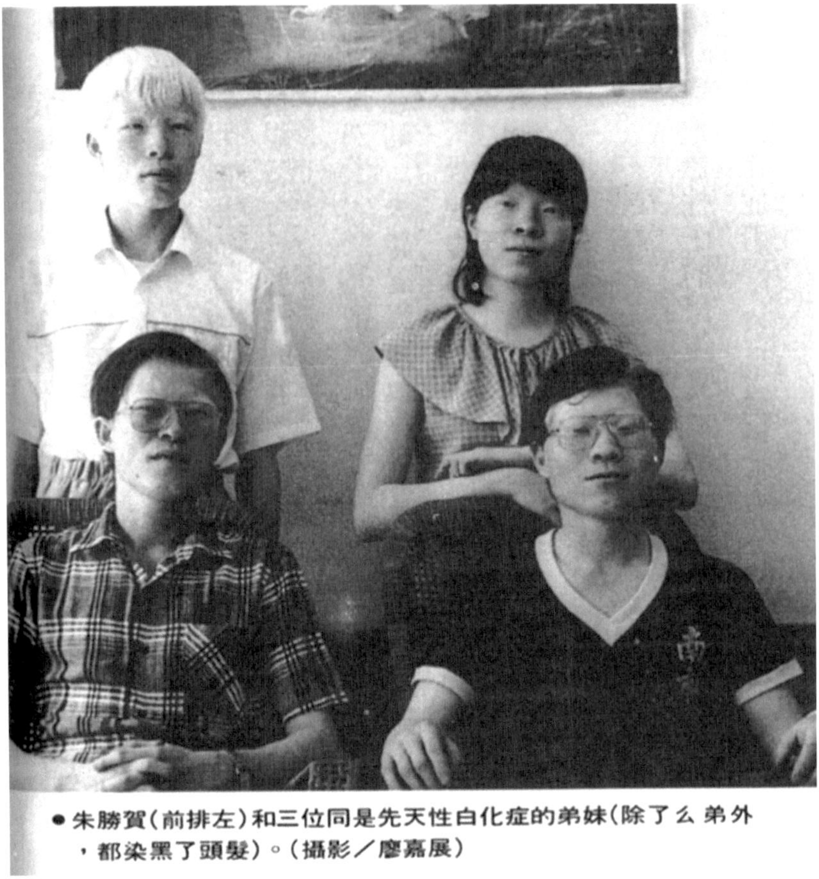

Fig. 6.2. The Chu siblings. (Reprinted by permission of Liao Chia-chan.)

ing at the camera amiably, while the younger brother and sister stand behind. Chu's gaze is trustful, but also has a weathered look; his brother on the right appears warm and cheerful. In the second row, the sister looks solemnly at the camera, while the youngest brother looks confidently to the right, not at the camera's lens. His natural white hair stands out among his siblings, who all dyed their hair black.

The photo's caption provides a framework emphasizing the visual differences in the siblings' hair. Further, the photograph registers *multiple layers of ekphrastic encounter* in the reportage, including the reportage author/photographer's on-site act of photographing the interviewees; his or her textual representation of the experience through narration and description; the reader's

Fig. 6.3. Chu and his youngest brother playing *erhu* and flute. (Reprinted by permission of Liao Chia-chan.)

encounter with the interviewed subjects by working through heterogeneous visual and verbal media, including the photo as a composite form of representation; and the reportage author/narrator's descriptions of the subjects and his re-memory of his subjective encounter with them through language and vision. This family photograph provides the context of the interviewees with albinism as sons and daughters with heterogenous experiences. The camera captures an atmospheric encounter between Liao and the Chu family members, as if allowing each to share a story of their own. Another photograph by Liao shows a leisurely moment of Chu and his youngest brother playing *erhu* and flute together (fig. 6.3). Despite their differences in visual composition and framing, both photographs demonstrate the dynamism and performativity of the photographed, with the photographer positioned as an engaged audience.

Two additional photographs capture scenes of Chu's life after he was dismissed from work. Shown in figure 6.4, Chu helps with harvest work in a fruit garden. During his dispute with the Farmers' Association's decision, Chu fell ill. His mother prepared him some ginger soup to help him recover

● 被解僱後的朱勝賀到果園幫忙採收梨子（爲避免對釋迦佛的不敬，南部人稱釋迦爲梨子）。（攝影／顏新珠）

Fig. 6.4. Chu helping with harvest work in a local fruit garden. (Reprinted by permission of Yan Hsin-chu.)

(fig. 6.5). Both photographs emphasize the photographer's engagement with Chu's struggles at the time and highlight a sense of "nowness." These images highlight photography as social documents by exposing Chu's suffering, and encourage the public to intervene to end the misfortunes of those in similar struggles. These two later photographs present a compelling sense of urgency and provide a concrete social context for Chu's struggles. In figures 6.4 and 6.5, the photographed subjects are looking down and away from the camera; the distance between the photographer and Chu and his mother, and Chu's and his mother's discernable silence, magnify the photographer's position as that of an external witness of Chu's suffering and resistance against injustice. In figure 6.5, the camera transforms a moment of shared silence between mother and son through its sympathetic gaze, presenting the voicelessness of Chu and his mother to the reader. Given that reportage registers a form of social encounter with the disenfranchised, these two photos reflect what Mitchell identifies as two fundamental epistemic questions about ekphrastic expression: "What lies beyond representation?" and "What is our responsibility toward it?"[26] The

● 在抗爭期間，不堪勞累的朱勝賀感冒了，朱媽媽熬半瓢的薑湯給他喝。（攝影／廖嘉展）

Fig. 6.5. While disputing the Farmers' Association's decision, Chu fell ill. His mother prepared some ginger soup to help him recover. (Reprinted by permission of Liao Chia-chan.)

contested relationship between representation and responsibility in ekphrastic reportage embodies the tension between reportage's desire to promote transformation and the actual sociopolitical constraints of reality.

Liao's reportage encompasses a variety of narrative forms, including subsections with "captions" for diverse aspects of Chu's life story, such as: "Are human beings that vicious?" "Education: a journey of challenge and warmth," "Deprived of rights in work," "Final disillusionment with the authorities," and "Illegally dismissed from work." Besides excerpts from interviews with Chu, his family, teachers, school principals, and law specialists, Liao includes the firing notice from the Farmers' Association, a quotation from a Japanese encyclopedia, Chu's appeal letter to the Farmers' Association, legal documents related to the operations of the Farmers' Association, and media coverage of Chu's unfortunate situation. The overriding presence of Chu's voice in the reportage, including interview excerpts, his letter of appeal, and personal recollections, enhances Chu's authority and power; he moves from the position of an interviewee to a storyteller of his own tale about the local authorities' dismissive reasoning and illegal discharge. As Liu Kang and Tang Xiaobing observe, the "textuality" of reportage "represents a transgression of accepted categories of fiction and history. It is also informed by the implacable tension between official ideology and the experience of everyday life."[27] Yingjin Zhang argues that reportage may construct a "subversive discourse," as displayed in works by Liu Binyan, Qian Gang, and Hu Ping.[28] Liao's reportage gains its sociopolitical impact by giving authority to Chu's resistant voice in expressing his grievances and eliciting public sympathy.

Several other examples in Liao and Yan's works cast an ironic look at the politics of "visibility" through ekphrastic inscription. The texts offer accounts of interviewees with albinism who are subjected to various forms of social stigma when their unique fair complexion, white hair color, and impaired vision bring them undesirable attention from others. Liao's reportage on these interviewees is ekphrastic in that it relies on iconic visual representations of the interviewees' images and graphic reconstructions of their experiences to make the readers "see" their encounters. Whereas albinism for the interviewees entails a form of "invisibility" reinforced by visual impairment and social stigma, it challenges the reportage authors to create "responsible representations" of their subjects in ekphrastic reportage.[29] An example is Liao and Yan's reportage on an elder interviewee, Mr. Li Huan-tien. Li is a villager from an impoverished family in Alian District, Kaohsiung, and has suffered from sun exposure and skin impairment, as well as frequent verbal slurs from others due to his albinism. A photograph by Yan Hsin-chu of Mr. Li presents him wearing a white sunhat (fig. 6.6). He is facing the camera, with his eyes casting a slanting look at the sunlight to the left; his weathered, splintered skin carries traces of sunburn from decades of field work without protection. Another photo by Liao captures the interior of Li's room and all his belongings, with Li resting on a thinly covered small bed (fig. 6.7). Li's half-length portrait, taken by Yan, is particularly compelling. While his body position indicates trust and willingness to communicate, his narrowed, averted eyes and his gaze at the blazing sunlight reveal the physical vulnerability of one with albinism. Against the dark backdrop, Li's skeptical and yet resilient gaze into the distance is given prominence, embodying the challenges of many like Li, the public's sympathy for such people, and the photographer's uncertainty in making their agony visible to others. These two photos make visible the intersectional themes of physical impairment and aging, suggesting Li's complex and challenging conditions.

The following section, "Snow White Also Has Fair Skin," illustrates the story of Liao Hong-lin, a four-year-old girl with albinism who is on the cover

Fig. 6.6. Li Huan-tien wearing a white sunhat. (Reprinted by permission of Yan Hsin-chu.)

image of the book. When Hong-lin asked her mother about her white hair color,

> Mrs. Liao would always tell Hong-lin in a frank tone, "Because of the lack of melanin!" She bought Hong-lin many picture books about characters with diverse skin color. A neighbor even bought Hong-lin a baby doll with purple hair. These efforts were meant to let Hong-lin know that there are people with different skin color in the world. Gradually, Hong-lin gained the understanding that Snow White has a white complexion because the white snow permeates her complexion; bamboos are green because of chlorophyll. Hence when someone questioned her

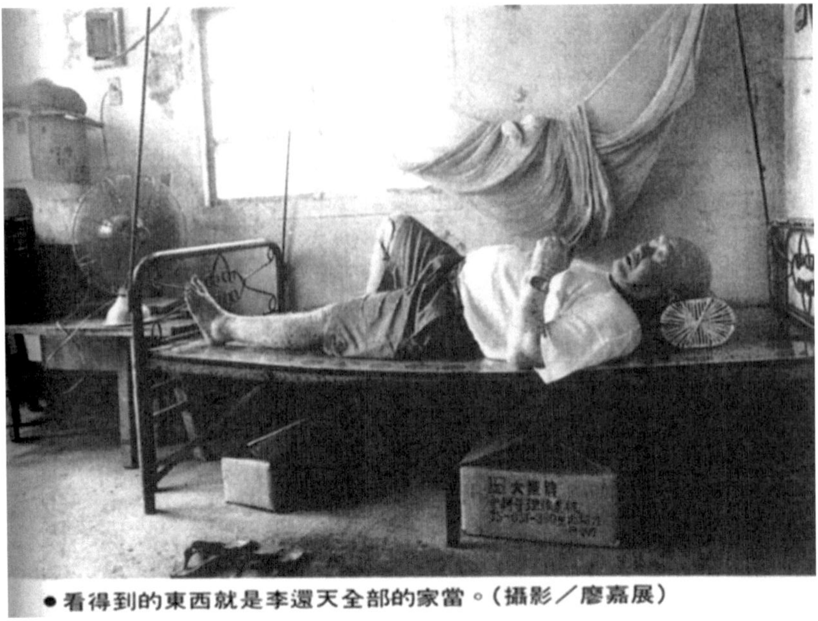

Fig. 6.7. The interior of Li's room and his belongings, with Li resting on a small bed. (Reprinted by permission of Liao Chia-chan.)

> about her white hair, she would always answer with candidness: I was born this way. I lack melanin.[30]

This section calls attention to children's marginalized social status as another intersectional issue in reportage coverage. The narrative takes on a stylized quality by including elements of a well-known fairy tale, expressing care and warmth in the portrayal of the child's life (figs. 6.8, 6.9, and 6.10). Because Hong-lin the child is too young to describe her situation or to have her own strong voice, the reportage draws extensively from her parents' affectionate responses to their daughter's situation. The couple deemed their daughter to be "an angel-like little fairy" who would bring endless joy to their lives.[31] Ekphrastic illustrations confront an ethical dilemma as they attempt to portray and speak for the vulnerable subject; drawing on the parents' words helps overcome such limitations and establish an empathetic context for Hong-lin's story to be heard.

Hong-lin's story calls for an ekphrastic imagination by incorporating fairy-tale elements and using the style of children's narratives. Ekphrastic reportage

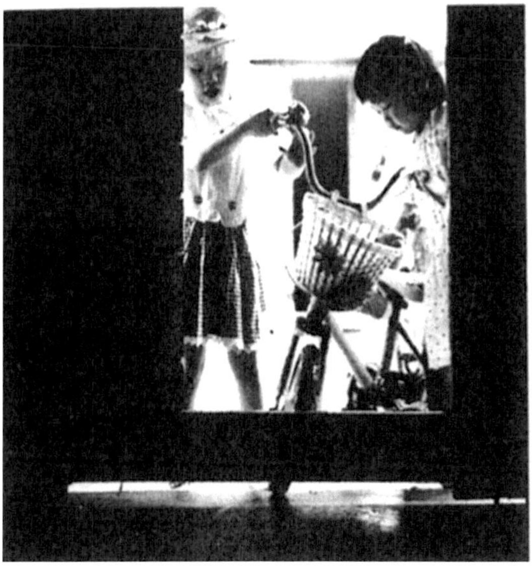

● 紅林與她的摯友胖美合力把脚踏車抬進屋裏。（攝影／顏新珠）

Fig. 6.8. Honglin with her friend taking a bike inside. (Reprinted by permission of Yan Hsin-chu.)

● 紅林和幼稚園的小朋友相處愉快。（攝影／顏新珠）

Fig. 6.9. Honglin got along with her friends in kindergarten. (Reprinted by permission of Yan Hsin-chu.)

● 紅林和她的「刎頸之交」，兩人可從早玩到晚。（攝影／顏新珠）

Fig. 6.10. Honglin playing with her best friend. (Reprinted by permission of Yan Hsin-chu.)

creates "textual pictures" in narration and introduces a childlike perspective in its figurative illustration of the subject and the world around her. Rather than being "read" as mere image/texts themselves, these photographs of Hong-lin from her everyday life allow her to "speak for herself" and tell her own story to the readers through the pictorial medium. This form of ekphrastic encounter between Hong-lin and her unmet audience permits both affective exchanges and potential resistances between the photographed child and her viewers. Yan's photographs of Hong-lin show her interacting with her close friends while doing chores, studying in the kindergarten, or playing at home, capturing her joyful moments of learning, playing, and enjoying friendship with other children. The captions of the photos highlight her joy in daily activities. In contrast with previous photos of interviewees with albinism, Hong-lin's photos do not show her consciously interacting with the camera, nor do any of these photos express anxiety or uncertainty about the possible spectator. This absence of anxious interactions with the camera could imply a trusting relationship with the photographer and the effectiveness of Yan's work to protect Hong-lin's sense of security. These photos of the worry-free child enhance a sense of care in the audience, suggesting to them the preciousness of such moments to the photographed, and the audience's responsibilities to protect the happiness of many children like Hong-lin.

These photographs invite a reconsideration of the photographer's role in socially committed documentary photography. As Walter Benjamin argues, to counterbalance and resist the ways in which photography has been deployed by capitalism, an alternative is to practice a form of participatory recording and to provide the full context for photographed subjects.[32] For Liao and Yan, the role of a reporter and that of an on-site recorder of those involved in the events are two constituent elements of producing photographic reportage. A photographer's complex subjective positions indicate his or her potential in creating ekphrastic encounters with the reported real people or live events, and affect the ethico-political risks in taking their pictures and telling their stories. The photographic works by Liao and Yan on albinism demand social empathy, and expose the anxieties produced by encountering new ethical choices that arise when viewing such evocative images and disseminating them for a public spectatorship. Whereas the photographs in these two works are candid, unpretentious, and even raw, the cover of the collection is different, displaying an aestheticized presentation of Hong-lin gazing into the distance with curiosity and hope. This aestheticization of Hong-lin's image does not undermine the photograph's authenticity or its affective and political significance. Rather, Hong-lin's close-up is instrumental in cultivating an empathetic audience for those who were often unjustifiably deemed to be "disabled" and "impaired" in the public eye. The cover image, juxtaposed with the figurative title "Moon Children," can be considered a reincarnated "imagetext" staging a form of poetic, aestheticized visibility for people with albinism.

"The Pig Master Ah Hsu": An Ekphrastic Portrait

As discussed, the reportage works by Liao and Yan could be considered ekphrastic reportage because of their "composite" nature. The use of mixed media of narrative portraiture and photographic images in their reportage creates an interactive mode of constructing personal stories by combining memories and on-site interviews with photographic images of joy and melancholy, motion and stillness. The descriptions in reportage connect the authors' formal experiments in diverse media with visions of the interviewee and his or her emotional world. Such is the case in "The Pig Master Ah Hsu," one of Liao's earliest reportage works. In 1983, Liao was attracted by a local news story about a blind man, Ah Hsu, in Linkou, Xiafu village, who was skillful at raising pigs, and visited him twice. Two decades earlier, an old grenade he picked up from a beach had exploded, costing Ah Hsu both of his eyes and severely injuring his right hand and right foot. Unwilling to succumb to the tragic incident, after a short recovery, Ah Hsu strove to earn a living by taking on various laboring jobs, first as a construction worker, then as a fisherman, before he took on pig raising. Liao recounts his interview with the Pig Master:

> When I reached out to Ah Hsu, I was curious about a blind and disabled man who could gain fame as a pig-raising master. Yet he turned out to be both humble and brilliant. He would never succumb to challenges in life and lose his faith in human nature, nor would he compromise his dignity at any price. *Since then, whenever I suffered thwarted emotional experiences or frustrations in my first twenty years' of life, when trivial feelings of self-pity, cynicism and distrust fill my heart, Ah Hsu's broad, fully smiling face and his blind eyes behind his sunglasses would resurface in front of my eyes, and give me unspeakable joy and strength. At such moments, I would always whisper, "Ah Hsu, please take good care . . ."* [my emphasis][33]

This passage captures a moment of ekphrastic encounter on multiple levels. First, the iconic image of Ah Hsu emerges from Liao's figurative descriptions as an intimate, approachable ekphrastic image. Second, the image invites an affective reaction from the first-person narrator/reporter and the readers, whose response to the Pig Master is cultivated through their exposure to the diverse cognitive and sensory motifs in a plurimedial reportage. Third, the dreamlike encounter with Ah Hsu invites us to consider a series of dialogic relations, including the relation between the narrator and the interviewee, the differences between Ah Hsu as an interviewee and him as an ekphrastic image visualized through writing, the narrator's anxiety about verbal/visual conjunctions in reportage, and how diverse modes of representation influence viewers' emotive responses.

The reportage offers an exciting depiction of the night when Ah Hsu was preparing a big pig for a local "Pig Contest" that was held once every nine years.

> On the eighth day of the sixth month of the lunar calendar, that night, Ah Hsu woke up early at around 1:00 a.m. . . . While eagerly waiting for daybreak, he kept asking me about the time. Just past 3:00 a.m., he could no longer stay seated to wait. Pacing up and down the road in front of the gate, he was like a nervous bear. *In this tranquil night, Ah*

> *Hsu's heart was beating with great excitement. He knew that to capture the pig for the seller, one must start in the chilly early morning. The giant pig would not be able to endure the labor and hardship if he were to be transported in daytime. The memory of another pig, Ah Pi, that suddenly died right after being weighed must have been haunting him even* [*on that day*]. (my emphasis)[34]

This passage entails an example of free indirect speech, a "technique of presenting a character's voice partly mediated by the voice of the author," with the voices effectively merged.[35] Free indirect speech yields a degree of narrative authority to the character.[36] The use of free indirect speech in Liao's reportage leads to an expanded understanding of the ekphrastic encounter between narrator and marginalized subjects. Laura M. Sager Eidt argues that "ekphrasis in free indirect discourse may be constituted by the character's pre-verbal thoughts and feelings, thus resulting in a verbalized (by the narrator) yet pre- or non-verbal ekphrasis (of the character)."[37] The above quoted passage stages an on-site narrator, whose voice signals reported speech, and Ah Hsu's psychological activity with himself as a character focalizor, that is, the narrative agent who perceives and facilitates the visions presented to the readers.[38] Ah Hsu's perspective gradually gains prominence, showing *his* excitement, uncertainty, and recollection of past memories. Yet this depiction is still framed through the narrator's perspective, as implied by the phrase "must have been haunting him." The scenario represents a case when ekphrasis, through free indirect speech, creates a compelling tableau of Ah Hsu the pig master in an intense moment. Free indirect speech has the creative potential to facilitate the transposition of the character's state of mind into the narrator's voice.

Another example is Ah Hsu's and his son's years of fish farming, in a section titled "The vines of bitter melons give birth to small bitter melons," with the section title deploying visual ekphrasis to express the characters' emotions. In a passage about the father and son being caught in a gale at the farm, the narrative comprises direct speech (in quotations in the original) and indirect speech (italicized by me), both of which depict the frightening situation of the stormy night.

> He [Ah Fa] kept crying out, "Papa! [I am] scared to death! Papa! [I am] scared to death! Where are you?" Following Ah Fa's voice, frantically crawling, shouting, touching around, Ah Hsu was finally able to find Ah Fa. *Father and son hugged each other tightly, and spent the night in the storm like that.* As he recalled this, in Ah Hsu's blind eyes, two drops of tears emerged but would not fall. [my emphasis][39]

Fig. 6.11. Ah Hsu singing songs and telling jokes to entertain his pig. (Reprinted by permission of Liao Chia-chan.)

This passage includes a mixture of the narrator's free indirect speech punctuated by Ah Hsu's direct speech. Ah Fa's exclamation of "Papa! [I am] scared to death! Papa! [I am] scared to death!" gives a direct psychological portrayal of the terrified child. Ah Hsu's reminiscing voice ("and spent the night in the storm like that") presents his direct speech embedded in free indirect narration, "*Father and son hugged each other tightly, and spent the night in the storm like that*" (父子兩人緊緊抱着，"就這樣被風吹雨打了一夜"). This italicized sentence, which vividly illustrates Ah Hsu and his son's experience in the storm in literary depiction, provides Ah Hsu (the interviewee)'s first-person experience through a third-person narrative point of view, and showcases a situation of free indirect speech. By deploying the device of free indirect speech, the text illustrates how Ah Hsu's position could be transformed from that of an interviewee to that of a reporter/narrator himself as he recalls that eventful night and describes his sensory experiences. The phrase "like this" (*jiu zheyang* 就這樣) implies Ah Hsu's intersectional positionality as focusing on his past experiences in the narrative, and also as an interviewee being seen and illustrated in text from a third-person voice. It presents a retrospective, self-reflective gaze—Ah Hsu at present examining his former self struggling against the vicissitudes of fate, a real-life experience revived through literary depiction. Here, the positions of the reporter and the interviewee are reversed, with the interviewee taking on a more authoritative position and even producing ekphrastic self-portrayal when reminiscing about his experiences.

Liao's ekphrastic writing allows readers to visualize the interviewee, and even lends an imaginative vision to the blind Ah Hsu as he recollects his earlier decades of striving to earn a meagre living after being disabled. In the text, the ekphrastic encounter engages the dialectics among different forms, styles, modes of representation, or frames of reference, and their corresponding affective affinities or political implications. Such is the case of the Pig Master story. Figure 6.11 indicates that the relations between Ah Hsu, his pig, and the camera entail multimodal sensory interactions. The photograph captures a moment when Ah Hsu was singing folk songs and telling jokes to entertain the pig. The photograph, featuring Ah Hsu in this dynamic moment, is meant to be "heard" as well as "seen." Ah Hsu's impaired vision hinders him from seeing the pig and interacting with the camera. However, losing his eyesight makes Ah Hsu extremely sensitive to other sensory experiences, including hearing, touch, taste, and smell. The photograph is shot from at eye level, showing a beaming Ah Hsu seated by his prized pig. Resting his right leg over his left knee, Ah Hsu holds up his cane in a horizontal position with both of his injured hands. He looks to the far right, smiling and talking joyfully to his pig, whose giant body is resting close in front of the camera. Ah Hsu's gaze is directed neither toward the pig to whom he is speaking, nor to the camera. This visual structure indicates his disability. It may also imply the lesser importance of vision in Ah Hsu's sensory experiences. The narrator observes that Ah Hsu's blindness paradoxically allows him to "recognize such rich and profound relations between human beings and heaven, between man and livestock, between man and animals in folk rituals."[40] The photographed pig Ah Pi used to be a feeble and unsightly piglet that could not be sold even at the lowest price in the livestock market. However, Ah Hsu really liked the piglet and prayed at a Buddhist temple for Boddhisatva's blessing for the piglet to grow up quickly and help Ah Hsu become a top winner in the local pig contest.

Fig. 6.12. Villagers chased Ah Hsu's pig into the gated sale area. Ah Hsu (*top left*) followed them, walking with a cane. (Reprinted by permission of Liao Chia-chan.)

After receiving a positive answer from the poe divination, he decided to take in Ah Pi and raise it with care to participate in the contest.[41] Trusting the Bodhisatva's blessing for Ah Pi and for himself, Ah Hsu developed a close bond with Ah Pi. The reportage invites audiences to view the photograph in figure 6.11 in light of this spiritual dimension of Ah Hsu's connection with Ah Pi. Here, Ah Hsu's bodily positions and expressions and his interaction with his pig invite a consideration of the affective bond underlying human and nonhuman relationships.

Liao resorted to a range of camera shots and techniques to emphasize the multilayered relations between man and animal, and among the disabled

●「 練下去！」阿旭餵豬公吃飯，總是這樣叨念著。(攝影／廖嘉展)

Fig. 6.13. Ah Hsu feeding his pig, gently murmuring, "Keep working on it!" (Reprinted by permission of Liao Chia-chan.)

subject, his surroundings, and viewers. Figure 6.12 is a high-angle shot of the scene in which a group of villagers managed to chase Ah Hsu's pig into the stockade sale area. The pig, and the crowd of men around it, are positioned in the foreground, with Ah Hsu walking in the background using a cane, his head tilted slightly toward the right, indicating his focus on listening to the sounds of his surroundings. The high angle and the distance between the camera and Ah Hsu (or the deep depth of field) render his image weaker, less powerful, and rather isolated in comparison with the villagers in the foreground. Figure 6.13 is an extreme high-angle shot of Ah Hsu feeding his pig, gently murmuring "Keep working on it!" as if also talking to himself. The photo emphasizes the intimate relation between man and animal, two resilient beings working against the vicissitudes of fate. Looking directly down at Ah Hsu and the pig, the camera makes both the pig master and the pig appear short and squat, displaying the more privileged position of the viewer in comparison with the disabled subject.

Figure 6.14 shows another side of Ah Hsu's life, as a popular writer and singer of Taiwanese *sio-po-kua* 相褒歌 songs.[42] Telling jokes to elders at the

● 在等待「相褒」的空暇，阿旭和公園的老人逗著玩。(攝影／廖嘉展)

Fig. 6.14. At the village's park, Ah Hsu telling jokes to the elders in the intervals between his singing of Taiwanese *sio-po-kua* songs. (Reprinted by permission of Liao Chia-chan.)

village's park, Ah Hsu, with his broad smile, is in high spirits during the intervals between his singing; his body is in motion and is partially blurred in the picture. The slightly elevated side view of the camera indicates the photographer's and viewers' positions as observer(s) of Ah Hsu in the small crowd. Ah Hsu is both the focus of the camera and the center of attention of a joyous and admiring crowd in the park; his expression and body language suggest an affective response to his approving audiences.

As these examples show, Liao and Yan's reportage captures and delivers their on-site sensory experiences through engagement with heterogeneous media, shifting between visual and verbal modes of expression. In Liao and Yan's reportage on the interviewees with albinism, ekphrasis activates the viewers' empathetic identification with the subjects and reclaims the subjects as elements of social histories and memories. In the above photographs from the story of the Pig Master Ah Hsu, ekphrasis carves out a new dimension of human understanding and showcases how the blind and disabled subject's unique sensory experiences could be made visible through camera work and photographic techniques. The camera sometimes activates a form of epistemic reversal, inviting viewers to imagine themselves in Ah Hsu's position, to take on his corporeal and emotional experiences, and to reconceive the relations between man and livestock, the disabled, and the crowds around them. Liao's photos of Ah Hsu activate an ekphrastic encounter between the disabled subject's sensory world and that of the viewers. The transferal between these two affective realms is facilitated through framing an empathetic bond between the viewer and the photographed, with the assistance of an assorted range of photographic techniques.

The rich description in "The Pig Master Ah Hsu" brings attention to the complexity of focalization in the text; it entails indirect speech (narrated by the first-person reporter Liao), direct speech (by Ah Hsu and other interviewees), and free indirect speech showing the transposition of the narrator's voice in depicting the interviewee's state of mind. Free indirect speech enriches the ekphrastic encounter between the reporter/narrator "I" and the marginalized interviewee, sets off subtle dynamics among different subjective positions, and may even challenge the narrator's authority and render the interviewee into the one with focalizing power. The key question underlying Liao's emphasis on lively portrayals of scenes is "Who sees?" in narration and description, and how plurimedial reportage contributes to new understandings of focalization. Liao's reportage complicates the question of focalization through visual representations of Ah Hsu and his affective bonds with livestock and the other people around him. In such an example, ekphrasis entails empathetic identification with the blind and disabled subject, whose inability to exchange gazes paradoxically magnifies a unique emotional world that is at once estranged from and intimate with viewers. Here camera shots, distance, angles, and various other techniques suggest diverse forms of focalization and ways to tell the Pig Master's story. The intervention of the first-person narrator often manifests the reportage author's subjective perspective and ethico-aesthetic anxiety about representation. However, Liao and Yan's work illustrates that truthful representation of Ah Hsu's story in itself is an ethical response to social reality and could in return register as a form of "co-respondence" between the reportage author and his/her readers.[43]

Epilogue: "Tender Lights of the Society"

Liao and Yan's approach in photography and reportage recalls the critical debate about high production values and sentimentalism in Taiwan's mainstream documentary films, including *Viva Tonal: The Dance Age* 跳舞時代 (dir. Chen-ti Kuo 郭珍弟, 2003) and *Gift of Life* 生命 (dir. Wu Yi-feng 吳乙峰, 2003).[44] In mainstream documentary films in Taiwan, Kuo Li-hsin identifies a collective trend toward sentimentalism that reinforces Taiwan's political isolation and discourages grassroots political activism.[45] Liao and Yan's work, however, avoids sentimentalism by validating a stance of social intervention and political activism. The aesthetic forms of Liao and Yan's reportage embrace the interactivity of, and even the dissonance between, language and images. Such stylistic complexity embodies the reporter/photographer's sociopolitical views by presenting feelings *of* and *for* the socially marginalized as contested experiences, rather than a unifying affective engagement. In his epilogue, Liao comments that this collection is somewhat "gray" in tone, with almost all included writings exposing the "scars of the era," such as stories of the blind, the disabled, and declining aboriginal tribes and cultures. His observation reiterates that reportage is an ekphrastic practice that renders such "scars of the era" in visualized and verbalized expressions. The subjects of his reportage are resilient and dignified subjects "who, despite their sufferings, are no less than tender lights of the society."[46] Embracing a plurimedial textuality that engages image and text as conversant components of the subject's story, Liao and Yan's reportage opens new spaces for considering reportage's personal, political, social, and aesthetic potentials. Besides creating and reinforcing aesthetic remediation through ekphrastic illustration and documentary photography, their works consciously cultivate an empathetic reading/viewing public. They explore the tensions between the reporter/photographer's objectivism and his or her on-site participatory reaction to the interviewed, along with the uneasiness of presenting or photographing the underprivileged and the ethical deliberations regarding the aesthetic appeal and political significance of the stories. Today, Liao and Yan's reportage remains visionary because of its pioneering plurimedial presentations of textual and visual sources, and its efforts to deepen the audiences' epistemic process of knowing the Other and develop intersubjective bonds with them.

NOTES

1. In college, Liao realized that it was impossible for a newspaper journalist to voice different opinions under Taiwan's martial law. He turned toward photojournalism and later reportage photography as alternative pursuits. Liao, "A Dream-Like Journey," 35. Also see the volume introduction for discussions of reportage's advantage in circumventing media censorship.
2. Tsai et al., "A Retrospection."

3. Kelsey and Stimson, "Photography's Double Index," xi.
4. Chung, "Maps of Life and Abjection," 354.
5. Tsai et al., "A Retrospection."
6. Mitchell, *Picture Theory*, 152.
7. Spitzer, "The 'Ode on a Grecian Urn,'" 207.
8. Spitzer, "The 'Ode on a Grecian Urn,'" 207.
9. Krieger, *Ekphrasis*, xv.
10. Mitchell, *Picture Theory*, 153.
11. Mitchell, *Picture Theory*, 153.
12. Mitchell, *Picture Theory*, 100.
13. On photographing human subjects as a social encounter between a disempowered individual and a more privileged observer, see Mitchell, *Picture Theory*, 288.
14. Berger, "Uses of Photography," 65.
15. Liao, "A Dream-Like Journey," 36.
16. Laughlin, *Chinese Reportage*, 188.
17. Shiu, "Reportage Literature." Following Yang Kui's arrest in 1949, reportage literature was censored. Reportage works published in the 1950s and 1960s include *Reports by Zhenying* 震瀛採訪錄 by Wu Xinrong 吳新榮 (1907–1967) and *The Alien Realm* 異域 by Bo Yang 柏楊 (1920–2008). In 1968, Zhang Renfei's journal *Scooper Monthly* 綜合月刊 became a forerunner of Taiwan's reportage literature. In 1975, a special issue, *Margins of Reality* 現實的邊緣, was published as a *Ren Jian* supplement under the editorship of Kao Hsin-chiang 高信疆 (1944–2009), and became a main force to promote reportage. In the late 1970s, the journal *China Tide* 夏潮, with a focus on "Critical Realism," published reportage works by Gu Mengren 古蒙仁 (1951–), Zhang Liangze, and others. In 1978, Kao established a special project in *Ren Jian*, "Reportage Literature." Leading works of the reportage include *Black Tribe* 黑色的部落 by Gu Mengren, *The Story of Hsi P'i and Fu Lu* 西皮福路的故事 by Chiu Kunliang 邱坤良 (1949–), *The World of a Leprosy Hospital* 痲瘋病院的世界 by Weng Taisheng 翁臺生, and *The Last Tribal Sword* 最後一把番刀 by Chen Ming-pan 陳銘磻 (1951–).
18. Chen, "Preface," 7.
19. Liao and Yan, *Moon Children*, 66.
20. Liao and Yan, *Moon Children*, 45.
21. Liao and Yan, *Moon Children*, 46.
22. Mitchell, *Picture Theory*, 154.
23. Mitchell, *Picture Theory*, 154.
24. Alian is a rural district located on the northeast side of the Kaohsiung Plain, in between Erren River and Agongdian River.
25. Liao and Yan, *Moon Children*, 49.
26. Mitchell, *Picture Theory*, 418.
27. Liu and Tang, "Introduction," 17.
28. Zhang, "Narrative," 211–42.
29. Mitchell, *Picture Theory*, 421.
30. Liao and Yan, *Moon Children*, 83.
31. Liao and Yan, *Moon Children*, 84.
32. Benjamin, "A Short History," 5–26.

33. Liao and Yan, *Moon Children*, 43.
34. Liao and Yan, *Moon Children*, 43.
35. Stevenson, *Modernist Fiction*, 32.
36. Genette, *Narrative Discourse*, 174.
37. Eidt, *Writing and Filming the Painting*, 123.
38. Mieke Bal defines focalization as "the relationship between the 'vision,' the agent that sees, and that which is seen" (Bal, *Narratology*, 146).
39. Liao and Yan, *Moon Children*, 30.
40. Liao and Yan, *Moon Children*, 21.
41. Liao and Yan, *Moon Children*, 19. Poe divination is a traditional religious practice in Taiwan and other parts of Asia. One may interpret divine will on personal matters by throwing two half-moon-shaped wooden or bamboo blocks on the ground and reading the patterns of the blocks' formulations.
42. *Sio-po-kua* are traditional mountain songs that "were chanted among the tea farmers of Pinglin, an area in southeastern New Taipei City. The melodies of *sio-po-kua* comprise simple three-note scales and are rich in expression" (Chang, "Duo Recital," 18).
43. On how responsible representation in ekphrastic encounter nurtures co-respondence between the representer and his or her audience, see Mitchell, *Picture Theory*, 421.
44. Wu directed *Moon Children* (1990), a documentary on Taiwan's albinist community.
45. Kuo, "Sentimentalism," 187.
46. Liao, "Epilogue," 298.

REFERENCES

Bal, Mieke. *Narratology: Introduction to the Theory of Narrative*. Toronto: University of Toronto Press, 2004.

Benjamin, Walter. "A Short History of Photography." *Screen* 13.1 (1972): 5–26.

Berger, John. "Uses of Photography." In John Berger, *About Looking*, 52–70. New York: Vintage International, 1980.

Chang, Ching-Ray. "Duo Recital Delivers Traditional Tea Harvest Chants." *NTU Highlights*, no. 61 (2017): 18. https://ntubeats.ntu.edu.tw/pdf/061fulltext.pdf

Chen, Yingzhen. "Preface I: Looking Forward to a New Departure for *Ren Jian*." In Liao and Yan, *Moon Children*, 4–8.

Chung, Jae Won Edward. "Maps of Life and Abjection: Reportage, Photography, and Literature in Postwar Seoul." *Journal of Asian Studies* 79.2 (2020): 335–65.

Eidt, Laura M. Sager. *Writing and Filming the Painting: Ekphrasis in Literature and Film*. Leiden: Brill, 2008.

Genette, Gérard. *Narrative Discourse: An Essay in Method*. Ithaca: Cornell University Press, 1983.

Heffernan, J. A. W. *Museum of Words. The Poetics of Ekphrasis from Homer to Ashbery*. Chicago: University of Chicago Press, 1993.

Kelsey, R., and B. Stimson. "Photography's Double Index (a short history in three parts).” In R. Kelsey and B. Stimson, eds., *The Meaning of Photography*, vii–xxxi. New Haven: Yale University Press, 2008.

Krieger, Murray. *Ekphrasis: The Illusion of the Natural Sign*. Baltimore: Johns Hopkins University Press, 1992.

Kuo, Li-hsin. “Sentimentalism and the Phenomenon of Collective ‘Looking Inward’: A Critical Analysis of Mainstream Taiwanese Documentary.” In Sylvia Li-chun Lin and Tze-lan Deborah Sang, eds., *Documenting Taiwan on Film: Issues and Methods in New Documentaries*, 183–204. New York: Routledge, 2013.

Laughlin, Charles A. *Chinese Reportage: The Aesthetics of Historical Experience*. Durham: Duke University Press, 2002.

Liao, Chia-chan; photography by Yan Hsin-chu. *Yueliang de xiaohai* 月亮的小孩 (Moon Children). Taipei: China Times Co., 1997.

Liao, Chia-chan. “A Dream-like Journey: On Reportage Literature.” *Bulletin of National Museum of Taiwan Literature* 9.44 (2014): 34–36.

Liao, Chia-chan. “Epilogue: In Search of a Tender Light in the Society.” In Liao and Yan, *Moon Children*, 297–98.

Liu, Kang, and Tang Xiaobing. “Introduction.” In Liu Kang and Tang Xiaobing, eds., *Politics, Ideology, and Literary Discourse in Modern China*, 8–22. Durham: Duke University Press, 1993.

Mitchell, W. J. T. *Picture Theory*. Chicago: University of Chicago Press, 1994.

Shiu, Wen-wei. “Reportage Literature.” *Encyclopedia of Taiwan*. October 28, 1998. https://nrch.culture.tw/twpedia.aspx?id=2293

Spitzer, Leo. “The ‘Ode on a Grecian Urn,’ or Content vs. Metagrammar.” *Comparative Literature* 7 (1955): 203–25.

Stevenson, Randell. *Modernist Fiction: An Introduction*. Lexington: University Press of Kentucky, 1992.

Tsai Ming-te, Liao Chia-chan, Tseng Shu-mei, and Ho Jung-shin. “A Retrospection: *Ren Jian*’s Historical Significance and Enduring Social Engagement.” *News Lens*, July 22, 2021. https://www.thenewslens.com/article/153983

Zhang, Yingjin. “Narrative, Ideology, Subjectivity: Defining a Subversive Discourse in Chinese Reportage.” In Liu Kang and Tang Xiaobing, eds., *Politics, Ideology, and Literary Discourse in Modern China*, 211–24.

III

Race, Indigeneity, and Border Crossings

SEVEN

Tales of Chinese Coolies in Late Qing Labor Reportage

Ping Zhu

Introduction: The Earliest Labor Reportage in China?

In the summer of 1872, the newly founded Shanghai-based newspaper *Shen Bao* 申報 published five essays, all on its front page, on the question of Chinese coolies, commonly called *zhuzai* 豬仔 (literally meaning "piglets"). Those essays were all submitted by Zheng Guanying 鄭觀應 (1842–1922) under various aliases.[1] Zheng, a thirty-year-old reformist during the late Qing period, had been closely following reports about the Chinese coolie issue and wanted to offer his own perspective on this troubling social issue. Written in classical Chinese, Zheng's works not only provided firsthand accounts of the rampant human trafficking and the miserable lives endured by Chinese coolies, they also conveyed the author's emotional reactions and deep humanistic concerns.

For example, "On Prohibiting the Slave Trade" (Lun jinzhi fanrenweinu 論禁止販人為奴), published on October 18, 1872, starts with Zheng mentioning a report that he came across in a Hong Kong newspaper about more than 900 Chinese men in Peru who were coerced into labor as indentured workers. He then references the ongoing María Luz incident, in which more than 200 Chinese coolies on a cargo ship to Peru were rescued by the Japanese government through diplomatic means. Afterward, in a sequence of emotionally charged rhetorical verses, Zheng implores readers to envision and feel the inhuman practice of enslaving and abusing Chinese coolies. He proposes to use universal moral principles (*yili* 義理) as the basis for solving the Chinese coolie problem at the international level.[2] Zheng wrote in one of the essays, "I am but a pedantic scholar who does not have the power to help [the coolies], but how can I sit idly when these things are happening in front of my eyes?"[3] Journalistic writing was Zheng's way of fighting against the draconian injustices within global commodity chains and labor relations.

One can observe in Zheng's writings how a late Qing merchant-scholar engaged the transnational media network with these visceral literary expressions. As Alex Des Forges summarizes, Ming-Qing literary critics put most emphasis on the "sensibility, clarity of moral vision, or depth of feeling" of the author.[4] This distinctive tradition is embodied in Zheng's writings, which heavily relied on moral logic and emotional appeal. In his well-crafted classical Chinese verses, Zheng portrayed the immense sufferings of Chinese coolies with the vividness of a firsthand witness. Simultaneously, he offered incisive critical commentary and imaginative solutions to the coolie problem. These writings not only reveal Zheng's deep empathy for his oppressed and enslaved compatriots; they demonstrate his distinct use of the modern medium of newspapers to promptly inject the Chinese voice into the global mediascape.

Journalistic writing was introduced to the Chinese by foreign missionaries in the mid-nineteenth century.[5] Founded in Shanghai in 1872 by a group of British businessmen, *Shen Bao* was the most important Chinese-language paper in the late Qing period.[6] Compared to other Chinese-language newspapers in the early 1870s, *Shen Bao* stood out for its original and timely coverage of both domestic and international events, drawing a wider readership, beyond officials and businessmen. Zheng was quick to seize on the newspaper as a new medium through which he could transform information into popular emotional responses, and in turn into social changes. In other words, writing for the newspaper became a weapon the writer wielded to transform the imagined national and international communities, which were infested with unequal power relationships and dehumanizing practices.

Zheng's journalistic writing can be regarded as the harbinger of late-Qing nonfiction or semifictional writings on Chinese overseas laborers, which proliferated in 1872 and culminated in around 1905 during the Chinese boycott against the US Chinese Exclusion laws. In those writings, Chinese authors consistently exposed the sufferings endured by Chinese overseas workers, both during the voyage and while on foreign soil, calling for intervention to rectify these injustices and uphold basic humanity.[7] Considering that Chinese overseas laborers constituted the first cohort of the Chinese working class in the modern sense,[8] these writings can be regarded as the earliest labor reportage in China and as precursors to the reportage literature that would be championed by leftist writers in the 1930s.

Translation played a critical role in the development of reportage as a self-conscious genre in China in the 1930s. The seminal 1929 essay "On Egon Erwin Kisch's Reportage" (エー・エー・キッシュの報告文学論 Ē Ē Kisshu no ruporutāju ron)[9] by Japanese literary critic Kawaguchi Hiroshi (1905–1984), which was excerpted and translated into Chinese by Shen Duanxian 沈端先 (aka Xia Yan 夏衍) and published in the leftist journal *Big Dipper* (北斗 *Beidou*) in 1932, set the tone for the definition and later development of reportage as a self-conscious genre in China. The earliest Chinese interlocutors of reportage literature, including Yuan Shu 袁殊 and Ah Ying 阿英, drew heavily on Kawaguchi's definition in their writings.

The Japanese proletarian literary movement that emerged after World War I was always part of the international proletarian cultural movement. Kawaguchi Hiroshi had been an avid translator and advocate of German proletarian literature since the late 1920s, and his own conceptualization of reportage was directly shaped by the theory and works of reportage of Egon Erwin Kisch (1885–1948), a Germany-based communist writer and journalist. Kawaguchi's conceptualization of reportage can be summarized in these terms: (1) It was a product of modern industrial society, namely, the rapid technological developments and the intensifying class struggle; (2) It included intense social criticism; (3) It was based on facts; and (4) It should show the reporter's close bond with the oppressed and the disenfranchised based on some "common ground" (*gongtong de jichu* 公共的基礎) of humanity.[10] In this context, reportage represented a modern response to the expanding capitalist system, with the goal of giving a voice to the disenfranchised and the oppressed, ultimately working toward the establishment of a more egalitarian society. This explains why in the early twentieth century this genre was quickly seized by communists and socialists all over the world as a proletarianized and combative form of literature to bring about social revolutions.

In China, reportage (*baogao wenxue* 報告文學) became a self-conscious and conspicuous genre in the 1930s and later advanced into the canon of modern Chinese literature.[11] However, as Laughlin points out in his groundbreaking study of Chinese reportage, "the genre had a notable *prehistory* in China [. . .]. Earlier writing practices that served as a foundation for the reportage form include travel literature since the Qing Dynasty as well as impressionistic accounts of historical events in progressive late Qing and early Republican journals and newspapers."[12] Regrettably, up to this date, the "prehistory" of

Chinese reportage remains understudied. Consequently, none of the Chinese anthologies of reportage has included any works from before the May Fourth Movement.[13]

By examining a group of essays and reports about Chinese coolies in late Qing newspapers, this chapter will show that reportage in the modern sense (exactly as defined by Kawaguchi) had already appeared in the early 1870s in China, long before the concept was introduced there. I will demonstrate that traditional Chinese aesthetics, centered on emotional authenticity, moral certainty, and the writer's ability to create and show mental images, were employed in early Chinese journalistic works, making them not only examples of the "repressed modernities"[14] in late Qing literature, but also examples of repressed *alternative* modernities.

A Chinese Coolie's Storytelling

The new media space, constructed by mushrooming newspapers in late Qing China, was a special contact zone. In Mary Louise Pratt's words, a "contact zone" is a social space "where cultures meet, clash, and grapple with each other, often in contexts of highly asymmetrical relations of power."[15] The early newspaper reports about coolies opened up an intense contact zone for the Chinese. On the one hand, the Chinese-language newspapers run by foreigners in mid-nineteenth-century China often featured various recruitment advertisements for Chinese laborers, enticing the Chinese poor to dig their first bucket of gold in a foreign land. On the other hand, it is noteworthy that the global demand for, as well as media attention on, Chinese indentured laborers coincided with the historical movement to abolish slavery and the transatlantic slave trade in the West.[16] In the late nineteenth century, reports of the Chinese coolie trade were widely disseminated in newspapers around the world, allowing people to read about the Chinese coolie traffic and the mistreatment of Chinese laborers in Cuba and Peru. The London-based newspaper *Anti-Slavery Reporter* and several US-based newspapers, including the *New York Times*, the *New York Herald*, and the *Chicago Daily Tribune*, continuously published reports on the Chinese coolie trade in Latin America and criticized this modern slavery. In self-defense, coolie traders and planters often cited international law and emphasized that the Chinese laborers were under "voluntary" contracts. These reports were often translated and published in Chinese newspapers in Hong Kong and Shanghai. Hence, when the educated Chinese audience encountered modern newspapers in the 1860s and 1870s and read news about Chinese coolies, they were immediately introduced to an international information network of power struggles, contentious debates, and fragmented truths.

As the modern newspaper was foreign and novel to the Chinese, there were very few Chinese voices in early Chinese newspapers. Consequently, amid the heated international discussion of modern slavery, the subject of the discussion—Chinese coolies—remained voiceless. For the Chinese authors who began experimenting with the new medium of modern newspapers in the early 1870s, the most pressing mission was to convey the authentic voice of Chinese coolies to their readers. This mission was also of global significance, because, as Lisa Yun puts it, Chinese coolies' voices could provide an alternative perspective on the "transitional narrative" in the global labor market that "provided currency for explaining [the Asian migrant laborers'] emergence and function as subjects in slave and free economies and as mediums for 'progress' and modernization."[17]

On May 2, 1873, one of Hong Kong's earliest Chinese-language newspapers, the *Chinese Mail* (*Xiangang huazi ribao* 香港華字日報), translated an in-depth report about Chinese coolies in Cuba from the *New York Herald*. The reporter visited a sugar plantation in Havana in January 1873, where he encountered a newly arrived cargo of 889 Chinese coolies, whom he referred to as "coolie celestials."[18] The reporter managed to talk to one of the Chinese coolies who knew some English, and the coolie's story was published in the section titled "Glimpse at a Cargo of Coolie Celestials" in the *New York Herald* on January 31, 1873. The Chinese version of the report, titled "On the Coolie Trade in Macao" (Lun Aomen zhuzai 論澳門豬仔), appeared on the other side of the Pacific three months later. However, the anonymous author for the *Chinese Mail* did not appear to be interested in faithfully translating this English-language report. Instead, they infused their rendition with numerous literary and emotional nuances.

In the original English report, the story of the Chinese coolie was directly relayed by the *Herald* reporter, who struggled to decipher what the Chinese man wanted to say due to the latter's "limited" English vocabulary. I include the whole passage of this story below for the sake of comparison:

> With the permission of the captain, I went through the ship until I found a Celestial who had the reputation of speaking English among his fellows. Unfortunately his vocabulary was very limited, or I should have been able to get a pretty history from the cargo. His story, so far as he could tell it, was no doubt representative of many of the rest. He had

> been to California some years ago, and had returned to his native land with some money. Having settled down, he married, and, things going wrong with him, accepted an offer of a situation in Macao, but, instead of being taken to Macao, he was put on board the immigrant ship and carried to Havana. The poor fellow seemed to feel very much for the two juvenile Celestials and his wife, who were left without protectors or support by his absence.[19]

The English report was written in a neutral, detached tone. Despite calling the Chinese "the poor fellow," the *Herald* reporter showed no sign in his writing of being emotionally stirred by the story. The "translator" for the *Chinese Mail*, in comparison, seized this rare opportunity to make a Chinese coolie's voice heard. He not only allowed the Chinese coolie to use a direct first-person narrative to vividly recount his own story, he added missing components to render it more integral and emotionally impactful. To achieve these goals, the *Chinese Mail* translator erased the part in the original report where the *Herald* reporter complains about the poor English of the Chinese coolie, and instead made the coolie fluent in English.

> 遍行船中，少有與該館之人談話相通，但得一人，頗識西語，乃與言。其人自云："餘曾往舊金山，少有所蓄，旋反家鄉。娶妻之後，不知生產，做事日匱，終無長策，以是從前儲積，至此一空。有謂偕予往澳門作傭工者，諾之。不意其人甫到，直擠予於'豬仔'船中，一路至此。念及家中有二子一妻，零丁孤苦，情何以堪？況乎作客他鄉，生為別世之人，死為異域之鬼，豈不痛哉！"言未畢，血淚沾襟，有如泉湧，其人之慘傷如此。

> [The *Herald* reporter] walked around in the ship, where there was barely anyone who could communicate with him, but eventually he found one person who knew English pretty well, so he spoke with him. The man said: "I had been to San Francisco, after I accumulated some savings there, I returned to my hometown. After I got a wife, I did not know how to farm the land, things I could do became more and more scarce, and I had no plan for the future. As a result, my savings eventually dried up. A man said he would take me to work in Macau with him, and I agreed. Unexpectedly, he didn't come at all, and I was squeezed in this 'piggy' ship all the way here. When I think of my two sons and my wife left alone at home, how can I not feel sad? How can I not feel the pain of being a guest in a foreign country, of living as a person in

> another world and dying as a ghost in a foreign land!" Before he ended his speech, blood and tears gushed out from his eyes and stained his lapel. This shows how miserable he was.[20]

Thanks to the creative translation, this was probably the first time a Chinese coolie directly narrated his story and expressed his feelings in a modern newspaper. Like Zheng Guanying, the translator appeared to be familiar with the many *zhuzai* stories circulating in Macao, hence he not only changed the title of the translated report to "Lun Aomen zhuzai 論澳門豬仔" (literally, "On the Macao Piglets"), he created a typical coolie trafficking story to fill the gap in the original report. The brief mention of "things going wrong with him" in the English report was transformed into a full story about how the Chinese man drained all his wealth in his hometown. The *Herald* reporter's neutral observation ("seemed to feel very much for the two juvenile Celestials and his wife") was turned into the climax of the coolie's speech in the Chinese report, in which the coolie expressed his worry for his sons and wife, along with the deep sorrow about being dispatched to a foreign land. The Chinese translator even added the imaginary description, "blood and tears gushed out from his eyes and stained his lapel," right after the coolie's speech.

The Chinese translator's literary touches can be found in other places in the report as well. For example, the *Herald* reporter writes about the difference between the new Chinese immigrants who were "full of strength and intelligence" and "the wretched wrecks of humanity who survive the contract system." The Chinese author translated this sentence by adding more vivid descriptions showing the shocking contrasts between the new and old Chinese coolies in Havana:

> When the workers first arrived at the port, their bodies were still healthy and sturdy. But when they complete the contract period, their appearances have become drastically different. They look emaciated, ashen, and can barely speak.[21]

Through the semi-imaginary descriptions of the Chinese coolie's stories, emotions, and appearances, the anonymous Chinese translator transformed the *Herald* report into a powerful indictment of the greedy capitalists behind the coolie trade. The Chinese version of the report contains a brief introduction to the capitalist operation in Cuba that brought in the Chinese coolies to replace black slaves. While the translation was basically summarized from the English report, the translator's own protest against the capitalists who owned the companies in

Cuba was added at the end: "Those who run the companies do not care about human feelings or moral principles. Even though they can make a huge profit, there is nothing noble about them!"[22] Refusing to succumb to such inhuman capitalist relations in the coolie trade, the Chinese report ends with the proposition that the Qing government should establish offices in those foreign countries to oversee the Chinese coolie trade and protect the Chinese people.

While holding on to the claim of authenticity, the Chinese version of the report made no pretense of being neutral; instead, it actively employed literary techniques to stir up readers' emotions. This is consistent with Zheng Guanying's writings on Chinese coolies that were published in *Shen Bao* in 1872.[23] Zheng's first essay published in *Shen Bao* on August 3, 1872, actually bears the same title, "On the Coolie Trade in Macao." In this essay, Zheng bewails that Chinese coolies' lives were "as low as the crickets and ants, and as light as the grass," lamenting, "Why are these innocent Chinese, having drifted tens of thousands of miles, subject to such cruelty?"[24]

Zheng also warns that the illegal coolie trade does not exclusively harm poor Chinese families, but can victimize any Chinese family:

> The bright sons from wealthy families often fall into the trap of deception. These young men leave home alone and travel far, with no relatives to support them. Even though their families are willing to pay a great sum, there is no way to find and redeem them. As a result, young couples cannot be reunited, and white-haired parents can only lean against the door, gazing into the distance.[25]

In addition to the "emphasis on authenticity and the moral certainty of historical experience"[26] found in the genre of reportage literature, these passages demonstrate how the inherent literariness of classical Chinese was employed to achieve maximum emotional appeal. Both Zhang's essay and the translated report covered current events, were addressed to a wide audience, and claimed to be based on authentic facts. However, the emotionally charged language sets them apart from other news reports on the coolie problem during this period.

The coolie's emotional discharge might appear excessive by the standards of modern journalism, but for Chinese readers, it was a mark of authenticity and the most natural way to indict the inhuman practices he had endured. Behind this distinction is a different conceptualization of representing truth. The traditional Chinese claim to truth hinged on the truthfulness of feelings. In *The Literary Mind and the Carving of Dragon* (*Wenxin diaolong* 文心雕龍), the most influential fifth-century book on Chinese literary aesthetics, the author Liu Xie 劉勰 commented that writings stemming from emotions were always "concise and truthful" (*yaoyue er xiezhen* 要約而寫真).[27] As Chinese cosmology idealizes the merging of the natural and human realms, the representation of the objective world became inseparable from the expression of the subject's feelings.

It is noteworthy that emotion and ethics are almost always intertwined in Confucian ideology. Summarizing the Confucian tradition, Li Zehou 李澤厚 has asserted that the ultimate Chinese aesthetic state is founded on the Confucian concept of "the unity of heaven and human" (*tianren heyi* 天人合一), wherein humans reach "a certain trans-moral sensual realm of life on the basis of morality."[28] In this state, humans enjoy a harmonious relationship with the highest moral order of nature, which is not perceived as a moral imperative but rather as a sensuous pleasure.[29]

Therefore, the "ethico-aesthetic paradigm" discussed by the editors in the introduction of this volume resonates with a core concept in the tradition of Chinese writing, which requires the writers' emotional investment to be inseparable from their moral critique. Viewed from this philosophical perspective, the separation of the description of people, events, or milieus from the subjects' emotions would not only hinder the truthfulness of a journalistic report, it would constitute a moral violation. This intertwined regime of truth and morality foreshadowed a unique preference in Chinese reportage writing from its inception, rendering it rather akin to the self-conscious genre of reportage in the 1930s.

Writing Autoethnographies of Chinese Coolies

Blending modern reportage with classical lyricism and commentary, the two pieces titled "On the Coolie Trade in Macao" discussed in the previous section were highly interventionist writings that asserted a Chinese voice and called for justice within the fledging network of newspapers in China. Pratt has used the notion of "autoethnography" to describe texts "in which people undertake to describe themselves in ways that engage with representations others have made of them."[30] The early Chinese newspaper essays on the coolie trade all bear this quality of autoethnography. The Chinese writers challenged the incomplete, vague, or abstract reports on Chinese coolies produced by foreign newspapers and endeavored to ensure that the authentic voice of the oppressed and marginalized social group, the Chinese coolies, was heard.

Zheng Guanying continued to employ the genre of reportage to create autoethnographies of Chinese overseas laborers. His "On the Coolie Trade in Macao Continued" (Lun Aomen zhuzai xu 論澳門豬仔續) was published in *Shen Bao* on August 6, 1872, only three days after the appearance of his first essay. It is noteworthy that Zheng's newspaper writing was rapidly evolving. He began his first essay, "On the Coolie Trade in Macao," with a quote from the Confucian classics, a typical opening in classical Chinese literati writings. In the second essay, however, Zheng had already abandoned this traditional style and began by explaining his engagement with the modern newspaper: "I record the recent events every day, so as to distinguish between good and evil in order to inspire people's minds, so that people from near and far will all follow the good."[31]

Zheng mentioned that he had read in Hong Kong newspapers the horrendous news about the Chinese coolie trade in Macao, along with the foreigners' rebuttal that all the coolies had volunteered. He boldly points out that Hong Kong newspapers "[do] not dare to expose the vices of this business," and continues with his direct observation:

> My family has lived in Macao for generations, so I know the inside stories well. [In Macao] there are not only houses for prostitution and gambling that drain thousands of silver coins each year, but also traffickers who ship people abroad. Ninety percent of those people were abducted or deceived. Fathers have lost sons, wives have lost husbands. Far from their homeland, forever drowning in the storm of life, the men left to mourn their separation in life and death, with no hope of ever returning home alive. It is heartbreaking to speak of or even hear about it. This is a trap set in our own territory. Since the establishment of the recruitment agencies [in Macao], countless men . . . have fallen prey to them, and this makes every Chinese either angry or heartbroken.[32]

In the late nineteenth century, human trafficking was more rampant in Macao because the city was a Portuguese colony.[33] Despite this, we can see in this passage that Zheng was already envisioning an imagined national "community of sympathy"[34] founded on the spread of information and emotional connections. The rise of the modern newspaper had greatly boosted the speed and scope of information transmission, facilitating the formation of the "imagined community" through sympathetic identification. By leveraging the newspaper's expansive network, Zheng strategically cultivated a sense of collective empathy among his fellow countrymen.

In the subsequent essay, "The Coolies Calling for Help" (Qiujiu zhuzai lun 求救豬仔論), published in *Shen Bao* on August 28, 1872, Zheng provides many details on human trafficking in Macao that other newspapers failed to cover, vividly describing the crime as though he were an eyewitness. Zheng's writing enables readers to envision the perilous, moonless night and to hear the desperate cries of the victims. Those horrendous details segue into Zheng's appeal at the end of the essay, in which he evokes "Heaven and Earth's love for all creatures" and "international law" to underscore the universal foundation of his plea.[35] The emotions that he conveys or seeks to evoke through his writings are not individualistic or random sensations; rather, his appeals transcend national or racial boundaries. Those appeals are consciously built on the "common ground" of humanity that can be found in Kawaguchi's definition of reportage.

Egon Erwin Kisch asserted that in reportage, "current events should be dealt with journalistically only from the angle of eternity and that each individual fate and each episode should mirror the great destiny of humanity."[36] We can imagine that for Zheng and his contemporaries, the need to appeal to the great destiny of humanity probably stemmed from the fact that they were writing in the contact zone of the modern mediascape, in which Chinese voices were extremely marginalized. Only by appealing to the common ground could Chinese writers promote and justify their own narratives of the Chinese coolie trade.

Zheng Guanying and his contemporaries were also learning the techniques of journalistic writing. One journalistic technique that was quickly adopted by the Chinese, for example, was the interview format. On October 17, 1872, Zheng published an anonymous essay titled "On the Human Trafficking in Peru's Slave Trade" (Lun Piluguo fanrenweinu shi 論皮魯國販人為奴事) in *Shen Bao*. Zheng prefaces this essay by saying that one day he was reading about the Maria Luz Incident in a newspaper and felt compelled to challenge the ship crew's testimony that the Chinese coolie trade was legal.[37] Zheng states that he interviewed "a friend" who had firsthand experience in Peru and could expose the numerous illegal practices in the Chinese coolie trade.

When this piece was collected in Zheng's *Important Suggestions for the Salvation of the Age* in 1873, it was renamed "The Grievance of an Escaped Coolie" (Ji zhuzai taohui suku lue 記豬仔逃回訴苦略) and included a revised opening. Zheng has removed the mention of the Maria Luz Incident and directly introduces the "friend," whose name he reveals as Li Decheng. According to Zheng's introduction, Li came from Zheng's hometown and had worked as a coolie in Peru for sixteen years before he finally escaped and returned to China. Li's background adds an extra layer of authenticity to Zheng's essay.

Li's recollection, as narrated by Zheng, covers various facets of the Chinese coolie trade, ranging from the deceptive contract signing to the wretched living and working conditions in Peru. It also contains a detailed depiction of guano mining:

> Near Peru there is an island that is extremely barren and filled with seabirds' droppings. The people of Peru do not like working in the field, so they always force the workers to go to the island to dig guano. Those workers who had contact with the filthy air and toxic gas [on the island] all died in a few years. After the workers have arrived in Peru and worked for a few years, they are all forced to go to the island. Therefore, I have only seen the workers leave for the island, never the workers return from the island.[38]

The description of the hellish working conditions on the guano island is followed by Zheng Guanying's, or Li Decheng's, vehement repudiation of the human trafficking and slave trade. Due to the emotional identification between the author and the witness in this example of Chinese reportage, it is sometimes hard to differentiate their voices.

Compared to the Western style of journalism, as seen in the *New York Herald* report discussed earlier, the merging of the author's voice and the witness's voice can be regarded as a unique feature of early Chinese journalistic writing. In his study of prose in early modern China, Alexander Des Forges shows that in the conventional idea of Chinese writing, "representation involves accessing and giving voice to a meaning that originally belongs to another."[39] In other words, attributing words to the individuals the author purports to speak for was a cherished aesthetic of representation among early modern Chinese writers. This again highlights the inherent connection between late Qing journalistic writings and the self-conscious genre of reportage.

Comparing novel and reportage, Theodor Balk comments: "In the novel reality is reflected in the consciousness of its personages; in reportage it is reflected in the consciousness of the reporter."[40] If this is true, then the fusion of emotions and voices between the subject and the reporter makes a work both reportage and literature. Perhaps for this reason, David Der-wei Wang has noted that the front pages of *Shen Bao* "often highlighted reports that combined journalistic reports and fictional imagination."[41] These hybrid texts both met the journalistic requirement for authenticity and the Chinese readers' preference for literary imagination and emotional appeal.

Representing "Logical Fantasy"

After accepting multiple submissions on the Chinese coolie trade, *Shen Bao* published an editorial, "On Stopping the Human Trafficking Abroad" (Jie guaifan renkou chuyang lun 戒拐販人口出洋論), on February 14, 1873. The author was listed as Shunyi Shizi Tanjingmizi 順邑獅子譚警迷子, but it seems to be a collective work because the editorial uses the plural subject "we" (余等 *yudeng*) and claims that those "truthful words" (*zhenyan* 真言) were written after they traveled around the world and witnessed the outrageous deeds done to Chinese coolies.[42] Crafted in the classical parallel prose style, the essay is filled with literary metaphors. For example, when describing how Chinese coolies were escorted to the cargo ship, the authors write:

> Under the guards' menacing gaze, the travelers lower their heads and scurry along like many rats. They go down to the lower cabin of the ship like a school of fish or a swarm of ants. In the cramped cabin in which they are immediately locked up, they have to crouch like dogs and creep like snakes. They cry and weep, faces covered in tears. Their clothes can barely cover their bodies, and the portion of food can barely fill their bellies. Suffering from hunger and cold, they are more subject to all kinds of illness. They live like cows and horses in a stable; there are no chopsticks for meals or beds for sleep. Tethered and chained, they are like the shrimp and fish caught in a net.[43]

Compared to the examples I discussed in earlier sections, this *Shen Bao* editorial is overtly lavish in the use of literary language. In this short passage, the authors used a string of metaphors (rats, fish, ants, dogs, snakes, cows, horses, and shrimp) to portray the miserable conditions of the Chinese coolies. They also employ literary devices such as contrast, parallelism, and hyperbole to create vivid images of the Chinese coolies' sufferings on the cargo ship.

In addition to the conspicuous use of parallel sentences, the plethora of metaphors and adjectives in this passage has endowed the editorial with a *visual* quality, indicating the performative aspect of the writing—of the authors' commitment to show images that could further authenticate the narrated events. We can again find the rationale for this impulse for visualization in traditional Chinese literary aesthetics. In *The Literary Mind and the Carving of Dragons,* Liu Xie asserts that the ideal writing should be the outcome of a dynamic and dialectic communicative process between the subject and the object: the subject's emotion is aroused by the object (*qing yi wu xing* 情以物興), then it is transplanted onto the object via the subject's emotional gaze (*wu yi qing guan* 物以情觀).[44] Liu actually proposed a kind of intersubjective mental image through an emotional gaze that is more complex than what is defined by sight. This gaze functions as a performative act of the subject, encompassing historical, cultural, and moral dimensions. Liu Xie's literary discourse continued to exert a dominant influence on Qing literati. In High Qing period scholar Pu Xian's 浦銑 *Commentaries on Rhapsodies* (Fu Xiaozhai Fuhua 复小齋賦話), he concurred with Liu Xie, asserting that "the most precious aspect of writing is its genuine emotion" (*wen yi youqing weigui* 文以有情為貴).[45] Pu viewed the literary subject's emotion as both a receptacle and a medium of reality: "Reality resides in emotions, emotions overflow in words."[46] The late Qing scholar Wang Guowei 王國維 also emphasized the dynamic exchanges between the feeling subject and the external world, famously stating in his *Poetic Remarks in the Human World* (*Renjian Cihua* 人間詞話), "All writings of the scenes are writings of emotions" (*Yiqie jingyu jie qingyu* 一切景語皆情語).[47] Based on this principle, late Qing writers would not be content with straightforward or factual depictions of an event; instead, they would seek to express their mental images through literary language to reveal the authentic "truth" underlying the events. Truth, in this context, extends beyond external facts and resides within the human heart, within the emotional connection forged among the reporter, the subject, and the readers.

This Chinese perception of truth is reminiscent of Egon Erwin Kisch's discussion of reportage: "The fact is merely the compass of [the reporter's] journey; he also needs a telescope, that of 'logical fantasy.'"[48] "Logical fantasy" seems to be an oxymoron, but it perfectly matches the preference for emotional gaze and mental imagery in the Chinese literary tradition. Fantasy, too, exists in mental images. It is the tendency to imagine and visualize what otherwise does not exist. Therefore, the highly literary and oftentimes imaginative mode of writing in the *Shen Bao* editorial was a deliberate aesthetic and ethical mode of representation. The authors had obviously resorted to the "logical fantasy" to fill out missing details with the many mental images they presented in the essay.

The incorporation of mental images or logical fantasy inevitably makes the representation heterogeneous and blurs the boundary between words and images. As the Chinese coolies' stories proliferated in Chinese newspapers, the demand also rose for supplementing textual narratives with visual components so that more illiterate Chinese could grasp the impending racial tragedy. In 1875, Fuwen Zhai 富文齋, a major commercial press in Canton, published

Illustrated Stories of the Living Hell (Shengdiyu Tushuo 生地獄圖說), a pamphlet that contains forty-two illustrated stories of Chinese coolies' miserable lives in Peru and Cuba. According to the preface written by the anonymous author, these real stories were selected from the many reports in various kinds of newspapers, and they represented "the most miserable cases."[49] The author also stated that he deliberately imitated the visual regime of the popular Daoist scriptures *Jade Calendar of Precious Records* (Yuli baochao 玉歷寶鈔) and *Illustrated Evidences on Secret Virtues* (Yinzhiwen tuzheng 阴隲文圖証) in order to "shock and startle" Chinese readers and viewers.[50]

Both *Jade Calendar of Precious Records* and *Illustrated Evidences on Secret Virtues* are Daoist books of persuasion (*quanshan shu* 劝善书) widely circulated during the Qing Dynasty. The former presents the Chinese folk perceptions of the Ten Kings of Hell (*Shidian yanwang* 十殿閻王) and the horrors of the underworld in gruesome detail, and the latter contains illustrated vignettes of people's good deeds. Both books heavily employed visual elements to complement, authenticate, and enhance the textual elements. Shih-shan Susan Huang points out that Daoist graphics often exhibit "the inextricable weaving together of representation and discourse," and "flexible, experimental, and 'high-tension' relations between words and images."[51] This feature is certainly inherited by the author of *Illustrated Stories of the Living Hell* and became an effective weapon for Chinese newspapers in the following decades, when pictorials (*huabao* 畫報) flourished in China.[52]

To visually represent the coolies' stories, which took place in Cuba or Peru, or on the cargo ships that the common Chinese had little knowledge of, it is necessary to rely on "logical fantasy" to recreate the full mental images. A couple of stories in this pamphlet echo the account of the Chinese coolies on the guano island in Peru that Zheng Guanying wrote about. One illustrated story states that each Chinese worker must dig two full carts of guano every day, otherwise they would be flogged and hanged. Exhausted and tortured, sometimes the coolies would bury themselves alive in guano.[53] In the accompanying image (fig. 7.1), in addition to the many flying seabirds and two carts of guano, we can see one Chinese coolie buried in guano, only exposing his face; two other Chinese coolies holding shovels are standing to the side, looking at each other. The one on the left is pointing, as if asking if they should report the incident to the supervisor; the one on the right is looking distressed and not giving an affirmative response. This echoes the last sentence of the narrative: "the Peruvians do not care [about the Chinese] at all."[54]

The illustrator's logical fantasy can also be demonstrated in another vignette, "Chinese coolies crushed by the train" (*huoche suiti* 火車碎體),

Fig. 7.1. A Chinese coolie burying himself alive in guano. (Reprinted from *Illustrated Stories of the Living Hell*, 21.)

which portrays Chinese coolies on a sugar plantation in Havana who cannot tolerate the continuous toil and choose to commit suicide by laying on the tracks. In the accompanying image (fig. 7.2), a train is running over two Chinese men laying on the railroad tracks. The half-naked Chinese man on the bottom is so skinny that his ribs are visible. From his posture, it seems that the excruciating pain is driving him to crawl away from the tracks, but his legs are already crushed under the train wheels. The other Chinese, whose right side is crushed by the train, is desperately trying to crawl closer to his fellow countryman and put his hands on him. Those visual details cannot be found in the text narrative and only originated from the illustrator's logical fantasy. It is noteworthy that the illustrator, who probably had never seen a train, had to recreate the train from his imagination. The "train" in the picture looks

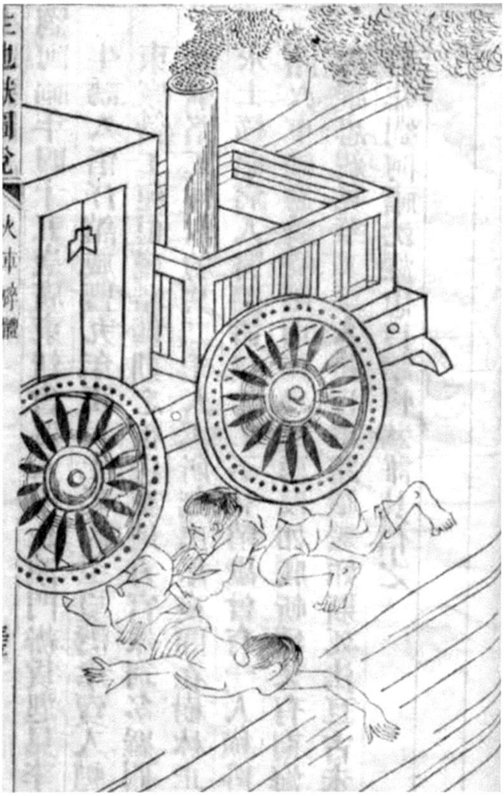

Fig. 7.2. Chinese coolies crushed by the train. (Reprinted from *Illustrated Stories of the Living Hell*, 3.)

like a cart with giant wheels and a chimney on top of the flatbed. Despite the amateurishness, the illustration successfully shows the crushing dominance of capitalism and modern technology over human beings.

Coupled with emotionally charged narratives and concrete personal details, the illustrations in *Illustrated Stories of the Living Hell* have a strong visual impact, leading people to imagine the "living hell" that the Chinese coolies suffered. The power of the visual representations is evidenced in the fact that on the publication of this pamphlet, the Spanish minister (Cuba was a Spanish colony in the 1870s) approached the Premier's Office of the Qing Dynasty and, claiming that this pamphlet was based on rumor and slander, requested that the Qing government destroy all copies.[55] This diplomatic reaction was a testament to the powerful claim to authenticity of those visualized narratives.

Conclusion

This chapter traces the origin of Chinese reportage in late Qing journalistic writings (and drawings) about Chinese coolies in the early 1870s. In the contact zone of the modern mediascape of the early 1870s, Chinese writers produced autoethnographic texts that allowed Chinese voices and images, and, more specifically, the Chinese coolies' voices and images, to be heard and seen. The works discussed in this chapter can be regarded as the earliest Chinese labor reportage in the modern sense. From journalistic writings in classical Chinese to illustrated stories in the pamphlet, it is evident that late Qing authors were striving to engage with more readers within the imagined national community. Even though they were not consciously employing reportage as a weapon for social reform yet, those emotionally charged and socially engaging works resemble Chinese leftist literature of the 1930s.

Although the examples I discuss in this chapter cannot be categorized as proletarian literature per se, they were highly progressive and "leftist" in their time. Since the authors were writing at a time when a proletariat class was still absent in China, they chose to focus on the earliest cohort of Chinese workers employed by capitalists—Chinese coolies—and to advocate for their rights and for justice. In these late Qing works, we can discern a commitment to authenticity and a strong aversion to capitalist greed. Additionally, since the writers emotionally identified with the coolies, their works also exhibit a keen awareness of China's racial and national crisis. All of these elements can be found in Chinese reportage literature of the 1930s.

There is a continuous lineage between late Qing journalistic works and the leftist reportage of the 1930s. The emotional engagement, moral certitude, and impulse for visual representations of the early Chinese journalistic writing continued in the vernacular works in later decades, as the writings about overseas Chinese workers had become a popular subject in newspaper essays and exposé novels. The later works covered not only the coolie trade, but also the mistreatment of Chinese immigrants in the United States during the Chinese Exclusion period (1882–1947).[56] These works, which persisted for another decade, shared a strong penchant for humanist emotions and social engagement that was eventually adopted in May Fourth literature. Due to space constraints, I do not examine those works in this chapter,[57] but we can nevertheless conclude that the earliest Chinese labor reportage in the modern sense can be traced back to the early 1870s.

NOTES

1. All five essays on the human trafficking problem published in *Shen Bao* in 1872 were collected in Zheng Guanying's volume *Important Suggestions for the Salvation of the Age* (Jiushi jieyao 救時揭要) in 1873.

2. Zheng Guanying, "Lun jinzhi fanrenweinu," 13.

3. Zheng Guanying, "Lun Aomen zhuzai xu," 9.

4. Alex Des Forges, *Testing the Literary: Prose and the Aesthetic in Early Modern China*, 22.

5. The earliest Chinese-language newspapers in the modern sense, such as *Chinese and Foreign Gazette* (Zhongwai xinbao 中外新報), founded in 1854 in Ningbo, and *Shanghai Gazette* (Shanghai xinbao 上海新報), founded in 1861, mainly published materials translated from foreign newspapers.

6. Barbara Mittler, *Joining the Global Public: Word, Image and City in Early Chinese Newspapers, 1870–1910*, 16.

7. Most of those writings were collected in Ah Ying's 1960 anthology *Fan Mei Huagong jinyue wenxue ji.*

8. Between 1848 and 1874, nearly 124,813 Chinese indentured workers arrived in Cuba (Turner 1974, 66); between 1849 and 1874, more than 100,000 Chinese indentured workers arrived in Peru (Lausent-Herrera 2009, 116). In comparison, there were fewer than 10,000 workers in China in 1870 (Zhu 1999, 27).

9. Kawaguchi's essay was originally published in the left-wing magazine *Bungei Sensen* 文藝戰線 (vol. 6, issues 1–3) in 1929.

10. Shen Duanxian, "Baogao wenxue lun," 242.

11. Charles A. Laughlin, *Chinese Reportage: The Aesthetics of Historical Experience*, 24.

12. Laughlin, *Chinese Reportage*, 13.

13. Most anthologies of Chinese reportage only include works produced after the January 28 Incident in 1932. The nineteen-volume *Compendium of Chinese Reportage Literature* (Zhongguo baogao wenxue congshu 中國報告文學叢書), published between 1981 and 1983, for example, includes selected works dating as far back as the May Fourth Movement in 1919.

14. David Der-wei Wang, *Fin-de-siècle Splendor: Repressed Modernities of Late Qing Fiction.*

15. Mary Louise Pratt, "Arts of the Contact Zone," 34.

16. The UK and the US banned slave trade between nations in 1807 and 1808, respectively. In 1817 Spain signed a treaty with the UK that abolished the transatlantic slave trade. However, Spain did not abolish slavery trade in its colony Cuba until 1886 (Corwin 1967). In Peru, slavery was abolished in 1854, but the Peruvian planters quickly shifted to international coolie trade, which was not abolished until 1874 (Stewart 2018).

17. Lisa Yun, *The Coolie Speaks*, 1.

18. During the Qing Dynasty (1644–1912), some Westerners used the term "Celestials" to refer to the Chinese people. The term was directly associated with the concept of "the Celestial Empire" (*Tianchao* 天朝), which was the self-proclaimed name of ancient China.

19. "Glimpse at a Cargo of Coolie Celestials," 4.

20. "Lun Aomen Zhuzai," 578–79.
21. "Lun Aomen Zhuzai," 579.
22. "Lun Aomen Zhuzai," 579.
23. Since Zheng could read English, it is possible that he translated the *Herald* report on *The Chinese Mail*. In fact, Zheng mentioned several times that he was a reader of the newspapers published in Hong Kong, such as the *Chinese Mail*.
24. Zheng Guanying, "Lun Aomen Zhuzai," 8.
25. Zheng, "Lun Aomen Zhuzai," 6.
26. Laughlin, *Chinese Reportage*, 7.
27. Liu Xie, *Wenxin diaolong*, 63.
28. Li Zehou, *Huaxia meixue: meixue sijiang*, 349–40.
29. Li Zehou, *Huaxia meixue: meixue sijiang*, 351.
30. Pratt, "Arts of the Contact Zone," 35.
31. Zheng Guanying, "Lun Aomen zhuzai xu," 8.
32. Zheng, "Lun Aomen Zhuzai Xu," 8.
33. The Qing government was not taking effective measures to halt human trafficking elsewhere in China. However, because Macao fell outside the jurisdiction of the Qing government, it became the favored location for coolie traffickers.
34. Haiyan Lee, *Revolution of the Heart: A Genealogy of Love in China, 1900–1950*, 7.
35. Zheng, "Qiujiu Zhuzai Lun," 11.
36. Egon Erwin Kisch, "Wesen des Reporters"; cited in Harold Segel, "The Career of Egon Erwin Kisch," 33–34.
37. The Maria Luz Incident (1872) occurred when a Peruvian ship carrying abused Chinese laborers docked in Yokohama. The Meiji Government of Japan detained the ship, conducted an investigation, and freed the Chinese laborers. The case was later taken to an international tribunal in Shanghai in November 1872, which ruled in Japan's favor. Zheng's piece was written before the tribunal.
38. Zheng Guanying, "Ji zhuzai taohui suku lue," 15.
39. Forges, *Testing the Literary*, 42.
40. Theodor Balk, "Egon Erwin Kisch und die Reportage"; cited in Harold Segel, "The Career of Egon Erwin Kisch," 76.
41. Wang, *Fin-de-siècle Splendor*, 2.
42. Shunyi Shizi, "Jie Guaifan renkou chuyang lun," 577.
43. Shunyi Shizi, "Jie Guaifan renkou chuyang lun," 576.
44. Liu, *Wenxin diaolong*, 16.
45. Pu Xian, *Fu xiaozhai Fuhua*, vol. 2, 95.
46. Pu Xian, *Fu xiaozhai Fuhua*, vol. 1, 39.
47. Wang Guowei, *Renjian cihua*, 32.
48. Kisch, "Wesen des Reporters"; cited in Segel, "The Career of Egon Erwin Kisch," 75.
49. *Shengdiyu tushuo*, 3.
50. *Shengdiyu tushuo*, 3.
51. Shih-shan Susan Huang, *Picturing the True Form: Daoist Visual Culture in Traditional China*, 21.
52. One salient example of the Chinese-style illustrated newspaper is the *Dianshizhai Pictorial* 點石齋畫報 (1884–1898).
53. *Shengdiyu tushuo*, 21.
54. *Shengdiyu tushuo*, 21.

55. Wu Jianxiong, *Shijiu shiji qianwang Guba de Huagong*, 45.

56. Some notable vernacular works include the illustrated "Story of Chinese Coolies" (Zhuzai ji 豬仔記) serialized in *Enlightenment Pictorial* (Qimeng huabao 啟蒙畫報) in 1903; Lin Xie's 林獬 reportage "Story of the Chinese Abuse in Honolulu" (Tanxiangshan huaren shounue ji 檀香山華人受虐記) serialized in the *Hangzhou Vernacular Paper* (Hangzhou baihua bao 杭州白話報) in 1905; Zhina Zifenzi's 支那自憤子 "Story of My Compatriots Being Abused" (Tongbao shounue ji 同胞受虐記), published in 1905; He Xiuxian's 何琇先 "Story of Preventing the Illegal Recruitment" (Fangzhi weiyue zhaogong shimo 防止違約招工始末) published around 1906; and several novels published during and right after the 1905 Chinese boycott against the US Chinese Exclusion laws, including *Bitter Society* (Ku shehui 苦社會, 1905), *Golden World* (Huangjin shijie 黃金世界, 1905), *Bitter Student* (苦學生 Ku Xuesheng, 1905), and *The Bizarre Tale of Opposing the Chinese Exclusion Law* (Juyue qitan 據約奇譚, 1906).

57. For a discussion of the Chinese Exclusion novels, see Ping Zhu, "The Chinese Exclusion Act and the Late Qing Chinese Cosmopolitanism."

REFERENCES

Ah Ying 阿英. *Fan Mei huagong jinyue wenxueji* 反美華工禁約文學集 (Anthology of Chinese Literature against the American Exclusion of Overseas Chinese Laborers). Shanghai: Zhonghua shuju, 1960.

Balk, Theodor. "Egon Erwin Kisch und die Reportage." *Internationale Literatur: Zentralorgan der Internationalen Vereinigung Revolutionärer Schriftsteller*, no. 3 (1935): 3–16.

Corwin, Arthur F. *Spain and the Abolition of Slavery in Cuba, 1817–1886*. Austin: University of Texas Press, 1967.

Des Forges, Alexander. *Testing the Literary: Prose and the Aesthetic in Early Modern China*. Cambridge, MA: Harvard University Press, 2021.

"Glimpse at a Cargo of Coolie Celestials." *New York Herald*, January 31, 1873, 4. https://www.loc.gov/resource/sn83030313/1873-01-31/ed-1/?sp=4&st=pdf&r=-0.488,-0.003,1.981,1.114,0 (accessed December 6, 2022).

Huang, Shih-shan Susan. *Picturing the True Form: Daoist Visual Culture in Traditional China*. Cambridge, MA: Harvard University Asia Center, 2012.

Kawaguchi Hiroshi. "Baogao wenxue lun" 報告文學論 (On Reportage Literature). Shen Duanxian 沈端先, translator. *Beidou*, no. 1 (1932): 240–45.

Kisch, Egon Erwin. [1918]. "Wesen des Reporters" (The Nature of the Reporter). In Kisch, *Mein Leben für die Zeitung 1906–1925: Journalistische Texte* (My Life for the Newspaper 1906–1925: Journalistic Texts). Berlin: Aufbau-Verlag, 1983.

Laughlin, Charles. *Chinese Reportage: The Aesthetics of Historical Experience*. Durham: Duke University Press, 2002.

Lausent-Herrera, Isabelle. "Tusans (tusheng) and the Changing Chinese Community in Peru." *Journal of Chinese Overseas* 5 (2009): 115–52.

Lee, Haiyan. *Revolution of the Heart: A Genealogy of Love in China, 1900–1950*. Stanford: Stanford University Press, 2006.

Li Zehou 李澤厚. *Huaxia meixue: meixue sijiang* 華夏美學· 美學四講 (Chinese Aesthetics: Four Lectures). Beijing: Sanlian shudian, 2008.

Liu Xie 刘勰. *Wenxin diaolong* 文心雕龍 (*The Literary Mind and the Carving of Dragons).* Shanghai: Shanghai guji chubanshe, 2010.

"Lun Aomen zhuzai" 論澳門豬仔 (On the Coolie Trade in Macao). 1873. In Ah Ying, ed., *Fan Mei Huagong Jinyue Wenxueji*, 577–80.

Mittler, Barbara. *Joining the Global Public: Word, Image and City in Early Chinese Newspapers, 1870–1910.* Albany: State University of New York Press, 2007.

Pratt, Mary Louise. "Arts of the Contact Zone." *Profession* (1991): 33–40.

Pu Xian 浦銑. *Fu xiaozhai fuhua* 复小齋賦話 (Commentaries on Rhapsodies). Shanghai: Shanghai guji chubanshe, 2007.

Segel, Harold. "The Career of Egon Erwin Kisch." In Harold Segel, ed., *Egon Erwin Kisch, the Raging Reporter: A Bio-Anthology*, 11–90. West Lafayette: Purdue University Press, 1997.

Shengdiyu tushuo 生地獄圖說 (The Illustrated Stories of the Living Hell). Guangzhou: Fuwenzhai, 1875.

Shunyi Shizi Tanjingmizi 顺邑狮子谭警迷子. 1873. "Jie guaifan renkou chuyang lun" 戒拐販人口出洋論 (On Stopping the Human Trafficking Abroad). In Ah Ying, ed., *Fan Mei Huagong Jinyue Wenxueji*, 575–77.

Turner, Mary. "Chinese Contract Labour in Cuba, 1847–1874." *Caribbean Studies* 14 (1974): 66–81.

Wang, David Der-wei. *Fin-de-siècle Splendor: Repressed Modernities of Late Qing Fiction, 1849–1911.* Stanford: Stanford University Press, 1997.

Wang Guowei 王國維. *Renjian cihua* 人間詞話 (Poetic Remarks in the Human World). Shanghai: Shanghai guji chubanshe, 2008.

Wu Jianxiong 吳劍雄. *Shijiu shijie qianwang Guba de huagong* 十九世紀前往古巴的華工 (The Chinese Laborers in Cuba in the Nineteenth Century). Taipei: Zhongyang yuanjiuyuan, 1988.

Yun, Lisa. *The Coolie Speaks: Chinese Indentured Laborers and African Slaves in Cuba.* Philadelphia: Temple University Press, 2008.

Zheng Guanying 鄭觀應. *Zheng Guanying ji* 鄭觀應集 (Works by Zheng Guanying), edited by Xia Dongyuan 夏冬元. Shanghai: Shanghai renmin chubanshe, 1982.

Zheng Guanying 鄭觀應. 1872a. "Lun Aomen zhuzai" 論澳門豬仔 (On the Coolie Trade in Macao). In *Zheng Guanying Ji*, 6–7.

Zheng Guanying 鄭觀應. 1872b. "Lun Aomen zhuzai xu" 論澳門豬仔續 (On the Coolie Trade in Macao Continued). In *Zheng Guanying Ji*, 8–9.

Zheng Guanying 鄭觀應. 1872c. "Qiujiu zhuzai lun" 求救豬仔論 (The Coolies Calling for Help). In *Zheng Guanying Ji*, 10–11.

Zheng Guanying 鄭觀應. 1872d. "Lun jinzhi fanrenweinu" 論禁止販人為奴 (On Prohibiting the Slave Trade). In *Zheng Guanying Ji*, 12–13.

Zheng Guanying 鄭觀應. 1872e. "Ji zhuzai taohui suku lüe" 記豬仔逃回訴苦略 (The Grievance of an Escaped Coolie). In *Zheng Guanying Ji*, 15–16.

Zhu Cishou 祝慈壽. *Zhongguo gongye laodong shi* 中國工業勞動史 (History of Chinese Industrial Labor). Shanghai: Shanghai caijing daxue chubanshe, 1999.

Zhu, Ping. "The Chinese Exclusion Act and the Late Qing Chinese Cosmopolitanism." *Comparative Literature Studies* 58, no. 4 (2021): 863–90.

EIGHT

Transforming the "Barbarian" Margins into Multiethnic National Centers

Photographic Reportage and Ethnic Imagination in Republican-Era China

Yanshuo Zhang

During China's tumultuous decades of the 1930s and 1940s, while the nation was mired in a destructive war with Japan, in the country's southwestern and northwestern ethnic frontier regions, several reportage projects were transforming the non-Han margins and their relationship to the newly established Republic of China. This chapter investigates how photographic reportage, as an emerging domain of national imagination, took root in China's southwestern and northwestern ethnic frontier regions in the Republican era. These photographic reportage projects helped envision new ethnic relations within China's western borderlands and contributed to shaping China's national identity in the 1930s and 1940s. The Republican era was a pivotal period in modern Chinese history, when a multitude of disciplines intersected to construct knowledge about ethnicity and the nation. At a time when such modern disciplines as ethnology and anthropology were first introduced to China from the West, photographic reportage assumed an important double role: On the one hand, it provided unprecedented aesthetic pleasure and exotic spectacles to China's reading public about its hitherto little-understood non-Han communities; on the other hand, photographic reportage appealed to the "real," reflecting an ethnographic realism much needed to imagine the transformation of China's former "barbarian" ethnic frontiers into the multiethnic centers of the new nation-state.

To illustrate both the affective and the epistemological function of photographic reportage in modern China, this chapter focuses on the renowned photographer Zhuang Xueben 莊學本 (1909–1984).* Recently hailed as China's first visual anthropologist,[1] Zhuang reported for the famous *Liangyou huabao* 良友畫報 magazine in Shanghai. He made several expeditions into the southwestern and northwestern frontier regions of China between 1934 and 1942. Zhuang tirelessly documented the cultural customs, social mores, religious institutions, and, most importantly, human faces of the Tibetan and other ethnic communities, in both his photography and travel writing. He refuted the traditional Confucian categorization of these non-Han people as "barbarians" by asserting that they were "noble and pure" citizens of the new Republic, highlighting the cultural details of the non-Han communities in his photography in an effort to imagine a colorful and rich multiethnic nation-state.[2]

This chapter reveals how Zhuang's reportage project was a unique product of a modernizing China straddling different epistemological and cultural worlds: Zhuang's reportage was simultaneously inspired by imperial China's gazetteer tradition of documenting local societies and the Western scientific desire for ethnographic objectivity. His photographic reportage created visual allure for a reading public eager to consume information about China's cultural "others" and offered serious anthropological accounts to recognize and investigate the multiethnic communities of China. Particularly, I theorize that Zhuang was engaged in efforts to create an "aesthetic regime" to promote an ethnically and culturally inclusive idea of Chineseness: He visualized and humanized the faces, bodies, and living environments of non-Han communities in China's southwestern borderlands with the artistic finesse of a master photographer informed by the nationalistic desire to (com)pose a multicultural Chinese republic. Importantly, Zhuang's photographic and textual portraits of minority women served as a productive site for articulating both a robust femininity for Chinese women and a healthy national identity defined by physical and cultural strength. Ultimately, Zhuang Xueben's photographic

*A note on Chinese characters: The author respects the original characters of the Chinese-language sources. If the original source is in simplified characters, the cited passage and/or titles from these sources in this chapter will also appear in simplified characters. Likewise, if the original source is in traditional characters, the author uses the traditional version. Zhuang Xueben's name is 莊學本 in traditional characters and 庄学本 in simplified characters.

reportage produced a deeply interwoven social space where ethnicity, nationhood, gender, visual culture, and anthropology came into intimate contact to redefine the complex and controversial ethnic frontier regions of a rapidly transforming multicultural Chinese nation.

The Obsession over Frontier Communities in Republican-Era Scholarly Practices

In this section, I investigate how the disciplinary and discursive practices of ethnology and anthropology in the 1920s and 1930s helped construct a multiethnic China. With the appearance of the modern disciplines in China, ethnic Han intellectuals themselves started frequenting the ethnic frontier regions, constructing a "symbolic regime of authenticity"[3] that centers around discovering and marking cultural and ethnic differences within China.

In 1926, the German-educated intellectual titan Cai Yuanpei 蔡元培 (1868–1940) authored one of the first academic pieces on ethnology in modern China, which helped construct ethnology as an academic discipline in China. In his article, "On Ethnology" (Shuo minzuxue 說民族學, 1926), Cai distinguished between what he called the "documentation-oriented" field of ethnographie/ethnography and the "comparison-driven" field of ethnology.[4] Cai evoked China's own tradition of "documentation" ethnography, such as the *Classics of Mountains and Seas* and various historical documents on the non-Sinitic "others."[5] Acknowledging that these earlier ethnographic accounts were mostly motivated by either the authors' cultural curiosity or a political necessity to govern various regions, Cai suggested that the modern practice of ethnography and ethnology is distinguished by a scientific quest for the "real":

> What distinguishes modern ethnography from that of the past is that [modern ethnography] is based on investigative research [*kaocha* 考察]. Sometimes this is combined with personal efforts, [as the researchers] go deep into the natural ethnic tribes, experience extremely harsh expeditions and endure great risks, sometimes to the degree of sacrificing one's own life. Those who are lucky enough to reach their research destinations can then write up *detailed and accurate* [*xiangque de* 詳確的] reports.[6]

Cai's emphasis on scientific empiricism, characterized by personally conducted ethnographic investigations as the benchmark of modern ethnology, testifies to the May Fourth faith in enlightenment and reason as the ultimate conduits to the pursuit of truth. It is systematic knowledge and rational investigations, rather than ideological and moral biases, that should govern the understanding of ethnic groups. In emphasizing scientific empiricism, the pursuit of the "real" can be defined as an epistemology: It is a way of knowing built on the modern disciplinary developments of observation-based, fieldwork-rich anthropology and ethnology. Even though anthropology and ethnology were still mediated through the researcher's interests and backgrounds, these disciplines were regarded by Republican scholars as the main path to a rational truth. This new "real" in the social sciences stood in stark contrast to earlier Confucian worldviews regarding the ethnic "others": In premodern China's artistic and literary accounts, ethnic "others" tended to be either romanticized as the guardians of lost rituals and innocent human emotions, or simply caricatured as barbarians.[7] By calling researchers to focus on personal investigations and to carry out adventurous expeditions in the process of obtaining scientific knowledge, Cai legitimated "detailed and accurate" accounts about ethnic groups and ushered in a new generation of Chinese ethnologists to travel to the distant ethnic frontiers of the nation.

Indeed, from the 1920s to the 1940s, China witnessed a golden era in the development of ethnology and other related social sciences. In 1928, Academia Sinica (*Zhongyang yanjiuyuan* 中央研究院), the highest academic and research institution of the Republic, was founded in the capital city Nanking, and Cai himself served as its founding president. In 1928, the Institute of History and Philology (*Lishi yuyan yanjiusuo* 歷史語言研究所) was established within Academia Sinica.[8] With the establishment of the Institute, many newly trained scholars went out in all directions to conduct the ethnographic investigations advocated by Cai Yuanpei. A new obsession with the nation's ethnic borderlands propelled scholars from Academia Sinica and beyond to venture into areas such as Guangxi, Hunan, Guizhou, Sichuan, and the Northeast, producing written and visual documents of the non-Han groups[9] inhabiting these regions as "indigenous residents."

As James Leibold observes, the rapid professionalization of ethnology, sociology, and anthropology as academic disciplines in China and their emphasis on "unmediated scientific field research" helped produce a "new discursive practice for representing and categorizing human variation."[10] Newly trained Han ethnologists and scholars enthusiastically embraced opportunities to conduct field research deep in the forests and mountains of China's ethnic borderlands, ardently using modern technologies such as ethnographic writing and photography to understand the variations and diversities of the myriad ethnic groups within the boundaries of China.

Granted, the emphasis on empirical reason and the systematic understandings of ethnic groups championed by modern ethnology and anthropology was not without its own problems: A colonial attitude of grappling with and conquering non-Western "others" characterized many of the modern West's early anthropological efforts to study indigenous societies. In fact, as Walter D. Mignolo points out, two earlier stages of globalization, the Christianization of the world promoted by the Spanish Empire and the "civilizing missions" of indigenous societies pursued by the British Empire and French colonization, blatantly set out to convert ethnic and cultural difference in accord with the West's imperial religious, economic, and "civilizational" agendas.[11]

However, when Han Chinese intellectuals imported Western ethnological and anthropological discourses and methodologies, they leveraged such methodologies and discourses toward the nationalist end of freeing China from the numerous imperial encroachments it was suffering from. Following the collapse of the Qing Empire, China was faced with an "identity crisis" as to who the ethnic groups of China were and how to incorporate them into a unitary Chinese polity.[12] This domestic issue was exasperated by incessant imperial Western and Japanese penetrations into China's hinterlands, particularly the ethnic frontiers.[13] Foreign imperial encroachments on China's national sovereignty and territorial integrity motivated Han scholars to study and incorporate frontier ethnic groups into a *Chinese* nationhood, energizing their intellectual pursuits with strong patriotic passions. Accordingly, the ethnic regions formerly known as the "barbarian" areas that lay beyond the pale of the Confucian moral and cultural world in premodern China were now transformed into the central sites of imagining a multiethnic, unitary China.

Zhuang Xueben's Photographic Reportage and the Construction of a Cultural Borderland

It is within the historical and political context of the emergence of a multiethnic, modern Chinese nationhood that the photographic reportage projects carried out by Zhuang Xueben became particularly salient in visually constructing and transforming the ethnic margins of China.

Zhuang Xueben was born in 1909 in the suburbs of Shanghai. Unlike the professionally trained ethnologists affiliated with Academia Sinica and other official organizations, Zhuang was a self-taught, self-made man who worked as a clerk in Shanghai's insurance companies and banks before finally embarking on the journey of becoming a reporter for prominent magazines of his time.[14] Despite—or perhaps because of—his lack of explicit affiliation with any official and professional institutions in the early part of his life, Zhuang had more freedom to roam—physically and metaphorically—the geographical and cultural terrain of the nation. As Zhuang Wenjun, Zhuang Xueben's son, remembers, his father helped form the Walking the Nation Association (*Quanguo buxingtuan* 全國步行團) in the 1930s.[15] Together with a few other young people, Zhuang Xueben set out from Shanghai to walk to different parts of China, investigating the social lives and livelihoods of different communities of the nation. Zhuang's determination to walk the landmass of China was only thwarted by the chaotic warfare that broke out among the warlords of northern China.[16]

This early experience of attending to the lived realities of a changing China informed Zhuang's later professional choice to become a reporter and photographer for the prominent Shanghai-based magazine, *Liangyou* (*Young Companion*). *Liangyou* allowed readers to imagine the non-Han groups that traditionally lay beyond the pale of "Chinese civilization" in the Confucian worldview, constructing a modern and multiethnic nation that revolved around the ethnic margins of China. *Liangyou* magazine was an important site of the cultural and visual construction of China's nationhood and civil life from 1926 to 1945. Founded in 1926 in Shanghai, probably the most cosmopolitan Chinese city during the Republican era, *Liangyou* was a semimonthly magazine published twenty-four times a year. This widely disseminated and popular magazine was pictorial, covering topics ranging from medical knowledge and popular science to literary fiction and women's fashion and style.[17] Most importantly, *Liangyou* routinely introduced and discussed both Chinese and foreign customs. Scholars have defined *Liangyou* as a kaleidoscopic "visual emporium of cosmopolitanism," as it offered diverse and hybrid ways to experience a dazzling urban-driven modernity.[18]

The fact that *Liangyou* was based in the alluring metropolis of Shanghai means that the magazine enjoyed a veil of cosmopolitanism—many issues of the magazine were accompanied by English translations of the titles and summaries of selected articles. Because of its bilingual and cosmopolitan appeal, we can infer that *Liangyou* mainly targeted young, educated, affluent middle-class readers of China, who were eager to learn about the world as China struggled to claim a place in the global community of independent nations.

If the earlier issues of *Liangyou* in the 1930s featured bourgeois displays of the hourglass figures of female stars clad in eye-catching *cheongsam* dresses, with the start of the Second Sino-Japanese War in 1931 marked by the Mukden Incident, the magazine took on a more didactic and stern tone. The outbreak of this war, known in China as the Anti-Japanese War, gave birth to a new wave of patriotism and nationalist fever among China's intellectual youth. The need to guard China's territories and sovereignty against Japanese invasion became a prominent concern for intellectuals like Zhuang.

From 1934 to 1942, Zhuang Xueben traveled to the vast territories of China's southwestern and northwestern provinces and regions, particularly Sichuan and Qinghai. As I have argued elsewhere, in the 1930s and 1940s, the western regions of China assumed the important function of symbolizing the ethnonational integrity of China: As many other Chinese frontiers, such as the northeast, fell under Western and Japanese occupation, many prominent Chinese scholars at the time and the national government treated the western regions as a strategic locale for ensuring China's territorial cohesion and ethnic unity.[19]

Liangyou magazine tapped into this popular sentiment of attending to the nation's western borderland regions and started a special column called *Liangyou Readers' Rail Tour* (*Liangyou duzhe lüxing lieche* 良友讀者旅行列車). Zhuang was commissioned to report for this special column with both his photography and travel writing in west China. The *Rail Tour* series became a pivotal locus for producing and imagining the multiethnic "margins" of China, constructing visually alluring images of China's "internal others," or ethnic minorities, for multifaceted ideological functions and cultural consumption.

As Charles Laughlin suggests, Chinese reportage can be defined as "deliberately literary nonfiction text that narrates or describes a current event, person, or social phenomenon."[20] Reportage literature is defined by its attention to current affairs and public concerns. Laughlin further maintains that reportage is characterized by its "exploration of modes of consciousness and identity" in a collective sense.[21] In other words, rather than focusing on the characters' individual dramas, which seems to be fictional literature's perpetual pursuit, reportage literature produces meaning from "places and events."[22] The urgency to build a collective sense of belonging in a China tormented by imperialist encroachments endowed Chinese reportage literature with a nationalistic function in the 1930s and 1940s. However, Zhuang Xueben's literary and photographic accounts of the multiethnic borderlands do not fully conform to a strictly political definition of reportage. In fact, Zhuang's visual and literary representations of west China's multiethnic margins sit creatively and somewhat uneasily at the intersections of reportage, spectacle, ethnography, travel writing, and premodern China's gazetteer traditions.

It is this creative intersectionality of Zhuang's work that lends itself well to rethinking the very category of reportage in modern China: Even though Zhuang was reporting for *Liangyou*'s urban readership, and readers relied on his images and words to understand China's western borderlands, Zhuang's photographic work and travel writing were by no means only expository and documentary. Zhuang interjected a strong personal pathos and often spectacular curiosity and exoticization into his work, conjuring up multifaceted images of China's western borderlands and minority groups that defy the realist conventions of what scholars normally think of as reportage. Zhuang's reportage emerged as a paradoxical double project: On the one hand, he maintained a didactic tone to spur modern development in the borderland regions and argued for cultural and territorial guardianship to keep western borderland regions an integral part of China under Japanese colonial threats. On the other hand, he skillfully capitalized on the exotic images of non-Han groups to create cultural spectacles for *Liangyou*'s urban Han readers, setting a powerful stage for his personal success and fame, as his borderland photography would become a benchmark of his career. In these regards, Zhuang was not a naïve reporter, but embodied the complex "ethico-aesthetic" mode of reportage discussed by Charles Laughlin and Li Guo in the introduction of this book: Zhuang manifested "a mode of activist artistic and cultural engagement" and embraced the "multiplicity within oneself" characteristic of modern Chinese reportage.[23]

The first defining feature of Zhuang's work is the language he uses to describe the non-Han groups, which testifies to the heterogenous and often even contradictory intellectual sources of his understanding of these groups. In the early 1940s, Zhuang frequently titled his reportage for *Liangyou* with "Exotic Accounts of Kham and Tibet" (康藏獵奇記 *Kangzang lieqi ji*, literarily "Hunting for the Exotic or Strange in Kham and Tibet"). Here, "Kang" (Tibetan Wiley: Kham) refers to Xikang province (西康省), a province newly established in 1939, which was west of Sichuan province and served as a middle point between Central Tibet and China proper. The establishment of Xikang province reflected the new Republic's determination to better govern the diverse ethnic minority groups in this area. Zhuang's exoticizing accounts of this region betray his indebtedness to not only modern Western racial discourses, but also his attachment to traditional Chinese epistemes regarding the ethnic "others."

In his reportage for a 1940 issue of *Liangyou*, Zhuang describes the Tibetan nomads as belonging to the "Xifan branch" (*Xifan xi* 西番系) of the Mongoloid race (*Menggu liya zhong* 蒙古利亞種).[24] Depicting the Tibetan Plateau as "Fan people's primitive cradle," (*Fanzu yuanshi de yaolan* 番族原始的搖籃), Zhuang marvels at the "mysterious Lamaism" (*shenmi de lamajiao* 神秘的喇嘛教) of Tibetan people, concluding that only in this region can one find the "true pure blood of the Fan people" (*Fanzu zhenzheng chunjie de xuetong* 番族真正純潔的血統).[25]

This passage is an uneasy juxtaposition of traditional Chinese and modern Western/Japanese epistemologies. On the one hand, the word "Fan" or "Fanzu" can trace its origin to premodern Chinese historiographies, such as *The Old Book of Tang* (舊唐書), as the Sinocentric Confucian scholars who compiled these historical books regarded the Tibetans as "Fan." Zhuang's reference to the Tibetan nomads as indigenous "Fan" betrays the strong influence of the traditional Chinese racial episteme on modern intellectuals. As the Fan groups were non-Sinitic groups beyond the reaches of the Confucian world, they were regarded as "primitives." Notably, Zhuang's passage is captured with the English title "Chinese Nomads" on the same page, showing Zhuang's (or the magazine editors') eagerness to include the former "barbarians" in a unitary Chinese nationhood. This small English caption is an important textual move to downplay a long history of Confucian racial hierarchy in order to assimilate the frontier nomads into a modern multiethnic Chinese polity.

On the other hand, Zhuang's depiction of the Fan nomads as part of the Mongolian race and his remark that the Tibetan Plateau is the site to discover the "true pure blood" of the Fan people were undoubtedly the result of the introduction of Western racial discourses into Republican China. During the Republican era, a new discourse emerged of constructing the ethno-racial lineage of China by combining traditional Chinese terminologies, such as "Fan," "Di" (氐), and "Rong" (戎), with Western racial classificatory system, evidenced in the books *History of the Races of China* (Zhongguo minzu shi 中國民族史), by Republican-era scholars Wang Tongling and Lin Huixiang.[26] The "Mongoloid race" was an invention of British-Darwinist colonial racial epistemology, which was introduced to China and combined with traditional Chinese racial knowledge to form a multiethnic national history of China. Apparently, Zhuang was under the sway of such a new epistemological shift. His reference to the Fan nomads as part of the Mongoloid race—the same as the Han people—testifies to his desire to construct a unitary ancestry of the various ethnic groups in China's land, another telling example of the nationalist tone of his reportage writing. Nevertheless, he seems to conjure up a fantasy of the "pure blood" of Tibetan nomads when he depicts them as occupying an untouched land of religious, cultural, and racial pristineness, contradicting his own statement about the shared ancestry of the Tibetan and the other groups within the "Mongoloid race."

Zhuang's reportage writing straddles the two worlds of traditional Chinese and modern Western racial discourses. By contrast, his photography creates an ethnographic visuality that tantalizes the senses of *Liangyou*'s urban readers. Xikang was one of Zhuang's major field sites. As Yajun Mo argues, during wartime China, Xikang was one of the most "written-about and photographed" sites.[27] The geographic frontiers of western China coincided with the ethnic boundaries of the country, igniting borderland imaginations that fueled the nationalist need to fend off Japanese imperialists.

Zhuang Xueben routinely published photographic works in *Liangyou* that portray the non-Han groups in their working and social environments. Many of his images of the nomadic groups also feature close-up portraits of the faces of non-Han peoples. In his photography, Zhuang strove to create a realist style that cast ethnic minorities in seemingly spontaneous settings in daily life. In a 1935 issue of *Liangyou*, Zhuang published his photographs of Tibetan nomads at work. Three of the photographs feature half-naked Tibetan men and women plowing, carrying wood, and doing other daily chores (fig. 8.1). These photographs have a strong ethnographic "documentation" flavor, because they capture the fleeting moment of Tibetan men and women in motion. Despite their seeming spontaneity, these photographs have carefully planned compositions that invite the reader's curious gaze: In the picture named "Most of the work is done by women," one of the nomad women is half-smiling and looking at the viewer, whereas her companion is a few steps back, creating an interesting depth that can be seen as a metaphor of the complex social space of the Tibetan nomads. In another picture, two young Tibetan boys are plowing with yaks, and their home is shown in the distance. The fertile farmland and forbidding mountains combine diverse visual elements to capture the attention of the reader.

In the English caption of these photographs, it is said that these people are "Tu Fan aborigines," which means that they are "primitive people [living] mostly in [the] northwestern part of Szechuen [Sichuan] Province." Once again, we see words such as "aborigines" and "primitives" permeating the textual construction of these nomadic peoples. On the previous page of the magazine, Zhuang marvels at the potential of this largely undeveloped land:

> The Aba region of this area is a virgin land [*chunü di* 處女地] suitable for agriculture and animal husbandry, with tens of thousands of *li* of plains. Alas, the Fan people have not come around to develop and cultivate [*kaifa* 開發] this land.[28]

Right next to this text, Zhuang presents a close-up image of a half-naked Tibetan/Tu Fan woman, who wears an elaborate necklace and directs a warm smile toward the viewer (fig. 8.2). This Tibetan woman looks directly into the eyes of the viewer; she appears confident and happy. Zhuang's sexual meta-

Fig. 8.1. Zhuang Xueben's photography and reportage on Tibetan nomads in *Liangyou*. (Reprinted from issue 112 [1935].)

Fig. 8.2. Zhuang Xueben's photography and reportage from the Tu Fan region in *Liangyou*. (Reprinted from issue 112 [1935].)

phor of the "virgin land" of the Tu Fan region and the juxtaposition of the image of a young Tibetan woman next to his text betrays the semicolonial, seminational attitude he and the editors of *Liangyou* magazine have toward frontier societies. On the one hand, these Tibetan groups were regarded as living in a "primitive" society rife with possibilities, awaiting cultivation and development from the Han "center." On the other hand, these nomadic communities were seen as part of the larger Chinese cultural and geopolitical entity, indispensable to national integrity.

Zhuang's photography was characterized by the style of photomontage and photo collage popularized by Shanghai-based magazines at the time. As William Schaeffer argues, "montage in Shanghai was not only a means of representing place; it was itself conceptualized pervasively as a spatial practice, a geographic aesthetic."[29] Image fragments, especially disembodied, dismembered, and dislocated images, were endowed with an agency and a voice in the photomontages published in Shanghai's magazines.[30] Even though Zhuang did not go so far as to include dismembered images, he freely juxtaposed landscape photos with portraits of Tibetan nomads. These montage photos create both exoticizing and intimate images of China's non-Han groups, highlighting both the geographic distance of the borderlands from urban China and the cultural and even sexual accessibility of the minority women for the visual consumption of Han readers. The bare-chested Tibetan women in his reportage look tantalizing and evocative of a tropical paradise. Yet such photos conceal the fact that the Tibetan Plateau can oftentimes be harsh and cold, and nomadic life was extremely unstable. Zhuang was somehow patching together a romanticized image of the Tibetan Plateau by rearranging the spatial aesthetics of the Plateau and placing human figures to accentuate his message of borderland cultural curiosity.

In addition to the visual and cultural appeal of his photographic reportage, during his journeys to the frontier regions, Zhuang repeatedly revealed his desire to contribute to the development of China's western regions.[31] This sentiment was infused with the nationalist call to guard and cultivate western China as a response to the Japanese occupation of northeastern China and other parts of the country in the 1930s. Even though he was not trained as a professional ethnologist, Zhuang exhibited great ethnological and ethnographic enthusiasm for studying China's frontier regions: He lamented the lack of *Chinese* ethnological studies of northwestern Sichuan, southwest Gansu, southern Qinghai, and northern Xikang and was determined to make his adventures part of China's national project to develop the western regions.[32]

As scholar Dong Weiming points out, Zhuang Xueben as a reporter enjoyed strong official and state support: Zhuang served as an advisory officer for the Steering Committee of the Xikang Provincial Government and later as an advisor for the Xikang Provincial Government.[33] Though he did not have a professional academic background in ethnology and anthropology, Zhuang shouldered important roles in academic organizations, such as serving as a council member of the China Border Studies Society.[34] Zhuang's wide political and social influence meant that his photographic and textual representations of west China's non-Han groups were much more than a personal endeavor or a particular intellectual taste, but epitomized the political and nationalistic need to imaginatively incorporate borderland communities into the core of a multiethnic China. As Zhuang's photographic and textual depictions of ethnic frontiers became widely disseminated through *Liangyou*'s urban readership, his efforts to visualize China's ethnic communities came to embody a "combination of state scrutiny, academic interests, and popular craze" toward the non-Han groups.[35] As such, his photographic projects and accompanying text endeavors carried a strong socionationalist incentive and an ethical urge to transform the "wasted" lands of the Tibetan Plateau into fertile lands for national development.

Despite Zhuang's efforts to forge a realist style of representing ethnic groups based on ethnographic documentation and his role as a cultural ambassador into the frontier regions, he was not immune to traditional China's epistemology about the ethnic "others." In his reportage, Zhuang repeatedly made moral judgements about the Tu Fan, such as characterizing Tu Fan society as one in which women are hardworking and men are "lazy in nature and idly wandering around" (*xingduo xianyou* 性惰閑遊).[36] He also concluded that since Tu Fan women work in men's place, they have developed a "strong and sturdy character" (*xingge qiangjian* 性格强健) and they look beautiful.[37]

In traditional China's gazetteer accounts, the descriptions of local societies and communities were almost always infused with moral judgments and a sense of cultural superiority from the Sinocentric writer. For example, Ming and Qing Dynasty accounts of the Miao tribes in southwest China routinely criticized the Miao for being unruly, rebellious, and having curious cultural customs.[38] Zhuang seems to have inherited this tradition of passing down moral judgments to indigenous societies by assigning essentialized attributes to "Tu Fan" men and women. His observations of indigenous societies bore a heavy stamp of the Confucian episteme and betrayed his somewhat Sinocentric view about the frontier societies. Zhuang formed moral judgments about gender relations in the Tu Fan society by overlooking the fact that the harsh environments and nomadic lifestyle of the Tibetans called for a more equal, if not somewhat matriarchal, relationship between the sexes, defying the rigid gender labor divisions and hierarchy of the Confucian society that he was more used to.

Furthermore, Zhuang's use of provocative words, such as "primitive" and "aborigines" (*yuanshi* 原始), is paired with half-naked portraits of the nomadic communities to create visually tantalizing cultural sensations for the consumption of *Liangyou*'s mostly urban, bilingual readers. By showing the Tibetan communities hard at work in a "pristine" landscape seemingly undisturbed by outside forces, Zhuang conjures up familiar images of the Noble Savage: The Tibetan nomads in his textual and visual representations exist as if "prior to any temporal alterations or corruption,"[39] showing timeless cultural traits and customs that were astounding to the Han reader. Therefore, despite Zhuang's quest for a realist style in his photography, his visual and textual constructions of the Tibetan borderland are mediated through an uneasy intersection of traditional Chinese and modern Western epistemologies about race, ethnicity, and indigeneity.

Minority Women and National Strength: Toward an "Aesthetic Regime" of Reimagining Ethnic Order in Republican-Era China

Perhaps the pinnacle of Zhuang Xueben's reporter role for *Liangyou* was the "Special Issue on New Sikong [Xikang]" (*Xin Xikang zhuanhao* 新西康專號) that the magazine published in 1940. At the height of the Second Sino-Japanese War, *Liangyou* started to adapt an increasingly didactic and patriotic tone, as the magazine routinely featured news reports about World War II and about Chinese soldiers and heroes who fought in the war. The "Special Issue" was premised on the fact that Xikang was the most recently established province of China, promising to be part of the future of a China characterized by interethnic unity and China's territorial integrity as it struggled to break away from Japanese colonization. The "Special Issue" features more than 100 photographs by Zhuang Xueben during his recent two-year journeys in Xikang.[40]

Importantly, this "Special Issue" attempted to reorient ethnic imagination in China in pivotal ways, somehow decentering the Han-centric ethnic order that was prevalent at the inception of the Republic. Late Qing to early Republican thinkers, such as Liang Qichao and Sun Yat-sen, valued the Han as the pillar of Chinese civilization. Contrary to this earlier trend, in the editor's note, the editors of *Liangyou* stated that with the growing tension of the Sino-Japanese War, the "heart of China has moved westward."[41] Indeed, with many academic institutions and universities relocated to Sichuan and Yunnan, and with the nation's capital itself moved to Chongqing, west China became the new political and cultural center of wartime China.

The editors went on to praise the pathbreaking Chinese immigrants who contributed to developing the various islands of the South China Sea, urging Chinese émigrés to return from overseas and start developing western China.[42] As a cosmopolitan magazine, *Liangyou* forged an outlook of a greater global Chinese community with multiple centers; it also started to envision a multiethnic, multicultural China not bound by the traditional Confucian worldview of the "civilized" Sinitic "self" pitted against the "barbarian" ethnic and foreign "others." In doing so, *Liangyou* became a pioneer of a multiethnic and even transnational imagination of Chinese-ness in Republican-era periodicals.

Similar to Zhuang's earlier photographic practice, in this "Special Issue," ethnic minority women figured prominently in Zhuang's and *Liangyou*'s construction of China's western multiethnic borderlands. The cover image of the "Special Issue" is a young "Lolo" (羅羅) woman smiling approvingly at the camera/viewer as she does embroidery work (fig. 8.3). The young woman, clad in a colorful ethnic costume, is captured at a happy moment of her work. This photo embodies Zhuang's ethnographic aesthetics, as the details of the woman's garment are touched up to mark her ethnicity, and she is presented in the context of her work. This portrait is also typical of Zhuang's photographic technique of creating intimate, close-up images of members of ethnic minority groups, especially minority women. These intimate portraits had a double function: On the one hand, they humanize and aestheticize ethnic groups for Han readers, destigmatizing the historical "barbaric" images of these groups that were deeply entrenched in the Sinocentric Confucian worldview. On the other hand, the images created a sense of familiarity between minority groups and Han readers, evoking a feeling of cultural pride by drawing attention to the multiethnic diversity of western China. In doing so, *Liangyou* achieved an "affective immediacy"[43] through its inclusive visual repertoire that embraced rural minority groups.[44]

Like Tu Fan, "Lolo" is a derogatory term from premodern China's historiographic traditions used to describe indigenous groups in Sichuan, Guizhou, and Yunnan, who are roughly categorized as the Yi (彝族) in the post-1949 ethnic classification system. Yet Zhuang reversed the historically negative connotations of Lolo by calling the cover girl "vibrant, healthy, and beautiful" (*huopo he jianmei* 活潑和健美) (fig. 8.3).[45] Elsewhere in his reportage for *Liangyou*, Zhuang admiringly called Tibetan women "strong and beautiful" (*qiangjian er mei* 强健而美),[46] attributing their physical strength and beauty to their hard work and the natural environment.

Fig. 8.3. The cover image of the "Special Issue on New Xikang" (*Xin Xikang zhuanhao*) is Zhuang's portrait of a Lolo woman. (Reprinted from *Liangyou*, special issue [1940].)

This aesthetic shift from calling frontier groups uncouth "barbarians" in earlier Chinese epistemology to regarding them as healthy and beautiful in the Republican era is crucial for understanding the changing representation of ethnic minority groups in modern China. Rather than blatantly throwing ethnic groups into a dry national ideology of multiethnic unity, later Republican-era reporters and artists like Zhuang Xueben endeavored to create what I call an *aesthetic regime* to foster embellished, visually inviting, ethnographically inspired images of ethnic communities in public discourses. Such an aesthetically motivated understanding of non-Han groups not only humanized and familiarized frontier groups to a Han intellectual public; it created a feeling of cultural intimacy and perhaps even cultural pride between the Han and the non-Han, despite the baggage of exoticizing and essentializing minority groups through an aestheticized lens.

Particularly, minority women, such as the "Tu Fan" and "Lolo" women

Fig. 8.4. Zhuang Xueben's photography of Rong women accentuates the ornamentality of the Rong's ethnic attire and conveys the aesthetic appeal of the Rong people. (Photograph courtesy of Beijing Fuzhuang Xueyuan.)

in Zhuang's photography, came to embody the Republican-era trend of constructing a new and robust femininity liberated from the shackles of traditional gender and social structures. As Maura Elizabeth Cunningham points out, from the late Qing to the early Republic, women's mobility, movement, and bodily autonomy were regarded as important signs of women's independence.[47] With an increasing interest in physical education and women's work in the first decades of the twentieth century, Republican-era China witnessed an ideological, social, and physical emancipation of women by valuing their lives outside of the family unit.[48] We can infer that this general social appreciation of women's autonomy and women's work contributed to Zhuang's favorable portrait of the beauty and strength of minority women (fig. 8.4).

In terms of his artistic technique, Zhuang played with different approaches, ranging from staging carefully posed portraiture of indigenous groups to capturing them at more spontaneous moments of their work and daily life. He was able to obtain aesthetically appealing and approving images of frontier groups

Fig. 8.5. The friendship Zhuang Xueben (*far left*) holds with local ethnic communities is evident in how he mingles with locals. (Photograph courtesy of Peng Xiaoling 第一财经.)

precisely because he built a friendly, harmonious relationship with local communities. Hiring local guides, Zhuang was frequently invited as a guest to local gatherings as he exercised the ethnographer's preference for staying with local communities and villagers, observing local life in great depth.[49] Zhuang's subjectivity as an empathetic reporter and his great enthusiasm for minority cultures were projected and translated in the smiling faces, aesthetic details, robust human images, and cultural curiosities that he tirelessly documented with his camera (figs. 8.5 and 8.6).

In creating culturally intimate portraits of minority groups, Zhuang epitomizes what Charles Laughlin and Li Guo call an "affective reversibility" in reportage in their introduction to this book: Zhuang's "ability to meet with and empathize with the subject and events" under his ethnographic investigations, and his acknowledgement of his "social relationality" as an urban Han reporter, contribute to transforming "aesthetic experiences [into] meaningful encounters to spark social change."[50] Zhuang's photographic reportage created an aesthetically appealing and affectively inviting repertoire of images for borderland communities. Captured during the years of China's struggles against Japanese invasion, the vibrant images of ethnic minorities served to uplift the national spirit for *Liangyou*'s urban readers and beyond. Even though some-

Fig. 8.6. Zhuang Xueben dressed in traditional Tibetan attire, appreciating Tibetan culture with locals. (Reprinted from Xin Xikang zhuanhao, *Liangyou*, issue 158 [1940].)

times Zhuang's images romanticized the environments and conditions of rural minorities, overall, they radically changed how non-Han groups could be understood and seen in modern China.

Coda: Zhuang Xueben's "Afterlife" and the Aesthetic Construction of Ethnic Minorities in Contemporary China

Zhuang Xueben continued to play an active role in ethnic minority cultural affairs in the late 1970s and early 1980s, until his death in his native Shanghai in 1984. Zhuang's black-and-white photography has assumed a vibrant afterlife in the twenty-first century. One day, I stumbled on Zhuang's photography in the virtual Ethnic Costume Museum (*minzu fushi bowuguan* 民族服饰博物馆) maintained by the Beijing Institute of Fashion Technology (*Beijing fuzhuang xueyuan* 北京服装学院). This virtual museum juxtaposes Zhuang's photography with videos on the skills involved in making ethnic costumes from various ethnic groups, as well as fieldwork videos depicting different ethnic traditions. The cover image for Zhuang's photography shows three young women from the Qiang 羌, Rong 戎, and Yi 彝 groups.[51] These young women look confidently at the camera with radiant smiles, creating an intimate visual interaction. These young women serve as a symbolic gateway and invitation

Fig. 8.7. The cover image of the virtual Ethnic Costume Museum at Beijing Fuzhuang Xueyuan. (Illustration courtesy of Beijing Fuzhuang Xueyuan.)

to explore minority cultures, as the viewer/user of the website can click on their images and enter the vast repertoire of Zhuang's visual documentation of each group (see fig. 8.7).

Indeed, Zhuang has now been widely proclaimed as the first "visual anthropologist" of modern China, and his legacy of creating aesthetically driven images of non-Han groups can be felt directly or indirectly in contemporary China. Zhuang's images of happy, smiling minorities might have inspired or served as a prototype for Mao-era propaganda posters about ethnic unity. From the late 20th century to the present, more contemporary reincarnations of Zhuang-style representations of minorities have been omnipresent in China. Whether it is the colorful new year's gala aired by CCTV or exotic ethnic tourism villages, minority groups in contemporary China tend to be constructed in aesthetic and visually alluring ways. Zhuang's photography has been increasingly used as historical-anthropological documents in today's China, while the elaborate details, artistic finesse, and careful compositions of his images also warrant a place in modern Chinese art history.

Zhuang Xueben's reportage projects embodied various epistemological and ideological transformations of his time; emphasizing empirical knowledge and personal investigations, the ethnological discourse of the Republican era propelled Zhuang to travel extensively and interact with indigenous societies in western China's borderlands. Driven by a nationalistic desire to foster interethnic unity, Zhuang became highly creative as he deployed artistic means and the visual technology of photography to portray the humanity and beauty of non-Han groups.

Zhuang imaginatively juxtaposed the search for the "real" with a quest for beauty as he shouldered the ideological baggage of a Republican-era scholar straddling different epistemological worlds. On the one hand, he set out to depict the true living conditions and acquire real knowledge about ethnic frontiers through personal and "objective" ethnological investigations; on the other hand, such investigations were partially filtered through traditional China's gazetteer conventions and Western racial discourses. At times, hints of exoticization were present in Zhuang's photography, as minority women were veiled in an eternalized sense of beauty. Zhuang's search for the "real" authenticated the desire of Han intellectuals of his time to construct a multiethnic Chinese nationhood by forging an inclusive visual imaginary that embraced the differences between the Han and the non-Han. He turned ethnic differences into visual symbols for the cultural consumption of *Liangyou*'s readership and for the nationalist imagination of a diverse, capacious Chinese identity.

Fig. 8.8. Zhuang Xueben wears Tibetan Buddhist regalia. (Courtesy Ma Xiaofeng and He Qing, Pengpai [澎湃].)

Zhuang's visualization of a new Chinese identity went beyond nationalistic discourses to denote cultural membership—the ethnic groups that were historically excluded from "Chinese culture" were now included in a more encompassing Chinese cultural membership. Through his search for the "real," Zhuang created embodied knowledge about ethnic groups: Not only did he personally travel to minority frontiers, he frequently mingled with local communities, donned ethnic costumes, and took on the persona of ethnic minorities to visualize cultural diversity and intimacy (fig. 8.8).

Zhuang used his own body as an experimental site for the artistic and cultural negotiation of the boundaries between the "Han" and the "non-Han."

Zhuang's efforts were both playful and serious: His playful gesture of appropriating minority cultures seemed to suggest that ethnic boundaries ought to be porous and flexible; his performative embodiment of minority identities also suggested a broader social and cultural desire in the Republican era to expand the conceptual and cultural boundaries of Chineseness by decentering the Han. The documentary *and* aesthetic, personal value of Zhuang's work poses interesting and important questions for researchers today: Zhuang's representation of ethnic groups was motivated by an aesthetic understanding of historically denigrated groups, and such an aesthetic and personal understanding in turn contributes to enriching the anthropological and cultural knowledge of different groups. Perhaps the construction of aesthetic and embodied knowledge does not have to involve caricatures or reductions of the subjects of research, but can illuminate the complexity of the research subjects and animate academic inquiries about the motivations and contexts of cultural representations across time and space.

NOTES

1. *Zaixian shijue zazhi* 在线视觉杂志.
2. Zhuang (1937), *Qiangrong Kaochaji* 羌戎考察記, 2.
3. Quoted in Leibold, *Reconfiguring Chinese Nationalism*, 7.
4. Cai, *Shuo minzuxue*, 1
5. Cai, *Shuo minzuxue*, 2.
6. Cai, *Shuo minzuxue*, 4; emphasis added.
7. See, for example, Hu Siao-chen's study of literary accounts about southwestern "barbarian" others in her book, *Ming-Qing wenxue zhongde xinan xushi* [The southwest in Ming-Qing literary imagination] 明清文學中的西南敘事; and David M. Deal and Laura Hostetler's translated volume, *The Art of Ethnography: A Chinese "Miao Album."*
8. Jianmin Wang, *Zhongguo minzuxue shi*, 110.
9. Ming-ke Wang, "Introduction," 19–20.
10. Leibold, *Reconfiguring Chinese Nationalism*, 134.
11. Mignolo, "Globalization," 36–38.
12. Mullaney, *Coming to Terms with the Nation*, chapter 1.
13. For example, during the Sino-Japanese War in the 1940s, Japan started dropping pamphlets announcing the Japanese government's support for creating an independent Huihui state in Xinjiang; Japanese secret agents also went to great lengths to "[promise] to support tribal and religious leaders" in China's ethnic frontier regions to help these groups "break away from Chinese control." Leibold, 137.
14. Zhuang Wenjun, "Wode fuqin Zhuang Xueben."
15. Zhuang Wenjun, "Wode fuqin Zhuang Xueben."
16. Zhuang Wenjun, "Wode fuqin Zhuang Xueben."
17. *Quanguo baokan suoyin.*
18. Paul G. Pickowicz, Kuiyi Shen, and Yinjing Zhang, "Introduction," 1–2.

19. Yanshuo Zhang, "Beyond Minority," 73–74.
20. Laughlin, *Chinese Reportage*, 2.
21. Laughlin, *Chinese Reportage*, 3.
22. Laughlin, *Chinese Reportage*, 3.
23. From Laughlin and Guo's introduction to this volume.
24. *Liangyou*, issue 154, 1940.
25. *Liangyou*, issue 154, 1940.
26. Yanshuo Zhang, *Beyond Minority*, 77.
27. Yajun Mo, "The New Frontier," 121.
28. Zhuang, "Jinri zhi Tufan minzu."
29. William Schaefer, *Shadow Modernism*, 148.
30. Schaefer, *Shadow Modernism*, 150.
31. Zhuang Xueben (2007), *Qiangrong Kaochaji*, 4.
32. Zhuang, *Qiangrong Kaochaji*, 4.
33. Dong Weimin, "Biandi yixiang," 46.
34. Dong, "Biandi yixiang," 46.
35. Yajun Mo, "The New Frontier," 124.
36. Zhuang Xueben, "Jinri zhi Tufan minzu," 14–15.
37. Zhuang, "Jinri zhi Tufan minzu," 14–15.
38. Janet Ng, "A Moral Landscape"; David M. Deal and Laura Hostetler, *The Art of Ethnography*.
39. Tony Brown, "The Primitive, The Aesthetic, and the Savage," 25.
40. Editors, Xin Xikang zhuanhao, *Liangyou* (special issue, 1940): 1. The general social excitement over the establishment of the new Xikang province was reflected in Zhuang Xueben's expeditions. He was mostly interested in the southwestern borderlands (sometimes called the Sino-Tibetan borderland in Western scholarship), rather than other borderlands, such as Xinjiang. Even though Zhuang did journey into Shaanxi province, there is no clear evidence that he went as far north as Xinjiang.
41. *Liangyou* (special issue, 1940): 1.
42. *Liangyou* (special issue, 1940): 1.
43. Paul G. Pickowicz, Kuiyi Shen, and Yingjin Zhang, "Introduction," 11.
44. It is interesting and important to note that *Liangyou* and Zhuang himself highlighted southwestern ethnic groups, rather than northwestern groups such as the Uighurs and the Kazaks, as the new "compatriots" of China. This may be due to the prevalent racial discourse of the Republican era, which classified southwestern ethnic groups, such as the Tibetans and the Lolo, as part of the "Monogloid" race that the Han belonged to. Northwestern ethnic groups were most often classified as belonging to the Caucasoid race.
45. Editors, "Special Issue on New Sikong [Xikang]," *Liangyou*, 1.
46. Zhuang Xueben, "Jinri zhi Tufan minzu," 14–15.
47. Cunningham, "Modern Girl," 99.
48. Cunningham, "Modern Girl," 99.
49. Zhuang Xueben (2007), *Qiangrong Kaochaji*, 4, 5, 38.
50. See Laughlin and Guo's introduction to this volume, "From Reportage to Nonfiction Art."

51. It is important to note that the terms "Qiang," "Rong," and "Yi" are not eternal ethnonyms but have their own complex histories of formation and transformation. For a discussion of the formation and transformation of the "Qiang" identity, see my dissertation, *Beyond Minority: Ethnicity, Modernity, and the Invention of the Qiang Identity*. This chapter has discussed a bit about the usage of "Rong" in Chinese historiography. "Rong" is not an officially classified ethnic minority group in post-1949 China, though certain Tibetan groups in Sichuan province continue to call themselves Jiarong Tibetans (嘉绒藏族). "Yi," or 彝族, was invented in the 1950s to replace the "Lolo" and is an officially recognized ethnic minority group in China today.

REFERENCES

Anderson, Benedict. *Imagined Communities: Reflections on the Origin and Spread of Nationalism*. London: Verso, 1991.

Beijing Fuzhuang Xueyuan 北京服装学院 [Beijing Fashion Technology]. Ethnic Costume Museum [Minzu fushi bowuguan 民族服饰博物馆]. http://www.biftmuseum.com/

Brown, Tony C. *The Primitive, the Aesthetic, and the Savage: An Enlightenment Problematic*. Minneapolis: University of Minnesota Press, 2012.

Cai, Yuanpei 蔡元培. Shuo minzuxue 說民族學 [On Ethnology]. In *Cai Yuanpei minzuxue lunzhu* 蔡元培民族學論著 [Cai Yuanpei's Works on Ethnology], edited by Zhongguo minzu xuehui [China Association of Ethnology], 1–11. Taipei: Taiwan zhonghua shuju, 1962.

Cunningham, Maura Elizabeth. "The Modern Girl in Motion: Women and Sports in *Liangyou*." In *Liangyou, Kaleidoscopic Modernity and the Shanghai Global Metropolis, 1926–1945*, edited by Paul G. Pickowicz, Kuiyi Shen, and Yinjing Zhang, 95–109. Leiden: Brill, 2013.

Deal, David, and Laura Hostetler, translators. *The Art of Ethnography: A Chinese "Miao Album."* Seattle: University of Washington Press, 2006.

Dikotter, Frank. *The Discourse of Race in Modern China*. London: Hurst, 1992.

Dong, Weimin 董卫民. "Biandi yixiang, guojia xiangxiang, xinmeiti: cong sange weidu zai sikao Zhuang Xueben xibu minzuzhi sheying." 边地意象 国家想象 "新媒体"-从三个维度再思考庄学本西部民族志摄影 [Image of borderland, image of nation and "new Media"—rethinking Zhuang Xueben's photography of northwest ethnology from three dimensions]. *Xibei Minzu Daxue Xuebao* 西北民族大学学报 [Journal of Northwest Minzu University] no. 6 (2017): 44–49.

Duara, Prasenjit. "Deconstructing the Chinese Nation." *Australian Journal of Chinese Affairs*, no. 30 (July 1993): 1–26. https://doi.org/10.2307/2949990

Hu, Siao-chen 胡曉真. *Ming-Qing wenxue zhongde xinan xushi* 明清文學中的西南敘事 [The Southwest in Ming-Qing Literary Imagination]. Taipei: National Taiwan University Press, 2017.

Laughlin, Charles A. *Chinese Reportage: The Aesthetics of Historical Experience*. Durham: Duke University Press, 2002.

Leibold, James. *Reconfiguring Chinese Nationalism: How the Qing Frontier and Its Indigenes Became Chinese*. New York: Palgrave Macmillan. 2007.

Ma, Xianfeng 马晓峰, and He Qing 何青. "Dangnian Zhuang Xueben zoude natiaolu, jiuxiang xitian qujing yiyang" 当年庄学本走的那条路，就像西天取经一样 [The road traveled by Zhuang Xueben back then was like a Buddhist pilgrimage to India]. Pengpai 澎湃 [The Paper], 2021. https://www.thepaper.cn/newsDetail_forward_15681107

Mignolo, Walter D. "Globalization, Civilization Processes, and the Relocation of Languages and Cultures." In *The Cultures of Globalization*, edited by Fredric Jameson and Masao Miyoshi, 32–53. Durham: Duke University Press, 1998.

Mo, Yajun. "The New Frontier: Zhuang Xueben and Xikang Province." In *Chinese History in Geographical Perspective*, edited by Yongtao Du and Jeff Kyong-McClain, 121–40. Lanham: Lexington Books, 2013.

Mullaney, Thomas. *Coming to Terms with the Nation: Ethnic Classification in Modern China*. Berkeley: University of California Press, 2011.

Ng, Janet. "A Moral Landscape: Reading Shen Congwen's Autobiography and Travelogues." *Chinese Literature: Essays, Articles, Reviews* (CLEAR) 23 (2001): 81–102.

Peng, Xiaoling 彭晓玲. "Ta yong guan'ai pingdeng de jingtou, paixiale bashiduo nian qian de xi'nan he xibei bianjiang" 他用关爱平等的镜头，拍下了80多年前的西南和西北边疆 [He used his caring attitude and his photographic lens equally in photographing the southwestern and northwestern frontiers from more than eighty years ago]. Diyi caijing 第一财经. https://m.yicai.com/news/101368994.html

Pickowicz, Paul G., Kuiyi Shen, and Yinjing Zhang. "Introduction: *Liangyou*, Popular Print Media, and Visual Culture." In *Liangyou, Kaleidoscopic Modernity and the Shanghai Global Metropolis, 1926–1945*, edited by Paul G. Pickowicz, Kuiyi Shen, and Yinjing Zhang, 1–13. Leiden: Brill, 2013.

Quanguo baokan suoyin 全国报刊索引 [Indexes to national newspapers and periodicals]. University of Michigan Chinese Studies Database. https://www-cnbksy-com.proxy.lib.umich.edu/literature/literature/cb6201d28ae43b25c62baa984950ff61

Schaefer, William. *Shadow Modernism: Photography, Writing, and Space in Shanghai, 1925–1937*. Durham: Duke University Press, 2017.

Wang, Jianmin 王建民. *Zhongguo minzuxue shi* 中国民族学史 [History of ethnology in China]. Kunming: Yunnan jiaoyu chubanshe, 1997.

Wang, Ming-ke 王明珂. "Introduction." In *Chuanxi minsu diaocha jilu 1929* 川西民俗調查記錄 1929 [Records of the 1929 folk and ethnic research studies in West Sichuan], by Li Guangming and Wang Yuanhui, edited by Wang Ming-ke. Taipei: Academia Sinica, 2004.

Zaixian shijue zazhi [Visual Magazine Online 在线视觉杂志]. "Zhuang Xueben: Zhongguo yingxiang renleixue xianqu." [Zhuang Xueben: The pioneer of China's visual anthropology] 庄学本：中国影像人类学先驱. http://www.imgii.com/archives/51205 (accessed July 18, 2022, no longer available).

Zhang, Yanshuo. "Beyond Minority: Ethnicity, Modernity, and the Invention of the Qiang Identity in China." PhD diss., Stanford University, 2018.

Zhang, Yanshuo. "Between Representation and Repression: The Photography of San Francisco's Historical Chinatown and the Visual Politics of Representing the Racial Other." *Stanford Journal of Asian American Studies* (2019): 10–26.

Zhuang, Wenjun 庄文骏. "Wode fuqin Zhuang Xueben" 我的父亲庄学本 [My father

Zhuang Xueben]. *Zhonghua wenhua huabao* 中华文化画报 [China Culture Pictorial] 2010 (3), 54–61.

Zhuang, Xueben 莊學本. "Jinri zhi Tufan minzu" 今日之吐蕃民族 [The Tufan aborigines today]. *Liangyou* 良友, issue 112 (1935): 14–15.

Zhuang, Xueben 莊學本. *Qiangrong kaocha ji* 羌戎考察記 [Expeditions into the land of the Qiang and Rong]. Shanghai: Liangyou tushu yinshua gongsi, 1937.

Zhuang, Xueben 庄学本. *Qiangrong kaocha ji: Sheying dashi Zhuang Xueben ershi shiji sanshi niandai de xibu renwen tanfang* 羌戎考察记：摄影大师庄学本二十世纪三十年大的西部人文探访 [Expeditions into the land of the Qiang and Rong: photographic master Zhuang Xueben's humanist explorations and visits to the West in the 1930s], edited by Ma Naihui 马鼐辉, Wang Zhaowu 王昭武, and Zhuang Wenjun 庄文骏. Chengdu: Sichuan chuban jituan, Sichuan minzu chubanshe, 2007.

NINE

Chinese-in-Japan Documentary and Media Reportage in the New Millennium

Toward a Disjunctive History of Transnational Affectivity

Ran Ma

Toward a Disjunctive History

This article focuses on the documentary and media (self-)representations of and by Chinese in Japan since the mid-1990s, emphasizing (im)migrants from the People's Republic of China. Specifically, I aim to foreground two disjunctive moments of the Chinese-in-Japan documentary and media reportage. The first centers on a four-episode television documentary series that aired in Japan between 2000 and 2006, *Our Days Studying Abroad: The Everyday in Japan* (私たちの留学生活—日本での日々, *Our Days* hereafter),[1] a collaboration between Fuji Television—one of Japan's major private broadcasters—and the self-made, independent documentarian Zhang Liling 张丽玲, a former international student from China who was working for a Tokyo-based company at the time.

The second line of inquiry looks at the nonfiction works centering on Li Xiaomu 李小牧 (Ri Komaki after naturalization). Born in 1960 in Hunan province, Li came to Tokyo in 1988 for self-funded study. While working as a "guide" (案内人) soliciting international customers for adult entertainment venues in Kabukichō, Shinjuku, Li quickly emerged in the pre–social media age as a celebrity of sorts. This chapter considers a web series titled *I Am Li Xiaomu* (我是李小牧, 2019, *Li Xiaomu* hereafter), directed by "Tokyo Wen'ge" (Wen Qiang 温强, a Tokyo resident from the PRC) and produced by NetEasy News Japan, as well as, among others, the documentary *I Want to Run for Office* (我要参选, 2016), directed by Xing Fei 邢菲, who used to study in Japan. The latter work chronicles Li's foray into Japanese politics, specifically his running for the Shinjuku Council of Tokyo in 2015 as a candidate of the Democratic Party of Japan; the former offers a meticulous look at Li's second—yet doomed—campaign for district councilor in the spring of 2019 as an unaffiliated candidate.

Aligned with the anti-Sinocentric, postcolonial underpinning of Sinophone studies, this chapter contemplates the development of Chinese-in-Japan subjectivity, viewing it in connection with diversified Sinophone/Xenophone positions and articulations including, but not limited to, the experiences of overseas Chinese (華僑・華人) and their communities, Japanese "war orphans" (残留孤児), "stranded war wives" (残留婦人) and their descendants, and, importantly, "newcomers" from the PRC who are "students, workers, family members, long-term residents and undocumented migrant workers."[2] Unlike the older generations of overseas Chinese who arrived in Japan before World War II, the inflow of the newcomers is directly related to China's policies of reform and opening-up since 1978. This new wave of immigration directly reflects the Japanese government's changing regulations over the decades, aspects of which cannot be fully explored here. Even though there is no lack of literary reportage and novels by Sinophone intellectuals and writers who came to Japan before 1949, as well as those by the mainland newcomer writers since around the late 1980s,[3] when it comes to Chinese-in-Japan cinema and media, one encounters a fragmented body of work that, regrettably, is under-archived and under-researched. Such conditions have made it challenging to develop a coherent account of the endeavors of Chinese-in-Japan documentarians and videographers. It is noteworthy that, unlike their *zainichi* (在日) Korean or Koreans-in-Japan counterparts, most Chinese-in-Japan filmmakers have not permanently settled in Japan, and the volatile experiences of being *zainichi*—meaning "residing in Japan"—constitute only a temporary stage of their lives.[4]

Zhang Yingjin shows that literary reportage and independent documentaries in China share a similar realistic pursuit of what Bill Nichols in his study of documentary unpacks as "epistephilia," which associates "a distinct type of pleasure" with not only acquiring knowledge, but with exploring "the various ways in which knowledge is acquired, disseminated, and contested."[5] Extending Zhang's discussion, one may argue that, like their literary counterparts, the documentary and media reportage under examination has an epistephilic dimension in bearing witness to the Sinophone subjects' lives being *zainichi*. Nichols has illustrated that epistephilia in documentary is imbricated with what he terms "gnostiphilia," that is, "knowledge not dependent on distance, objectivity, and reasoned analysis alone but also on empathy, identification, feeling, tone, and sensibility."[6] Foregrounding the affective dimension of documentary media, and also echoing Moran's chapter regarding the "emotional knowledge" one obtains from documentary,[7] this study looks at the film and media representations of affects, emotions, and affective life—here examined under the umbrella term of "affectivity"—related to the Chinese students and migrants in Japan. Following Lily Wong, I do not separate affect from emotion, but view their relationship as "a spiral feedback loop instead of being a linear genealogy"; I also consider "affect as a politics of emotional mobilization—the power to move and be moved by others," an analytical perspective that incorporates "arguments for flow and fixity as well as extratextual and representational characteristics of affect."[8]

Associating reportage with documentary realism and particularly the observational mode, I emphasize how the filmmaker adopts "a peculiar mode of presence 'on the scene'" as the events unfold in front of the camera, hence exhibiting "a sense of duration of actual events."[9] For the viewers, the "on-the-spot" aesthetics "yields an impression of observing at the scene, in the here and now, as if the real is unfolding unmediated."[10] As elucidated by Laughlin and Guo in the introduction to this volume, reportage concerns an "affective community" that correlates with "the transversal communication among the author, the reader/audience, and the subject in reportage."[11] For them, reportage is underpinned by an ethico-aesthetic paradigm envisioning "a pluralistic subjectivity through aesthetic evocation of audience responses and meaningful configurations with varied affective relations."[12] This chapter considers how *Our Days* and *Li Xiaomu* leverage disparate transnational media-technological assemblages in engaging the ethico-aesthetics. Particularly, I examine affectivity generated by and circulated through these film and media works, first by looking at their production and circulation and then by turning to the multilayered sociopolitical interrelations that Chinese in Japan are situated within, contending with, and working through. In the context of social transformations in both China and Japan since the mid-1990s and considering shifting transnational film and media ecologies, my aim is to (re-)align a minor history of Chinese-in-Japan documentary media with a focus on affectivity.

From TV to the Web

It is useful to first sketch out the production and distribution of the documentary and media reportage in question. This needs to be contextualized vis-à-vis the diplomatic rapprochement of, and tensions between, China and Japan since the pivotal year of 1972, a detailed account of which is beyond the scope of this chapter. Unpacking Sino-Japanese relations under the two administrations led by Abe Shinzō (2006–7 and 2012–14), for example, Kinnia Yau presents analytics indexing the changes in public opinion and feelings on the part of the citizens of each nation over the decades. Nevertheless, grounded in methodological nationalism, Yau's analysis overlooks subjects whose identities or residential statuses do not easily fit into the distinct categories of either Chinese or Japanese nationals—an aspect my study aims to address and further complicate.

Our Days (2000–2006) was mainly self-funded by Zhang and her family and friends until they secured a broadcasting partnership in China, which qualified the documentary series as an "independent" project in a transnational context.[13] That said, the production entirely relied on professional support from Fuji TV (see fig. 9.1).[14] Foregrounding the life stories and everyday struggles of several Chinese students in Japan from the mid-1990s to the 2000s, episodes often wrap up on an uplifting note, endorsing the characters' perseverance and determination to "eat bitterness" (吃苦) in a challenging environment. The Chinese version of *Our Days* premiered on Beijing Television in 1999 with the title *Our Days Studying Abroad* (我们的留学生活).[15] The Japanese version debuted on Fuji TV a year later, kicking off with an episode titled "A Young Overseas Student" (小さな留学生, May 2000), which follows nine-year-old schoolgirl Zhang Su, who, having recently arrived in Japan due to her father's job transfer, finds herself having to cope with the totally strange environment at a local primary school without knowing much Japanese language or culture. The final episode, "Persisting with Tears in Eyes" (泣きながら生きて, *Persisting* hereafter), which I shall turn to later, aired in November 2006.

The Chinese version of *Our Days* was publicized as "the first-ever documentary series produced by overseas students." In "post-socialist subject-making China," television "has become a particularly important resource for projects geared toward constructing a sense of national, ethnic, gendered, generational identity."[16] After it aired, the CCP-affiliated *Guangming Daily* (光明日报) organized a symposium of TV professionals and researchers on the series, where experts expressed admiration for its realistic aesthetics and reportage value, suggesting that the episodes contributed to reimagining the

Fig. 9.1. Zhang's visit to Fuji TV in 1995: "[P]lease loan me a camera!"

lives of Chinese students overseas and the national spirit (民族精神) in a new era.[17] The Japanese version gained recognition within the Japanese TV industry as well as popularity among transnational audiences, enabling Zhang Liling to build her career as a media entrepreneur and realize her "Japanese Dream." In 1998 Zhang became the chairperson of CCTV Daifu 大富, arguably the first satellite TV channel broadcasting Chinese-language programs in Japan.[18]

Moving to Li Xiaomu, his extraordinary transborder trajectory has inspired several transmedia works, including but not limited to various Kabukichō-themed autobiographies, photobooks, and transnationally produced feature films, such as *Shinjuku Incident* (新宿事件, 2009). Publicizing itself as a "reportage reality show" (纪实真人秀), *Li Xiaomu* consists of bilingually subtitled episodes, each ten to twenty minutes long. It primarily relies on the privately run video accounts of Live Japan (日本现场) on video-streaming and -sharing platforms such as YouTube and Bilibili 哔哩哔哩—the latter being the largest video-streaming platform in China today—for distribution and as spaces for user interactions.[19] The series should be seen within a wider spectrum of digital technology–powered networks that have facilitated the production, circulation, and distribution of image works about and by Chinese in

Japan. These networks converge with a media landscape Tianqi Yu characterizes as China's "post-cinematic era" since the 2010s, wherein personal videos "are produced with DV cameras, webcams and smartphones, are streamed on domestic video-sharing sites and watched on personalised portable digital devices."[20] However, although Live Japan promised that the users would "witness the birth of the first Japanese councilman who's from mainland China," Li's defeat was already announced *before* most of the episodes were streamed online. Transnational viewers thus do not follow Li's campaign with an acute sense of real-time participation or suspense. As I discuss below, in leveraging Li's overabundant online celebrity presence (e.g., X/Twitter and Weibo accounts, videos circulated on social media platforms), along with his prominent career as a "cosmopolitan public intellectual,"[21] this series serves as a key component of Li's reality media assemblage.

To Eat Bitterness and to Persist with Tears

Echoing Lily Wong, who views the "work(ing) of affect" in terms of process, Chang Hsiao-hung in her insightful analysis of "trans-national affect" suggests how the first usage of affect as "personal affection" and the second usage as the "pre-personal, non-subjective force of assemblage" could "superimpose upon each other," which can be considered the "*double entendre*" of affect.[22] Chang offers a critical lens to ruminate on the potential of "trans" as in "trans-national," as she pushes for a rethinking of its habitual association with border crossing. "Trans" is thus envisioned as "an affective assemblage endowed with an intensity to illustrate the complex theoretical linkage of trans-historicity and trans-nationality in the current discourses on the globalization of culture."[23]

Inspired by the framework offered by Wong and Chang, I turn to how the works in question have configured discursive, textual surfaces wherein a spectrum of affects/emotions associated with diasporic and migrant experiences, displaced/dislocated bodies, and senses of un/belonging can be registered and worked through. Second, I interrogate the dynamics underlying the transnational and transmedia production, circulation, and distribution of the film and media works by means of the following questions: How do the nonfiction works mediate/mediatize the migrant experiences of Chinese in Japan (including experiences of studying abroad) concerning affective registers such as tears, hope, and optimism? How should we approach the affective connectivities between the filmmaker (videographer), the filmed, and the translocal audience (users) concerning the (self-)representations of Chinese im/migrants at the textual, discursive level and beyond? Together with *Our Days*, *Li Xiaomu* registers and manifests "the multiple modes of attachment, endurance, and attunement to the world and to the contemporary world of spreading precarity and normative dissolution" present for Chinese migrants in Japan.[24]

The production of *Our Days* spanned the latter half of the 1990s and early 2000s, with most of the shooting taking place in Japan. Although Japan was home to the world's second-largest economy in the 1980s, the 1990s came to be known as its "lost decade(s)" following the collapse of its economic bubble. The number of Chinese students in Japan began to grow dramatically after China relaxed overseas travel restrictions in 1988. However, many newly arrived Chinese students back then "dropped out of school and turned to illegal employment and crime," which was complicated by widely reported cases of "illegal entries, overstays, and felonies involving Chinese."[25] This social reality forms the backdrop for Zhang Liling's focus on students from China. Interpreting a lineup of Japanese films and TV dramas since the 2000s, Yau observes that "over 90% of Japanese have a negative view of China and Chinese people," despite the dramatic increase in the number of Chinese tourists to Japan since 2000.[26]

Yet the contemporaneous conflicts between the two nations as expressed in public opinion are hardly touched on in *Our Days*. As each episode opens, audiences see newcomers from China arrive in Japan and be instantly overwhelmed by the dazzling modernity of Tokyo. Most of them believe that being accepted into Japanese universities ("The Young People"/若者たち, 2000) and earning their desired degrees ("My Sun"/私の太陽, 2001) will ensure the fulfillment of their "Japanese Dream."[27] Most episodes of *Our Days* foreground and end in this stage of "study abroad," with the protagonists' future remaining open. The Chinese students' struggles onscreen can be grasped by attending to the affective work of "eating bitterness," namely enduring all forms of hardship, with the implication that the protagonists will overcome these challenges to embrace the "good life" to come. As is common in Japanese TV documentaries, the episodes blend the observational and the expository—"on-the-spot" observations and interactions with the protagonists are sometimes complemented by Zhang Liling's voice-over, which offers restrained explanations in soft tones. Even though Zhang navigates viewers through life experiences that are not her own, her accented narration registers a layer of subjectivity rather than authority, leading viewers to perceive that the individual students and their stories on screen embody structures of feeling that resonate with a broader affective community. This sense of collectivity, though loosely and contingently formed, is funneled through the first-person plural used in the series title.

"The Young People" is emblematic. Two Chinese students from Zhejiang arrive in Tokyo in the spring of 1996. Han Song, twenty-six years old, has quit his job to pursue overseas study in Japan, though he has a comfortable life at home. A nineteen-year-old girl, Wang Ermin, comes to live with her aunt in suburban Tokyo. Like other episodes in the series, "The Young People" does not try to tone down the bitterness, conflicts, and disappointments. As Han and Wang are busy attending Japanese-language schools and preparing for their college entrance exams, they are seen juggling the part-time jobs they need due to the extraordinarily high cost of living in Tokyo. Understandably, the documentary does not merely focus on classroom activities. Han and Wang work in restaurants and convenience stores, the typical three-K jobs (*kiken*/dangerous, *kitsui*/painful, *kitanai*/dirty) normally available to foreign immigrants and overseas students in 1990s Japan.

At a certain point, Han disappears, and the documentary crew loses contact with him. Months later he reaches out again, with the reunion triggering mixed feelings. Accompanied by Zhang's gentle voiceover, the hand-held camera follows Han back to his newly rented place at night. Aware of how the dimly lit, dilapidated building might appear to the crew and viewers, Han looks right into the camera and mildly mocks himself, saying, "There are lots of poor Japanese too. . . . They are also staying here, just like me." Then, in an indoor sequence, Han in silence first rubs his eyes and nose subtly to suppress his emotions, and turns to the camera and asks, earnestly, whether everybody feels "the first year is the bitterest [最苦的]," adding, "I mean, mentally speaking, the toughest [最苦的]," before the viewers see him resuming the study of his Japanese-language textbook that will run late into the night. By the episode's end, two and a half years have elapsed since shooting began. By this point, both protagonists have survived their extremely tough work/study schedules. They have seemingly grown into different, more-mature individuals, ready to move on to new stages of their lives in Japan.

The final episode of the series, *Persisting*, pushes the affective trope of "eating bitterness" to its extreme. It chronicles the fifteen-year struggle of its protagonist, Ding Shangbiao. Ding, from a lower-working-class Shanghai family, works in Tokyo as an illegal migrant enduring the unbearable solitude of being separated from his family while working hard to fulfill his dream of saving enough money to support his daughter's overseas studies in the United States. When Ding's wife flies to New York to reunite with their daughter, who has begun her studies there, she briefly stops in Tokyo, where the couple reunites

Fig. 9.2. Ding and his wife's reunion. (From "Persisting with Tears in Eyes" [2009].)

after thirteen years before parting again (fig. 9.2). Highly acclaimed by domestic audiences in Japan when it was aired on Fuji TV, *Persisting* was released in Japanese cinemas in 2009. In her analysis of this documentary, Yiman Wang carefully unpacks the affective discharges—tears—by interlacing them with Ding's personal saga, the documentary's rave reception among both Chinese and Japanese audiences, and Zhang Liling's documentary style, marked by her camera's zooming "onto family members' faces from different angles, capturing every muscle movement as they try to fight back the tears, only to be reduced to inconsolable weeping at home, in the subway, and at the airport."[28]

Dreaming the Japanese Dream

The leitmotif of "eating bitterness" is juxtaposed with the hopeful sequences about the Chinese students' dreams and "good life" prospects for a better career and livelihood (for the family) and for individual achievement, which in the series are partially historicized within and contrasted with tumultuous periods in the PRC (e.g., the Cultural Revolution). Therefore, in *Our*

Days, studying abroad does not simply indicate geographic movement per se, but also movement in time and ontological transformation, from the less-developed to the super-developed, and from the semimodern to the futuristic, while being voluntarily integrated into the system of global capitalism and its urban infrastructures. Noteworthy is Han's exclamation when he first sets eyes on the Shinjuku area, which looks to him like the "paradise" broadcast on TV. "Eating bitterness" thus has configured a mechanism/process through which Chinese students have their individual values and affective affiliations—familial, national, socialist, or cosmopolitan—reterritorialized by neoliberal aspirations. "Studying abroad" is foregrounded as an unprecedented, liberating opportunity for Chinese students and migrants to get connected to the developed world and its affective regime—a Japanese Dream, despite the concomitant outcomes of self-sacrifice for the family by Old Ding and vice versa (the caring wife and her researcher husband in *My Sun*).

However, despite its lack of interest in dealing with national identities and the issues of multiculturalism, the series foregrounds how the temporal-spatial configuration of Chinese students' lives—classrooms, dorms and apartments, part-time workplaces—is not in sync with and very much remains marginalized vis-à-vis the polished, hypermodern metropolitanism of Japan and its spectacular infrastructure. Except for in "A Young Overseas Student," the (adult) Chinese individuals onscreen rarely interact with ordinary Japanese people deeply or with much sophistication. Somewhat unexpectedly, one becomes aware of a strong anachronism if one watches a version of this documentary series from its broadcasting period on a Japanese TV screen during the early 2000s. Between segments about the personal struggles and tear-jerking stories of the suffering and endurance of the Chinese students and migrants, commercials bombard audiences with montages of euphoric high consumerism, beaming faces, and cosmopolitan coolness, contrasting sharply with the cramped rooms and endless menial chores such as dishwashing that the students and migrants must undertake. If Chinese-in-Japan subjectivity can be grasped as a becoming that has generated its own affects and is part of a larger assemblage of affects, the trans-affectivity is arguably located in anachronism, in the interstices between the disjointed, heterogeneous temporalities of modernities.

Commenting on the Japanese audiences' reactions to *Persisting*, Wang observes, "Battling current financial crisis and collective despair, the audience found solace and inspiration in the family's perseverant love that enabled it to get through difficult times while empowering the younger generation."[29] In relation to the socioeconomic situation in Japan in the 1990s and early 2000s,

Wang's comments on the series' therapeutic, cathartic effects are relevant to the entirety of *Our Days*. Yet one may also want to interrogate whether viewers in Japan in the early 2000s found "solace and inspirations" in the understanding that the Chinese/students were safely caught up in their own "bitterness-eating" efforts or the disjointed interstices of temporalities. Throughout the series, the Chinese migrants' dreams might also reassure audiences that "Japan" was still a desirable place and could provide hope for a future. In other words, instead of closing the gaps between "Japan" as ultramodern and "China" as less modern, affective connectivities help configure and maintain the differentiations between Japan and its Other. With *Persisting*, the (Japanese) audience is compelled to react, viewing the Chinese working-class family from a perspective that is both humane and yet somewhat privileged, superior, and distanced. The hot tears alleviate, if not defuse, the possible moral judgment of Ding's prolonged stay in Japan and his illegal status, yet they coexist in the public sphere with racist discourse that makes associations in Japan's mass media between the Chinese(-looking) migrants and criminality, rightist politicians' aggressive speeches on foreigners, and the xenophobic public imagination.[30]

Our Days constitutes one side of the same coin representing the Chinese in Japan stranded in anachronism, the other side being a lineup of Japanese and Hong Kong (coproduced) genre films from the same period—the mid-1990s and early 2000s—that feature Sinophone migrants (and their communities in Japan) from heterogeneous backgrounds as delinquents and criminals. These films, several of which were inspired by Li Xiaomu's Kabukichō stories (i.e., *Shinjuku Incident*), offer a nightmarish alternative to the attainment of the neoliberal dream and the therapeutical force that underpins *Our Days*. In these works, the aspirations of the Chinese (im)migrants to gain a foothold in Shinjuku/Japan invariably end in disillusionment. Seemingly the only way to break free from the abysmal living of the Real as the Other in Japan—namely, to transcend anachronism—is violence and aggression, which often lead to mental breakdown and death.

Li Xiaomu's Reality Show

Shot on digital equipment, each episode of the web series *Li Xiaomu* starts with a carefully edited sequence showing a long night shot of Kakukichō's landmark red neon gate. After quick glimpses at the glittering billboards advertising adult entertainment businesses, the camera swiftly descends to pavement level, cutting to the back of a tall, thin man in a deep-blue uniform

Fig. 9.3. Li walks toward Kabukichō. (From the opening sequence to the web series *I Am Li Xiaomu* [2019].)

(such as are often seen in electoral campaigns) walking against the crowd in slow motion (fig. 9.3). As the camera follows him, the scene culminates with the camera looking up at the neon gate. Simultaneously, viewers hear a coarse voice as Li proudly introduces himself in Mandarin, "I am the infamous Li Xiaomu. I have lived in Kabukichō for 31 years . . . , which is one of the largest red-light districts in Japan and even in Asia." This opening sequence showcases an infrastructural imagination of Kabukichō that is intriguingly distinct from those illustrated in *Our Days*. Back in the mid-1990s, on their arrival the Chinese students seemed invariably engulfed by Shinjuku's futuristic urban landscape; they were seen gazing up at the skyscrapers and billboards. However, the brief yet dynamic camerawork canvassing the sleepless neighborhood from various angles in the web series reveals a different way of seeing and perceiving, emphasizing the vantage point of a self-assured knowing subject—this "I" who is speaking, thereby enhancing Li's sense of confidence and authority.

Li Xiaomu exemplifies "reality media" by offering the viewers an intimate survey of Li's "public private self."[31] Reality media consist of "Reality TV, social networking sites, blogs, YouTube, mobile phone technology," the "tools for turning oneself into media material and for sharing the consumption of media."[32] Despite their Eurocentric approach, Biressi and Nunn's insights into the second phase of reality TV development (since the early 1990s) align with the series, which is characterized by an "observational format series involving intertwining stories driven by strong 'characters' or 'personalities' and taking place in a huge range of settings and scenarios from the intimate (home, marriage) to the public arena (work, public organisations), but all of them with an emphasis on people playing themselves."[33] While both *I Want to Run for Office* and *Li Xiaomu* are collaborative and participatory, with Li performing in his "campaign mode," the titles of both works underpin his first-person perspective, stressing his performativity and, notably, his agency in making the great leap from media representation to political representation. Writing on Li's performed masculinity, Jamie Coates indicates that Li's "claim to authorship allows him to convey truths that are purportedly typical to the Chinese migrant experience," wherein Li weaves various stories and voices of Chinese migrants, not necessarily his own, to enact his "citational practice" in everyday life and also to leverage such "citations" to generate and reproduce new "texts" to configure his "star persona."[34] Arguably, the web series intersects with China's "post-cinematic" ecology, where "mediated first person self-expression," facilitated by social media, has become both necessary and ubiquitous.[35] The episodes thus create a loop of self-reference, with titles often drawn directly from Li's quotes, such as "I'd Be Grateful that No Japanese Asks Me to 'Get Out,'" (episode 2) and "Even If You Do Not Vote, You'd Still Remember Me" (episode 4). Whereas Coates cautiously celebrates how Li's "boisterous insistence has positioned him as a spokesperson for reimagining local Sino-Japanese relations,"[36] the politician persona of Li in the series seems to outgrow his (trans)media persona, yet it remains unable to sustain itself independent of the latter persona.

The opening of the first episode, for instance, intercuts between an array of unrelated sequences. The viewers first see Li tirelessly making appearances and posing at various social occasions such as TV and radio interviews and talk shows, book-signing events, and a local cultural festival. At night, when the crew eventually returns to Li's home turf, his Hunanese restaurant, a tracking shot follows Li from behind as he navigates through the bustling streets of Kabukichō. As Li enters the restaurant and starts to entertain his old and new customers, the camera cues the audience to a web of images of Li on the wall that includes film posters, a photograph with the megastar Jacky Chan shot on the set of *Shinjuku Incident*, book covers, news clippings, and finally, Li's campaign poster. It is not until a third of the way into the twelve-minute-long video that Li is seen talking about his campaign. He emphasizes that it is not that he is better off or more influential than most Chinese migrants; rather, he is simply more courageous: "At least I have a sense of social responsibility," he says. Conveying a sense of triumph, the inaugural episode is aptly titled, "In Stepping Out, I Have Already Won."

Cruel Optimism

Li's political ambitions—represented in the series and circulated among viewers, followers, users, and so forth—have registered what Lauren Berlant calls cruel optimism, wherein "the object/scene of desire is itself an obstacle to fulfilling the very wants that bring people to it."[37] For Berlant, cruel optimism "is the condition of maintaining an attachment to a significantly problematic object."[38] Whereas optimism subscribes to "a cluster of promises," the optimistic attachment to "the object of desire" can feel cruel when the very attachment frustrates and compromises its realization, which then becomes "*im*possible," turned into "sheer fantasy," or "*too* possible, and toxic."[39] Insofar as *Li Xiaomu* has configured a mediatized event as well as an interface for approaching Chinese migrants' affective connectivity with Japanese society and the world today, the potentialities of Li's activism, if any, have been at the same time compromised by the cruel optimism underpinning his political vision and practice.

Li's campaign attaches to a vision of transnational political participation, considerations further clarified in his Japanese monograph, *Originally Chinese, Aiming to Become a Politician in Japan* (元・中国人、日本で政治家をめざす, 2015). First, he promotes the political engagement of the younger generation of voters, for example, by addressing the problem of the low voting rate of that group in Japan. Second, he aims to convey to the Chinese people—in Japan and in the PRC—messages about the "excellence of democracy" (民主のすばらしさ). Additionally, Li wants to advocate for equal rights for what he calls "minority groups," such as foreign residents and adult entertainment workers; one of his manifestos mentions "elevat[ing] the social statuses of hosts and hostesses" (ホスト・キャバ嬢の社会的地位向上). Despite the random encounters captured by the series showing Japanese-speaking interviewees on the street reacting positively to Li's campaign, however, his 2019 defeat—he received only 1,036 votes, just 18 more than he had in 2015—was also indicative of how Li's political ideals were difficult to pitch to his constituency.

According to Yau, since the latter half of the 2010s, while statistics show that Chinese sentiment toward Japan "has been improving dramatically," the Japanese impressions of China have not improved accordingly.[40] For her, the fact that Japanese media (including TV, journalism, and film) pay little attention to China or make few efforts to portray China and the Chinese people positively, instead investing overwhelmingly in construing China as a "threat" to Japan, has led to a disproportioned media discourse.[41] Meanwhile, over the same period, Chinese TV dramas set during the Anti-Japanese War (1937–45) became a phenomenon. In the "anti-Japanese drama" (抗日剧), not only are Japanese "Others" demonized and the CCP core ideology legitimized, "the collective memory of the country's great national disaster and the humiliations of the past" are reinforced.[42] It then becomes important to consider how Li's cosmopolitan personas "straddl[ing] between China and Japan"[43] point to the critical potentiality of "Chinese in Japan" as an assemblage of commingled affects, which may potentially complicate the facile imaginations and representational tropes about the Other in the national film and media spheres in Japan and China.

Berlant holds that that impasse can be grasped as "a stretch of time in which one moves around with a sense that the world is at once intensely present and enigmatic," wherein the "cruelty" concerns exactly the aspiration of living in and through an "impasse."[44] In the series, though Li is seen trying to leverage his Chineseness/minority status as an edge to address the impasses characterizing the political imaginations on both the Japanese and the Chinese sides, he appears to be less outspoken with his political opinions onscreen than in his monograph. In *I Want to Run for Office*, Li is still meeting with party leaders and seeking suggestions from young people working in Kabukichō. However, with *Li Xiaomu*, except for Li's lecturing and confessions in front of the camera, no in-depth exchanges of political ideas or debates seem to take place on screen.[45] Biressi and Nunn insightfully observe that instead of relying on "evidential documentary modes" and "macro socioeconomic frameworks," reality TV "offer[s] micro frameworks of intimacy, game-playing and the personal journey of self-realisation in order to understand everything from personal relationships, family and small group dynamics to class structures, globalisation and gender roles"; that is, it engages the social to "reveal the personal."[46]

The perspectives offered partially illuminate why *Li Xiaomu* does not focus on political activism. For example, in her director's statement, Xing indicates that *I Want to Run for Office* seeks to "depict the hardships faced by Chinese when they aspire to become politicians in Japan and the authentic perspective of Japanese society on China's rise."[47] In contrast, rather than tackling the metanarrative of international relations or critiquing democratic institutions, the web series aspires to "present a comprehensive, in-depth, and authentic portrayal of Li," in highlighting his campaigning as micropolitical engagements of the "self" at a mundane level. Additionally, it is exactly because Li envisions his campaign to enlighten PRC citizens about the electoral system in a democracy like Japan that he approaches the system in a positive light. Instead of voicing criticism, Li emphasizes the need for individual determination and actions to improve the system. Presenting himself as transcending

Fig. 9.4. Li's campaign mode. (From episode 5 of *I Am Li Xiaomu* [2019].)

the Chinese migrants' aspirations for materialism (as depicted in *Our Days*), Li asserts his evolution as he strives for political participation and rights as the new "object/scene." However, the need for the Chinese in Japan to self-engineer still operates as a narrative constructed on neoliberal governmentality and its prescribed mandates of the self.

The title of episode 5, "If the Youth Don't Care about Politics, the Country Won't Have a Future," ostensibly addresses a key concern of Li's agenda, the low voting rate among young people in Japan. Nevertheless, most of the video follows Li's unextraordinary campaign routine around the Shinjuku area. He is seen diligently greeting passers-by, delivering speeches on the street, preparing and distributing his campaign posters, and visiting local residents, restaurants, and shops, through which he is rebranding himself by presenting "images of earnest and powerful athleticism and clean salaryman attire"[48] (see fig. 9.4). Toward the end, the crew captures Li's nighttime street speech, in which he promises to be a "bridge between foreign residents and the Japanese." This is intercut with shots of beaming faces and favorable reactions from the crowd, accompanied by an uplifting soundtrack. The problem of the voting rate, however, is not explored in the video. It is also intriguing that the series does not effectively position Li within any affective community in which political ideas are exchanged (except for an episode on his conversion to Christianity). In contrast to the isolated Chinese students in *Our Days*, the series presents Li with the streets of Shinjuku and the Hunanese restaurant as his stages, where he is capable of mingling with an array of Japanese and Chinese individuals. However, interactions with his supporters in situ are mostly brief, episodic, and rather business-oriented.

A sense of community can be nevertheless grasped by turning to the online space. A transnational body of Chinese-language audiences and social media platform users engage more actively with the YouTube version, as most comments are written in (simplified) Chinese or occasionally in English by self-identified Sinophone individuals living in Japan and elsewhere. Neither Li, the production team, nor Live Japan provided any response. The online interactions, such as comments and "like" reactions, though I cannot fully explore them through a sociological survey grounded in quantitative viewership data, provide an entry point for considering a virtual public space where people form contingent connections to exchange views on Li's reality show and discuss electoral democracy and political rights. Analyzing a sample of these online commentaries can elucidate how the "good life" promise for PRC viewers and Sinophone audiences/users in Japan and beyond is discussed and circulated, albeit with complexities.

The most viewed episode on the YouTube channel is the third one, sensationally titled "Divorced Six Times, and Never Thinking of Getting Married Again" (uploaded on May 3, 2019), having garnered 278,000 views and 714 comments. Despite Li's self-confessional account of his problematic relations with his female partners, the majority of comments express a feeling of affirmation rather than offense. Several of the most "liked" ones highlight the idea of *zhen* (真, "being true" or "authenticity"), as observed in the frequent use of terms such as "real," "authentic" (真实的), "real man" (真男人), "genuine character" (真性情), and so forth. These terms are employed not only to applaud the on-the-spot style of the video but to endorse Li's candid reflections on his failed marriages, framing them as the defining characteristics of his personality and masculinity. One comment that received many likes reads, "Li's great, and it's all down to one thing: 'zhen.' He doesn't fake it, sticks to his guns, and really goes for it. Thick-skinned? Yep, but totally sincere. A genuinely good guy, no doubt about it."[49] I am not concerned here with whether viewers are too naïve to engage critically with Li's reality media assemblage and the series' observational mode. Rather, *zhen* should be seen as an affective trope that channels the viewers' perceptions of the realistic value of the reportage, as well as their feelings about Li's weakness and frustration expressed onscreen, simultaneously serving as a framework Sinophone viewers use to "measure and re-evaluate their own identities, values and behaviours."[50]

As a foil to the overall positive reactions toward Li in episode 3, one viewer-user who self-identifies as a Chinese living in Japan for seventeen years argues that the show fails to represent Li's political persona as one built on convincing political acts or visions. Written in the second-person singular, the comment goes,

> If you aim to become a local politician in a foreign country, it's essential to completely immerse yourself within the Japanese and *zainichi* Chinese community and genuinely engage in actions (such as serving the people). . . . After watching all the episodes, my impression is that, besides getting to know your difficulties, there's not much else to it. The content of your talk lacks substance.[51]

Consequently, for this viewer, Li's performance on screen as "true to himself" hardly translates into any substantial campaign leverage. The fact that the interactive platform constitutes an interface that enables a wide spectrum of Sinophone individuals to ruminate on their political participation in Japan and beyond, partially fulfills Li's dream of using his campaign as a pedagogical project, even though Li doesn't win. To illuminate the political predicament or impasse that underpins the cruel optimism of Li's campaign saga, I turn to the dramatic finale, "I Spent 10 Million Japanese Yen to Buy What I Cannot Purchase in China" (uploaded on July 13). This episode documents Li's press conference before midnight on April 21, 2019, after hearing the election result; he is seen mumbling before he unexpectedly collapses, possibly due to exhaustion or the devastating news—an unforeseen incident that the camera captures in a hand-held style. At the time of writing, it had already accumulated more than 165,749 views and 599 comments, many of which encourage Li and offer appreciation of his courage and efforts. One of the most-liked comments reads,

> I've been in New York for more than 10 years, but I've never seen any Chinese congressman on the road meeting people to get votes. I am very touched by Xiaomu's campaign, and I really hope that Chinese people all over the world can fight for the welfare of the Chinese community [华人群体] like Xiaomu, so that people in any country will know that we Chinese are united wherever we are![52]

It is intriguing that several users who posted follow-up comments debate, however briefly, whether an elected Chinese politician, in either the United

States or Japan, should be committed solely to the Sinophone community or to "everybody living on this land."[53] This points to the thorny questions concerning Li's ethno-national identity in connection with community representation: Who are the people for whom Li is speaking, and to which community/ies does he belong? Meanwhile, several other comments unpack the "reasons" for Li's defeat, such as the one (originally in English) by *janeinflushing*, "Japanese society is still conserved [*sic*] to give chance to a naturalized person. Most Japanese still think Mr. Li is a foreigner who knows less than a Japanese candidate about this society,"[54] which echoes the opinion of another commenter: "I also worked in a Japanese company for 2 years, and the harmony at the surface cannot rule out problems of racism. Without finishing the episodes I already know that he has little hope to win. However, Li dares to take the action and it's already much better than most of us!"[55]

Concerning the commentary on the web series, a voice critical of the socio-institutional problems faced by foreigners living in Japan should be foregrounded. Unless foreign nationals are naturalized like Li, they are not entitled to voting rights, and therefore the politically passive, docile foreigners in Japan—Chinese in Japan included—are produced and precluded partially because of systematic and institutional segregation. Most of Li's potential voters might be those who have not yet or will not "become" Japanese: PRC citizens or netizens who are, in actuality, living with and enduring a totally different election system with a different version of hope with regard to political participation, or those foreign residents (including Chinese) whose political aspirations remain unaccounted for in Japan's political theater.[56] Li's campaign and defeat to some extent are symptomatic of such multilayered incongruencies. Hence many Chinese-language viewers prefer to take Li's adventure as one of obtaining experiences and emphasizing participation as well as the process, wherein the multivalent *zhen* mentioned earlier configures an affective trope about sharing and embracing the impasse that underpins Li's campaign and the rebranded Japanese dream for Chinese in Japan. If *Our Days* can be approached as a bildungsroman that offers a type of broadly defined "coming-of-age" narrative pertaining to the Chinese in Japan by illustrating how international students trapped in the interstices of disparate temporalities can still leap into a future via the mechanism of "eating bitterness," with *Li Xiaomu*, one contemplates the actual form of the future expected in *Our Days* once it has materialized. Li Xiaomu's reality show concerns the present, which documents and mediates how the political impasse of the Chinese in Japan is being confronted and lived through with as much aspiration as cruelty.

NON-ENGLISH LANGUAGE TERMS

抗日剧 anti-Japanese drama
小さな留学生 *A Young Overseas Student*
哔哩哔哩 Bilibili
华人群体 Chinese community
大富 Daifu
吃苦 eat bitterness
ホスト・キャバ嬢の社会的地位向上 elevat[ing] the social statuses of hosts and hostesses
民主のすばらしさ excellence of democracy
真性情 genuine character
中国からの贈りもの *The Gift from China*
光明日报 *Guangming Daily*
我是李小牧 *I Am Li Xiaomu*
我要参选 *I Want to Run for Office*
李小牧 Li Xiaomu (Ri Komaki)
日本现场 *Live Japan*
私の太陽 *My Sun*
民族精神 national spirit
新华侨华人文学 new overseas Chinese literature
元・中国人、日本で政治家をめざす *Originally Chinese, Aiming to Become a Politician in Japan*
我们的留学生活 *Our Days Studying Abroad*
私たちの留学生活—日本での日々 *Our Days Studying Abroad: The Everyday in Japan*
華僑・華人 overseas Chinese
泣きながら生きて *Persisting with Tears in Eyes*
真实的 real, authentic
真男人 real man
纪实真人秀 reportage reality show
新宿事件 *Shinjuku Incident*
残留婦人 stranded war wives
东京梦 Tokyo Dream
留东外史 *Unofficial Records of Studying in Japan*
残留孤児 war orphans
温强 Wen Qiang
邢菲 Xing Fei
若者たち *The Young People*
在日 zainichi
张丽玲 Zhang Liling
真 *zhen* being true; authenticity

ACKNOWLEDGMENTS

The author expresses gratitude to the editors, as well as the organizers and participants of the ACLA 2022 Annual Conference seminar, "Rethinking Heterogeneity: Sinophone Reportage and Beyond." This article is accomplished with the support of the Harvard-Yenching Institute and JSPS KAKENHI Grant Number 22K00230.

NOTES

1. References are to the Japanese edition, unless otherwise specified. All English-Chinese and English-Japanese translations are mine, unless stated otherwise. All Chinese terms are in simplified Chinese.

2. Liu-Farrer, "Chinese Newcomers in Japan: Migration Trends, Profiles and the Impact of the 2011 Earthquake," 231. As of June 2023, Japan's immigration bureau reported 3.22 million foreign residents, with 788,495 (24.5%) from the PRC, including Hong Kong (Immigration Services Agency); "Japanese war orphans," children abandoned in China after 1945 and raised by locals; and "stranded war-wives," Japanese women who married locals for survival in postwar Manchuria; both faced hardships but predominantly repatriated to Japan in the 1980s (see Chan 2011).

3. The Qing government sent thirteen students to Japan in 1896, which marked the beginning of a significant trend of Chinese studying in Japan during the late Qing and Republic of China periods. Novels such as 东京梦 (*Tokyo Dream*, 1909) by Lübing and 留东外史 (*Unofficial Records of Studying in Japan*, 1916–22) by Buxiaosheng (Xiang Kairan) provide early insights into Chinese students' lives in Japan (Shi 2010). Chinese intellectuals' cultural and literary activities in Japan are also closely connected with the early development of modern Chinese literature. For more on the so-called "new overseas Chinese literature" (新华侨华人文学) in Japan since the 1980s, see Lin (2023).

4. As Liu-Farrer elucidates, "Japan is not considered an immigrant destination, and many aspects of this country . . . remain uncompromisingly ethno-nationalistic. As a result, at least initially, migrating to Japan means a temporary sojourn" (2020, 60).

5. Zhang, "Perseverance through Aftershocks," 129.

6. Nichols, *Representing Reality: Issues and Concepts in Documentary*, 194.

7. See Moran, "The Poetics and Praxis of Zhang Mengqi's Documentary Films," this volume.

8. Wong, *Transpacific Attachments*, 8, 10.

9. Nichols, *Introduction to Documentary*, 135.

10. Zhang, "Perseverance through Aftershocks," 146.

11. Laughlin and Guo, *Reportage in the Chinese-Speaking World*, 10.

12. Laughlin and Guo, *Reportage in the Chinese-Speaking World*, 10.

13. Zhang used her own savings and ended up borrowing money. She also persuaded her family members to work with her, eventually interviewing hundreds of people, following sixty-six Chinese students, and accumulating video footage on around 1,000 cassettes (Liu et al., 2000, 5). I am referring to its Japanese version unless otherwise indicated.

14. As revealed in the "making-of" documentary about the series, *The Gift from China* (中国からの贈りもの, 2002), the main purpose of Zhang's very first visit to Fuji TV in 1995 was to borrow the shooting equipment from the TV station. Fuji's veteran producer Yokoyama Yoichi later also participated the project.

15. The Chinese version was also aired by TV broadcasters in Shanghai, Jilin, Chongqing, Nanjing, and on Phoenix TV from December 1999 onward, eliciting strong reactions among audiences.

16. Song, "All Dogs Deserve to be Beaten: Negotiating Manhood and Nationhood in Chinese TV Dramas," 205. Despite the systematic reform, all TV stations and channels in China remain state-owned.

17. *Guangming Daily*, "Selected Discussions from the Forum on Our Days Studying Abroad," December 2, 1999.

18. Daifu TV's official site reads, "The aim is to provide the latest cultural and current information on China for Chinese residents in Japan, to deepen Japanese understanding of China and the Chinese people, and to play a role in building friendly relations between Japan and China" ("Company Profile of Daifu," n.d.).

19. There is a temporal gap in the episodes' release dates between YouTube and Bilibili. The YouTube version includes seven episodes, whereas the Bilibili version consists of five, but discrepancies exist. This article refers to the YouTube version unless otherwise indicated.

20. Yu, *"My" Self on Camera*, 187.

21. See Coates, "Persona, Politics, and Chinese Masculinity in Japan," 132, 137.

22. Chang, "Transnational Affect," 35; italics in original.

23. Chang, "Transnational Affect," 34.

24. Berlant, *Cruel Optimism*, 13.

25. Tsu, "Black Market, Chinatown, and Kabukichō," 144.

26. Yau, "Japanese Media and China-Japan Relations."

27. See also Coates, "The Cruel Optimism of Mobility: Aspiration, Belonging, and the 'Good Life' among Transnational Chinese Migrants in Tokyo."

28. Wang, "Alter-Centering Chinese Cinema," 536.

29. Wang, "Alter-Centering Chinese Cinema," 536.

30. Tsu, "Black Market, Chinatown, and Kabukichō."

31. Silverstone, *Why Study the Media?*, 70.

32. Biressi and Nunn, "Reality TV: A Sign of the Times?," 301.

33. Biressi and Nunn, "Reality TV: A Sign of the Times?," 303.

34. Coates, "Persona, Politics, and Chinese Masculinity in Japan," 136.

35. Yu, *"My" Self on Camera*, 187.

36. Coates, "Persona, Politics, and Chinese Masculinity in Japan," 143.

37. Berlant, *Cruel Optimism*, 227.

38. Berlant, *Cruel Optimism*, 24.

39. Berlant, *Cruel Optimism*, 24; italics in original.

40. Yau, "Japanese Media and China-Japan Relations," 22.

41. Yau, "Japanese Media and China-Japan Relations," 2.

42. Song, "All Dogs Deserve to Be Beaten: Negotiating Manhood and Nationhood in Chinese TV Dramas," 205.

43. Coates, "Persona, Politics, and Chinese Masculinity in Japan," 142.

44. Berlant, *Cruel Optimism*, 4.

45. That said, in the YouTube "bonus edition," after his defeat Li meets Puranik Yogendra, a Mumbai-born councilman elected to Edogawa City Council, who came to Japan as a student in 1997.

46. Biressi and Nunn, "Reality TV: A Sign of the Times?," 300.

47. Xing, "Wo Yao Canxuan."

48. Coates, "Persona, Politics, and Chinese Masculinity in Japan," 141.

49. HK-bc9hh, "HK-bc9hh's YouTube Comment."

50. Biressi and Nunn, "Reality TV: A Sign of the Times?," 303.
51. happyya77, comment on *I Am Li Xiaomu.*
52. User1, comment on *I Am Li Xiaomu.*
53. user-xr5pz3pv3p, comment on *I Am Li Xiaomu.*
54. Janeinflushing, comment on *I Am Li Xiaomu.*
55. Yuzhenwang, comment on *I Am Li Xiaomu.*
56. Hwang, "Resident Foreigners in South Korea and Japan," 719. Whereas the Supreme Court in Japan ruled that "local suffrage for resident foreigners is not opposed to the constitution in principle but only subject to the policy decision of the state administration," permanent residents cannot vote in national or local elections.

REFERENCES

Berlant, Lauren. *Cruel Optimism.* Durham: Duke University Press, 2011.

Biressi, Anita, and Heather Nunn. "Reality TV: A Sign of the Times?" In *The Documentary Film Book*, edited by Brian Winston, 299–305. London: Palgrave Macmillan, 2013.

Chan, Yeeshan. *Abandoned Japanese in Postwar Manchuria: The Lives of War Orphans and Wives in Two Countries.* New York: Routledge, 2011.

Chang, Hsiao-Hung. "Transnational Affect: Cold Anger, Hot Tears, and 'Lust, Caution.'" *Concentric: Literary and Cultural Studies* 35, no. 1 (2009): 31–50.

Coates, Jamie. "Persona, Politics, and Chinese Masculinity in Japan: The Case of Li Xiaomu." In *Cosmopolitan Dream: Transnational Chinese Masculinities in a Global Age*, edited by Derek Hird and Geng Song, 127–48. Hong Kong: Hong Kong University Press, 2018.

Coates, Jamie. "The Cruel Optimism of Mobility: Aspiration, Belonging, and the 'Good Life' among Transnational Chinese Migrants in Tokyo." *positions* 27, no. 3 (2019): 469–97. https://doi.org/10.1215/10679847-7539277

"Company Profile of Daifu." n.d. Accessed November 23, 2022. http://www.daifutv.com/j/index.php?option=com_content&view=article&id=214&Itemid=96

Guangming Daily. "Women de liuxueshenghuo—zairiben de rizi yantaohui fayan xuandeng" [Selected discussions from the Forum on Our Days Studying Abroad]. December 2, 1999. https://news.sina.com.cn/comment/1999-12-2/37231.html

happyya77. Comment on *I Am Li Xiaomu.* May 3, 2019.

HK-bc9hh. Comment on *I Am Li Xiaomu.* May 3, 2019.

Hwang, Jung-Mee. "Resident Foreigners in South Korea and Japan: A Comparative Policy Analysis." *Asian Perspective* 40, no. 4 (2016): 699–730.

Janeinflushing. Comment on *I Am Li Xiaomu.* July 13, 2019.

Immigration Services Agency. "Regarding the number of foreign residents." 2023. https://www.moj.go.jp/isa/content/001403955.pdf

Lin, Qi. *Fenggu yu wu'ai zhijian: Riben xin hua qiao huaren wenxue sanshi nian (1990–2020)* [Between Feng Gu and Wu Ai: thirty years of Japanese new overseas Chinese literature 1990–2020]. Beijing: China Social Sciences Press, 2023.

Liu, Fang, et al. *Zhui meng nüren: Zhang Liling he "Women de liuxue shenghuo"* [A female chasing her dream: Zhang Liling and *Our Days Studying Abroad*]. Beijing: Guangming Daily Publishing House, 2000.

Liu-Farrer, Gracia. "Chinese Newcomers in Japan: Migration Trends, Profiles and the Impact of the 2011 Earthquake." *Asian and Pacific Migration Journal* 22, no. 2 (2013): 231–57.

Liu-Farrer, Gracia. *Immigrant Japan: Mobility and Belonging in an Ethno-Nationalist Society*. Ithaca: Cornell University Press, 2020.

Nichols, Bill. *Representing Reality: Issues and Concepts in Documentary*. Bloomington: Indiana University Press, 1992.

Nichols, Bill. *Introduction to Documentary*. Bloomington: Indiana University Press, 2017.

Ri, Komaki. *Moto Chūgokujin, Nihon de seijika o mezasu* [Originally Chinese, aiming to become a politician in Japan]. Kindle. Tokyo: CCC Media House, 2015.

Shi, Ye. "Cong Dongjing meng dao Liudong Waishi—Qingmo minchu liuri xiaoshuo de lanshang he fazhan [From 'Tokyo Dream' to 'Unofficial Records of Studying in Japan': the origin and development of studying-in-Japan novels in late Qing and early Republican era]." *Journal of Ming-Qing Fiction Studies* 95, no. 1 (2010): 202–11.

Silverstone, Roger. *Why Study the Media?*, 70. Quoted in Anita Biressi and Heather Nunn, "Reality TV: A Sign of the Times?" In *The Documentary Film Book*, edited by Brian Winston, 299–305. London: Palgrave Macmillan, 2013.

Song, Geng. "All Dogs Deserve to Be Beaten: Negotiating Manhood and Nationhood in Chinese TV Dramas." In *Changing Chinese Masculinities: From Imperial Pillars of State to Global Real Men*, edited by Kam Louie, 204–19. Hong Kong: Hong Kong University Press, 2016.

Tsu, Yun Hui Timothy. "Black Market, Chinatown, and Kabukichō: Postwar Japanese Constructs of 'Overseas Chinese.'" *Positions: East Asia Cultures Critique* 19, no. 1 (2011): 133–58. https://doi.org/10.1215/10679847-2010-027

user-xr5pz3pv3p. Comment on *I Am Li Xiaomu*. July 14, 2019.

User1. Comment on *I Am Li Xiaomu*. July 14, 2019.

Wang, Yiman. "Alter-Centering Chinese Cinema: The Diasporic Formation." In *A Companion to Chinese Cinema*, edited by Yingjin Zhang, 535–51. Hoboken, NJ: Wiley-Blackwell, 2012.

Wong, Lily. *Transpacific Attachments: Sex Work, Media Networks, and Affective Histories of Chineseness*. New York: Columbia University Press, 2018.

Xing, Fei. "Wo Yao Canxuan [I want to run for office]." Cinephilia.Net (June 2017). https://cinephilia.net/58457/

Yau, Shuk Ting Kinnia. "Japanese Media and China-Japan Relations: From the Normalization of Diplomatic Relations to the Second Abe Regime." *Asia-Pacific Journal: Japan Focus* 19, no. 14 (2021). https://apjjf.org/2021/14/Yau.html

Yu, Kiki Tianqi. *"My" Self on Camera: First Person Documentary Practice in an Individualising China*. Edinburgh: Edinburgh University Press, 2019. https://doi.org/10.1515/9780748698226

Yuzhenwang. Comment on *I Am Li Xiaomu*. July 14, 2019.

Zhang, Yingjin. "Perseverance through Aftershocks: Epistephilia in Chinese Reportage and Independent Documentary." *Modern Chinese Literature and Culture* 31, no. 2 (2019): 129–61. https://www.jstor.org/stable/26895774

Epilogue

The Rebirth of Reportage in the New Age

Charles A. Laughlin and Li Guo

This volume identifies reportage not as a genre of writing, but rather as a mode or function that can be activated in *any* form of creative expression, including photography, film, and writing (among others). Importantly, in nonfictional expression we also often see the plurimedial coordination of artistic vehicles, as in photography and writing on Po-hsi Chen's and Li Guo's contributions, or dance and film as we see in Thomas Moran's. Essential to this mode is ethical engagement between creator, subject, and audience. If we set aside the tendency to define reportage in terms of the ontology of the subject matter ("real people and events"), we still observe the ethical exploration of social and political themes in reportage texts, through which we can highlight their kinship with artistic works of all kinds that share this trait. Rather than viewing "reportage" as a *representation* of social reality, we affirm the semiotic nature of the actual projected in these works to emphasize their aesthetic and moral complexity. It is specifically an ethico-political semiotics, so that the layer of the real can be understood not as content, but as a relation of engagement among creators, subjects and audiences on issues that matter to them.

By shifting attention to visual expression (photography and film) and especially its combinations with texts, we are able to see, for example, how when filming an actual person (or nonhuman subject such as Yan Wang Preston's trees in Federica Mirra's contribution), creators intervene by projecting what that subject is being portrayed "as"—what referents are they the signifier for?—and how that is aesthetically communicated to the viewer. What subjects signify in practice involves issues such as exploitation, environmental precarity, identity, and historical witnessing, among others. Rather than explicitly defining these layers of reference, creators express or channel significance through aesthetic choices. Because the subjects are marginalized, silenced, and invisible, these strategies of expression challenge the conventional associations of the subject-as-referent. For example, in the system of Yan Wang Preston's photography, the relocation of trees signifies care for the environment to Chongqing government agencies, while to Preston and her audience, the consequences of their mistreatment instead signify neglect and environmental degradation.

Similarly, the albino "moon children" of Liao Chia-chan and Yan Hsin-chu's writing and photography in Li Guo's article, typically stigmatized for their differences, are artfully humanized through the aesthetic choices and creativity of the artists, engendering the possibility of new relationships between the subjects and the viewer/reader. Subjects' stories also show how their stigmatization unfairly hinders their daily life and work, not to speak of hindering the fulfillment of their human potential. Gu Mengren portrays indigenous Atayals' struggle for survival in a society that neglects them under the stigma of primitiveness. The figure of darkness Gu Mengren sustains throughout the narrative is part of their identity, but also their burden, while the contrasting imagery of enlightenment that should be their beacon of hope is unintentionally complicated by its possible complicity with the many layers of colonization and imperialism in Taiwan's history.

All of these expressions partake of an ethico-aesthetic paradigm by which the work is already politicized at the outset by readers' and viewers' awareness of subjects' precarity and marginalization, while creators' pushback against this marginalization ethically challenges the audience: What assertions and implications will the reportage audience glean from these works? What relationships will they imagine with the creators and their subjects? Does the work challenge them to reassess their worldview/lifestyle? These questions come up in narrative/imaginative/fictional art as well. If we acknowledge that there are fictional works in which these questions do arise, we can see the ethico-aesthetic paradigm as definitive not of an artistic genre, but of a transgeneric mode of artistic expression. These constellations of ethical engagement include the reader-audience in addition to creators and subjects. In addition to nonfiction writing, the reportage mode may be recognized in other nonfictional forms not included here, such as dramatic performance, dance, and poetry, historical and contemporary, that can be studied from the same conceptual framework.

Using the study of reportage to inspire a different framework for experiencing and interpreting art, we invite readers to reenvision creative expression and its relation to society generally. Viewing art primarily as dynamic and reciprocal affective engagement among creators, subjects, and audiences illuminates how it can generate empathy and create the conditions for greater understanding and positive change. For more than a century in the Chinese-speaking world, under many different historical and political circumstances, performing artists, writers, and filmmakers looked to creative expression as a powerful means to effect social change through impassioned and emotionally moving expressions of actual people's social and historical experiences. They may bring the audience to feel poverty, oppression, dehumanization, marginalization, and trauma, but also the joy, fulfillment, and identification accompanying individual and collective forms of empowerment and liberation. These special functions of art as a form of social intervention are manifested not only in the creative works themselves, but in readers' responses to them, especially when they feed back into social life.

As the introduction of this volume states, the chapters expand "the legacy of earlier women reportage authors in deploying the form of reportage writing to explore 'new social, political terrains across national boundaries' and to imagine alternative aesthetic and political sentiments beyond a nationalistic framework." Current scholarship could benefit from more studies on plurimedial reportage by women based in mainland China, Taiwan, and diaspora culture. Besides renowned wartime women reportage writers such as Bai Lang, Ding Ling, and Hu Lanqi, leftist filmmaker, writer, and activist Chen Bo'er 陳波兒 (1907?–1951) also left a rich legacy of reportage works that deserve scholarly attention. Wang Zheng has offered a substantial discussion of two of Chen's battlefield reportage works on peasant women's participation in war-resistance movements, titled "Chen Bo'er's Letters from the Battlefield" (陳波兒從戰地的來信, 1939) and "Impressions of Three Women Representatives with Bound Feet" (三個小腳代表印象記, 1940), which were published in *Women's Life* (Funü shenghuo 婦女生活).[1] Further, Chen Bo'er's documentary filmmaking could be reconsidered through the lens of women's aesthetic and political intervention through plurimedial reportage. Prominent examples include the first documentary of socialist China, *The Democratic Northeast* (Minzhu dongbei 民主東北, 1947, by Northeast Film Company), and six documentaries released by state-owned film enterprises in 1950.[2] In addition, as Thomas Moran observes, women authors continued with reportage writing during the Maoist period. Yang Gang 楊剛 (1905–1957), Moran observes, "wrote about the pomp and ceremony that accompanied the formation of the new state" in 1949 and 1950 in her reportage works.[3] Furthermore, as Moran also observes, there were many influential women reportage authors in mainland China during the early Reform and Opening period who have been largely neglected in extant scholarship and deserve further attention, including Huang Zongying 黃宗英 (1925–2020), Chen Zufen 陳祖芬 (1943–2019), Li Lingxiu 李玲修 (1944–), and Tao Siliang 陶斯亮 (1941–), to whom we could add Dai Qing 戴晴 (1941–) and Zhang Xinxin 張辛欣 (1953–) from later years.[4] *Fish and Elephant* (Jinnian xiatian 今年夏天, 2001) directed by Li Yu 李玉 (1973–), is an example of a narrative film that also activates the ethico-aesthetic function of reportage by responding to women's lived conditions in the Reform and Opening period. In Taiwan, women authors Ma Yi-kung 馬以工 (1948–) and Han Han 韓韓 (1948–) cowrote the book *We Only Have One Earth* (Women zhiyou yige diqiu 我們只有一個地球, 1983), described as "very influential in the early 1980s" and "[laying] the ground for Taiwanese nature writing."[5] Taiwanese filmmaker Hu Tai-li's acclaimed documentaries such as *Voices of Orchid Island* (Lanyu guandian 蘭嶼觀點, 1993), *Passing through My Mother-in-Law's Village* (Chuanguo pojia cun 穿過婆家村, 1997), and *Stone Dream* (Shitou meng 石頭夢, 2004), along with her nonfiction writings about women, also deserve more scholarly attention.[6]

Children's and young adult reportage in China, Taiwan, and Hong Kong also remains an urgent yet notably understudied topic. *Twelve Months in the Empty Nest* (Kongchao shier yue 空巢十二月, 2021), by Sichuan-based author Qiu Yidong 邱易東 (1952–), provides accounts of eighteen left-behind children, one of China's most marginalized and vulnerable segments of society. Qiu's reportage illustrates how these children struggle against the lack of long-term parental companionship, family care, and educational opportunities, and how their agonies expose the human cost of rapid economic growth and massive rural-urban migration. A similar work, *Transparent Children: Illegal Migrant Workers' Children in Taiwan* (Touming de xiaohai: wuguoji yigong ertong de gushi 透明的小孩：無國籍移工兒童的故事, 2017), covers Taiwanese children's reportage. Written by the award-winning writer Hsing Chia-hui 幸佳惠 (1973–2019) and illustrated by Chen Yu-ling 陳昱伶, this reportage work provides truthful accounts of illegal international migrant workers' children, their stateless status, and their consequently unseen, "transparent" lives at the margins of society. Hsing and Chen's work draws attention to migrant workers' children as a growing yet invisible social community, as well as to their marginalized social status under intersectional forms of oppression because of race, class, youth, and health conditions. Turning to young adults, a trailblazing work is *A Rose Hidden in the Backpack: Middle School Students' Perceptions of Sexuality* (Cang zai shubao li de meigui: xiaoyuan xingwenti fangtan shilu 藏在書包裏的玫瑰：校園性問題訪談實錄, 2004) by Sun Yunxiao 孫雲曉 (1955–) and Zhang Yinmo 張引墨. As the first mainland Chinese reportage exploring middle school students' sexual activities as a social issue and a reality, the book is comprised of interviews with sixteen students from various parts of China about their sexual relations, exposing the inadequacy of extant sex education and providing young adults with suggestions and sources of psychological counsel and social assistance. Warmly received by students as well as by scholars in youth education, gender studies, and social work, the book was praised as a much-needed textbook of sex education that had a long-term beneficial impact among young adult readers.

Reportage's coverage of queer communities and their ongoing struggles for civil rights in mainland China, Taiwan, and Hong Kong still awaits scholarly engagement and examination. In Taiwan, a pioneering queer reportage work, "A Confession of Forbidden Love" ("Jinji de gaobai" 禁忌的告白, written by Tseng Shu-mei, photography by Yan Hsin-chu), was published in *Ren Jian* in July 1988. It includes interviews with Chi Chia-wei 祁家威 (1958–) and three anonymous queer interviewees. As the first person in Taiwan to come out as queer on national television, Chi worked as one of Taiwan's earliest AIDS/HIV activists. The reportage praises him as "the only unconcealed emissary" (唯一不隱身的使者) whose dedication and enthusiasm contributed to the beginning of a new path for Taiwan's bourgeoning queer activism and social engagement with AIDS/HIV prevention.[7] A documentary film on Chi's activist endeavors *When the Dawn Comes* (Liming daolai de na yitian 黎明到來的那一天), directed by Zhang Hong-jie 張弘榤, was released in 2021. A prominent mainland Chinese work that could be considered as queer reportage is *A Brochure for Lesbians* (Lala shouce 拉拉手冊, 2012), written by Meng Meng 朦朦, which is a series of ebooks focusing on providing "truthful accounts" (*jishi* 紀實) of lesbians' lives and emotional experiences, suggestions and sources on mental health, guidelines on "coming out," and personal reflections on the contemporary LGBTQ community in China. In Hong Kong, whereas LGBTQ cinema suffered a visible decline as a result of increased censorship following the "Handover" in 1997, the impact of the Closer Economic Partnership Arrangement in 2003, and the Hong Kong National Security Law (2020), queer cinema nonetheless has taken on a new role as a vehicle for articulating Hong Kong citizens' conflicts in reconciling personal beliefs and values with intersecting forms of heterosexism, nationalism, and ethnocentrism. A prominent example of Hong Kong's queer reportage is the exhibition "Unruly Visions: Selected Works of Queer Photography" (Xiao'ao zhi xiang: kuer zhi yingxiang xizuo 嘯傲之相：酷兒之影像習作) at the Hong Kong International Photography Festival in 2021. The exhibition claimed to provide "witness, remembrance, agency, and affirmation" (見証，記憶，行動，認同) to queer communities, and brought together works by nine leading Hong Kong LGBTQ+ artists.[8] Low Ai Lok observes that these photographic works resort to diverse visual aesthetics and respond to a range of social topics, including "Hong Kong's socio-political crisis, same-sex marriages, sexual identifications, and shifting discourses about queer futurity and utopianism."[9]

A roundtable discussion was convened at the Modern Language Association's annual meeting in January of 2025.[10] The topic—exploring the relation between reportage and the politics of visibility—invited reflections on intersectional forms of oppression induced by race, disability, urban displacement, or political marginalization. Thus, the politics of visibility illustrates many possibilities for broader investigation of the many variations of nonfiction art discussed above. In the roundtable proposal, Jie Guo observes that random notes, sketches, and essays from the borderlands in the Republican period "facilitated the political visions of the indigenous groups who are constantly resisting being absorbed into the utopian political order of a new China as a multiethnic nation," while Steven Riep points out that transmedial representation of disability (in vision, hearing, physical impairment, or mental disorder) in Chinese and Sinophone photographic reportage and nonfiction films not only "expands the audiences' epistemic horizons," it also "celebrates their activity, mobility, and empowerment." Dorothee Hou explains how Cong Feng's documentaries on urban development and displacement in postreform China illustrate "how documentary filmmakers' efforts to excavate and reexamine 'stolen footages' from the public domain yield new insights on the issues of spatial justice, both locally and globally, and on the ethics of looking in an age assailed by pervasive media and ubiquitous surveillance." Louisa Wei identifies "an activist mode of production" in Hong Kong protest documentaries that function in many different ways, from "closely follow[ing] an event's progress to screening protest videos for participants to improve their strategies, serve as visual evidence in court, or even engage the attendance of victims/participants at screenings to meet with the audience."

In sum, the humanist value of reportage and its varied forms, as a reader of *Ren Jian* puts it, is to "send warmth and care to the run-down and deprived ones in this world."[11] Or, as a reader describes, reading reportage works is rejuvenating because it allows readers to see "certain precious qualities of mankind gleaming on an industrial wasteland."[12]

NOTES

1. See Wang Zheng, "In Search of Feminism: Chen Bo'er and the Founding of Chinese Socialist Cinema," 128–34.
2. See Wang Zheng's discussion of Chen as a pioneering figure in establishing a feminist paradigm of socialist film, in Wang, *Finding Women in the State*, 143–69.
3. See Moran, "True Stories: Contemporary Chinese Reportage and Its Ideology and Aesthetic," 116.
4. See Moran, "True Stories," 127–28, and note 128.
5. Kuei-fen Chiu, personal correspondence with Charles A. Laughlin, June 8, 2024.
6. Though an academic, Hu's collections of ethnographic essays, such as *Sex and Death* (Xing yu si 性欲死; 1986) and *Guide for Wives* (Xifu rumen 媳婦入門; 1997), are numerous and widely read.
7. Tseng and Yan, "A Confession of Forbidden Love," 20. Notably, Tseng and Yan's reportage on Chi received warm and sympathetic responses from readers. In the section of "Readers' Letters" of issue 35 of *Ren Jian*, for example, Rong, a nineteen-year-old reader, identified with the "wandering and restless souls" of underground queer people who lived under a mask during the daytime and had to force themselves to accept heterosexual relations.
8. See Low, "Dark Night and Varied Lights."
9. See Low, "Dark Night and Varied Lights."
10. See Li Guo, Jie Guo, Riep, Hou, Wei, and Laughlin, "Reconsidering the Politics of Visibility."
11. Yang Guoshu, "Readers' Letters," *Ren Jian*, issue 3 (November 10, 1986).
12. Li Yifeng, "Readers' Letters," *Ren Jian*, issue 3 (November 28, 1986).

REFERENCES

Guo, Li, Jie Guo, Steven Riep, Dorothee Hou, and Charles A. Laughlin. "Reconsidering the Politics of Visibility through Sinophone Non-Fiction Writings and Film." MLA 2025 Convention Roundtable Proposal, January 2025.

Li, Yifeng, "Readers' Letters." *Ren Jian* 3 (November 28, 1986).

Low, Ai Lok 勞緯洛. "Heiye yu guangcha: zenme yang de kangzheng? 'Xiao'ao zhi xiang: kuer zhi yingxiang xizuo' zhanlan hougan" 黑夜與光差：怎麼樣的抗爭？——《嘯傲之相：酷兒之影像習作》展覽後感 (Dark Night and Varied Lights: What Kind of Resistance? Reflections on the Exhibition *Unruly: Selected Works of Queer Photography*). *p-articles*, March 16, 2021. https://p-articles.com/critics/2059.html

Moran, Thomas Elton. "True Stories: Contemporary Chinese Reportage and Its Ideology and Aesthetic." PhD thesis, Cornell University, 1994.

Rong, "Readers' Letters." *Ren Jian* 35 (September 1, 1988).

Tseng, Shumei, and Yan Hsin-chu. "Jinji de gaobai" "禁忌的告白" (A Confession of Forbidden Love.) *Ren Jian* 33 (1988): 10–20.

Wang Zheng. "In Search of Feminism: Chen Bo'er and the Founding of Chinese Socialist Cinema" (女權尋蹤:陳波兒與中國社會主義電影範式的創立). In *Gender and the Visual: 100 Years of Chinese Image Researched*, edited by Wang Zheng and Lü Xinyu, 113–60. 性別與視覺:百年中國影像研究. Shanghai: Fudan University Press, 2016.

Wang Zheng. *Finding Women in the State: A Socialist Feminist Revolution in the People's Republic of China, 1949–1964*. Berkeley: University of California Press, 2017.

Yang, Guoshu, "Readers' Letters." *Ren Jian* 3 (November 10, 1986).

Contributors

Po-hsi Chen is Assistant Research Fellow at the Institute of Modern History, Academia Sinica. He holds a PhD in East Asian Languages and Literatures from Yale University. Prior to joining Academia Sinica, he was postdoctoral fellow in Taiwan studies at the University of Cambridge. He is working on a manuscript tentatively titled *Writing an Impossible Revolution: Transnational Radical Thoughts in Cold War Taiwan Literature*. His research interests include modern and contemporary Chinese literature, global leftism, and the cultural Cold War.

Li Guo is Professor of Asian Studies at Utah State University. Guo's research bridges gender studies, narrative theory, vernacular cultures, film, visuality, and animation. She is the author of *Writing Gender in Early Modern Chinese Women's Tanci Fiction* (Purdue University Press, 2021) and *Women's Tanci Fiction in Late Imperial and Early Twentieth-Century China* (Purdue, 2015). She has coedited two volumes: *Ecologies of Translation in East and South East Asia, 1600–1900* (with Patricia Sieber and Peter Kornicki, Amsterdam University Press, 2022), and *Games and Play in Chinese and Sinophone Cultures* (with Douglas Eyman and Hongmei Sun, University of Washington Press, 2024).

Charles A. Laughlin is Ellen Bayard Weedon Chair Professor of East Asian Studies at the University of Virginia. He received his BA in Chinese Language and Literature from the University of Minnesota in 1988, and his PhD in Chinese Literature at Columbia University in 1996. Laughlin has published two monographs, *Chinese Reportage: The Aesthetics of Historical Experience* (Duke, 2002), and *The Literature of Leisure and Chinese Modernity* (Hawai'i, 2008). He also edited *Contested Modernities in Chinese Literature* (Palgrave Macmillan, 2005). Laughlin's current research includes the dynamics of desire in revolutionary fiction and film, and images of aging in Chinese film.

Ran Ma is Associate Professor in the international program of "Japan-in-Asia" Cultural Studies and Screen Studies (Eizogaku) at Nagoya University, Japan. Her research interests lie at the intersection of inter-Asia studies, transnational film and screen cultures, and film festival studies, on which she has published chapters and journal articles in English, Chinese, and Japanese. Currently, her research focuses on exploring the dynamics of translocality, infrastructure, and affect within the context of transnational media across East Asia. Ma is also the author of *Independent Filmmaking across Borders in Contemporary Asia* (Amsterdam University Press, 2019).

Federica Mirra is Leverhulme Early Career Research Fellow, currently leading a three-year project titled "The City as Art: Living Aesthetics in Twenty-First-Century China" at the Centre for Chinese Visual Arts, Birmingham City University (BCU). She completed her PhD, "Urban Imaginaries: Contemporary Art and Urban Transformations in China since 2001," at BCU, sponsored by the Midlands3Cities AHRC Doctoral Studentship Award. She worked as a research fellow at St. Gallen University, Switzerland, and as a curatorial assistant for the Thailand Biennale 2018–19.

Thomas Moran is Professor Emeritus at Middlebury College, where he taught Chinese language, literature, and film. His 1994 Cornell dissertation, "True Stories: Contemporary Chinese Reportage and Its Ideology and Aesthetic," focuses on reportage from the 1980s. He provided the English translation of the intertitles for Wu Wenguang's 2016 documentary film *Investigating My Father*. He has edited or coedited and contributed to three volumes of the Dictionary of Literary Biography series: *Chinese Fiction Writers 1900–1949*, *Chinese Fiction Writers 1950–2000*, and *Chinese Poets Since 1949*. His translation of a 2010 novel by Ning Ken, *Tibetan Sky*, was published by Sinoist Books in 2025.

Federico Picerni is Assistant Professor at the University of Bologna. He obtained his PhD in Asian studies from Ca' Foscari University of Venice in a double degree program with Heidelberg University. His broad research interest is the relationship of literature and society in China. Specifically, he works on worker writers and poets, amateur/grassroots cultural productions, and Sinophone cultural productions in Europe.

Yanshuo Zhang is Assistant Professor of Asian Languages and Literatures at Pomona College. She is the principal investigator for "Diversifying Humanistic Pedagogy in China Studies: Incorporating Ethnic Minority Literary and Cultural Productions into North American College Classrooms" (collaborators: Mark Bender, Robin Visser, Jiajun Wang, and Jingui Zhang), which won the inaugural Luce/ACLS Collaborative Grant in China Studies in 2024. Her scholarly monograph, one of the first English-language monographs on the creative cultures produced by China's ethnic minorities, is forthcoming with the University of Michigan Press. Zhang is committed to advancing a multicultural, multiethnic understanding of China. Her publications have appeared in *Journal of Asian Studies*, *positions: asia critique*, *Journal of Urban Cultural Studies*, and *Prism: Theory and Modern Chinese Literature*, among other journals.

Ping Zhu is Professor in Transnational Chinese/Sinophone Literary, Film, and Media Studies at UC San Diego. She serves as the editor-in-chief of *Chinese Literature and Thought Today* and is an editorial board member for *World Literature Today*. She is the author of *Gender and Subjectivities in Early Twentieth-Century Chinese Literature and Culture* (2015); coeditor (with Zhuoyi Wang and Jason McGrath) of *Maoist Laughter* (2019); and coeditor (with Faye Hui Xiao) of *Feminisms with Chinese Characteristics* (2021). She is currently working on a monograph titled "The Cult of Labor in Modern China."

Index